Ethics and Representation in Qualitative Studies of Literacy

Ethics and Representation in Qualitative Studies of Literacy

Edited by

Peter Mortensen
University of Kentucky

Gesa E. Kirsch
Wayne State University

National Council of Teachers of English
1111 W. Kenyon Road, Urbana, Illinois 61801-1096

Grateful acknowledgment is made for permission to reprint the following:
"You Have to Be Deaf to Understand," © 1971 by Willard J. Madsen.

Staff Editor: Sheila A. Ryan

Interior and Cover Design: Doug Burnett

NCTE Stock Number: 15969-3050

Library of Congress Cataloging-in-Publication Data

Ethics and representation in qualitative studies of literacy / edited
    by Peter Mortensen, Gesa E. Kirsch.
        p.   cm.
    Includes bibliographical references and index.
    ISBN 0-8141-1596-9
    1. English language—Rhetoric—Study and teaching—Theory, etc.
I. Mortensen, Peter, 1961–   . II. Kirsch, Gesa.
PE 1404.E86 1996
808'.042'07—dc20   96-28521
                                                    CIP

Contents

Foreword: Considering Research Methods in Composition and Rhetoric

Andrea A. Lunsford, Melissa A. Goldthwaite, Gianna M. Marsella, Sandee K. McGlaun, Jennifer Phegley, Rob Stacy, Linda Stingily, and Rebecca Greenberg Taylor
The Ohio State University

> *[C]omposition scholars need to develop a sophisticated understanding of the methodological, ethical, and representational complexities in their research.*
>
> —Gesa E. Kirsch and Peter Mortensen,
> "Introduction: Reflections on Methodology in Literacy Studies"

As a graduate student trying to find my way into the study of rhetoric and composition in the early and mid-1970s, I felt like a rider on a somewhat out of control merry-go-round, grasping whatever methodological gold (or brass) rings came my way, hoping to cobble together research projects that would help me learn the field as well as write my way into it. I conducted case studies, carried out quantitative analyses, used tests of significance, compared t-unit lengths—all enthusiastically, and, for the most part, uncritically. While I cared deeply for students and for their writing, while I worried a great deal over how (or whether) I could be of help to them, and while I thought of my stance as grounded in an ethical system I could defend and live by, I did not fret about appropriation, about erasure, about (mis)representation in my role as teacher-researcher. Even when I began teaching "methods" in the early 1980s, I taught what I had learned, using my experiences with various research methods as a touchstone for inviting graduate students to begin their own research projects.

That was then, however, before I embarked on the collaborative research that would change my life and my work, before I began to immerse myself not simply in feminist activism but in the rich discourse of feminist theory, before I underwent a personal crisis of self-representation that shattered any confidence I had ever had in my own sense and ways of knowing. That was then, before I began to question my all-too-easy assumptions, to write differently, to teach differently, to conduct research differently, and to teach "methods" differently. That was then, and now is now, when I have just finished teaching-learning English 895: Research Methods in Composition and Rhetoric with twelve talented graduate student teacher-researchers who had an opportunity to work with a large part of the manuscript of this book.

Receiving permission to read these essays before publication was a great stroke of good fortune for our seminar, for we[1] were working toward articulating research projects of our own, and we found ourselves living out many of the dilemmas contained in its pages, grappling with just those personal and ethical and political issues its essays bring to light. We were, in at least this important sense, just the audience that editors Gesa Kirsch and Peter Mortensen invoke when they say that "we hope the collection will be especially useful in graduate seminars, introducing advanced students and novice researchers to representational and theoretical issues not readily apparent from reading research reports alone." Thus we began to talk to, and to talk back to, this text, engaging its essays and themes individually and collaboratively, in class and out of class, and always in terms of our own work.

The seminar is long over now, but a group of us continued to meet, to read and reread parts of this text, and to explore its implications for our lives and work. What follows are fragments of these discussions, all multivocal, all collaboratively produced, and all aimed at demonstrating how one particular graduate seminar made points of contact with the timely and deeply significant issues raised by this text.

Researcher/Self

> *[A]ny account we produce must simultaneously inscribe and transcend the self who produces it.*
>
> —Patricia A. Sullivan, "Ethnography and the
> Problem of the 'Other'"

Issues of the self-as-researcher became very important to students in our seminar as we struggled to write research proposals (which in some cases were to serve as dissertation prospectuses) and to come to terms with how graduate students could conduct research that would gain prestige within the academy while questioning the positivistic paradigms upon which such research is traditionally based. While institutional constraints generally require factual, solid conclusions that would allow us as researchers to write ourselves into the academic community, this seminar asked us to question ourselves and our methods. As a result, we strove to think critically and self-reflectively while simultaneously attempting to demonstrate expertise. We had to fight the desire for easy answers, and we were forced to recognize that we could not look through our own subject positions and our methods as if they were transparent. We realized that researchers' multiple identities and subjectivities manifest themselves and shape both the inquiry and the interpretation of results. As Elizabeth Chiseri-Strater states, "All researchers are positioned whether they write about it explicitly, separately, or not at all."

This book brought the issues of self-representation and self-critique to the forefront of our class discussions, and, through the examples set forth in essays such as Brenda Jo Brueggemann's and Chiseri-Strater's, we were given models of research that carry out self-critique which does not undermine the work, but makes it stronger. We read many essays that addressed the importance of self-critique, but even as we struggled to understand just what such a critique might entail, we were learning the degree to which self-reflection is not a panacea. As Brueggemann points out, self-reflection poses risks such as rewriting ourselves to the exclusion of our subjects on the one hand, and remaining silent on the other. However, this book is an apt testimony that we can, finally, get the work of research done without abandoning the examination of our own subject positions at the same time. One project in our seminar, a project that focused on student responses to teacher comments on essays, led to intense self-reflection on the part of the graduate student researcher who recognized that much of the motivation for exploring this issue stemmed from her frustration with deciphering teacher comments on her own papers. Like Helen Dale's project, this inquiry demonstrated that "researching one's own teaching offers the possibility of meaningful change in classrooms and rich contexts for reflection." In many other instances as well, we found that self-reflection led not only to a sophisticated examination of the researcher's motivations and biases, but to questions of the ethical representation of others.

Researcher/Subject

> *Does she think I have misunderstood, misrepresented her? Is she confused by where she stands in the spaces between . . . researcher-subject? I simply don't know.*
>
> —Brenda Jo Brueggemann, "Still-Life: Representations and Silences in the Participant-Observer Role"

Our positions as graduate students—as teachers, students, activists, researchers-in-training, and sometimes subjects of the research of others—left us with a special concern about the relationships between researchers and subjects. We could not help but feel anxiety when human subjects seemed subordinate in the hierarchy of research because we recognized that qualitative research could not exist without the subject's willingness to be observed and to participate.

The essays in this book help us to consider the complexity of the researcher-subject relationship. Cheri L. Williams's discussion of Cathy in "Dealing with the Data: Ethical Issues in Case Study Research" reminds us that subjects are in vulnerable positions when they find themselves under the scrutiny of the researcher's eye. It is with no small measure of uneasiness that we consider how such scrutiny can have negative consequences in the lives of subjects despite a researcher's best intentions. Thomas Newkirk helps us confront this uneasiness when, in "Seduction and Betrayal in Qualitative Research," he encourages researchers to "question the automatic belief in our own benevolence, the automatic equation between our own academic success and ethical behavior." He also reminds us that good research requires integrity and honest attention to complexity and that a complex research report will probably contain both good and bad news. Similarly, Williams's essay forces us to consider not only issues affecting our own academic success, but the importance of the lives of subjects who, though valuable to the research, can be left emotionally and socially displaced within their world long after the researcher has disappeared from the scene of inquiry. Such was the concern of one of our classmates as she struggled to allow subjects to define and represent themselves in ways that challenged traditional paradigms of race and ethnicity. Other seminar participants who chose to examine texts from centuries past expected to take some comfort in studying subjects made distant by the passage of time; however, they too found that they needed to negotiate issues of representation and to confront the possibilities of appropriation and misrepresentation.

Readers of this volume are encouraged to regard the relationship between subjects and researchers as mutually interdependent, even though traditional research reports do not always figure the relationship as such. Writers in this volume present examples of mutually respectful relationships that are negotiated up front and checked continuously during the research process to lessen the ethical dilemma Newkirk describes, in which the subject enters unwittingly into a tangled relationship of subordination and judgment. Even in the best circumstances, when researchers and subjects are viewed as teachers and learners simultaneously, dilemmas may still exist. Despite such hazards, the researchers in this book are willing to explore possibilities and negotiate challenges.

We see in many of these essays a commitment to establishing and maintaining mutually beneficial relationships between subjects and researchers, a commitment that often calls for collaboration. Ann M. Blakeslee, Caroline M. Cole, and Theresa Conefrey describe a subject's and a researcher's divergent interpretations of collaboration and also explain how research can be affected when subjects are highly regarded professionals. Russel K. Durst and Sherry Cook Stanforth share the problems of collaboration they faced as co-researchers when Stanforth was both researcher and subject and Durst was her academic adviser. It is only in the context of such interdependent relationships that issues of authority and trust can be negotiated and we can, as Williams encourages, begin to "find better ways to honor those people who make our 'tales of the field' possible."

Researcher/Text

> [T]hose who turn other people's lives into texts hold real power.
>
> —Thomas Newkirk, "Seduction and Betrayal in Qualitative Research"

The powerful "tales" told by researchers are complex textual constructions, records of careful observation, reports of equally careful composition. The researchers represented in this collection have made conscious and self-reflective choices about how to represent the subjects of their inquiries, as well as themselves, in their texts. In negotiating those representations, they are also negotiating the relationships between themselves and their texts—the "unfinished" and unpublished texts of field notes, interview protocols, and transcripts, as well as the "finished" and frequently published texts of dissertations, essays, and books. In selecting material and in making choices about how to order it, researchers face questions about how the words they choose to describe also inevitably (re)inscribe.

Lucille Parkinson McCarthy and Stephen M. Fishman address this issue in "A Text for Many Voices: Representing Diversity in Reports of Naturalistic Research." They note that the three goals of such reports— "[to] represent diverse voices . . . reveal the researcher's influence . . . [and] describe the emerging research design"—are often not well served by traditional academic language. McCarthy and Fishman engage in a self-conscious discussion of the relationship between text and researcher;

others in this volume actually perform their challenges to traditional paradigms within the texts themselves. All of these researchers are conscious of the ethical implications of the textual choices they make, recognizing that texts are not always received in the same manner in which they are deployed and that readers read themselves into texts and construct meaning according to their own lives, experiences, and needs.

Researchers, then, must be doubly aware when figuring audience(s) in their texts, when telling their tales. Who is—or should be—the audience of composition research? Is research written up *for* the subjects of the study, *on behalf* of them, or merely *about* them? How do researchers' identities and subjectivities (and those of their subjects and audiences, although they are not always separate groups) shape their interpretation and representation of findings? How does the text of the research report register the diversity of voice and meaning that inevitably proceeds from qualitative research studies? Researchers face a persistent double bind: while traditional research genres elide or erase voices of participants, challenges to those genres are often read as less rigorous "storytelling" and thus are less likely to be published.

In asking and attempting to answer these questions, the writer-researchers in this volume led members of our seminar to reflect on text-related issues in our own research projects. One proposal focused on the ways in which several women researchers in rhetoric and composition, seeking alternative ways to represent the complexities of their research, experiment with conventions of creative nonfiction in the writing of their research reports. Another explored the question and possibility of whether the academy can consider the novel a valid form for reporting research. In opening our eyes not only to the "real power" held by the researcher wielding the pen (or keyboard), but also to the power of the text itself, these creative and nontraditional research reports provided us with more complex and imaginative ways of thinking about our own particular textual choices.

Researcher/Context

> [R]esearchers and readers of research alike need to remember that ethnographic inquiry . . . puts us all into political and ethical spaces even when we do not actively seek them.
>
> —Jennie Dautermann, "Social and Institutional Power Relationships in Studies of Workplace Writing"

As beginning researchers, we are faced not only with the ethical dilemmas which emerge in the relationships among ourselves, our subjects, and our texts, but with the additional knowledge that these already perplexing relationships unfold within equally complicated and constraining sociocultural and institutional contexts. This volume makes us aware that the scenes of our research have ethical implications that are as intricate as those arising from the relationships among researcher, subject, and text; indeed, the contexts of such relationships are as integral as the subject(s) and researcher(s) themselves. Context, these authors assert, is not merely a peripheral consideration, but is central to the research process itself.

While all of the researchers in this volume demonstrate the influence of context upon their projects, the writers in the final section problematize context in particularly provocative ways. In these four essays the consequences of cultural, institutional, and material exigencies on research processes are foregrounded and reflected upon at length. Roxanne D. Mountford situates readers within a web of contextual relations, problematizing first the lack of representation of feminist ethnographers within postmodern anthropology, and then framing this critique within a reading of Zora Neale Hurston's ethnographic work, reminding us that Hurston bridged several contexts as an African American woman writing ethnography. Jabari Mahiri also articulates an awareness of the delicate relationship between researcher and context, which he developed as he worked to bring rap music ("an authentic cultural experience" for his subjects) into the formal educational setting of an urban high school. These difficulties do not end with qualitative research undertaken in academic settings, as Jennie Dautermann demonstrates in examining the workplace writing of hospital employees and the ethical treatment of research subjects in such contexts. Paul Anderson discusses the historical context surrounding the implementation of the U.S. *Code of Federal Regulations* regarding human research subjects and in doing so addresses many of the institutional "constraints" alluded to by nearly all of the researchers in this collection.

As student-researchers, we too faced institutional constraints. Writing a qualitative research proposal within the confines of a graduate seminar necessitated a multitude of elaborate negotiations. Among other challenges, we battled the limited availability of time and resources, the pressure of impending evaluation, and the hierarchical power structure endemic to the academy. The essays in this collection are especially useful to us as graduate students, because the constraints we face now will extend beyond graduate seminars to our dissertation work and, in fact, will be a presence throughout our professional lives, shifting and refiguring as we enter different contexts as teachers, writers, research-

ers. For students in composition studies who are pursuing widely varying projects situated in a diversity of contexts, this volume models qualitative inquiry as it is enacted both inside and outside the academy, simultaneously interrogating the opportunities and constraints that these
research sites present.

Such interrogations were especially relevant to the research proposal developed by one seminar participant studying how context functions not only in contemporary ethnographic studies but also in historical rhetorical acts. Careful examination of interacting contextual factors
helped illuminate this student's explication of the rhetorical situations
of three American nature writers and their audiences. In similar ways,
our class discussions about context were confirmed and enriched by the
essays in this volume and led us to realize that descriptions of context
can never be total or stable. When we began to account for the complicated web of generic expectations, institutional constraints, conflicting
perceptions, and personal motives that constitute the contexts of research,
we found ourselves entangled in, and puzzled by, the intricate components of context. A second equally important realization was that we
could not and should not attempt to remove ourselves, as researchers,
from this always uncertain but rich tangle. As writers in this volume
repeatedly demonstrate, attempting to "think through the tangle" and
working to participate actively in the very contexts we seek to describe
are both essential aspects of self-reflective and informed research.

Conclusion

> *Our guilt, our art, and our scholarly rigor are both professional and personal,*
> *at once a dilemma and a delight.*
>
> —Bonnie S. Sunstein, "Culture on the Page: Experience,
> Rhetoric, and Aesthetics in Ethnographic Writing"

At many points in our Research Methods in Composition and Rhetoric
seminar, one or another of us raised a question always hovering on the
periphery of consciousness: If the project of research is so fraught with
dangers of misrepresentation, appropriation, and violence, why not just
give up the enterprise entirely? Indeed, by midterm, and particularly as
we attempted self-critiques of our own projects, many felt close to paralysis. Thus what makes *Ethics and Representation in Qualitative Studies
of Literacy* finally so valuable for us is its refusal of such paralysis and its
concomitant insistence, in the face of enormous problems of ethics and
representation, on *getting work done*. On a personal level, this move is
enormously reassuring, quite literally authorizing us to keep on keep-

ing on, learning from our ongoing introspection—and mistakes. On the level of praxis, this concentration on getting work done points to the deeply collaborative nature of all research and to the need for constant interrogation of the power relations inscribed in these collaborative acts. And on a theoretical level, this move seems tied very closely to the discipline of composition itself. Patricia A. Sullivan (in "Ethnography and the Problem of the 'Other'") perhaps puts it best when she says, in another context, that compositionists cannot easily engage in a "refusal of writing. The refusal to write," she goes on to say, "banishes from the scene of inquiry the very medium that defines composition and circumscribes our work." And, we would add, that makes our work, at least potentially, both usable and useful. This volume helps us remember, then, that writing is always an act of composing, of re-presenting. Without the risk of linguistic representation, we could not compose, we could not communicate, we could not get our work done.

More than many disciplines, composition aims not only to get work done but to hold that work up to the criterion Marge Piercy sets out in her powerful poem "To Be of Use." Real work, Piercy argues, is that which has the "massive patience . . . to move things forward" and which does "what has to be done, again and again." "The pitcher cries for water to carry," Piercy says, "and a person for work that is real." The essays in this volume have provided glimpses of researchers attempting "work that is real" and thereby have helped us come closer to understanding just how much is at stake for teachers and researchers of writing in trying to achieve this goal.

Notes

1. The shift from first person singular to plural here is, of course, deliberate, and the use of the plurals "we" and "us" and "our" in the remainder of this Foreword refers specifically to the eight people who worked on it together. After discussion and experimentation with other ways of representing plural voices in this text, we agreed to work through our drafts collaboratively until we each felt ourselves "voiced" by this text, although to different degrees and, certainly, never fully. We wish especially to thank the editors for offering us the opportunity for this rich collaboration.

Works Cited

Piercy, Marge. "To Be of Use." *Circles on the Water: Selected Poems of Marge Piercy.* New York: Knopf, 1982. 106.

Acknowledgments

We asked this volume's contributors to engage in the difficult, provocative task of reflecting on the practice of qualitative literacy research. For their efforts, their patience, and their cooperation, we are most grateful. Our thanks, too, to Marlo Welshons and Dawn Boyer at NCTE, who carefully tended to this project through its development. Their support, as well as that of NCTE's manuscript reviewers and its Editorial Board, is sincerely appreciated.

Brenda Weber Ijams read early and late drafts of the manuscript, pointing out lapses in good sense and form that might have otherwise slipped into print. Ijams's work was funded by Dean Richard C. Edwards of the University of Kentucky College of Arts and Sciences.

Gesa Kirsch would like to thank Janet Webster at the Guin Library, Hatfield Marine Science Center in Newport, Oregon, for providing a wonderful space to work—an office, computer, and library access. And thanks go to Anthony Schreiner for his willingness to listen, for encouragement and support, and most of all for times of laughter and play that helped keep everything in perspective.

Peter Mortensen wishes to acknowledge the generosity of the University of Kentucky Department of English and its chair, David Durant. At home, Karen Pinney Mortensen's personal interest in—and mathematician's amusement with—this project has been a constant source of encouragement. And for laughter, play, and perspective, not to mention joyful sleep deprivation, nothing could have done so well as the arrival of Sarah Elizabeth Mortensen just weeks before *Ethics and Representation* went to the publisher.

Introduction: Reflections on Methodology in Literacy Studies

Gesa E. Kirsch
Wayne State University

Peter Mortensen
University of Kentucky

Qualitative approaches to research—ethnographies and case studies in particular—continue to gain prominence in composition studies as researchers strive to enrich our understanding of literacy in its myriad cultural contexts.[1] This arrival of qualitative research has been signaled in many of our professional forums. In recent years, for example, an increasing number of submissions to the NCTE Promising Researcher competition have featured qualitative research methodologies.[2] The *CCCC Bibliography of Composition and Rhetoric* each year lists more and more dissertations that involve case study and ethnographic inquiry.[3] Journals in composition studies seem more willing now than ever to publish segments or summaries of ethnographic fieldwork. And academic publishers are meeting the challenge to bring out qualitative research in long form.[4] Further, teacher research on writing—largely qualitative in nature—is finally receiving due notice, professionally and institutionally.[5] Yet despite the popularity of qualitative research, scholars in composition studies are only beginning to examine the informing assumptions of this work: assumptions that, when analyzed, yield difficult questions about ethics and representation that demand our consideration.

Wendy Bishop recalls that in 1986, while planning an ethnographic study, she felt that she was practically "inventing ethnography"—inventing it in the sense that her only guidance came from texts "written for social scientists and anthropologists" (148). These texts did not address issues of language and literacy in ways that were especially useful to her. Since the mid-1980s, a number of new books have appeared that discuss qualitative research design, and scholars in composition may no longer feel the distress that Bishop did, at least not in terms of procedural questions: the mechanics of gaining access to, making observations in, and collecting data from writing communities. Also, there exist now a number of book-length ethnographic studies in composition that model good practice (e.g., Chiseri-Strater; Cross; Goldblatt; Schaafsma; Sunstein) as well as chapters and articles that render specific methodological advice (e.g., Bleich; Bridwell-Bowles; Brodkey; Calkins; Chin; Cintron; Herndl; Kleine; Moss, *Literacy*). All of this work makes clear the interdisciplinary borrowing that has animated qualitative research in composition. But there remains a pressing need to scrutinize what it means to import, adapt, select, and transform ethnographic and case study methods in order to investigate literacy and writing communities. As Bishop's comment attests, this need is recognized, but unmet.[6] A desirable critical conversation about qualitative research and its theoretical underpinnings cannot be borrowed from other disciplines; the conversation must begin with and be sustained by scholars in composition studies themselves.

One starting point for such a conversation takes us back some fifteen years to a time when composition researchers began sharing critical reflections on conducting and reporting ethnographic studies of literacy. In their 1981 article in *Research in the Teaching of English*, Kenneth Kantor, Dan Kirby, and Judith Goetz comment on the growing popularity of ethnographic studies in English education and composition. After detailing good and bad ethnographic practice, they examine five problems they believe qualitative researchers must account for: "Reliability and Validity," "Interpretive Language," "Data Collection and Analysis," "Correspondences with Experimental Research," and "Resources for Research" (302–05). As these categories suggest, Kantor, Kirby, and Goetz attend mainly to the integrity of *processes* through which observation becomes data, and through which data become report. In only one section do the authors speak directly of the *people* whose literate lives are taken up in qualitative research, and that is in "Data Collection and Analysis." In that section, prospective researchers are urged to choose their "key informants" carefully, for such informants have the potential to greatly enhance the validity of ethnographic narratives (303). Implicit here is that by foregrounding key informants, researchers may maintain a distanced, objective stance—both in the field and in its reconstruction on the page. Throughout the 1980s, this positioning of researcher and subject remained fairly stable in arguments about how to do and how to read qualitative composition research, especially case studies and ethnographies (see, for example, Calkins; Doheny-Farina and Odell; Lauer and Asher 23–53; Myers 9–25; North 273–74; Odell).

In recent years, criticism of the positivist assumptions characterized in Kantor, Kirby, and Goetz's article has prompted recastings of qualitative inquiry in composition. The urgency to fix hard standards of reliability, validity, and generalizability has given way to a provocative range of questions about power and representation that are manifest in the field and on the page. Many scholars now assume that interpretation is central to all research, that researchers' values permeate and shape research questions, observations, and conclusions, and that there can be no value-neutral research methodology.[7] With interpretation a crucial issue, researchers must grapple with the rhetorical construction of interpretive authority. And attendant upon rhetorical construction are a host of ethical questions regarding the rights and responsibilities of representation.

This ethical turn springs from developments within several of the intellectual traditions composition scholars routinely draw upon. Take academic feminism, for example. Its practitioners' interest in ethics arises from frustration with a kind of ethical relativism that has often overtaken—and paralyzed—discussions of subjectivity and agency in postmodern theories of culture. And despite great diversity among the various schools of feminisms, most feminists agree on some basic ethical principles, such as that feminist research should aim to validate and improve women's lives, not simply observe and describe them. (For statements about research *for* women rather than *on* women, see Fonow and Cook; Kirsch and Ritchie; Smith.) This commitment to emancipatory goals leads many feminist scholars to reassert the importance of agency, a move that departs from and sometimes stands in opposition to postmodern perspectives. But in so doing, feminists do not propose a return to an unproblematic, unified, Cartesian subject. Instead, feminist scholars recognize the multiple and shifting subject positions we inhabit at work and play, and they aim to develop ethical principles that foreground such questions as the following: Who benefits from the research? Whose interests are at stake? What are the consequences for participants? In developing a feminist ethics, scholars are not generating a foundational code; rather, they are reconceiving ethics with the knowledge that subjects and agency may take many forms within and against normalizing rules of culture.[8] In other words, feminists wish to avoid reinscribing a single ethical code, such as the traditional "ethics of rights," for they recognize the folly of developing "universal principles" that turn out, time and again, not to be universal at all, but to privilege only those values held by a dominant group.

So as a consequence of feminist interventions, as well as (sometimes conflicting) contributions from poststructural and postcolonial theorists, we have come to recognize how hierarchies and inequalities (marked by gender, race, class, social groupings, and more) are transferred onto and reproduced within participant-researcher relations. On this count, James Porter summarizes pointedly: "Ethics is not a set of answers but a mode of questioning and a manner of positioning" (218).

In *Ethics and Representation in Qualitative Studies of Literacy*, contributors take up this project of questioning and positioning with respect to their own research and the research of others. They reflect on their past and present practice: on how they have addressed (or failed to address) ethical dilemmas, on how they have represented others in the ethnographic narratives they have written, and on the political, institutional, cultural, and gendered contexts in which they have conducted their work. In speaking to a broad range of issues that bear on the representation of literate lives in research reports, contributors to this volume explore questions like the following:

- How do power, authority, and equity figure into researchers' relationships with their subjects? How is the position of the subject defined by the role of the researcher, and vice versa?

- What ethical issues must composition scholars consider when undertaking qualitative research?

- How do researchers' identities and subjectivities (e.g., gender, sexuality, race, ethnicity, and class) shape their cognition and interpretation of "data" at the site of inquiry?

- How do institutional and historical contexts shape the conduct and outcomes of qualitative research?

- How are ethnographic data transformed into narratives? What happens—what is gained and lost—in this transformation?

- What narrative and rhetorical strategies do authors of ethnographies and case studies invoke in their writing—and toward what ends?

Ethics and Representation in Qualitative Studies of Literacy, then, is not so much a "handbook" of qualitative research techniques as it is a book that illuminates the complex ethical and representational questions that are rarely discussed in research manuals. The chapters collected here are amplifications of dialogues already begun in recent articles scattered in composition journals and edited collections. The chapters are also infused with strains of conversations taking place in anthropology and sociology, disciplines in which practitioners have for some time reflected critically on the nature of fieldwork (e.g., Van Maanen's *Tales of the Field* or Wolf's *A Thrice-Told Tale*).

The authors in this collection do not all share the same views, nor do they speak with a singular voice. In fact, many differences of opinion are audible within and at the margins of every chapter. For example, Thomas Newkirk, whose chapter opens this book, views the researcher's "consent form," designed to protect participants' rights and choices, as part of the "seduction and betrayal" that participants in qualitative research often suffer. Yet Paul Anderson, whose chapter concludes the book, stresses the importance of consent forms as part of the federal and local regulations aimed at preventing harm to research participants. Somewhere between these two views lies the perspective of Cheri Williams, who notices that the strict guidelines designed to protect the privacy and anonymity of study participants can actually have unanticipated negative effects: she argues that we may lose opportunities to publicly recognize the achievements of research participants who could serve as important role models in their communities.

Another set of contrasting views is provided by Ann Blakeslee, Caroline Cole, and Theresa Conefrey on the one hand and Roxanne Mountford on the other, all of whom draw on feminist theory in their work. Blakeslee, Cole, and Conefrey contend that there is epistemological and methodological coherence in blending postmodern and feminist stances, and they make this claim by appealing to the authority of social constructionist ideology. But Mountford turns this argument on its head, claiming that much postmodern theorizing—in anthropological circles particularly—focuses on subjects in ways that undermine the very social gains that feminists seek to achieve.

Clearly, our goal is not to provide in this collection a smooth, seamless narrative aimed at containing the discourse on ethics and representation in qualitative research. Rather, we wish to stake out spaces that permit disciplinary dialogue, debate, and dissensus and to bring into public view the many kinds of ethical and representational quandaries researchers tend too often to keep to themselves. But having stressed the diversity of thought exhibited herein, it is important also to illuminate one concern contributors in this volume share: all view research as a complex of rhetorical acts, and so they are sensitive to the power of spoken and written words to liberate as well as to regulate experience in public and private life.

In creating a forum for debate and discussion, we hope to provide both new and experienced researchers with the opportunity to better anticipate the conditions and decisions they will encounter in the field. We hope the collection will be especially useful in graduate seminars, introducing advanced students and novice researchers to representational and theoretical issues not readily apparent from reading research reports alone. The book is also intended for composition teachers and writing program administrators interested in learning more about the subtleties of composition research. We want to encourage such teachers and administrators to view their own classrooms and writing programs as sites of inquiry. Finally, we wish to advance methodological know-how in composition studies: knowledge of how to design, conduct, write, and read ethnographic narratives; of how to address ethical and representational questions in qualitative research; of how to think through the tangle of conflicting literacy narratives circulating in our profession, in the academy, and in the culture at large.

Ethics and Representation in Qualitative Studies of Literacy is arranged in three sections that address, in order, ethical dilemmas in qualitative research; questions of representation, voice, and subjectivity; and the nature of institutional and social contexts. These issues overlap to a certain extent, as our contributors make quite evident. In fact, for many contributors, particular ethical dilemmas are a point of departure for thinking through subsequent problems of representation. The arrangement of sections, then, is not meant to define static boundaries; section headings are instead signposts that mark the terrain traversed in the collection. Chapters that could fit into more than one section (because they take up several issues) are located at the beginning or end of sections so as to underscore their bridging function.

Part I, Confronting Ethical Dilemmas, explores the complex and at times vexing ethical predicaments inherent in qualitative research, such as how to write revealing and "truthful" accounts of fieldwork while also honoring the interests, trust, and privacy of subjects. The chapters in this section illustrate just how common ethical dilemmas are in qualitative research, how difficult they can be to address, and what compromises researchers have had to make in negotiating them.

In "Seduction and Betrayal in Qualitative Research," Thomas Newkirk maintains that the close, even intimate, relationships researchers establish with their subjects constitute a form of seduction. This said, he examines a major ethical quandary faced by qualitative researchers: how to be critical of study participants without violating their trust and (sometimes) friendship. Newkirk observes that when researchers withhold judgment during observations, participants and researchers lose valuable opportunities for dialogue, growth, and insight. Furthermore, participants often feel betrayed because they only learn about the researcher's judgment from the final report of the study. Looking at published work in which subjects are portrayed negatively, Newkirk asks whether the "greater good" of a project ever justifies betrayal. He concludes that researchers need to address this ethical dilemma by committing themselves to sharing "bad news" with participants during the research process, by granting participants rights to co-interpretation, and by taking on the responsibility of intervention.

In the next four chapters, researchers offer critical reflections on their research processes and their responses to ethical dilemmas. Brenda Jo Brueggemann interrogates how her role as participant-observer in a study of deaf student writers at Gallaudet University colored her representation of those students, their literacy, and their culture. She describes her efforts to participate in both the Deaf and the Hearing cultures of the university and recounts the difficulties and pain she encountered when she was not being fully accepted by members of either one. Attending to the institutional, educational, and cultural debates surrounding the university, Brueggemann argues that the role of participant-observer carries with it some serious liabilities that can ultimately undermine the researcher's ostensible respectability. Cheri Williams also takes us into the world of Deaf culture, but her research focuses on young deaf children's language and literacy development. Williams continues the discussion begun by Newkirk about when and how to intervene at the scene of observation, referring to an incident in which she watched a teacher engage in potentially abusive treatment of a deaf student. Williams also candidly reflects on coming to terms with parents' pain at discovering, through reviewing her research, that they treat their deaf and hearing children quite differently, to the detriment of the deaf child. Finally, Williams addresses questions of anonymity, giving the topic an interesting twist: instead of emphasizing the importance of protecting participants' confidentiality, she asks what is lost when researchers conceal participants' identities.

The next chapter, by Russel Durst and Sherry Cook Stanforth, examines collaboration and conflict in composition research, focusing on a study conducted by the authors, an experienced researcher and writing program administrator and a junior colleague whose own classroom was the site of the research. Durst and Stanforth investigate power relationships, researchers' multiple roles, and the politics of studying scenes of instruction. They offer an honest description of the personal and professional tensions they encountered in the research process, tensions they attribute to differing genders, ranks, and roles in the university setting. Unlike other, more celebratory descriptions of collaborative research practices, this chapter cautions those who engage in collaborative research to expect conflict to be part of the experience.

Helen Dale concludes Part I by revisiting the ethical dilemmas she faced in a study of ninth-grade collaborative writing groups. Like Newkirk and Williams, Dale examines how she negotiated the roles of "participant" and "observer" when she felt the need to intervene in, and not just observe, the emotionally scarring behavior of students in a collaborative writing group. Further, she looks at the institutional constraints at school which made for multiple and conflicting loyalties to the participating teacher, to the students in the classroom, to the school district, and to her dissertation committee. Importantly, Dale notes that dilemmas of fidelity experienced by researchers often resolve into choices among equally valid priorities—choices that many times, unfortunately, must be made with little time for reflection.

Part II, Representation: Positionality, Subjectivity, and Voice, charts the ethical and rhetorical problems entailed in representing others— their voices, experiences, and lives—in qualitative research. With the decline of esteem for positivist research paradigms (at least outside the natural sciences), scholars of many stripes are experiencing a "crisis of representation": they are questioning their authority to speak for and about others. Contributors ask such questions as: What does it mean to speak for others, to render their experiences in writing? Can we speak for and about others without appropriating their experiences or violating their realities? What happens to their experiences—and their right to claim their experiences—after they have been passed through the critical filter of the ethnographer? And does that critical filter necessarily essentialize the "subject" of research? Addressing these questions, authors in this section draw on feminist and postmodern theory to explore new ways of working with research participants and of translating that work into ethnographic reports. They argue that a major task facing composition scholars is the development of new rhetorical strategies for representing sites of inquiry and the figures populating them. Specifically, there is a need to foreground rather than conceal conflicting perspectives that emerge in the analysis of data, so that research reports register the diverse voices of research participants as well as the multiple subject positions of researchers (see Peshkin). Finally, this section's contributors also evaluate some recent experimental ethnographies and speculate about researchers' responsibilities to readers, sponsors, and participants. Some argue that, for experimental ethnographies to succeed, researchers need to help readers (including journal and press editors) understand the unfamiliar discursive conventions they employ.

Patricia Sullivan opens Part II by exploring the problem of representing "others," particularly when they are members of the same community as the researcher. She examines alternative forms of presenting ethnographies (e.g., Denny Taylor's oral performances at conferences to which she invites her research participants) and of writing ethnographies (e.g., Elizabeth Chiseri-Strater's work on academic literacies) that intentionally include and amplify the voices of those being studied. Sullivan notes that we can never escape the "room of mirrors" we create in self-reflective ethnographic narratives, particularly when we study literacy and writing, because the subject we study and the medium we use to report our findings are one and the same.

Following Sullivan's lead, Elizabeth Chiseri-Strater argues that researchers need to make themselves—as subjects—the objects of contemplation and reflection. She illustrates her argument by tracing her own development as a researcher over the course of two ethnographic projects, her master's thesis and her book, *Academic Literacies.* In doing so, Chiseri-Strater uncovers how, each time, her own subjectivity as well as the dominant research paradigm influenced the kind of data she observed, her interpretation of those data, and her discursive voice. Finally, she articulates the thin line between self-centered display and revealing positionality that researchers must negotiate when they foreground themselves in their texts.

Continuing the discussion of voice and positionality, Ann Blakeslee, Caroline Cole, and Theresa Conefrey argue for the integration rather than the appropriation of the voice and authority of the ethnographic "other." Drawing on feminist scholarship, the authors urge researchers to treat the "other" as a thinking subject who can collaborate with the researcher in authoring ethnographic narratives. They illustrate their argument with a study in which the research participant, a physicist, disagrees with the researcher (Blakeslee) on a key interpretive issue. Only through ongoing conversations do researcher and research participant come to new understandings of a disputed term ("collaboration"). Blakeslee, Cole, and Conefrey stress the importance of negotiating authority and voice with participants while realizing that such negotiation always contains the potential for further conflict.

In the next chapter, Lucille Parkinson McCarthy and Stephen Fishman explore how to create "A Text for Many Voices." They argue that reports of naturalistic inquiry should be heteroglossic—that is, they should represent and respect the diverse voices speaking at the scene of research. In so arguing, they evaluate two recent articles that attempt to capture multiple voices and perspectives. McCarthy and Fishman also reflect on their own collaborative practice and the difficulty they have encountered in their efforts to create an egalitarian research relationship.

Although equal in academic rank and status, the authors work in separate disciplines, a difference that has contributed to conflicts of voice, authority, and commitment in their research. Such problems notwithstanding, the authors conclude by suggesting that heteroglossic reports may have a liberating effect on researchers as well as on the ethnographic others they represent.

In "Culture on the Page," Bonnie Sunstein examines rhetorical and aesthetic features of ethnographic discourse. Drawing on her published work about a summer institute for English teachers, Sunstein describes the process of collecting, selecting, and transforming data into ethnographic narratives, and comments on the uneasiness and guilt researchers often experience in that process. She explores representational and rhetorical issues involved in writing ethnographies, compares her textual strategies to those used by other ethnographers, and calls for self-reflexivity in the field and on the page.

Part III, Social and Institutional Contexts, addresses the ways in which institutional, social, and historical factors can at once enrich and constrain ethnographic and case study inquiry. Of special interest here are the anthropological origins of ethnographic inquiry. To what extent, one contributor asks, must researchers in composition studies accept methodology flawed by the sexism that marks another discipline's history? Two other contributors find that the institutional forces at play in qualitative research are best accounted for outside academic disciplines, outside the university. They report insights from work conducted in an urban high school and a metropolitan hospital. Yet another chapter takes up a thread that runs through many contributions to this collection by investigating how federal and local regulation of human participant research determines what we can know about literacy in various communities.

The first chapter in Part III, "Engendering Ethnography: Insights from the Feminist Critique of Postmodern Anthropology," addresses both representational and institutional contexts for ethnographic work. Roxanne Mountford traces disciplinary forces in anthropology that have led to the degraded position of gender in postmodern anthropology, and she assesses critical responses of feminist anthropologists to this significant oversight. Drawing numerous examples from the work of Zora Neale Hurston, whose innovative ethnographies of African American culture were suppressed because of their reflexivity, Mountford offers ways for ethnographers in composition studies to foreground gender in their research. Noting that composition researchers often look to postmodern anthropologists for insights into the rhetoric of ethnography (e.g., Geertz and Clifford), she suggests that better models of reflexive cultural accounts can be found in the marginalized work of women anthropologists.

In "Writing, Rap, and Representation," Jabari Mahiri documents how capturing and representing lived experiences in the context of formal schooling requires considerable attention to students' lives outside the classroom. Mahiri illustrates his argument with excerpts from his ethnographic research on African American and popular youth culture, research in which he used rap music as a bridge between students' extracurricular experience and school literacy. He recounts how he had to negotiate different and at times competing interests of funding agencies, participating teachers, concerned parents, and students participating in the project.

Jennie Dautermann takes us into the domain of workplace writing, where she examines the complex social fabric that supports writing in a hospital setting. She focuses on two crucial yet often contradictory needs in ethnographic inquiry: the need to maintain informants' trust and the need to explore freely the power arrangements at work in institutional circles. Dautermann describes how she negotiated her dual roles as writing consultant and researcher, roles that led to loyalty divided among the nurses participating in the writing project, the head nurses who provided her link to the hospital administration, and the hospital administrators who financed her labors as a consultant.

In the chapter that concludes Part III, Paul Anderson traces the history of U.S. government regulations intended to protect human participants in research. He identifies underlying regulatory principles, describes the administrative structures within which human participant research is governed, and discusses several areas in the regulations where ambiguities and controversies have arisen to perplex administrators and researchers alike. Four areas of controversy are found especially pertinent to researchers in composition studies: special exemptions for educational research, applicability of guidelines to qualitative research, questions of boundaries between research and practice, and relevance of guidelines to research conducted by students. Anderson's chapter, written from the perspective of someone who submits proposals to institutional review boards (IRBs) and who has served on a university IRB, makes a valuable contribution to composition studies. He demystifies the review process and its implications for composition by outlining the federal regulations that guide IRB decision making; he also describes local factors, such as individual institutional history, size, and board membership, that affect the review process.

As our introductory discussion suggests, composition scholars need to develop a sophisticated understanding of the methodological, ethical, and representational complexities in their research, understanding similar to that in fields where such discussions already have a considerable history. We are just entering an era when the canon of qualitative research in composition is deep and broad enough to enable thoroughgoing analysis and critique of this sort. Part of our critical effort must be to examine precisely how qualitative methods from other fields have been *transformed* as they have been adapted to study literacy. The moment has arrived for reflection on methodological issues specific to literacy studies. It will no longer suffice to glimpse such reflections in mirrors polished by practitioners in other disciplines.

Notes

1. When illustrating what we mean by "qualitative research," we often refer to its most popular forms—ethnographic and case study inquiry. But we recognize that there are many other forms of qualitative research: oral histories, narrative inquiry, craft interviews, observational-descriptive narratives, introspective reports, and more.

2. Information provided by Russel Durst, University of Cincinnati, chair of the NCTE Promising Researcher Award Committee, 1993–95.

3. Recently, the Conference on College Composition and Communication's dissertation award has gone to emerging researchers who work in an ethnographic vein: Harriet Malinowitz in 1993 and M. A. Syverson in 1994.

4. See, for example, Eli Goldblatt's *'Round My Way* and David Schaafsma's *Eating on the Street* (in the Pittsburgh Series on Composition, Literacy, and Culture), and Beverly Moss's edited collection, *Literacy across Communities* (in the Hampton Press Written Language Series).

5. See, for example, Ruth Ray's recent work on teacher research, as well as important contributions by Miles Myers, and Dixie Goswami and Peter Stillman.

6. So far, most published work on research methods in composition either prescribes how projects ought to be designed (e.g., Lauer and Asher's *Composition Research: Empirical Designs*) or critiques already completed research studies (e.g., North's *The Making of Knowledge in Composition*). The book Kirsch edited with Sullivan, *Methods and Methodology in Composition Research*, begins to address epistemological and ethical research questions, but it is much broader in focus than the present volume in that *Methods and Methodology* also includes chapters on historical, cognitive, and experimental approaches to composition research.

7. For more detailed histories of the ascent of qualitative research, see Athanases and Heath; Beach, Green, Kamil and Shanahan; Bridwell-Bowles; Denzin and Lincoln; Gere; Hillocks; Lunsford.

8. A diversity of approaches exists here as well: for example, "an ethics of care" (Noddings; Tronto) and "lesbian ethics" (Frye). For recent books on feminism and ethics, see Card, *Feminist Ethics*; Tronto, *Moral Boundaries*; Young, *Justice and the Politics of Difference*.

Works Cited

Alcoff, Linda. "The Problem of Speaking for Others." *Cultural Critique* 20 (1991–92): 5–32.

Athanases, Steven Z., and Shirley Brice Heath. "Ethnography in the Study of the Teaching and Learning of English." *Research in the Teaching of English* 29 (1995): 263–87.

Beach, Richard, Judith Green, Michael Kamil, and Timothy Shanahan, eds. *Multidisciplinary Perspectives on Literacy Research.* Urbana: NCRE and NCTE, 1992.

Bishop, Wendy. "I-Witnessing in Composition: Turning Ethnographic Data into Narratives." *Rhetoric Review* 11 (1992): 147–58.

Bleich, David. "Ethnography and the Study of Literacy: Prospects for Socially Generous Research." *Into the Field: Sites of Composition Studies.* Ed. Anne Ruggles Gere. New York: MLA, 1993. 176–92.

Bridwell-Bowles, Lillian. "Research in Composition: Issues and Methods." *An Introduction to Composition Studies.* Ed. Erika Lindemann and Gary Tate. New York: Oxford UP, 1991. 94–117.

Brodkey, Linda. "Writing Ethnographic Narratives." *Written Communication* 4 (1987): 25–50.

Calkins, Lucy McCormick. "Forming Research Communities among Naturalistic Researchers." *Perspectives on Research and Scholarship in Composition.* Ed. Ben W. McClelland and Timothy R. Donovan. New York: MLA, 1985. 125–44.

Card, Claudia, ed. *Feminist Ethics.* Lawrence: UP of Kansas, 1991.

Chin, Elaine. "Ethnographic Interviews and Writing Research: A Critical Examination of the Methodology." *Speaking about Writing: Reflections on Research Methodology.* Ed. Peter Smagorinsky. Vol. 8 of Sage Series in Written Communication. Thousand Oaks: Sage, 1994. 247–72.

Chiseri-Strater, Elizabeth. *Academic Literacies: The Public and Private Discourse of University Students.* Portsmouth: Boynton/Cook, 1991.

Cintron, Ralph. "Wearing a Pith Helmet at a Sly Angle: Or, Can Writing Researchers Do Ethnography in a Postmodern Era?" *Written Communication* 10 (1993): 371–412.

Clifford, James. "On Ethnographic Authority." *The Predicament of Culture: Twentieth-Century Ethnography, Literature, and Art.* Cambridge: Harvard UP, 1988. 21–54.

Clifford, James, and George E. Marcus, eds. *Writing Culture: The Poetics and Politics of Ethnography.* Berkeley: U of California P, 1986.

Cross, Geoffrey A. *Collaboration and Conflict: A Contextual Exploration of Group Writing and Positive Emphasis.* Cresskill: Hampton P, 1994.

Denzin, Norman K., and Yvonne S. Lincoln, eds. *Handbook of Qualitative Research.* Thousand Oaks: Sage, 1994.

Doheny-Farina, Stephen. "Writing in an Emerging Organization: An Ethnographic Study." *Written Communication* 3 (1986): 158–85.

Doheny-Farina, Stephen, and Lee Odell. "Ethnographic Research on Writing: Assumptions and Methodology." *Writing in Nonacademic Settings.* Ed. Lee Odell and Dixie Goswami. New York: Guilford P, 1986. 503–35.

Fonow, Mary Margaret, and Judith A. Cook. "Back to the Future: A Look at the Second Wave of Feminist Epistemology and Methodology." *Beyond Methodology: Feminist Scholarship as Lived Research.* Ed. Mary Margaret Fonow and Judith A. Cook. Bloomington: Indiana UP, 1991. 1–15.

Frye, Marilyn. "A Response to *Lesbian Ethics:* Why *Ethics?*" *Feminist Ethics.* Ed. Claudia Card. Lawrence: UP of Kansas, 1991. 52–59.

Geertz, Clifford. *Works and Lives: The Anthropologist as Author.* Stanford: Stanford UP, 1988.

Gere, Anne Ruggles. "Empirical Research in Composition." *Perspectives on Research and Scholarship in Composition.* Ed. Ben W. McClelland and Timothy R. Donovan. New York: MLA, 1985. 110–24.

Goldblatt, Eli C. *'Round My Way: Authority and Double-Consciousness in Three Urban High School Writers.* Pittsburgh: U of Pittsburgh P, 1995.

Goswami, Dixie, and Peter Stillman, eds. *Reclaiming the Classroom.* Upper Montclair: Boynton/Cook, 1987.

Herndl, Carl G. "Writing Ethnography: Representation, Rhetoric, and Institutional Practices." *College English* 53 (1991): 320–32.

Hillocks, George Jr. "Reconciling the Qualitative and Quantitative." Beach, Green, Kamil, and Shanahan 57–65.

Kantor, Kenneth, Dan Kirby, and Judith Goetz. "Research in Context: Ethnographic Studies in English Education." *Research in the Teaching of English* 15 (1981): 293–309.

Kirsch, Gesa E., and Joy S. Ritchie. "Beyond the Personal: Theorizing a Politics of Location in Composition Research." *College Composition and Communication* 46 (1995): 7–29.

Kirsch, Gesa E., and Patricia A. Sullivan, eds. *Methods and Methodology in Composition Research.* Carbondale: Southern Illinois UP, 1992.

Kleine, Michael. "Beyond Triangulation: Ethnography, Writing, and Rhetoric." *Journal of Advanced Composition* 10 (1990): 117–25.

Lauer, Janice M., and J. William Asher. *Composition Research: Empirical Designs.* New York: Oxford UP, 1988.

Lunsford, Andrea A. "Rhetoric and Composition." *Introduction to Scholarship in Modern Languages and Literatures.* 2nd ed. Ed. Joseph Gibaldi. New York: MLA, 1992. 77–100.

Malinowitz, Harriet. *Textual Orientations: Lesbian and Gay Students and the Making of Discourse Communities.* Portsmouth: Boynton/Cook-Heinemann, 1995.

Moss, Beverly. "Ethnography and Composition: Studying Language at Home." *Methods and Methodology in Composition Research.* Ed. Gesa Kirsch and Patricia A. Sullivan. Carbondale: Southern Illinois UP, 1992. 153–71.

———, ed. *Literacy across Communities.* Cresskill: Hampton P, 1994.

Myers, Miles. *The Teacher-Researcher: How to Study Writing in the Classroom.* Urbana: ERIC and NCTE, 1985.

Noddings, Nel. *Caring, a Feminine Approach to Ethics & Moral Education.* Berkeley: U of California P, 1984.

North, Stephen. *The Making of Knowledge in Composition: Portrait of an Emerging Field.* Upper Montclair: Boynton/Cook, 1987.

Odell, Lee. "Planning Classroom Research." Goswami and Stillman. 128–60.

Peshkin, Alan. "In Search of Subjectivity—One's Own." *Educational Researcher* 17.7 (1988): 17–21.

Porter, James E. "Developing a Postmodern Ethics of Rhetoric and Composition." *Defining the New Rhetorics.* Ed. Theresa Enos and Stuart C. Brown. Vol. 7 of Sage Series in Written Communication. Newbury Park: Sage, 1993. 207–26.

Ray, Ruth E. *The Practice of Theory: Teacher Research in Composition.* Urbana: NCTE, 1993.

Schaafsma, David. *Eating on the Street: Teaching Literacy in a Multicultural Society.* Pittsburgh: U of Pittsburgh P, 1993.

Smith, Dorothy E. "Some Implications of a Sociology for Women." *Woman in a Man-Made World: A Socio-Economic Handbook.* 2nd ed. Ed. Nona Glazer and Helen Youngelson Waehrer. Chicago: Rand McNally, 1977. 15–29.

Sunstein, Bonnie S. *Composing a Culture: Inside a Summer Writing Program with High School Teachers.* Portsmouth: Boynton/Cook-Heinemann, 1994.

Taylor, Denny. *Family Literacy: Young Children Learning to Read and Write.* Exeter: Heinemann, 1983.

Tronto, Joan. "Beyond Gender Difference to a Theory of Care." *Signs* 12 (1987): 644–63.

————. *Moral Boundaries: A Political Argument for an Ethic of Care.* New York: Routledge, 1993.

Van Maanen, John. *Tales of the Field: On Writing Ethnography.* Chicago: U of Chicago P, 1988.

Wolf, Margery. *A Thrice-Told Tale: Feminism, Postmodernism, and Ethnographic Responsibility.* Stanford: Stanford UP, 1992.

Young, Iris Marion. *Justice and the Politics of Difference.* Princeton: Princeton UP, 1990.

I Confronting Ethical Dilemmas

1 Seduction and Betrayal in Qualitative Research

Thomas Newkirk
University of New Hampshire

"But I am mightily pleased, Signor Bachelor Sampson Carrasco, that the author of the history has not spoken ill of me; for, upon the faith of a trusty squire, had he said anything of me unbecoming an old Christian, as I am, the deaf should have heard of it." "That would be working miracles," answered Sampson. "Miracles or no miracles," quoth Sancho, "people should take heed what they say and write of other folks, and not set anything down that comes uppermost."

—Miguel de Cervantes, *The Adventures of Don Quixote*

Every qualitative researcher I know has an ethical story to tell, one in which he or she wrestled with what I will call "the ethics of bad news." Jack Douglas poses this issue well:

> Whenever people let us into the private realms of their lives as friends they implicitly impose on us, and we accept, the obligation of not telling anyone things that will hurt them, but we also know that there are some implicit limits to the waiver of moral denunciation. What are the limits? Nobody knows until they face the situation at hand and construct their meanings and course of action—in anguish. (30)

Part of this anguish comes from our rarely making clear to the person being studied that there are, in fact, limits to the implicit waiver of denunciation. In the opening encounters with those we study, we may give no indication that our rendering of them may be partially or wholly negative. We may even suspect that our pose of friendliness (the way we emphasize our good will, our interest in the subject, in students, in gaining knowledge useful to teachers—our "ethos") was a strategy to disarm the person we study, an act of seduction. Because we present ourselves as completely well-meaning, we find ourselves in moral difficulty when we write "bad news" in our final rendering. Even though the negative might be balanced by the positive, and even though we have carefully disguised the identity of the person we render, we (and often the subject) feel as if a trust has been betrayed. And it often has.

Janet Malcolm, in her extraordinary look at journalistic ethics, *The Journalist and the Murderer,* sees this form of betrayal as virtually inevitable. In a paragraph that set the profession's teeth on edge, she writes:

> Every journalist who is not too stupid or full of himself to notice what is going on knows that what he does is morally indefensible. He is a kind of confidence man, preying on people's vanity, ignorance, or loneliness, gaining their trust and betraying them without remorse. . . . Journalists justify their treachery in various ways according to their temperaments. The more pompous talk about freedom of speech and "the public's right to know"; the least talented talk about Art; the seemliest murmur about earning a living. (3)

Convinced of our own benevolence, we may recoil from Malcolm's characterization, yet a more disciplined response is to acknowledge the exploitative potential of qualitative research and to consider guidelines that may do what traditional consent forms clearly fail to do—protect the person being rendered.

Paradoxically, the measures devised to protect those being studied often aid the researcher in the seduction. An opening ritual is to sit down with prospective subjects and go over an "informed consent form" approved by the institution's committee on human subject research. Typically these forms provide a very brief and often vague description of the project, and then provide a number of assurances—that the subject can decline to participate and can withdraw at any point, that he or she will remain anonymous, and that results of the study will not affect grades in any course related to the research or be communicated to supervisors.

The form helps to reinforce the impression of the researcher's solicitousness; in Erving Goffman's terms, the consent form is part of our "sign-equipment" (*The Presentation of Self* 36). It is one of the props that all professions use to enact idealized roles. For example, the biological researcher's white lab coat may have a sanitary function, but it also *signifies* integrity, discipline, care; it enables the researcher to carry off an idealized performance. Charles Cooley writes that the

> impulse to show the world a better or idealized aspect of ourselves finds an organized expression in the various professions and classes, each of which has to some extent a cant or pose, which its members assume unconsciously, for the most part, but which has the effect of a conspiracy to work upon the credulity of the rest of the world. (qtd. in Goffman, *The Presentation of Self* 35)

The consent form tends to heighten the sense of importance of the study about to be undertaken, and, most significantly, by being filled with assurances it stresses our own benevolence. Then, in a moment of great irony, the subject signs a form indicating he or she was fully informed—even though the American Psychological Association grants researchers the right to deceive in the interests of science (633–38).

My guess is that outright deception, such as Stanley Milgram carried out in his infamous obedience study, is not the major problem. The problem arises in the neutral, benign, and general way in which the project is often described to those involved. For example, in a study of teacher-student discourse, the teacher being recruited for the study may learn that it "will look at the ways in which culture and gender influence classroom interaction." This statement is not directly deceptive, but it may hide the researcher's true interest, which is to document the ways in which teachers silence or dominate students. This truer intent may well be hidden for fear of tipping the study and scaring the teacher away from participating. Because of this benign description, the teacher is given no inkling that bad news may become an issue, and consequently there is no procedure in place for handling bad news.

University researchers who study the classrooms of public school teachers and subordinates (students and teaching assistants, nontenured faculty) have a special obligation to recognize the vulnerability of those they study (see also Anderson's discussion, this volume). Literacy researchers operate in hierarchical systems in which they typically "study down," creating descriptions of those with less education, professional status, economic resources. In many cases, the teachers being studied feel some professional discomfort (no matter what the consent form says) in saying no. Just as in cases of sexual harassment, it is clearly unethical to use our position in the hierarchy to place those lower in the hierarchy in a professionally embarrassing situation (i.e., for them to unwittingly provide "bad news" for our critical descriptions of their practices).

I will approach this issue more concretely by examining two widely read studies that explore the ways in which gender, class, and culture contribute to miscommunication and flawed evaluation in classroom situations. The first study will be Hull, Rose, Fraser, and Castellano's "Remediation as Social Construct: Perspectives from an Analysis of Classroom Discourse," winner of the 1992 Braddock Award, given by the Conference on College Composition and Communication. The second is Linda Brodkey's "On the Subjects of Class and Gender in 'The Literacy Letters.'" From this specific examination I will move to some very provisional guidelines for university researchers who "study down."

The Ethics of Intervention

"Remediation as Social Construct" is a subtle study that examines the classroom discourse of June, a doctoral student presumably teaching college composition as an adjunct or teaching assistant, and Maria, who was born in El Salvador and learned English as a second language. The study shows how June classifies Maria as deficient in sequential thinking when, in fact, her primary "difficulty" is her failure to fit into a fairly restrictive initiate-respond-evaluate pattern of classroom conversation (see Mehan). She would, for example, persist in developing *her* topic when the teacher had indicated she wanted to move on. Thus what is at most a different conversational style is transformed into a cognitive deficit. Using a micro-macro pattern of investigation, the authors move from their fine-grained look at classroom talk to a survey of the broader cultural assumptions that have historically "constructed" remediation by turning differences such as the one they identified into cognitive deficits.

I want to read this study against the grain by focusing on the situation and depiction of June as a research subject. The authors take pains to mitigate their criticism of her; she is introduced as follows:

> The teacher in this study was June, a recent and respected graduate of a long-standing composition program and a candidate for an advanced degree in literature. Our work with June confirmed her commitment to teaching. She spent a great deal of time responding to papers at home and meeting with students in conferences, and she was interested in discussing composition research and finding ways to apply it in her classroom. In fact, she volunteered to participate in our study because she saw it as an occasion to be reflective about her own teaching and to improve instruction for students in remedial classes. (Hull et al. 300)

It is not clear whether June understood when she volunteered for the study that her teaching practices might be so publicly exhibited as prejudicial. But I want to focus on the "occasion to be reflective" that drew June to the study because these reflective interviews seem to have been less than candid.

After a class in which she appeared to dismiss Maria's contribution about systems for rating videos, June commented on Maria's classroom talk:

> Maria is becoming to me the Queen of the Non Sequiturs. You know, she really is just not quite. . . . That's, that's why I'm sort of amazed at times at, at her writing level, which is not really too bad. . . . Because her thinking level seems to be so scattered that I would expect that her writing would be a lot more disorganized and disjointed. (310)

We do not get the interviewers' reply to this problematic interpretation, but there is no evidence that they put forward to June their counterhypothesis that Maria was simply having trouble with the structure of classroom discussion. In fact, there is no evidence that June learned of this hypothesis until the study was published. It appears that the reflection was one-sided: June would offer up her reflections on Maria, but the researchers did not tip their hand about what they saw as the unfair stereotyping that was going on. Although the authors later advocate work that "look[s] closely at writing instruction to identify moments when teachers transcend deficit attitudes," they seemed to have had such a moment in the interview but remained silent about what they saw (318). Our image of June would be much more positive if we saw her reflecting on this issue and perhaps monitoring her own classroom talk to give students like Maria greater space.

It is also possible that the failure to intervene and reveal their concerns may have hurt Maria herself. The authors note that the course sapped Maria's confidence:

> By the end of the semester, the mismatch between Maria's discourse style and that of the classroom seemed to be taking a toll. Maria told us in her last tutoring session that she now "had some problems with . . . English," that her writing had gotten "longer" but not necessarily better, and that she was "not a very good speaker." (317)

It may be that the conversational patterns that helped cause this evaluation were so deeply ingrained that researcher intervention may have had little effect. But the decision not to discuss with June their counterhypothesis raises the ethical question of what researchers' responsibilities to students are. If they saw Maria sinking—and had a clear idea why she was sinking—what justification do they have for not saying something?

There are a couple of ethical justifications that might be offered. It might be claimed that June, in agreeing to the study, should have realized that negative results were possible, no matter how solicitous the researchers appeared. An analogy might be made to chess, a game filled with deceptions. If someone entices me with a pawn and takes my rook,

I may be upset with myself, but I am not likely to be morally outraged. Deception is an openly agreed part of the game. Similarly, if Bill Clinton is being interviewed by William Buckley, they might small talk about common acquaintances at Yale before getting down to business. Yet if Clinton thinks this friendliness means Buckley will write a positive column—and if he is outraged when he doesn't—we are more likely to think Clinton a fool than Buckley a deceiver. This kind of deception is part of the game.

It seems less likely, though, that a research subject will (or should) see deception as an expected stance from one's teacher or from a scholar at an institution where one works. The subject in this case is more likely to see the solicitousness as a genuine reflection of the researcher's attitude.

It could be argued that a utilitarian cost-benefit analysis might show that the "greater good" of the published study, in this case the insights into stereotyping, outweighs the costs. It could also be argued that the harm to June (who, after all, remains anonymous) is more than balanced by the good that comes from bringing this issue to the attention of the profession, perhaps preventing mismatches like the one illustrated. This benefit outweighs the professional embarrassment (and perhaps feeling of betrayal) that June may feel when she reads her class portrayed this way. It also outweighs other "harms"—Maria's lessened self-esteem, the moral discomfort researchers may have felt in depicting June, and the possibility that such treatment may make teachers reluctant to take part in such studies.

But ethicists have regularly noted the limitations of this utilitarian attempt to balance benefits and harms in the social sciences. Unlike in medical research, benefits and harms are not equally distributed; that is, in a heart bypass operation the benefits and harms *both* accrue to the patient. In qualitative research critical of classroom practices, the most direct benefits accrue to the researcher and the most direct harms often to the subject. The value of a study to the profession, its wider influence, as any researcher knows, is easy to overestimate. In practice, "this philosophical outlook tends, generally, to discount local harm by appeal to the general balance of good over evil and to neglect systematically the indebtedness of the researcher to the researched" (May 363).

This ethical perspective needs to be balanced by one which gives more weight to local harms. As a simple rule of thumb, we might ask how we would feel if *we* were the subject of this study, if we were June. I suspect we would have wanted to know more about what judgments researchers were making. I would have wanted a chance to talk about this problem and, if possible, an opportunity to try to be open to "digressive" classroom contributions. It may well have been these types of opportunities June wanted when she agreed to participate.

Speaking "Over" the Subjects

Linda Brodkey's study, "On the Subjects of Class and Gender in 'The Literacy Letters,'" raises the question of our obligations to our own students whom we involve in our research. Her study examines a letter-writing project she conducted in a graduate class on the teaching of writing, what she calls "a pen-pal experience for adults" (282). Six of her middle-class graduate students corresponded with six white working-class women in an adult basic education (ABE) class taught by one of the students in Brodkey's class.

It seems from her description that participation was voluntary, but clearly an "invitation" of this sort from one's own teacher for her research project carries some coercive force. There was one key prohibition: the participants could not contact each other, either in person or by telephone, at any time during the study (no reason is given for this prohibition). Students gave Brodkey permission to photocopy the letters, though she agreed not to read the letters until the end of the semester to protect the educational rights of those who agreed to participate.

Brodkey claims that her own students were almost completely unable to engage the narratives of the ABE students, and, though she acknowledges that the teachers in her study "were not ogres," she condemns their efforts in particularly harsh terms:

> [T]he teachers' markedly inept responses to their correspondents' narratives suggest that the hegemony of educational discourse warrants teachers not only to represent themselves as subjects unified by the internal conflicts like guilt that preoccupy professionals, but to disclaim narratives that represent a subject alternatively unified in its conflicts with external material reality. This refusal to acknowledge the content of their correspondents' narratives, most explicable as a professional class narcissism that sees itself everywhere it looks, alienates the ABE writers from educational discourse and, more importantly, from the teachers it ostensibly authorizes. (285)

We get almost no indication of the ABE students' understanding of these letters (and it seems it was not elicited as part of the study). Brodkey offers no direct evidence that they *were* alienated. The only hint we get about her own students is that they found the letters "stressful" (282). And well they might.

To examine the justice of Brodkey's condemnation, we need to imagine ourselves in the rhetorical situation she placed her students in. They were asked to correspond with people they had never met, people whom they were enjoined from meeting. This lack of common ground is clearly a major impediment. Their communication was part of a research project, and they had given their teacher permission to quote from their letters for publication. We should ask of this "task" the same kinds of questions we ask of experimental research: Are the results of the study more a reflection of the task itself, and perhaps not of the inability of these teachers to engage with narratives of people from a different socioeconomic-discursive class? To put it more bluntly: Were the students set up for failure?

In this situation, I would be tentative and evasive, as if I were on the blindest of blind dates. I might be hesitant to engage the reality of the "other" because I lacked the common ground, the standing, for such an engagement. My own narratives might be an evasion of engagement (I suspect this is common in enforced pen-pal situations). As I read these responses, I sense the awkwardness of people thrown into an almost impossible rhetorical situation. I will look at one example, Brodkey's commentary, and a possible alternative that her student might have given (had he been asked).

I will quote from the Dora-Don correspondence, which in the early exchanges consisted of Dora's responses to the self-mocking stories that Don, Brodkey's student, told. After a few weeks Dora reverses roles and writes:

> I don't have must to siad this week a good frineds husband was kill satday at 3:15 the man who kill him is a good man he would give you the shirt off his back it is really self-defense but anyway I see police academy three it was funny but not is good as the first two (286)

Don responds as follows:

> I'm sorry to hear about the problem that you wrote about last week. It's always hard to know what to say when the situation is as unusual as that one. I hope that everything is getting a little better, at least for you trying to know what to say and do in that situation. (287)

Brodkey sees this response as typical of her students' failure to engage with the content of the ABE students' narratives:

> Don might have assisted her by simply responding to the content of her story. He might have asked about motive or even asked

> why she says nothing about the victim. But Don's response suggests only that he is nonplussed. . . . Don's linguistic facility, under the circumstances, only amplifies the discursive inadequacy of this passage as a response to the content of her narrative. (286–87)

My reading of Don's response is entirely different. He seems to be trying to extend sympathy to a woman in a difficult position; she must offer solace to her friend—while believing in the essential goodness of the man who shot her friend's husband. To use Don's words, "know[ing] what to say and do" in this situation is no easy thing. As to the "inadequacy" of the message, one wonders how Brodkey can make this judgment without learning the reaction of the recipient. In effect, Brodkey has silenced both groups of students so that she can allow her own interpretation to stand uncontested.

Since Don is not allowed to speak, I will try to imagine a response he might have made if Brodkey had shared her opinion that he should have engaged the content of the narrative and asked Dora why she has said nothing about the victim:

> It took me a long time to write this letter. In fact, I was surprised she shared this news with me since we really hardly know each other. It would seem rude to ask her why she said nothing about the victim—like I'm accusing her of not being sensitive. I finally just tried to offer her my sympathy and hope that she can deal with it. As I read it over it sounds euphemistic—I say "problem" instead of "murder." It's like when you learn someone has cancer, you might say "illness."

If a rationale like this had been included in Brodkey's account, her own completely uncontested interpretation might have been challenged. Don almost surely would be viewed more sympathetically, and his response, awkward as it is, might be seen as an attempt to make human contact in a highly contrived situation. It might have happened.

The great paradox of Brodkey's study is that she illustrates the hegemonic practices that she deplores in her students' letters. Just as her students may not have engaged the narratives of the ABE students, she herself has neither elicited nor allowed any interpretive scope to the students writing the letters. She has so privileged her own reading of the letters that we hear nothing from those, subordinated in the educational hierarchy, who engaged in the correspondence.

Brodkey seems to imply that her ethical obligations to her students were met when they signed an agreement to have the letters photocopied with an understanding that they would not be read before the end of the semester. In retrospect, this protection seems flimsy indeed. Could they have even imagined that their consent would lead to what amounts to professional condemnation in a leading journal in the field? And can it plausibly be argued that the students from both groups, who have offered their time to advance the professional career of the author, did not deserve a chance to qualify and challenge her reading of their work? I would even argue that this study and many others would benefit from polyvocality, a chorus of competing and perhaps irresolvable readings of the same "text."

Toward an Ethics of Rendering

The solution to the dilemma of "bad news" is clearly not to insist that renderings of classrooms and teachers should avoid the negative, for the researcher has ethical obligations to the reader to honestly represent the data he or she gathers. If bad news is screened, the depiction can lose integrity, complexity, and even plausibility. Much of the classroom research coming out of the whole language-writing process movement, for example, seems to exclude instances where the approach did not work, where, for example, students misused the freedom they were given. What we often have is *research as advocacy,* a selectively chosen sample of the most convincing examples of student success. Such an approach to rendering shifts the terms of deception—here the contract with the reader seems to be broken.

It is also unwise to suggest any inflexible rule for dealing with "bad news" because qualitative research, and the relationships created in studies, are so diverse. In some cases, a researcher's candor may close the doors of an important site, allowing those responsible for unwise or harmful practices to successfully prevent disclosure. Had Erving Goffman been very specific about his theories of "total institutions," St. Elizabeth's Hospital might well have prevented him from gathering data for *Asylums.* I would argue, though, that literacy researchers, particularly as they work with teachers, can rarely claim this necessity of deception so that they might expose educational malpractice (though there may be such cases).

To preserve flexibility, and at the same time suggest some principles of action, I will try to outline a "default" position. This will be, in effect, the standard "setting," the general procedure for working with teachers in classroom-based qualitative research. Like the default setting on a computer program, this procedure can be changed—but the researcher is responsible for explaining why he or she chose to vary the default position. In Brodkey's case, for example, this default rule would not require that she solicit the interpretations of the students in both classes, but it would require her to explain why she did not. In the Hull, Rose, Fraser, and Castellano study, there may have been reasons why June was not told of their counterhypothesis (the pattern may have appeared to them too late), but those reasons for moving off the default position should be given.

1. "Bad News" and the Consent Agreement

Anyone who spends a great deal of time in a teacher's classroom, particularly someone who has experience in a similar teaching situation, will observe practices that seem ineffective. And some of these will probably relate to the issues the researcher is examining. It is naïve to pretend otherwise, although in the early courtship this possibility may be momentarily put aside. As part of the initial agreement, the researcher should state a willingness to bring up issues, problems, or questions (and a corresponding willingness on the part of the teacher to have them brought up). If this mention of possible "bad news" is disturbing or alarming to the teachers, they should be encouraged *not* to participate—that, after all, is the primary intent of the informed consent agreement. The researcher is then obligated to raise issues as they occur, and not to avoid discussing them, and then to raise them in print. It is of course naïve to believe that this alteration of the consent arrangement will *solve* the problem because at the start of the project the possibility of "bad news" may seem so hypothetical. Even so, I would argue that laying out a process for talking about issues at least provides a foundation for later discussions.

2. The Rights of Co-interpretation

The researcher should grant the teacher (and, when relevant, her students) the opportunity to respond to interpretations of problematical situations. When, as outlined above, those being studied have access to the researcher's emerging questions and interpretations, there is an opportunity to offer counterinterpretations or provide mitigating information. Ideally these exchanges should be part of the data gathering and not be postponed for the time when a full manuscript has been prepared. My experience is that, at that point, research "subjects" may be reluctant to amend a report that seems so final.

In addition, the researcher has the responsibility to include participant interpretations even if they conflict with the judgment the researcher is making. In the case of Brodkey's study, the effectiveness or ineffectiveness of the letters was surely open to multiple views—hers, her students, and those of the students in the ABE class. The default position would be to solicit and juxtapose these multiple perspectives.

3. The Responsibility of Intervention

If the researcher notes teaching practices that seem ineffective, I would also argue that there is an ethical responsibility to work with the teacher to deal with problems the researcher and teacher identify. This kind of activism, it seems to me, does not contaminate the study. (The idea that activism can contaminate seems a vestige of positivism still alive in ethnography.) "Going native" in this way is a natural and productive challenge for those involved; it is the payoff that teachers and schools hope for when they volunteer for a study. The best example of this form of intervention is the curricular work Shirley Brice Heath did in the Piedmont Carolina school attended by the children in her study. She could have taken a noninterventionist stance and documented the ways in which home language patterns interfered with school expectations. Instead, she worked with teachers in the school to train students to be ethnographers of language, to play school language off against home language. What could have been an indictment of school was transformed into an illustration of educational possibilities. Other examples are Elizabeth Chiseri-Strater's collaboration with an art history teacher she studied, and Walvoord and McCarthy's work with a large naturalistic writing-across-the-curriculum study.

Ultimately those of us in the university must question the automatic belief in our own benevolence, the automatic equation between our own academic success and ethical behavior. For the stakes are high. Anyone who spends time with public school teachers—or even overhears community college teachers trying to find a relevant session at the Conference on College Composition and Communication convention—senses the fissure between those who teach literacy and those who study or theorize about it. Often those of us who teach at the university are viewed as comically out of touch with the professional lives of those who teach literacy in this country. If we are to be players at all in educational reform, we will have to solicit the "readings" teachers offer of their situations and enter into dialogue with them.

As Sancho Panza so eloquently reminds us, those who turn other people's lives into texts hold real power. Sancho of course lacks this power by his class, and not coincidentally by his illiteracy. In the second part of *Don Quixote,* he is disadvantaged in a complex way. Again and again, he hears of a book about his master and him, written by the Moor Cid Hamet Benengeli and translated into Castilian—in fact the book we, as readers, have just finished. (Cervantes adopts the conceit that he *found* the book.) We have the advantage over Sancho, who can only learn about this story and his role in it from those who have money and literacy. He interrupts one of his master's long disquisitions on the truthfulness of art to worry aloud about his characterization:

> "Well, then," said Sancho, "if this Signor Moor is so fond of telling the truth, and my master's rib-roastings are all set down, I suppose mine are not forgotten; for they never took measure of his worship's shoulders, but at the same time they contrived to get the whole length and breadth of my whole body." (306)

He never gets an answer, though. His master silences him with "Sancho, thou art an arch rogue" (306). He is a character denied access to his own characterization. From this vulnerable, subordinated position, he reminds us that "people should take heed what they say and write of other folks" (307).

Works Cited

American Psychological Association. "Ethical Principles of Psychologists." *American Psychologist* 36 (1981): 633–38.

Brodkey, Linda. "On the Subjects of Class and Gender in 'The Literacy Letters.'" *College English* 51 (1989): 125–41. Rpt. in *Rhetoric and Composition: A Sourcebook for Teachers and Writers.* Ed. Richard L. Graves. 3rd ed. Portsmouth: Boynton/Cook, 1990. 279–95.

Cervantes [Saavedra], Miguel de. *The Adventures of Don Quixote de la Mancha.* 1605 and 1615. New York: Dodd, Mead, 1962.

Chiseri-Strater, Elizabeth. *Academic Literacies: The Public and Private Discourse of University Students.* Portsmouth: Boynton/Cook, 1991.

Douglas, Jack D. "Living Morality versus Bureaucratic Fiat." *Deviance and Decency: The Ethics of Research with Human Subjects.* Ed. Carl B. Klockars and Finbarr W. O'Connor. Beverly Hills: Sage, 1979. 13–33.

Goffman, Erving. *Asylums: Essays on the Social Situation of Mental Patients and Other Inmates.* Chicago: Aldine, 1962.

———. *The Presentation of Self in Everyday Life.* New York: Doubleday Anchor, 1959.

Heath, Shirley Brice. *Ways with Words: Language, Life and Work in Communities and Classrooms.* Cambridge: Cambridge UP, 1983.

Hull, Glynda, Mike Rose, Kay Losey Fraser, and Marisa Castellano. "Remediation as Social Construct: Perspectives from an Analysis of Classroom Discourse." *College Composition and Communication* 42 (1991): 299–329.

Malcolm, Janet. *The Journalist and the Murderer.* New York: Knopf, 1990.

May, William F. "Doing Ethics: The Bearing of Ethical Theories on Fieldwork." *Social Problems* 27 (1980): 358–70.

Mehan, Hugh. *Learning Lessons: Social Organization in the Classroom.* Cambridge: Harvard UP, 1979.

Milgram, Stanley. *Obedience to Authority: An Experimental View.* New York: Harper and Row, 1974.

Walvoord, Barbara E., and Lucille P. McCarthy. *Writing and Thinking in College: A Naturalistic Study of Students in Four Disciplines.* Urbana: NCTE, 1990.

2 Still-Life: Representations and Silences in the Participant-Observer Role

Brenda Jo Brueggemann
The Ohio State University

Hold still, we're going to do your portrait, so that you can begin looking like it right away.

—Hélène Cixous, "The Laugh of the Medusa"

I want to take a picture and frame issues of "representation" in qualitative composition research here. In doing so, I will be considering both general issues and my own specific qualitative research in a "critical gesture" (Herndl 323). This gesture indicates my ever stronger (and ever more troubled) belief that, as Herndl himself makes clear, "constructing the ethnographic account is a rhetorical activity" (321), governed in part, large or small, by institutional practices. As I wrestle with the troubling issues this belief has left me with, I will open a Pandora's Box that (be forewarned) I do not necessarily intend to close again. Be further forewarned: the subject of my portrait here—"the crisis of representation," as Yvonna Lincoln and Norman Denzin have called it (577)—is not likely to hold still or be necessarily accurate.

In addressing "the crisis of representation" I want to ask, as Michel Foucault does at the end of his essay "What Is an Author," "What does it matter who is speaking?" (101). What difference, I ask, does it make *who* researches, *who* writes about, *who* represents "subjects" in composition research? And what difference does it make *how* these subjects are represented?

Exploring these questions, I will first turn to a more general theoretical examination of what the participant-observer role, so central to ethnographic and qualitative research, currently seems to be. But I also intend, in a second section, to explore this question within the more specific frame of the ethnographically oriented case studies of deaf student writers I conducted a few years ago at Gallaudet University.[1] Finally, in a third section, I will summarize by suggesting a list of guiding questions we might use to consider issues of representation and silence in our qualitative research. These three sections of my essay will be concerned with representative roles and role playing—with both researcher and subject roles, both self-constructed and socially constructed roles, both preestablished and constructed-in-the-process roles, and both participant and observer roles. Just as Michelle Fine has recently "worked the hyphen" in the self-other relationship of qualitative research, I plan to explore, both generally and specifically, what goes on in the hyphenated space of the participant-observer role. And I also plan to show how that hyphenated space has worked and continues to work me as I have tried to work it.

Participation, Observation, Representation

> *Often this speech about the "other" annihilates, erases: "no need to hear your voice when I can talk about you better than you can speak about yourself. No need to hear your voice. Only tell me about your pain. I want to know your story. And then I will tell it back to you in a new way. Tell it back to you in such a way that it has become mine, my own. Re-writing you, I write myself anew. I am still author, authority. I am still the colonizer, the speaking subject, and you are now at the center of my talk." Stop.*

> —bell hooks, *Yearning: Race, Gender, and Cultural Politics*

As Clifford Geertz makes clear in his essay on "'The Native's Point of View'" (*Local Knowledge*), the posthumous publication of Malinowski's myth-shattering *A Diary in the Strict Sense of the Term*—in which Malinowski tells the "real" story behind his fieldwork for the anthropological classic *Argonauts of the Western Pacific*—significantly altered previous conceptions of the much celebrated participant-observer role in ethnographic fieldwork. With this publication, the Janus-faced participant-observer, capable of maintaining some sort of objective observer distance while simultaneously "going native" as participant, was unmasked. Until this point in anthropology (and indeed, probably for some time after it), the dangers of too much objectivity *and* the dangers of too much subjectivity were supposedly kept neatly in checks and balances by the so-called participant-observer role. But Malinowski's *Diary* toppled that system of checks and balances as "the myth of the chameleon fieldworker, perfectly self-tuned to his exotic surroundings, a walking miracle of empathy, tact, patience, and cosmopolitanism, was demolished by the man who had perhaps done most to create it" (Geertz, *Local Knowledge* 56). Far from being either empathetic or objective, the man who was largely responsible for the fashioning of anthropology as a serious academic discipline (and ethnography as a serious methodology) "had rude things to say about the natives he was living with, and rude words to say it in. He spent a great deal of time wishing he were elsewhere" (Geertz 56).

In 1967, Malinowski's brazen (albeit posthumous) confession that things political and personal did, in fact, grossly affect one's "research" reeked of scandal. But since then qualitative research (and composition studies) have both been through the 1980s and postmodernism. Today rhetoric, politics, and the personal are very much with us; and they are with us as we do fieldwork, as we write it down, write it up, and as we represent our selves and the "others" we study in this writing. The words of Edward Bruner stand as near-dogma on this account: the qualitative researcher is now "historically positioned and locally situated [as] an all-too-human [observer] of the human condition," and the meaning such a researcher might make is "radically plural, always open, and . . . there is politics in every account" (1).

This plural, open, radicalized meaning makes for what Lincoln and Denzin have named as two of the most pressing issues for qualitative research today: "the crises of representation and legitimation" (576). And they are not alone in naming representation as a qualitative research crisis; others in their impressive *Handbook of Qualitative Research* offer counsel and further critique on qualitative researchers' reproduction of a "contradiction-filled . . . colonizing discourse of the 'Other'" (Fine 70).[2] "Self-reflexivity" has lately been lauded as an antidote to such colonizing discourse. Yet I would suggest that such self-reflexivity, turning as it does on issues of representation, risks turning representation into a solipsistic, rhetorical position in which the researcher (the self)— ah, once again—usurps the position of the subject (the other). For in being self-reflexive, we turn the lens back on ourselves, put ourselves at the center of representation. We are still, then, as bell hooks mocks in this section's epigraph, "author, authority" as we rewrite *ourselves* anew. Yet instead of the "other," we have now put *ourselves* back at the center of our talk.

And when we are back in the center, as such, being reflexive only further complicates the issue of representation, only further undercuts the possibilities (and sensibilities) of being the "chameleon fieldworker," the mythical "participant-observer." If we choose to be reflexive, to put the roles and representations of our subjects and our selves under scrutiny, we cannot possibly be the chimeric, both/and, distanced yet near, objective yet subjective, participant-observer. We can be neither exclusively participant nor wholly observer because, in order to be reflexive in our roles and representations as qualitative researchers, our frames must always be ready to shift; they cannot be contained in any of these entities. We must instead "work the hyphen," traverse the terrain of what is "happening between" participant and observer, learn to negotiate the "zippered borders" of our various roles and representations (Fine 70).

It is this kind of ethnographic work that David Bleich has recently (and rather idealistically, I think) suggested might offer "prospects for socially generous research" in literacy studies (176). But again, beware: I do not think this kind of work will solve the issues of the crisis of representation—or at least not solve them in a way that will give us solid answers. In fact, I think we risk encountering moments of our own stillness—our own silence, stasis, and absence—when we stay in the space between participant and observer. Not an always comfortable role, to be sure. (But certainly one, at least, that qualitative researchers have long placed their own subjects in.)

Of Knowledge Ownership, Unclear Messages, and Silence

> *What is it like to be curious,*
> *To thirst for knowledge you can call your own,*
> *With an inner desire that's set on fire—*
> *And you ask a brother, sister, or friend*
> *Who looks in answer and says, "Never mind"?*
> *You have to be deaf to understand.*
>
> . . . .
>
> *What is it like to have to depend*
> *Upon one who can hear to phone a friend;*
> *Or place a call to a business firm*
> *And be forced to share what's personal, and,*
> *Then find that your message wasn't made clear?*
> *You have to be deaf to understand.*
>
> . . . .
>
> *What is it like on the road of life*
> *To meet with a stranger who opens his mouth—*
> *And speaks out a line at a rapid pace;*
> *And you can't understand the look in his face*
> *Because it is new and you're lost in the race?*
> *You have to be deaf to understand.*
>
> —Willard J. Madsen, "You Have to Be
> Deaf to Understand"

Let me move into specifics here—into the admittedly personal and political—as I try to re-represent my roles as a qualitative researcher investigating the writing processes of deaf students at Gallaudet University. This study, initially completed in the latter half of 1991, is now several years old as I write. Since coming home with my boxes of data, I have written a rather large dissertation and several journal articles and given about a dozen formal and informal talks from the data. But I still do not know where I stood, or where I stand now for that matter, in the space between participant-observer. I still question my representations—of my "self" and my "others"—in this study. I am still trying to be self-reflexive and in that process find myself often feeling like I am "wearing a pith helmet at a sly angle" (Cintron 371).

In trying to think of what to say next—or if ever to say anything again—I often read bits of the three journals I kept during this research experience. And I come away from those rereadings repelled by how much I must sound like Malinowski in his *Diary*, spending "a great deal of time wishing he were elsewhere." Lately, for that wishful absence and a host of other crises of representation, I think I have found myself, in moments of silence and reflexive stasis, caught (and squirming) in the zipper of the participant-observer role.

And ironically, my recent feelings of muteness, mutability, and (the truth may as well be known) mutiny in the face of my original representations and writing about these deaf student writers are tied up in the issues of their own figurative and literal silence. For these deaf students are members of a classically colonized culture (still often not granted status as a culture, but rather labeled as "disabled," "hearing-impaired" individuals) whose language, sign language, occurs silently (and therefore suspiciously in an otherwise oral world) and is also often not granted status as "real" language.[3] In short, they have usually not owned any knowledge (because they have not been allowed to own any culture or language); their messages—and thus their very lives—have often been misunderstood (because, again, of the ways their language and culture have been disregarded and even dismantled); and they have been silenced—more by the dominant "hearing world" ideologies than by their own physical incapacities to verbalize.[4] In the years since I left the "field" at Gallaudet, hardly a day has gone by that I have not questioned my own (ever shifting and various) representations of them; not a day has gone by that I have not agonized over my own "ownership" of their knowledge, about the unclear messages I might give when I speak, write, represent them, and finally about the ways I may have silenced them.

What I want to do in the rest of this section, then, is explore some of the crises of representation I have encountered in setting up, conducting, and writing up these ethno-oriented case studies of deaf student writers at Gallaudet. As I see it, these crises are all located in the deceit of trying to represent myself as the so-called participant-observer, and I will try to keep that theme central to each exploration.[5]

The crises I present center around four periods of my research: (1) the conflicts between my preestablished participant-observer roles and those particular participant and/or observer roles that were constructed in the process after the study began; (2) the conflicts of interpretation, unclear messages, and representation that occurred as I first tried to write the study for my dissertation; (3) further conflicts that occurred as I began trying to present and publish my results in various literate and oral settings; and (4) the ongoing conflicts, throughout the entire study and the years since, arising from my attempts to involve the subjects, to let their own voices become a part of my representations of them.

Rolling Out a Map of Preestablished Roles

I went to Gallaudet to do a sociocognitive study of the writing processes of deaf students in "remedial" English courses. I rolled my way in on the powerful locomotive of a prestigious research grant from the National Council of Teachers of English. That fact in itself marks my participant-observer role as potentially pretentious, suspicious, even antagonistic. As David Bleich has pointed out, "even politically sympathetic ethnographers seem to require for themselves *some* elevated position relative to the studied culture" (179). Thus I too, as Bleich claims ethnographers Fetterman, Clifford, and Marcus have done, "assume[d] the political legitimacy of members of privileged societies who use their superior wealth to enter, or travel to, less privileged societies in order to bring home a new understanding of these societies" (179).

The role of the colonizer. No wonder, then, that I found myself labeled, treated with much suspicion, and by and large not granted much "reality" status. It was clear that a good number of the faculty members did not want me there.[6] But how could they say no and save face in light of the grant I held? How could they say no and not risk the things I might say about them for refusing me entry in the first place? And how might that look when it came time for them to seek any individual or departmental funding of their own?

At the time, of course, their predicament in this proverbial space between a rock and a hard spot simply did not occur to me. For most of my four months there, I felt instead confused, angry, crushed, belligerent, beleaguered, weepy, and vindictive by the ways they repeatedly made it clear that I was suspicious at least, intolerable at most. I had wanted to roll with the flow; I took a lot of punches instead. For the most part, the representative participant-observer roles I tried to play were either rearranged or ignored by the "natives" at Gallaudet. They would have me represented otherwise.

Before I even entered the field and set foot on Gallaudet's campus, I had decided upon several distinct roles I might occupy or play in an attempt to carve out a space for myself as the well-balanced participant-observer. I found instead that I could be neither participant nor observer—or even participant-observer—with any consistency or self-agency; I felt, in short, carved up and imbalanced most of the time.

I thought, for example, that my status as "hearing-impaired" from birth would gain me substantial insider status, would make my entry and acceptance considerably smoother and larger. I thought wrong. In fact, my status as a hearing-impaired (not Deaf) woman who had clearly made it in the hearing world became the platter I was most often carved on.[7] Because of the pattern and severity of my hearing loss, I have poor discrimination abilities for normal human speech—particularly the higher frequency consonants and particularly in situations where there are multiple voices, background noises, or white noises. In other words, I am "deaf" where hearing counts the most—in discriminating normal human speech. In this regard, I am like most of the deaf students at Gallaudet (and, in fact, my hearing loss is enough to have qualified me as a potential student there). My difficulty and fatigue in many social and educational situations, I hoped, would construct a role for me as possible empathetic "participant." In the initial entry into the field, this role did actually provide me with a small amount of credibility and certainly a large amount of interest from faculty and students alike.

"Are you Deaf or Hearing?"[8] From the first day I arrived at Gallaudet, this was always the initial question asked of me. And as I have indicated, it was a hard question for me to answer—a multiple choice to which I often believed the best answer was "yes" or "all of the above." One of the strongest cultural imperatives I encountered at Gallaudet was the effort—made by both hearing and deaf persons—to define individuals as simply, starkly either "Deaf" or "Hearing." It never seemed quite that simple to me.

For most of my time in the field, my representations (self- or other-imposed) as either Deaf or Hearing (which is essentially how Deaf culture labels those who call themselves hearing-impaired) were caught and confused somewhere in the hyphen of that word itself. Thus I often found myself between the two cultural borders, caught in the crossfire, as I ran across the hyphen, waving a tattered representative flag on both sides.

Another set of tattered roles I attempted to carry out simultaneously in my efforts to be a good participant-observer were those of both the "novice" and the "expert." I had thought, before entering the field, that it would be best to portray myself as a total novice in deaf education. So, while I had read most of the important sources on deaf education and literacy instruction for deaf students before I arrived at Gallaudet—in an effort to illustrate from the outset that I was aware of and sensitive to most of the issues surrounding deaf education—I did not impose my book-learned knowledge in this area. I tended to play the role of someone who knew *some* things, but admittedly did not know enough. I asked other faculty members many a simple, practical classroom-related question those first few weeks, even though I thought I already knew the answers; I also asked for further direction in reading research in the area, even when I was relatively sure I had already read the significant related research.

Admittedly, I was not presenting my true self on these occasions. I was trying instead to present myself as a noninterfering and nonjudgmental, somewhat objective and distanced observer, but also as an eager, interested, and intelligent potential participant. And I was trying this primarily on the advice of David Fetterman, who maintains in his handbook *Ethnography: Step by Step* that such "nonjudgmental orientation" on the part of the researcher is a crucial, key concept of ethnography (32). (Never mind the inherent deceit such a role represented—a deceit that Clifford Geertz in 1973 and Maurice Punch in 1994 have claimed is the trademark of participant-observation.)

Yet while maintaining and embellishing a novice profile in the area of deaf literacy education, I worked equally hard—and honestly here—to establish, maintain, and embellish a relative "expert" profile in the area of general literacy education. This embellishment was necessary, I thought, in order to give myself and my research project some credibility among both students and teachers at Gallaudet.

Many conflicts between these two representations arose. Ironically enough, most at Gallaudet chose to see me in my deceitful role—as a novice. And the more they represented me that way, the more it seemed I tried to abandon that novice portrait and live out my expert role instead. A long tug of war over those roles went on for my four months in the field, particularly in the two "basic" English classes where I worked as a teaching assistant. I often felt as if that teacher and I were engaged in a dance of mutual deceit (another characteristic of the participant-observer role that Punch claims is "virtually inherent to the deeply engaged fieldwork role" [93]): while I saw myself as capable of doing more with the remedial English 50 students we taught than I was allowed or encouraged to do, the teacher I worked with seemed to think differently. My opinion, for example, was rarely asked about a day's lesson plans, or about strategies for working with any one student on a particular literacy problem. Instead, my time, both in class and outside, was usually spent grading the kind of work that could be checked with a preestablished answer sheet, keeping student files in order, typing up worksheets for class. And for the most part, I carried out my secretarial duties with a pleasant smile plastered to my face, rumbling all the while inside at my deceit.

In large part, I felt trapped in this deceit because this particular teacher was my "representative"—my official research sponsor on campus. Had it not been for his signature on a letter, for his willingness to let me work as a teaching assistant with him, I might not have been at Gallaudet to complete the study in the first place. I rubbed pretty sorely in between that rock and hard spot, chafed by how much I wanted to be a participant in the teaching and was only, for the most part, allowed to be an observer.

Another role and representation that chafed more often than not was my attempt and desire to be a friend or familiar colleague to fellow English department members. It just didn't work that way. At least half of the faculty are hearing, and I had somehow imagined that they would welcome a hearing-impaired teacher who had been successful in their world, too—if for no other reason than the perspectives I might offer. But instead, they were without doubt more hostile and suspicious than anyone else of my presence there.[9]

Likewise, I had envisioned the deaf faculty members as interested, if not eager, to learn from me and my successful literacy experiences. By and large, they were less hostile and suspicious than the hearing faculty members, but they remained predominantly aloof. So much, then, for establishing myself as a friendly, empathetic "other" on either account. I was reminded that, as Denzin has pointed out, "clearly, simplistic classifications do not work" (512).

This is not to say that I did not make some significant friends and colleagues in the department. I did. But what is most significant about these relationships is that they were mutually made—not ones I expected or preconceived before entering the field. They grew not from some research agenda, but—even in spite of those agendas—from natural affinities. In short, they were not self-conscious or even unconscious representations; they were, simply, just real friendships. Two were with the student subjects I studied (both older, nontraditional students) and three were with English department faculty members. The trouble with all five of these friendships was that, once home from the field and left with the always political, rhetorical, artful act of interpreting and writing up my study, I found that these five had been, of course, my key informants. So much of what I knew, thought, and wrote about in my field journals was connected to things I had talked about with these five people that my own still-forming interpretations were fused with direct quotations, paraphrases, and interpretive leaps I had "borrowed" from them. Yet to write about and with them as such would be to betray an enormous trust, to possibly demolish friendships I had come to value. Again, I danced in deceit in that space between participant and observer.

How could I adequately represent the intensely political, colonial, downright degenerative situation of literacy education at Gallaudet—a situation I was greatly troubled by—without betraying their confidences in me (and moreover without perhaps putting those people at risk within their own department and university)? For the sake of *my* research agenda, *my* representation, they could well stand to lose much that they had gained within the Gallaudet community and Deaf culture at large. Through my relationships with them, I had come to know too much and, to be honest, I feared for my own authority in this regard. Through them, I had lost the nonjudgmental observation of the participant-observer role. I had, in effect, gone native.

And once home, I found that some members of my dissertation committee were not particularly happy about my native status. Torn now between my own fears and the concern of my committee over what I could or should write about and how I had essentially failed to be a participant-observer (or even simply an observer or a participant), I lapsed into silence while trying to write up my study. I had never known a writer's block like this. That hyphenated space between participant-observer worked hard on me; I would have to work it back. This is where the second period of representational difficulties began for me.

Representation, Interpretation, and Writing It Up

Every time I sat down to review some of my data or to stare at the blank computer screen and cursing cursor, the issues of knowledge ownership, unclear messages, and silence that Madsen writes about in his poem "You Have to Be Deaf to Understand" held me fast and still (qtd. in Gannon 380). My problems negotiating and mediating interpretation were (and are) not, of course, particularly unusual in qualitative research.

In considering both of the subjects-informants I focused on in my dissertation and in interpreting their own interpretations, I found myself caught in "nothing more than relativism" (Marcus and Fischer 33). I was asked, for example, as I wrote up my concluding chapter, to be sure to include a section about the "representativeness" of these two subjects. I was concerned both theoretically and practically about the possibilities for successfully doing this. I felt, for one, that such a request stemmed from an attempt to place phenomenological research in a positivistic frame—to somehow attempt to universalize and validate results that were indeed relative. But of course I did it as best I could, wanting the dissertation done more than I wanted to quibble over this point. (Again, the inherent deceit resurfaces.)

What troubled me was that in writing about my subjects' representativeness, I was not representing my beliefs very well. For the two students I wrote up in the dissertation, Anna and Charlie, were not necessarily representative of all deaf students, nor even of all deaf students at Gallaudet, nor even of other deaf students in their basic writing classes. Their literacy pasts and presents were unique and relative, as I could say about virtually every student I worked with at Gallaudet.[10] A representative interpretation simply was not possible—or even desirable.

And the problem of interpretation was more than just a figurative one: because of Anna's and Charlie's use of American Sign Language (ASL), interpretation became a very real, literal concern as well. Anna, for example, wished to conduct the interviews without an interpreter (mostly because she is extremely proud of her ability to lip read and voice). And so I honored her wish, and our conversations and interviews took place in something like Pidgin Signed English (PSE), a composite of ASL and spoken English. Yet upon completion of my fieldwork, as I transcribed the videotaped interviews two months later and seven hundred miles away, I often found it difficult to make sense of Anna's equally "ungrammatical" spoken English and sign language, occurring simultaneously in our interviews. I found myself frustrated trying to interpret and make sense of either language, let alone both.

With Charlie, there was an even more interesting and deeply embedded interpretation problem. Profoundly and prelingually deaf and faced with a researcher (myself) whose signing skills were barely more than intermediate, Charlie chose to use an interpreter for our interviews. While she was an interpreter I trusted, I found myself frustrated on many accounts as I reviewed and transcribed the tapes several months later. First, as Charlie began signing an answer to a question I had just asked, I would inevitably find myself beginning my own translation of his signing *in process.* And just when I would have my own translation working silently at the speed of his communication, my interpreter would interrupt (in a fashion) and begin her own voiced translation—about a sentence or two behind where I was already in my own translation. The result was a frazzled researcher trying to comprehend and interpret not only two conversations at once, but two languages at once, out of phase with each other by a sentence or two.

Often, I also found myself torn between wanting to transcribe my own interpretation of what Charlie had signed instead of the interpretation the interpreter voiced as she sat behind me and off screen. For the most part, for the sake of interpretative consistency, her interpretation was the one I recorded. But the whole interpreting and tape-transcribing process was still agonizing—and certainly a profound lesson in the "always interpretative, critical, and partial" nature of "translation," both literally and figuratively (Haraway, "Situated Knowledges" 195).

Trying to represent two discourses at once also went well beyond those practical language interpretation problems. For a long time I tried in vain to write for two different audiences—my dissertation committee and the Gallaudet community. On the one hand, there was the academic (dissertation) audience. If I did not address and represent them, I would not be likely to complete my dissertation, to earn the Ph.D. degree that had been my lifetime personal goal. Yet on the other hand, there was the home audience—the Gallaudet community and Deaf culture to which I now, in part, felt I belonged. If I did not address and represent them, I would not be likely to maintain my newly gained and desired identity among them.[11] And no more than I could be a both/and participant-observer, could I write for—and represent—both these audiences in one piece of discourse. Trying to do so silenced my writing for some time.

Representation in Publishing

A somewhat similar representational dilemma has silenced me now in recent efforts to publish and speak about pieces of the case studies. On several occasions, I have been asked to speak about—to represent, as it were—the problems that deaf students encounter in college literacy situations: my university's Disability Services has sent several deaf/hearing-impaired students my way, hoping that I might offer them advice, if not individual tutoring; and my university's Writing Center, a tutoring center for any and all students having writing difficulties in any or all of their courses, recently encountered quite a number of deaf students and asked me to lead a discussion with its staff about how to work with deaf students on their writing problems.

I have felt less than competent or helpful in both of these situations. That is, I have felt less than competent or helpful in how well I might represent all or any particular deaf students that Disability Services and the Writing Center might encounter. For if there is but one thing I have learned well from my experiences tutoring and researching deaf student writers at Gallaudet it is that the diversity of their audiological, educational, family, linguistic, and cultural backgrounds makes characterizing a "representative" profile of such a student virtually impossible: there is simply no way to sum up what literacy skills might be expected from such students by the time they reach college-level course work. Thus my attempts to represent them in these situations have seemed futile, if not downright dangerous.

Another exercise in futility has come in my efforts to represent Anna, one of the deaf students I studied and tutored at Gallaudet. So far, I do not feel I am doing a very good job of it. Some time ago, I sent a rather long piece about Anna to one of the major journals in composition studies. It came back with lengthy comments from four reviewers and the journal's editor. In sum, they wanted me to revise and resubmit and were, in the end (as a few of my colleagues have assured me), quite encouraging about my doing so. And yet I have not felt very encouraged.

Several of my reviewers seemed dissatisfied with my representations of Anna—questioning everything from how I described her to what the whole purpose of my representation was in the first place.[12] It seems that they see Anna differently than I do, and that moreover they see the moral of my story about her as something different than what I try to present. There is a disconcerting amount of seeming and seeing otherwise going on here. A great deal of unclear messages.

While I would be the first and loudest to admit that my representations of Anna and her story are neither clear-cut nor objective, this whole attempt to publish a piece about her has raised, yet again, more issues of representation for me. (And therein it has raised even more issues about the place and possibility for publication of qualitative research in composition studies journals.) These issues now blanket me in suffocating layers: I attempted to represent Anna, but my reviewers and editor wanted my representation changed. Their concerns, as I read them, are based largely on how my work will look (i.e., be represented) in their journal; on how I, as a qualitative researcher, will look in their journal; on how Anna, as an "other," will look in their journal; and finally, on how qualitative research at large (as represented by my study) will be represented in their journal. Whew.

And I still have not been able to revise a single word of that piece. I have, in effect, been silenced by their attempts to re-represent my own representations. But the silence has not been all bad. In fact, I have come to understand another telling incidence of silence in this research process *because* of the silence encountered here. It should come as no surprise by now, of course, that this incidence of silence is yet another of the crises of representation I believe we must consider in qualitative research.

Involving Our Subjects in Our Representations of Them

Launching "new research principles" for composition studies from the work of scholars in women's studies, particularly from Sandra Harding, Gesa Kirsch has recently suggested that we make every effort not to silence our subjects. Instead, Kirsch asks that we consider "opening up the research agenda to subjects, listening to their stories, and allowing them to actively participate, as much as possible, in the design, development and reporting of research" (257). She specifically calls for composition studies to undertake these new research principles by paying particular attention to the "researcher-subject relationship" (261) and by assuring that our research is "grounded in subjects' experiences and designed to benefit both researchers and subjects" (263). Here, I hear Kirsch asking us to work the hyphen between researcher-subject relationships and to work against silencing our subjects.

While conducting and writing up my research in the year before Kirsch published these suggestions, I tried to work against this silence and pay much attention to my relationships with my subjects. For instance, I made sure that the students in my study were not students I would be grading—I simply did not want to place myself in such a power position and to place them in such a vulnerable position. As already mentioned, I worked only as a teaching assistant in the course they were enrolled in and had no real input in actually evaluating them. In addition to my individual work with them (and the other class members) as a teaching assistant, I offered them free tutoring in exchange for the hours of additional interviews with me.

Often at the end of either a tutoring or an interview session, Anna and Charlie would ask me questions like, "What have you learned so far? Have I been helpful? Are you finding out anything?" And always I would answer as honestly as possible—usually by summarizing patterns I had begun to see in their (past) literacy history and (present) literacy skills, by paraphrasing some of the things they had told me in the interviews, by offering suggestions for how they might best conquer (or at least encounter) their specific literacy problems, and finally by asking them if they thought I was on the right track with my summaries, paraphrases, and suggestions. I would also ask if they thought I was helping them in any way, or if I could do something more to be helpful. They seemed to like this give and take, and I, at least, felt I was learning even more from it.

In both of the final interviews with Anna and Charlie, I wound up crying, certainly not an objective participant-observer strategy. In fact, it was not a strategy at all—just an honest response made to the honesty they were sharing with me. It was in both of these exit interviews that Anna and Charlie made clear their life-long frustrations and failures with acquiring English literacy: Anna was crying, partly out of joy and disbelief for just having passed English 50, partly out of frustration and anger for all the incredible self-motivation she had drummed up to pass the class; Charlie, who had not yet taken the exit exam, was clearly just angry, frustrated, and fearful that he would fail again—for the third time. And as an observer of what I felt was the oppressive, degrading nature of basic literacy instruction at Gallaudet, yet also as a participant in Anna's and Charlie's lives (they, too, counted me as a friend), I felt all of these emotions with them. (Charlie, by the way, did pass the course this time.)

At this point in my study, I had much invested in my subjects—both personally and professionally, both as a participant and an observer. And there was no way by the end of my fieldwork that I felt I could neatly separate out my personal and professional roles and feelings, or my positions as participant and observer. I had come to claim what Donna Haraway calls "feminist accountability" and "feminist science"—that which "requires a knowledge tuned to resonance, not to dichotomy," that which is "about the sciences of the multiple subject with (at least) double vision" ("Situated Knowledges" 194–95).

In becoming involved and invested in Anna's and Charlie's literacy successes, I myself had become one of the multiple subjects of my own study. Professionally, I did not by any means approve of the oppressive and rote literacy instruction I felt they had been given. To be quite honest, their success in passing out of that system felt like a moral, personal victory for me because of my part in tutoring and talking to them about their own writing. Their success represented (to me, at least) survival in spite of what J. Elspeth Stuckey has called "the violence of literacy," where little if any regard is paid by those privileged enough to be literacy instructors to the particular cultural, communal, and linguistic losses an "illiterate" student might suffer as she acquires the language of the master, the "gift" of the dominant culture's literacy.

Now that they had been "gifted," I still wanted very much to stay in touch and remain friends with Anna and Charlie, still wanted very much to have them read and respond to what I might write about them. And so, as I left the field, we exchanged addresses and best wishes. Over the next six months as I was writing up my dissertation, I heard from both of them, both directly and indirectly. Anna reiterated that she wanted to see what I had written about her when I was finished, while Charlie seemed interested in maintaining our acquaintance but not particularly keen on reading anything I had written about him. I respected both their interest and lack thereof—mailed Anna a copy of the chapter about her when it was finished, sent Charlie nothing.

A troubling silence has mushroomed out of that mailing. For since I have given Anna a copy of "her" chapter, I have not heard from her. (Charlie continues to send greetings via another mutual friend on electronic mail, although he himself no longer sends me messages.) Now I could imagine numerous reasons for Anna's silence: everything from "she's just too busy" and "she's just no longer interested in maintaining a long-distance acquaintance that will most likely be nothing more than that" to "I've greatly offended her" and "she's confused by what I wrote because (as a dissertation chapter) it was simply over her head."

But the truth? I simply don't know.

Does she think I have misunderstood, misrepresented her? Is she confused by where she stands in the spaces between participant-observer and researcher-subject? I simply don't know. Two attempts on my part to reestablish communication have been met with further silence—one with no answer, one with a "returned to sender; no forwarding address" sticker. And so the mystery and myth of representation continues.

Anna's silence has been matched by what I think is a telling silence on other accounts. While many faculty members in the English department at Gallaudet (both friends and otherwise) expressed a great interest in seeing my dissertation when it was finished (and, indeed, part of my "contract" with the department for being allowed to conduct the study in the first place was that I would give them a completed copy), only one person has yet responded to it.

And ethically, I am simply not comfortable in requesting specific responses from any of them. That is, I do not feel that my attempts to represent the students or the literacy instruction situation at Gallaudet necessarily obligate any of them to respond (no more than I feel that, just because the phone rings, someone is obligated to answer it). While I would agree with Kirsch (and the feminist scholars like Sandra Harding and Donna Haraway that she builds her suggestions for "new research" on) that we ought to try to collaborate with our subjects, I do not think it entirely ethical that we unequivocally assume that they *want* to be involved, to collaborate, to respond, to co-construct representations with us.[13]

We cannot make them participate if they only want to observe. We cannot require them to speak if they only want to remain anonymous or silent. Those positions are ones we need to consider and respect as well. Those positions represent something meaningful (if not painful). They are positions in the space between researcher-subject and participant-observer, in the "split and contradictory self" that both Michelle Fine and Donna Haraway (*Primate Visions* 70) claim is the position of real accountability.

Conclusion: Still Being Split

It's so hard to believe that you pass. . . .

—Anna

My left foot is hearing, my right is deaf. I feel pulled in both directions. That's been the struggle and fight of my life.

—Charlie

Even if our subjects choose to speak and share (as Anna and Charlie did while I was in the process of collecting data about them), I do not think we will be able to co-construct a final, situated representation—a still-life—of either them or us as the subjects. We will not be able to represent fully or accurately because, as Haraway and a host of other feminist scholars and postmodern ethnographers claim, all knowledge is "situated and embodied"; we have only and always the "privilege of partial perspective" (Haraway, "Situated Knowledges" 183). We are always partially subject, partially researcher; partially participant, partially observer; partially self, partially other—never exclusively one or the other, never wholly one or the other.

And if our subjects should choose silence? Then I think the question for us, as researchers, becomes how—or even whether—we should try to represent out of, or in spite of, this silence. It is through this question that my own work currently sifts as I encounter silence from myself and the others I have studied. Can I—or even should I—speak out of these silences? How might I represent the silences themselves?

My answer, partial (in both senses of the word) though it may be, to these questions is to suggest (yet even more) questions that might guide us concerning representation in our qualitative research:

- What representations do we enter our research with? From the outset, how do we represent ourselves as participant-observer? as researcher-subject? as self-other?

- What representations inform and grow out of our ongoing interpretations of our data? Where and how do they conflict with those we entered with?

- What representations inform and grow out of our writing up the data?

- What representations are required or influenced by our various audiences?

- Which of our representations intersect, parallel, conflict with those of the subjects we are representing? Which give them voices, make them silent?

- Which of our representations give us voice, make us silent?

- And finally, is there yet another way we might ask these questions? Is there yet another way to represent?

And so I am asking myself now: Can I write it again another way? Can I write from the hyphen?

Because I am currently asking myself these two final questions the most often and energetically, I chose to begin this final section with two connecting quotations from Anna and Charlie. Like Anna, I see my life—both personal (as a hearing-impaired person) and professional (as a qualitative researcher in the postmodern era)—as a perpetual rite of "passing." Like Charlie, I see my life—both personal and professional— "caught between . . . pulled in both directions." And because of those views I am trying, for one thing, to respect the spaces between, and the silence within, those spaces while at the same time I try to re-write, re-re-represent, re-vision. My life as a participant-observer has been anything but that—has been anything but still.

Acknowledgments

The research in which this essay is rooted was made possible by a grant from the National Council of Teachers of English.

Notes

1. Elsewhere I have called this research "ethno-oriented case studies" because, while I used ethnographic techniques for most of my data collection during the four months I researched and taught at Gallaudet, and while I have boxes of these ethnographic data stored in my study, the focus of my work thus far has been on individuals, on case study subjects within that ethnographic setting. The title of the original research is "Context and Cognition in the Composing Processes of Two Deaf Student Writers."

2. Michelle Fine, for example, explores the "happening between" self and other representations by collecting "a messy series of questions about methods, ethics, and epistemologies" that are meant to unearth "the contradictions that percolate at the Self-Other hyphen" (70). Maurice Punch also unearths issues of representation as he examines "entry and departure, distrust and confidence, elation and despondency, commitment and betrayal, friendship and abandonment" in researcher-subject relations (84). In large part, entrenched still in the necessity of the participant-observer role (and *because* of this very role), Punch proclaims that "the notion of *mutual deceit* [is] virtually inherent to the deeply engaged fieldwork role" (93).

Norman Denzin also illustrates how representation possibly relies on deceit, since it is an issue of writing and, as such, is rhetorical and "speaks to such topics as voice, audience, the 'Other,' and the author's place in the reflexive texts that are produced" (503). Finally, George Marcus follows the "crucial turn . . . [in] the position taken toward self-critical reflexivity in ethnographic writing" (568). This self-reflexivity has become the mantra of postmodern research, although it exists in many different forms, as Marcus himself points out. For some examples of the various calls for self-reflexivity see Bourdieu; Clough; Haraway, *Primate Visions* and "Situated Knowledges"; Myers; Stacey; and Watson.

3. For example, the Modern Language Association still does not feature any sessions that include sign languages, and it has been my own experience that attempts at such inclusion have been fruitless.

4. A sampling of some of the more recent work addressing these issues of colonization, "disability," cultural identity, and language status for deaf people might include Harlan Lane's *The Mask of Benevolence: Disabling the Deaf Community*; Oliver Sacks's *Seeing Voices: A Journey into the World of the Deaf*; and Edward Dolnick's essay, "Deafness as Culture."

5. My recent stance on the participant-observer role has come to mimic that taken by Clifford Geertz, now two decades ago. In a footnote early in *The Interpretation of Cultures*, he claims that

> So far as it has reinforced the anthropologist's impulse to engage himself with his informants as persons rather than as objects, the notion of "participant observation" has been a valuable one. But, to the degree it has led the anthropologist to block from his view the very special, culturally bracketed nature of his own role and

to imagine himself something more than an interested (in both senses of the word) sojourner, it has been our most powerful source of bad faith. (20)

Perhaps, I rationalize, it is because Geertz hid this profound insight in a footnote that it has taken me so long to truly "see" it.

6. One of the strongest rejections I encountered from English department faculty members came in the weeklong inservice workshop held the week before fall classes began at Gallaudet. I secured permission from the department chair to attend this workshop, but on the first day one of the workshop leaders himself stood before the group and queried, "Perhaps BJ [my sign-name] would prefer to spend her time more valuably elsewhere?" Thus the question was put to the other faculty members—as if I were not even in the room. It seemed clearly a move to make me uncomfortable at least, to cast me out at most. All eyes turned to me as I stood and signed, simply, in response: "I would prefer to stay." That one scene was repeated, in many varied instances, throughout my four-month stay in the English department at Gallaudet.

7. Let me give but one small (and yet so large) example of the way in which my representations of myself have continued in metamorphosis. Before I went to Gallaudet, I considered myself either "hard-of-hearing" or "hearing-impaired"—both terms the hearing world has imposed on deaf persons and thus terms they reject in favor of calling themselves "deaf" (to represent their audiological condition) and/or "Deaf" (to represent their cultural and linguistic affiliation). While at Gallaudet, largely because of the empathy I felt and friendship I was offered by several Deaf faculty members and students, as well as because of my increasing skills in American Sign Language, I began to call myself "Deaf." Five years later now, acknowledging (for better and worse) that I am indeed more a member and product of the hearing world, I have reverted back to the hearing-world label of "hearing-impaired." This does not, by the way, mean that I necessarily approve of the rather colonial naming game inherent in this term; to me it simply means that I am what I am—predominantly a member of the hearing world, the dominant culture.

8. The use of capital letters is significant here. In Deaf culture, the capital letter *D* is used to denote one's cultural affinity, while the use of the lower case *d* ("deaf") indicates one's audiological condition. Thus a person can be deaf (audiologically) but not Deaf (culturally)—and even more rarely, Deaf (culturally) but not in any way deaf (audiologically).

9. My previous example of an attempt to exclude me from the inservice workshop serves again here. The workshop leader who posed the question of my presence to the others was "hearing," as were, in fact, all those who made overt (and covert) attempts to exclude me from departmental life during that semester. I am reminded of the description one Gallaudet student's mother used to describe the relationships between "Deaf" (primarily students) and "Hearing" (primarily faculty) cultures at Gallaudet: in an essay in *The Nation* on the volatile situations at Gallaudet, Judith Treesberg called Gallaudet "occupied territory" (155).

10. Here I am reminded of Hull, Rose, Fraser, and Castellano's powerful argument in "Remediation as Social Construct" for interrogating the all-too-easy ways we construct similarities and differences among our students—particularly among our "remedial" students.

11. This is an ethnographer's potential dilemma that Beverly Moss addresses in her essay "Ethnography and Composition: Studying Language at Home."

12. One reviewer, for example, called my use of the word "hysterical" to describe Anna in her final interview "patronizing." (This was the interview where she sums up her experiences in English 50 that semester and talks about all the self-motivation she had to muster against the system to pass that class.) The same reviewer pointed to several other instances and terms where he/she felt I was less than objective. While this reviewer's remarks have indeed made me question the possible perniciousness of my description here, I am still puzzled as to how a reviewer, who has never met Anna, might have a better sense of what terms to describe (represent) her in than I have.

13. I feel it worth mentioning that I have, over the years, engaged in several collaborative projects with some of the faculty I worked with during this ethnographically oriented study: I have collaboratively designed a junior-senior-level course on "writing and learning" for the deaf students at Gallaudet, and I have organized two conference panels centered on issues of deafness and literacy instruction with colleagues from Gallaudet.

Works Cited

Bleich, David. "Ethnography and the Study of Literacy: Prospects for Socially Generous Research." *Into the Field: Sites of Composition Studies.* Ed. Anne Ruggles Gere. New York: MLA, 1993. 176–92.

Bourdieu, Pierre. *The Logic of Practice.* Stanford: Stanford UP, 1990.

Brueggemann, Brenda Jo. "Context and Cognition in the Composing Processes of Two Deaf Student Writers." Diss. U of Louisville, 1992.

Bruner, Edward M. "Introduction: The Ethnographic Self and the Personal Self." *Anthropology and Literature.* Ed. Paul J. Benson. Urbana: U of Illinois P, 1993. 1–26.

Cintron, Ralph. "Wearing a Pith Helmet at a Sly Angle: Or, Can Writing Researchers Do Ethnography in a Postmodern Era?" *Written Communication* 10 (1993): 371–412.

Cixous, Hélène. "The Laugh of the Medusa." *Signs* 1 (1976): 875–93. Rpt. in *The Rhetorical Tradition: Readings from Classical Times to the Present.* Ed. Patricia Bizzell and Bruce Herzberg. Boston: Bedford-St. Martin's P, 1990. 1232–45.

Clough, Patricia T. *The End(s) of Ethnography: From Realism to Social Criticism.* Newbury Park: Sage, 1992.

Denzin, Norman K. "The Art and Politics of Interpretation." Denzin and Lincoln 500–15.

Denzin, Norman K., and Yvonna S. Lincoln, eds. *Handbook of Qualitative Research.* Thousand Oaks: Sage, 1994.

Dolnick, Edward. "Deafness as Culture." *Atlantic Monthly* Sept. 1993: 37–51.

Fetterman, David M. *Ethnography: Step by Step.* Newbury Park: Sage, 1989.

Fine, Michelle. "Working the Hyphens: Reinventing Self and Other in Qualitative Research." Denzin and Lincoln 70–82.

Foucault, Michel. "What Is an Author?" *The Foucault Reader.* Ed. Paul Rabinow. New York: Pantheon Books, 1984. 101–20.

Gannon, Jack R. *Deaf Heritage: A Narrative History of Deaf America.* Ed. Jane Butler and Laura Jean Gilbert. Silver Spring: National Association of the Deaf, 1981.

Geertz, Clifford. *The Interpretation of Cultures.* New York: Basic, 1973.

———. *Local Knowledge: Further Essays in Interpretive Anthropology.* New York: Basic, 1983.

Haraway, Donna J. *Primate Visions: Gender, Race, and Nature in the World of Modern Science.* New York: Routledge, 1989.

———. "Situated Knowledges: The Science Question in Feminism and the Privilege of Partial Perspective." *Simians, Cyborgs, and Women: The Reinvention of Nature.* New York: Routledge, 1991. 183–201.

Herndl, Carl G. "Writing Ethnography: Representation, Rhetoric, and Institutional Practices." *College English* 53 (1991): 320–32.

hooks, bell. *Yearning: Race, Gender, and Cultural Politics.* Boston: South End P, 1990.

Hull, Glynda, Mike Rose, Kay Losey Fraser, and Marisa Castellano. "Remediation as Social Construct: Perspectives from an Analysis of Classroom Discourse." *College Composition and Communication* 42 (1991): 299–329.

Kirsch, Gesa E. "Methodological Pluralism: Epistemological Issues." *Methods and Methodology in Composition Research.* Ed. Gesa Kirsch and Patricia A. Sullivan. Carbondale: Southern Illinois UP, 1992. 247–69.

Lane, Harlan. *The Mask of Benevolence: Disabling the Deaf Community.* New York: Knopf, 1992.

Lincoln, Yvonna S., and Norman K. Denzin. "The Fifth Moment." Denzin and Lincoln 575–86.

Malinowski, Bronislaw. *Argonauts of the Western Pacific.* London: Routledge and Kegan Paul, 1922.

———. *A Diary in the Strict Sense of the Term.* New York: Harcourt Brace, 1967.

Marcus, George E. "What Comes (Just) After 'Post'? The Case of Ethnography." Denzin and Lincoln 563–74.

Marcus, George E., and Michael M. J. Fischer. *Anthropology as Cultural Critique: An Experimental Moment in the Human Sciences*. Chicago: U of Chicago P, 1986.

Moss, Beverly J. "Ethnography and Composition: Studying Language at Home." *Methods and Methodology in Composition Research*. Ed. Gesa Kirsch and Patricia A. Sullivan. Carbondale: Southern Illinois UP, 1992. 153–71.

Myers, Fred. "Locating Ethnographic Practice: Romance, Reality, and Politics in the Outback." *American Ethnologist* 15 (1988): 609–24.

Punch, Maurice. "Politics and Ethics in Qualitative Research." Denzin and Lincoln 83–97.

Sacks, Oliver. *Seeing Voices: A Journey into the World of the Deaf*. Berkeley: U of California P, 1989.

Stacey, Judith. "Can There Be a Feminist Ethnography?" *Women's Studies International Forum* 11 (1988): 21–27.

Stuckey, J. Elspeth. *The Violence of Literacy*. Portsmouth: Boynton/Cook, 1991.

Treesberg, Judith. "The Death of a 'Strong Deaf.'" *Nation* 11 Feb. 1991: 154–57.

Watson, Graham. "Make Me Reflexive—But Not Yet: Strategies for Managing Essential Reflexivity in Ethnographic Discourse." *Journal of Anthropological Research* 43 (1987): 29–41.

3 Dealing with the Data: Ethical Issues in Case Study Research

Cheri L. Williams
University of Cincinnati

What does it mean to do the right thing?
—William Ayers and William Schubert, "Do the Right Thing"

When I began my case study investigation, I had just completed a sequence of qualitative research courses designed specifically for educators. I was armed with a host of methodology texts and related articles, sophisticated audio and video recording equipment, a stack of tablets for all those field notes I would write, a high-tech computer program for the manipulation of qualitative data, and the support of a peer research group. For the most part, I felt both theoretically and methodologically prepared to begin my investigation. I was (and still am) a novice researcher, however, and in my naïveté I lacked an understanding of the *nature* of qualitative research, particularly with regard to the ethical issues that all qualitative researchers face. I knew something about how *to do* research but very little about how *to be* a researcher.

As this book demonstrates, researchers are beginning to explore what it means to be a qualitative researcher and to explicate what constitutes ethical behavior in the conduct of ethnographies and case study research (see also Cassell, "Ethical Principles"; Punch, *The Politics and Ethics*; Stake). What is ethical behavior? When can we say that a researcher has acted ethically? In this chapter, I discuss several ethical issues that confronted me as I conducted a qualitative investigation of deaf children's language and literacy learning and as I wrote individual case reports based upon that research. I describe specific dilemmas and my struggles with and attempts at ethical behavior within each situation. In endeavoring to provide a reflexive account, I am, in some sense, owning up to the ways in which I solved, or more often failed to solve, these dilemmas.

The Ethical Dilemmas

Maintaining Anonymity and Acknowledging Accomplishments

There is a longstanding practice among qualitative researchers to protect the identity and privacy of research participants. Generally speaking, researchers believe that participants and sites should not be identifiable in print or during formal presentations of the research. The protection of informant anonymity is so elemental in qualitative research that Marycarol Hopkins argues that "anthropologists do not even have to explain that [they] have used pseudonyms" (124). But the practice of preserving informant anonymity often presents perplexing ethical dilemmas for those who conduct ethnographies and case study research. While most researchers disguise participants' names and associations to protect them from potential embarrassment or harm, this strategy also prevents participants from receiving recognition. In fact, as researchers paper over participants' identities, they eliminate any opportunity for public acknowledgment or praise. Such was the case in my investigation. Given the longstanding and rather heated theoretical and pedagogical debates surrounding studies of young deaf children's language and literacy development, it seemed essential that I maintain the participants' anonymity. Consequently, informants chose their own pseudonyms or asked me to do so. Using pseudonyms proved problematic, however, in two instances. In both cases, the pseudonyms prevented key participants from receiving recognition for their success in supporting the language and literacy development of children in the study.

Sue's Parents

Sue (a pseudonym) was the youngest child who participated in the research, and like the other case study children, she was profoundly deaf.[1] Her receptive language development was severely delayed, and her parents, particularly her mother, worked painstakingly to increase Sue's vocabulary and verbal language use. Her parents believed they had been successful in supporting their daughter's language and literacy development, and during the initial stages of the investigation, they requested that I use their real names and their daughter's real name in the written report. I, too, felt they deserved public recognition, and I wanted to acknowledge and honor them for their diligence and success. Yet to use their names in the written report I would have had to sacrifice the anonymity of other participants, in particular, their daughter's preschool teacher and her classmates. Since Sue's case study contained "bad news"

(Newkirk, this volume) regarding several preschool teachers' instructional practices, I could not comply with this request. I discussed the confidentiality issue with Sue's parents, and in the end they chose pseudonyms which they found acceptable.

Anna

Anna was one of the preschool teachers I observed. She taught the four- and five-year-old children who used total communication[2] to interact. One of the case study children (Andrew) was in Anna's class. When teachers use total communication to interact with students, they attempt to sign and speak simultaneously. This is an extremely difficult task (see Williams for a thorough description), yet Anna was adept in her use of simultaneous communication. Her signing vocabulary was very large; her signs were clear, sharp, fluid, and easy to understand; and she was able to sign the majority of words she spoke. In every way, Anna's proficiency in this area was remarkable. Furthermore, she did an outstanding job of integrating signed language, spoken language, and written language in authentic ways throughout the curriculum.[3] On a daily basis, she engaged her students in meaningful learning experiences which required them to use language for a variety of authentic purposes. From my perspective, Anna was successfully implementing a holistic learning approach, and she deserved recognition and praise for her work. She received it as "Anna," but I wished a more personal recognition for her. I found that maintaining her anonymity was often difficult and frustrating.

It appears that most researchers have yet to find a balance between confidentiality and public commendation in the writing of ethnographies and case studies. Feminist scholar Gesa Kirsch struggled with this issue as she was interviewing women for *Women Writing the Academy: Audience, Authority, and Transformation.* She was torn between protecting interviewees' privacy and acknowledging their scholarly accomplishments in fields historically dominated by men. Teacher educator Susan Tancock also labored with this issue in the writing of *At-Risk Students: The Social Construction of Status,* an ethnographic investigation of two at-risk first-grade girls. One of the teachers in that study consciously included all students in the social milieu of the classroom, despite middle-class students' alienation of children from lower-income families. Tancock wanted to acknowledge this teacher's success in demonstrating respect for all children, but issues of anonymity prevented personal recognition. Interestingly, sociologist Gary Alan Fine experiments with such a balance in *Shared Fantasy: Role-Playing Games as Social*

Worlds. In the book, Fine refers to one of his informants, M. A. R. Barker, by name. Barker is a professor at the University of Minnesota and creator of Empire of the Petal Throne, a popular game of the fantasy role-playing genre. Fine argues that Barker "deserved the credit that his role in the hobby brought him and [that] there was no effective means of talking about him without his identity being revealed" ("Credit" 79). Importantly, however, Fine used a pseudonym for Barker in instances where "the emotions and attitudes expressed in his gaming groups [might be] connected to him to his embarrassment and discomfort" (79). To test the success of this strategy, I read several chapters of Fine's book, focusing primarily on the excerpts from personal interviews and field notes. I specifically looked for attempts to conceal Barker's identity. It appears that Fine's strategy was successful, for I was unable to identify Barker in instances where he was not specifically named.[4]

While I could not acknowledge Sue's parents' or Anna's accomplishments in any personally meaningful way in the research report, I tried to recognize them in other ways. I wrote a letter of support for Sue's parents as they attempted to secure financial assistance for their daughter's auditory-oral education from the Alexander Graham Bell Association for the Deaf. I nominated Anna for the Outstanding Teacher Award given each year by the Convention of American Instructors of the Deaf. The award is presented "to an individual who exemplifies the highest standards of the teaching profession and who demonstrates extraordinary commitment to educational excellence and the learning and welfare of hearing-impaired children."[5] These were small efforts, but they demonstrated my respect for Sue's parents and for Anna. Perhaps most important is that I have maintained personal contact with each of them over the years, which may be more meaningful to parents and teachers than the honors we typically recognize within the academy. Even so, I believe that discovering innovative ways to publicize the accomplishments of research informants is an understudied ethical issue, one that deserves our attention and interest. We must find better ways to honor those people who make our "tales of the field" possible (see Van Maanen).

Choosing between Loyalties

Establishing rapport with informants is of paramount importance in the conduct of qualitative inquiry; in fact, the success of this kind of research often rests on the relationship developed between the researcher and the informants. Close rapport opens doors to more informed research (Fontana and Frey). Getting close, however, is not without its problems. Researchers often find themselves in difficult positions as a consequence of the intimacies they have developed with respondents (see, for example, Roman).

Throughout the course of my investigation, I talked with many of the preschool teachers and developed both a professional and personal rapport with several of them. On their invitation, I observed their classrooms, attended after-school activities, and joined field trips. During these observations and activities, I occasionally saw teachers employing instructional techniques or taking disciplinary measures that seemed to me inappropriate and potentially harmful to the children, both physically and, especially, emotionally.[6] I was faced with a serious ethical dilemma: What was I to do with these very sensitive data?

On the one hand, I felt a responsibility—an obligation—to speak on the children's behalf and report the teachers' actions to the school administrator. I believed the teachers' behaviors were potentially harmful to the children, so the ethical thing to do was to act as the children's advocate. On the other hand, I felt a responsibility to protect the confidentiality of the teachers. I believed that reporting these data would embarrass them and, more importantly, that it could have significant implications for their careers. This was a perplexing ethical dilemma, and I was torn between my loyalty to the children and my loyalty to the teachers.

I struggled with my thoughts: Surely the teachers realized that their behavior was inappropriate? If so, however, why would they engage in such behavior in my presence? Did our familiar relationship and comfortable rapport lead them to believe I would keep this information confidential? Or did they think nothing of their behavior? My readings in critical ethnography (e.g., Denzin, *Interpretive*; Simon and Dippo) urged me to take action on the children's behalf, but at the same time a "covenantal ethic" cogently argued against betraying the teachers' trust (May 367); I was both grateful and indebted to them for opening their classrooms to my research project.

For weeks I wrestled between my professional responsibility to the teachers and my personal commitment to the welfare of the children. I argued with myself: I was not studying the teachers, I was studying the children, and the ethnographer's paramount responsibility is to those she studies. I was supposed to do everything in my power to protect the children's "physical, social, and emotional safety and welfare"— or so said the American Anthropological Association—so, wasn't my moral obligation to the children? Yet the teachers were also participants in the research project. To what extent should I continue to protect their confidentiality? How could I report their behavior and at the same time maintain their anonymity? What was ethical here?

When I was most honest with myself, however, I knew I faced a third and perhaps more personal issue. For all practical purposes, reporting the teachers' behavior would have ended my research project— my dissertation—and postponed the completion of my graduate degree. As I struggled between loyalties, I also wrestled with my own ambitions, purposes, and agenda. Whose interests were really being served? Was I truly willing to act on the children's behalf? If so, why hadn't I? How important was this research project *in itself*? Was it more important than what might be done for the children? While I labored with these issues, I conveniently avoided any responsibility to the children. They were "rescued," however, by a parent who also witnessed what she believed to be inappropriate instructional and disciplinary behavior. She reported the incident to the administrator, who dealt with it immediately.

Sharan Merriam suggests that "knowing when to intervene is perhaps the most perplexing ethical dilemma facing case study investigators" (181). I would argue that knowing when to intervene is only half the dilemma; *doing so* is the other. If this parent had not spoken on the children's behalf, would I eventually have done so? I could answer a hasty, after-the-fact "yes," but how important is that response now? The fact is, I did not intervene. Of course I could say, "If I had it to do over again, I'd intervene." But that response seems overly simplistic as well. Tenure calls as loudly now as the Ph.D. did then. Besides, the purpose of this chapter is to be up front and honest about my struggles with and attempts at ethical behavior. Yet I am not as ruthless as this may sound; I still (five years later) feel a sense of guilt about my inaction on the children's behalf. I want to believe I would do things differently "next time." I believe I understand more about conducting qualitative research, collaborating with participants, and, most importantly, knowing myself.

Dealing with Issues of Representation

Throughout the literature, social scientists argue that no harm should come to any informant as a direct result of participating in the research (see Anderson, this volume). To this end, researchers are called to safeguard the "rights, interests, safety, and *sensitivities* of those who entrust information" to them (American Anthropological Association, emphasis added). This ethical code is often compromised, however, when the results of research are disseminated or published (see Cassell, "Risk and

Benefit"). When informants read what researchers have written, they may feel hurt, embarrassed, outraged, or deceived. Consider, for example, the reactions in "Cornerville" (the North End of Boston) to the publication of Whyte's *Street Corner Society,* an ethnography of the social structure of an Italian neighborhood, or the furor among the literate, articulate pillars of "Springdale" over Vidich and Bensman's *Small Town in Mass Society,* a controversial study of class, power, and religion in a rural community in upstate New York.[7] As these cases illustrate, the informants' response to the researcher's text often raises questions about objectivity, truth, and modes of representation.

Representing the beliefs and behaviors of others in ethnographic reports often requires difficult and uncomfortable, but important, ethical decisions; in fact, in their landmark *Handbook of Qualitative Research,* Norman Denzin and Yvonna Lincoln suggest that "how best to describe and interpret the experiences" of others poses a *crisis* for qualitative researchers, a "crisis of representation" (577). This is particularly the case when the ethnographic account involves what Thomas Newkirk (this volume) calls "bad news," information that has the potential to hurt or embarrass those who have participated in the research. How does the researcher deal with these data in an ethical manner? How does she solve this crisis of representation in ways that protect informants yet fulfill her interpretive responsibility to readers?

In the final stages of my investigation, while writing the case report, I distributed copies of the provisional text to all research participants and requested that they respond to its "truth and validity." At least two informants were confronted with "bad news" in the narrative, and their reactions indicated that my representations of them may have been problematic.

Cathy

Cathy was the single mom of one of the case study children. Her son Andrew had a profound hearing loss and used signs as his primary mode of communication. Cathy, however, knew very few signs, and her interaction with her son was limited and difficult. She frequently used the wrong signs, and since she did not know many of the signs Andrew used, she often misunderstood his communication. Importantly, she interacted much less frequently with Andrew than she did with her younger, hearing son Bradley. In fact, Cathy and Bradley often talked in Andrew's presence without including him in the conversation.

In our final session, Cathy told me that reading the draft of the case study about Andrew was painful for her. In the report, I described the nature of the interactional patterns that took place in each child's home. The narrative descriptions illustrated Cathy's difficulty in communicating with Andrew and indicated that she interacted more with her hearing son than with her deaf son. She stated that while she was unaware of this behavior, she "knew [the words] were true" when she saw them in the draft, and they bothered her. In some sense, my critique set Cathy on "a collision course with reality," and we both struggled with her pain (Ayers and Schubert 23).

Although "Cathy" is a pseudonym, almost everyone at the preschool knew about the investigation and could easily identify the research participants. Because the researcher works closely and regularly with case study informants, anonymity within the research site is often impossible (Deyhle, Hess, and LeCompte; see also Merriam). Cathy and I both knew that the administrator, the preschool teachers, and the parents of the other two case study children would be reading the written report. There were specific examples (raw data) of Cathy's interactions with Andrew in the report, and Cathy's failure at communication would be apparent to all. This was more than just an embarrassing issue, however. The previous year, Andrew had failed his oral preschool class (where no signs are used). That is, because he did not make satisfactory progress in oral language development, he was retained and moved into the total communication classroom where he would learn to sign. Clearly, many readers of the case report would make connections between Cathy's failure at communication within the home and Andrew's recent failure in the preschool.

I considered withdrawing the descriptions from the final report to spare Cathy this embarrassment. Wasn't it enough that she should come to terms with this situation? It seemed harsh and unfair to broadcast it. Yet this was a real-life description of the ways in which a deaf child experienced verbal language, and I considered it to be crucial to my research and, ultimately (I hoped), to disciplinary knowledge. Cathy's and Andrew's crisis of communication posed a crisis of representation for me. I discussed the issue with Cathy, and when I suggested withdrawing the descriptions, she declined. She stated, "I'm going to be more aware of it, and this might help someone else." I gained a greater sense of respect for Cathy because of her courage and willingness to be vulnerable and in some sense to endure suffering—the very thing I was to protect her from—as a result of participating in the research project. Furthermore, I found that engaging in a joint decision concerning whether or not to publish the "bad news" was an important and ethical move, and I argue for the importance of such negotiation and collaborative behavior among qualitative researchers and their participants.

Still, there is another ethical question: Did Cathy's willingness to suffer embarrassment negate my ethical obligation to her? Was the knowledge gained worth the pain she suffered? Robert Stake argues that the "value of the best research is not likely to outweigh injury to a person exposed" (244). Although Stake gives us something important to think about, I believe that balance on this issue is ultimately a question for the individual researcher in each investigative context. Researchers must deal with these kinds of problems on a case-by-case basis. Much of qualitative research is by nature evaluative (see Patton), and participants undoubtedly will confront data that are uncomfortable to them. Dealing with these data in a manner that is both palatable to research participants and informative for the larger research and teaching community is at the heart of what it means to conduct ethical research.

Elizabeth

The second participant confronted with "bad news" was Elizabeth, one of the preschool teachers. (Sue was the case study child in Elizabeth's class.) Despite numerous attempts on my part to arrange meeting times or telephone conversations, Elizabeth would not discuss with me the draft of the case study which I had shared with her. Although I cannot be sure, I believe Elizabeth's unwillingness to participate in the final "member check" was primarily due to statements I made in the case report about her theory of how deaf children learn to read and write and about her instructional practices (Lincoln and Guba 314).

Elizabeth's theory and her classroom practice reflected the reading readiness paradigm, an epistemological stance which espouses a linear approach to language development and literacy learning. That is, those who embrace a reading readiness perspective believe that children must be proficient language users before literacy instruction will be effective. They typically focus on language development activities in the preschool setting and postpone literacy instruction until the primary grades. This position is at odds with my own emergent literacy perspective, which suggests that children's language and literacy develop simultaneously, mutually reinforcing one another in development, and, therefore, should be taught in an integrated fashion in the early childhood program.

In the case report, I described each teacher's theoretical stance on deaf children's language and literacy learning (based primarily on formal interviews with each teacher), and I provided examples of classroom practice that reflected these theories. While I tried to write objectively, reporting only what I had seen and heard, it is quite likely that my educational values (based upon my emergent literacy perspective) were reflected in the narrative descriptions and that they were less than "emicly sensitive" (Pitman and Maxwell 768).[8]

Was Elizabeth so hurt by my descriptions of her theory and practice that she refused to assist me further? Did she feel betrayed or deceived? Or was she enraged? Perhaps Elizabeth saw herself portrayed in the case report in ways that did not mesh with her own perspective. Did she think I had misrepresented her? Would she give a different telling of her story? Were the descriptions hurtful because of their accuracy? Or did Elizabeth simply lack the time or interest to respond?[9]

Elizabeth's unwillingness to participate may also have been a consequence of my own inability to identify and explicate all necessary facets of the study before beginning the investigation. When I negotiated the research project with the teachers, I described the kinds of observations and video recordings to be made of the case study children. Of course, these observations would include the teachers and the other children, so I asked the teachers and all parents to sign consent forms.[10] At that time, however, I did not realize the extent to which I would be observing and, more importantly, describing the teachers' instructional practices as a part of my description of the children's experiences with oral language, signed language, and written language. That is, to provide "thick description" of the children's experiences with verbal language and literacy, I described in great detail the teachers' classroom practices in the case study report (see Geertz). In some sense, I wrote these descriptions without *informed* consent, and perhaps this is the reason Elizabeth would not respond to the report.[11] Unintentionally, my consent form was a seductive device, luring Elizabeth into the research project without explaining to her the possible consequences of participation (see Newkirk, this volume).

While I did not provide the informants with extensive information about all facets of the research, neither did I intentionally misrepresent the character of my study.[12] Clearly, it is impossible to predict the exact course of a qualitative investigation before the research is initiated. Qualitative researchers have a sense of direction, and they may seek to answer specific questions, but the research itself is evolutionary in nature and must be constructed in the field. New issues surface and additional questions are raised throughout the research project because the researchers largely work inductively. This must be the case, for limiting oneself to predetermined research agendas will certainly limit the potential for discovery (Peshkin). Nevertheless, all participants have the right to be informed about the nature of the research. To meet the ethical requirement that informants give their consent, I should have discussed methodological and conceptual changes with the teachers (and parents) as soon as I recognized them, before writing the case report. Indeed, Barrie Thorne suggests that changes in one's research "may warrant a new, explicit effort to communicate one's purpose and one's methods as a researcher, and to ask for a renewed granting of consent" (290). This is, obviously, risky business. On learning of new developments, participants might decline further participation. And this process could become endless, as researchers continually refine and redefine their research focus and questions. Nevertheless, I would argue for renewed consent as a useful principle. How often and when to engage in this process of negotiation becomes an individual decision for each researcher. In my case, data collection and analysis were complete; I did not recognize this ethical dilemma until the initial stages of writing. At that point, I should have discussed with the preschool teachers my predicament and attempted to negotiate an acceptable solution. I did not; I was afraid of the consequences. I wrote the provisional draft and gave it to the teachers, assuring them of my willingness to change any statements they found inaccurate or unacceptable. It was at this point that Elizabeth refused to respond.

It may be that my descriptions *silenced* Elizabeth. Perhaps the discourse I used in the narrative had a regulatory impact, silencing her rather than helping her articulate her perspective (Simon and Dippo). At the time of that writing, I tried to give Elizabeth voice by quoting her throughout the narrative, especially when describing her theoretical paradigm. I was attempting to ensure that she was in the text. But those quotations were taken from formal interviews; they were answers to *my* questions. And I used those quotations to develop *my* theory about Elizabeth's philosophy. As I read the narrative now it is univocal, for in my talking about Elizabeth, I took over her voice (see Denzin, "The Art and Politics").

Whatever the reasons, Elizabeth did not respond to the provisional report, and, consequently, I had no member check on my interpretations of her theory or classroom practice. According to Lincoln and Guba, the member check, whereby the informants scrutinize the researcher's interpretations, is "the most crucial technique" for establishing the credibility or internal validity of the report (314). I recognize that there is currently a serious rethinking of the ways in which qualitative researchers attempt to legitimate their studies (Denzin and Lincoln, "Introduction" 11), and that issues of validity mask issues of the researcher's and the text's authority (Lincoln and Denzin 579). Nevertheless, I continue to believe that qualitative research gives birth to an interpreted world which needs to be examined and scrutinized by the participants in that world (Altheide and Johnson 486). Without Elizabeth's perspective, I cannot be sure of the interpretative accuracy of the case study. I reported what I saw and heard, but, as is always true of qualitative research, my observations were undoubtedly ethnocentric, filtered through my own ethnographic lens, replete with its theoretical and pedagogical positions and biases.

I have learned that, while unable to script every aspect of the research, I can discuss with the participants the general nature of qualitative inquiry—its open-endedness and evolving dimensions. Certainly, my consent form should include an explicit statement concerning the potential for "bad news" and an agreement that such issues will be discussed, negotiated, and reported in print. I recognize the limitations of seeking to explain the nature of this kind of inquiry to those who have little knowledge of qualitative research, the roles of the researcher, or the consequences of the case report. Yet I have a responsibility, an ethical obligation, to see that the informants have some understanding of what I am doing and how the research could affect their lives.

Dealing with Ethical Issues

In thinking through each of the ethical issues discussed in this chapter, I am coming to believe that collaborative research may be the method of choice—an ethical choice to be sure.[13] When research is truly collaborative, the researcher and the informants participate as a team; they become co-researchers who explore an issue of common interest and concern. They co-author the research questions, co-collect, co-analyze, and co-interpret the data, and they co-construct the final products (e.g., written reports, public presentations). The researchers develop an interactive, dialogic, reciprocal relationship that mitigates the strictures of traditional, imperialistic hegemony. They learn to respect one another's perspective and honor one another's trust (e.g., see Branscombe; Carr and Allen; Klassen and Short; and Heath and Branscombe; see also Bickel and Hattrup).

In their powerful book *Engaging Children: Community and Chaos in the Lives of Young Literacy Learners*, teacher educator JoBeth Allen and classroom teachers Barbara Michalove and Betty Shockley describe their collaborative research relationship:

> Betty Shockley (first grade) and Barbara Michalove (second grade) invited JoBeth to study with them in their classrooms. The research

team worked together all year, not because we were paid (we were not), or because someone was doing doctoral research (no one was at that point), or because we just liked each other (although we did). We worked together as a community of learners ... because we had very important questions driving our teaching and thinking, and this seemed like one way of investigating those questions with other experts interested in the same issues. (4–5)

It seems significant to me that the classroom teachers invited the university professor to collaborate *with them*. Shockley and Michalove made the decision to conduct research to find answers to their own questions about teaching and learning, and they initiated participatory inquiry with Allen. This is very different from my own research project. Without fully realizing it at the time, I was studying down, conducting research *on* participants, a methodology which perpetuates the hierarchical relationship between university researchers and classroom teachers.[14] If Elizabeth and I had been collaborating, we would have co-examined the data, and we could have negotiated its meaning from the emic perspective. We would have co-authored the case study, juxtaposing multiple interpretations if necessary. We could have prevented Elizabeth's (distressing?) encounter with the unexpected "bad news" and what I suspect were feelings of betrayal and distrust.

Despite my growing support for participatory inquiry, however, I do not believe that collaborative relationships will eliminate difficult choices or solve the ethical dilemmas of qualitative research. Any relationship, regardless of how egalitarian, is framed by ethical dimensions. Collaborative research relationships may, however, provide a powerful avenue for dealing with the crisis of representation. Further, collaborative research relationships may move us closer to a rigorously examined, richly contextualized, and emicly sensitive ethnographic "truth" which honors multiple interpretations and voices, a "truth" that will contribute to our understanding of people and their lives.

Some Closing Thoughts

In this chapter, I have attempted to provide a reflexive account about the ethical dilemmas I faced while conducting my first qualitative investigation, dilemmas that can compromise case study research. I have been honest and open about the manner in which I solved, or failed to solve, these issues—a kind of "owning up" strategy. I hope that in this writing I have contributed to the development of an accepted genre for talking about our attempts at solving ethical issues, what Maurice Punch calls "coming clean" on predicaments in the field ("Politics and Ethics" 90). I realize, however, that simply discussing, in retrospect, the issues I faced does not justify my decisions or actions; that is not my intent. Rather, thinking through these dilemmas and discussing them openly is an important first step toward ethical research. The next step is to *learn* from these discussions, to let them influence future research projects. I invite and welcome other shared accounts of the ethical dimensions of qualitative research and the ways in which investigators have faced these challenges. A kind of "coming clean" genre would be especially beneficial as we continue to learn how to be and become better qualitative researchers.

Although we have various guidelines and professional codes of ethics for conducting qualitative research in an ethical manner, these can only serve to raise our consciousness and, I hope, our sensitivities. No set of principles will hold for every situation or answer every question. We must continually ask ourselves, and each other, what it means to "do the right thing" and what it means to act ethically. Dealing with ethical dilemmas moves qualitative research into the course of everyday living for each of us. Perhaps this is where an ethics of research properly begins.

Notes

1. The term *profoundly deaf* refers to individuals who have very severe (<91 dB PTA) hearing losses (Paul and Quigley).

2. Total communication is a philosophy requiring incorporation of appropriate aural, manual, and oral modes of communication in order to ensure effective communication among hearing-impaired persons.

3. I realize that this is a value-laden statement, an outgrowth of my own theoretical and pedagogical paradigm.

4. This outcome may have been different if I had read the entire text. Fine's descriptions of the behaviors and actions that occur within the games, particularly the treatment of women characters, was disturbing for me, and after reading several chapters of the text, I aborted my attempt to complete it. As Fine notes, "[W]ithin the context of the game, players are oriented toward murder and death without considerations of any moral niceties" (*Shared Fantasy* 43).

5. From a memorandum of the Awards Committee of the Convention of American Instructors of the Deaf, April 1995.

6. For example, one teacher, who was clearly angry, grasped a four-year-old child by the shoulders and shook him harshly as she reprimanded him. Another teacher slapped the hands of children in the auditory-oral classes who

used sign language instead of oral language to communicate with their peers. An auditory-oral teacher stuck her first three fingers vertically into the mouth of a three-year-old child to pry it open as she told him he had to open his mouth if he was going to learn to talk. The child looked frightened; his eyes filled with tears, and his face blushed a deep scarlet. I felt physically ill as I watched this incident. *As I write this footnote, I struggle with the ethics of printing these data.*

7. More recently, consider the reactions of community members of "Frenchtown" to Caroline Brettell's lecture on priest Charles Chiniquy and the settlement of French-Canadian immigrants in Illinois.

8. The emic stance focuses on the insider's perspective on reality, in this case, Elizabeth's perspective on her own theory and classroom practice. Mary Anne Pitman suggests that "emicly sensitive" research focuses on the informants' issues and meanings (Personal communication). The researcher does not simply learn what informants think, feel, say, and do. Rather, she learns what *they believe* they are thinking, feeling, saying, and doing. The researcher's responsibility is to elicit the informant's issues and meanings and represent them as authentically as possible.

9. Although I struggle with the reasons for Elizabeth's silence, I agree with Brenda Jo Brueggemann (this volume), who cogently argues that researchers must respect participants' silence as an important position. She states, "We cannot require them to speak if they only want to remain anonymous or silent. Those positions are ones we need to consider and respect as well. Those positions represent something meaningful (if not painful)."

10. The consent forms briefly explained that I would be conducting "a research investigation" which would focus on "how very young hearing-impaired children learn to use language for beginning reading and writing." These forms secured permission from parents to record, using videotape, audiotape, and photography, "the children's participation in early reading and writing activities." Teachers and teachers' aides consented to being videotaped, audiotaped, and photographed as they "engaged in literacy-related events" with the children. The consent forms stated that the recordings would be used for "both research and instructional purposes" (in university teacher education courses) and that "a case study report of the research findings" would be provided at the end of the study.

11. Through informed consent, research informants are made aware that their participation is voluntary and that they may choose to discontinue their participation at any time. Informants are provided an explanation of what their participation will entail, and they are informed of any aspects of the research that could affect their well-being (Lincoln and Guba; see also Anderson, this volume).

12. I believe that my own inexperience in conducting qualitative research was a factor in this dilemma. We learn by doing, and I had never done this before.

13. I am intentionally using the phrase "coming to believe." An important issue here is whether or not all qualitative research should be collaborative. That is, what do researchers do if, as Brenda Jo Brueggemann (this volume)

suggests, informants agree to the research project but do not want to collaborate? Should we proceed and do research *on* these individuals? Or should we seek another research site—continue to look for informants who do want to collaborate? If such a site cannot be found, should we abandon the research project altogether? These questions have ethical dimensions. At this point, I desire a collaborative relationship for my next research project. I am interested in a particular area of literacy learning and instruction, and I am now trying to locate early childhood educators who are interested in, and already asking themselves, the same questions.

14. Interestingly, throughout the data-collection period I felt the study might collapse at any time. I believe this was true primarily because of the very controversial and sensitive nature of the education of deaf children. It was not until the writing phase that I began to feel some control. And that power, I believe, is what makes "studying down" so problematic.

Works Cited

Allen, JoBeth, Barbara Michalove, and Betty Shockley. *Engaging Children: Community and Chaos in the Lives of Young Literacy Learners.* Portsmouth: Heinemann, 1993.

Altheide, David L., and John M. Johnson. "Criteria for Assessing Interpretive Validity in Qualitative Research." Denzin and Lincoln 485–99.

American Anthropological Association. *Statement on Ethics: Revised Principles of Professional Responsibility.* Washington: American Anthropological Association, 1990.

Ayers, William, and William Schubert. "Do the Right Thing: Ethical Issues and Problems in Qualitative Research." *Teaching and Learning* 6.2 (1992): 19–24.

Bickel, William E., and Rosemary H. Hattrup. "Teachers and Researchers in Collaboration: Reflections on the Process." *American Educational Research Journal* 32 (1995): 35–62.

Branscombe, Amanda. "I Gave My Classroom Away." *Reclaiming the Classroom: Teacher Research as an Agency for Change.* Ed. Dixie Goswami and Peter R. Stillman. Upper Montclair: Boynton/Cook, 1987. 206–19.

Brettell, Caroline B. "Whose History Is It? Selection and Representation in the Creation of a Text." *When They Read What We Write: The Politics of Ethnography.* Ed. Caroline B. Brettell. Westport: Bergin and Garvey, 1993. 91–105.

Carr, Emily, and JoBeth Allen. "University/Classroom Teacher Collaboration." *Qualitative Research in Education.* Ed. Judith Goetz and JoBeth Allen. Athens: U of Georgia P, 1988. 123–31.

Cassell, Joan. "Risk and Benefit to Subjects of Fieldwork." *American Sociologist* 13 (1978): 134–43.

———. "Ethical Principles for Conducting Fieldwork." *American Anthropologist* 82 (1980): 28–41.

Denzin, Norman K. "The Art and Politics of Interpretation." Denzin and Lincoln 500–15.

———. *Interpretive Interactionism.* Newbury Park: Sage, 1989.

Denzin, Norman K., and Yvonna S. Lincoln, eds. *Handbook of Qualitative Research.* Thousand Oaks: Sage, 1994.

———. "Introduction: Entering the Field of Qualitative Research." Denzin and Lincoln 1–17.

Deyhle, Donna L., G. Alfred Hess, and Margaret D. LeCompte. "Approaching Ethical Issues for Qualitative Researchers in Education." LeCompte, Millroy, and Preissle 597–641.

Fine, Gary Alan. *Shared Fantasy: Role-Playing Games as Social Worlds.* Chicago: U of Chicago P, 1983.

———. "Credit and Blame in Ethnographic Publishing." *American Sociologist* 21 (1990): 76–79.

Fontana, Andrea, and James H. Frey. "Interviewing: The Art of Science." Denzin and Lincoln 361–76.

Geertz, Clifford. *The Interpretation of Culture.* New York: Basic, 1973.

Heath, Shirley Brice, and Amanda Branscombe. "'Intelligent Writing' in an Audience Community: Teacher, Students, and Researcher." *The Acquisition of Written Language: Response and Revision.* Ed. Sarah Warshauer Freedman. Norwood: Ablex, 1985. 3–32.

Hopkins, Marycarol. "Is Anonymity Possible? Writing about Refugees in the United States." *When They Read What We Write: The Politics of Ethnography.* Ed. Caroline B. Brettell. Westport: Bergin and Garvey, 1993. 119–29.

Kirsch, Gesa E. *Women Writing the Academy: Audience, Authority, and Transformation.* Carbondale: Southern Illinois UP, 1993.

Klassen, Charlene, and Kathy G. Short. "Collaborative Research on Teacher Study Groups: Embracing the Complexities." *Literacy Research, Theory, and Practice: Views from Many Perspectives.* Ed. Charles Kinzer and Donald Leu. Chicago: National Reading Conference, 1992. 341–48.

LeCompte, Margaret D., Wendy L. Millroy, and Judith Preissle, eds. *The Handbook of Qualitative Research in Education.* San Diego: Academic P, 1992.

Lincoln, Yvonna S., and Norman K. Denzin. "The Fifth Moment." Denzin and Lincoln 575–86.

Lincoln, Yvonna S., and Egon G. Guba. *Naturalistic Inquiry.* Beverly Hills: Sage, 1985.

May, William F. "Doing Ethics: The Bearing of Ethical Theories on Fieldwork. *Social Problems* 27 (1980): 358–70.

Merriam, Sharan B. *Case Study Research in Education: A Qualitative Approach.* San Francisco: Jossey-Bass, 1988.

Patton, Michael Quinn. *Qualitative Evaluation and Research Methods.* Newbury Park: Sage, 1990.

Paul, Peter V., and Stephen Quigley. *Education and Deafness.* New York: Longman, 1990.

Peshkin, Alan. "Understanding Complexity: A Gift of Qualitative Inquiry." *Anthropology and Education Quarterly* 19 (1988): 416–24.

Pitman, Mary Anne. Personal communication. Aug. 1994.

Pitman, Mary Anne, and Joseph A. Maxwell. "Qualitative Approaches to Evaluation: Models and Methods." LeCompte, Millroy, and Preissle 729–70.

Punch, Maurice. "Politics and Ethics in Qualitative Research." Denzin and Lincoln 83–97.

———. *The Politics and Ethics of Fieldwork.* Beverly Hills: Sage, 1986.

Roman, Leslie G. "The Political Significance of Other Ways of Narrating Ethnography: A Feminist Materialist Approach." LeCompte, Millroy, and Preissle 555–94.

Simon, Roger I., and Donald Dippo. "On Critical Ethnographic Work." *Anthropology and Education Quarterly* 17 (1986): 195–202.

Stake, Robert E. "Case Studies." Denzin and Lincoln 236–47.

Tancock, Susan M. *At-Risk Students: The Social Construction of Status.* Diss. Ohio State U, 1991.

Thorne, Barrie. "'You Still Takin' Notes?' Fieldwork and Problems of Informed Consent." *Social Problems* 27 (1980): 284–97.

Van Maanen, John. *Tales of the Field: On Writing Ethnography.* Chicago: U of Chicago P, 1988.

Vidich, Arthur J., and Joseph Bensman. *Small Town in Mass Society: Class, Power, and Religion in a Rural Community.* Garden City: Doubleday, 1960.

Whyte, William F. *Street Corner Society: The Social Structure of an Italian Slum.* Chicago: U of Chicago P, 1955.

Williams, Cheri L. "The Language and Literacy Worlds of Three Profoundly Deaf Preschool Children." *Reading Research Quarterly* 29 (1994): 125–55.

4 "Everything's Negotiable": Collaboration and Conflict in Composition Research

Russel K. Durst and Sherry Cook Stanforth
University of Cincinnati

A researcher sits in a first-year composition class, observing and jotting down field notes, occasionally taking part in discussion. His collaborator, who is also the teacher, stands at the blackboard, leading a lively classroom conversation. On this day the teacher focuses on two Studs Terkel profiles; she wants students to contrast Mike LeFevre, a caustic but witty steelworker in a dead-end job, with Stephen Cruz, an idealistic Mexican American who gives up a successful corporate career to farm and to teach in a small college. In an attempt to provoke critical analysis, the teacher makes the following assertion:

> Cruz just quits, leaves it all behind for the farm. He won't buy into your magic formula for personal happiness because he's tired of being labeled a minority. Yes, he holds a good position, but in the eyes of the company, Cruz is no better than (she makes a quoting gesture with her hands) "a good working nigger."

The researcher at his seat squirms a little over his colleague's choice of language. And yet the students appear undisturbed, and discussion proceeds apace. After class, however, the collaborators argue heatedly about the teacher's use of the "N" word. He says it is a word which could easily be taken out of context, capable of alienating, outraging, or deeply hurting individual students. He refers to an experience from his own undergraduate days when a teacher used an ethnic slur several times in a lecture. He had been offended and shocked, yet felt powerless to protest in what seemed to be a class full of indifferent students. She points out that the word came from the assigned text. She draws on feminist theory, insisting that teachers cannot hide behind polite and tidy language, especially in a class where students are asked to challenge their own cultural assumptions. He refers to some very real problems which have occurred in multicultural classrooms, suggesting that she did not contextualize the reference sufficiently; students, especially African Americans, might easily misconstrue her usage as insensitive, even racist. She, on the other hand, claims confidence in her relationships with individual students and refers to past teaching experiences where she made a whole host of ethnic slurs the center of discussion. Both struggle to maintain the role of collaborative partner. Eventually, after some days of discussing the matter with each other and with colleagues, she agrees that certain words should only be used in class with very careful bracketing; he admits to overreacting initially. They resume the collaboration, each finally understanding a little better what the other was trying to say.

What complicated this dispute is the fact that these were not just two friendly colleagues collaborating. Key differences in status, power, and experience separated the two. He is a tenured professor, veteran researcher, and director of the composition program in which she teaches. She is a graduate student and teaching assistant pursuing work in composition. As they argued their respective cases, he found himself instinctively pulling rank. Suddenly their individual roles began to blur; they shifted from collaborative partners to senior researcher and junior researcher, to professor and graduate student, to program director and less experienced teacher. Such shifting made for a complex and multilayered discussion.

The foregoing conflict took place between the two of us, co-authors of this chapter, during a two-quarter-long study of students and student-teacher interaction in a first-year English classroom. Together, we were investigating ways in which students and teacher understand and negotiate ground rules underlying academic discourse. The study focused on the development of students' critical reading, writing, and thinking and on their understanding of the teacher's expectations. As part of the research, Russel sat in on Sherry's class, regularly meeting one-on-one with a group of case study students from the class and collecting and examining all students' writing. The two of us also met throughout the project to discuss the course in general, writing assignments, class activities, and the progress and problems of particular students.

It was while reflecting on this larger research project about students' writing development that we began to see another story unfolding. This story told about the varying degrees of institutional authority represented by a program director, a graduate teaching assistant, and undergraduate students—and the problems that such status roles posed for reading qualitative data. We had embarked upon the collaborative, classroom-based study with what we thought were the best of reasons. For Sherry, the project offered the chance to work with an experienced faculty member who could provide both a significant research opportunity and insights about her own teaching. For Russel, the project involved an opportunity to study the classroom of one of the department's most innovative teachers. It was a chance to work closely with and give research experience to a talented student specializing in composition studies, and providing such experience is an important part of the job for faculty teaching in a doctoral program. The project also made sense, given the impetus in composition studies to undermine traditional notions of hierarchy and power relations (Bullock, Trimbur, and Schuster; Mortensen and Kirsch) and to encourage collaborative projects (Bruffee; Ede and Lunsford).

However, our conflict over language, and other situations that took place over the course of the project, helped to illustrate for us the very complex nature of our collaboration, a complexity we had not fully understood at the outset of the study and one not often articulated in published discussions of collaborative research. Such discussions tend to be exceedingly sanguine about the appeal of collaboration. Hudelson and Lindfors, in an early book on collaborative inquiry in language education, describe the pieces in their collection as "positive, strong, warm, upbeat" (ix). Other published discussions of collaborative research similarly emphasize the positive, feel-good aspects of such work. In an enthusiastic defense of collaborative scholarship, Roen and Mittan extol the virtues of collaboration as multiperspectival, rigorous, full of heuristic value for researchers and for readers, and more enjoyable than solo study. The authors do point out that collaboration can "lead not to dialogue but to misunderstanding and acrimony," can be "vulnerable to conflicts in personality type and work habits," and is "not . . . immune from such social and political concerns as gender and status differences" (295–96). But, as in the Hudelson and Lindfors book and in an essay by Roen and McNenny, Roen and Mittan quickly move past such caveats to sing the praises of collaboration. Advocates of collaborative research, like those of collaborative writing and learning in the classroom, cite social constructionist theories of language and development (Bakhtin, Vygotsky) to support the view that working together, besides being politically progressive, is beneficial to learning. Indeed, the term *collaboration* appears to have achieved "keyword" status in composition research, in that it "seems never to be used unfavourably" or to be interrogated critically (Williams 66).

We began our work together examining the inner workings of a classroom. But as our research progressed and as the political complexities of our collaborative activity became more evident, studying scenes of instruction evolved into an examination of the politics of studying scenes of instruction. In this chapter, while acknowledging its benefits and unique strengths, we would like to examine in greater detail some of the tensions involved in classroom-based collaborative research. We focus in particular here on negotiations of power and authority in a collaboration between colleagues at different levels of the academic hierarchy, using examples from our own collaboration. Our purpose is not in any way to discourage or disparage collaborative research. Rather, in presenting a less celebratory, more critical, and, we believe, more realistic picture of such research, we hope to raise awareness of the complex politics and the sometimes overlapping, sometimes conflicting roles which affect collaborators who study classrooms. We argue that conflict or "dissensus" (Karis; Trimbur) can in fact be a critical and even productive part of the collaborative process. Because an important aspect of the complexity of collaborative research involves making sense of the differences in collaborators' perspectives, we will each consider our roles in the collaboration, framed by a jointly authored discussion. We will conclude by presenting some reflections about preparing for and dealing with problems and conflicts that might arise during collaboration.

Sherry Cook Stanforth's Perspective on the Collaboration

"Could you give me a couple of days?" I asked him after our initial discussion. "I'd really like more time to think about it." For a graduate student in the field of composition studies, the invitation to do collaborative classroom research with the director of freshman English seemed almost too good to be true, except for one small detail: many of the actions under scrutiny would be my own. Despite the confidence I had built over four years of teaching and presenting work at academic conferences, I worried about a "collaboration" where my classroom identity would be fully exposed to someone who played an important role in my professional development. I took my first graduate course in the field from Russel. He guided one of my research projects; he acted as my academic adviser; he wrote my recommendations. His title was "Director of Freshman English" and mine was "Graduate Assistant." How could I forget, when acting as a kind of writing authority for twenty-two students, that traditionally my collaborator had served as my evaluator? This addition to my classroom audience complicated my struggle to fulfill the role of "effective teacher." As usual, Russel would supervise and respond to my professional performance. But in this situation, he was a "partner" who first watched and scribbled notes in a yellow legal pad—then returned to his office to render "my" experiences into text.

As a teacher who emphasizes dialogic participation, I have grown to appreciate how sitting in a circle makes it difficult for anyone to hide. Such a classroom structure recalls the theoretically charged vocabulary of negotiated authority, polyvocality, egalitarianism, demarginalization, pluralism, Bakhtinian heteroglossia. As we face each other's "alien word[s]" (Roen and Mittan 293), we must decide how, or if, we will respond with our own. This interaction forms the basis for relationships, identified by Edelsky and Boyd as "the one constant feature" in collaborative work. Negotiators are constantly confronted by surprises, and before arriving at their common goal they must forage through a "jumble of thorns and roses" (5).

But traditionally, institutional settings have resisted alien words, and as a student and a teacher, I have often experienced those uncomfortable situations where the circle-of-equals philosophy won't do. Authority ultimately shapes itself to the organizational context surrounding collaborators—in this case, the English department, where performance evaluation and decision making occur daily. Varying levels of identification and commitment to the perceived interests of that organization, along with the agendas which have been informed by superordinate groups (Cheney and Tompkins 2–3), imply a hierarchy between the director who has a hand in designing the curriculum, the teaching assistant who has been "chosen" to interpret and carry out that curriculum—and the students who must fulfill its requirements.

My job teaching English 102 required that I guide my students toward analyzing, synthesizing, and evaluating arguments on political and cultural topics. Drawing on class discussion, assigned reading, and journal entries, students were to write short essays and a self-reflexive research project—all of which critically examined the beliefs and values informing their own and other positions within complex social discourse. In my ideal class, I visualized myself as facilitator of a decentralized classroom where my (mostly white, conservative) students carefully considered the alien word. At the end of the quarter, my writers would leave the circle shuddering at positivism, ready to expose rhetorical manipulation, and they would never, ever tune in to Rush Limbaugh again.

But I faced the reality of students like Joshua writing about women who refused to know their God-given role in life—that of the happy homemaker. Mindy, Jan, and Stephanie fixated on the "gross injustice" of affirmative action and the "overboard" political objections of African Americans. The heated discussion which followed a classroom visit from the director of Affirmative Action confirmed my suspicion that the three had a strong following. In yet another discussion, Karen mentioned that her AIDS-infected uncle "deserved to die." I struggled with the silence. Russel waited, pencil poised—and somewhere in my periphery, a hand waved eagerly. What I thought would be a challenge to Karen's views turned out to be Donald's "making sure" that she didn't mean that *all* people with AIDS deserved to die. After all, his research project was about AIDS-infected hemophiliacs as victims of discrimination, and his initial thesis—his rhetorical emphasis—designated that they were the "innocent" AIDS sufferers.

Ken, who told me in a conference that his father was homosexual, chose not to participate at all in the discussion. Jack, who wrote his first paper about the struggle to repress his homosexuality and his suicidal tendencies, chose not to participate in the discussion either. Nor did Jeff, a minority prelaw student who told me in a conference that he wanted to fight social injustice, choose to participate in the discussion. And Katie and Chelsea passed up a golden opportunity to draw on Gordon Allport's group-norm theory of prejudice (from *Rereading America*), despite the fact that it had served as a key citation in their recent essays.

I do not remember exactly what I contributed to the discussion. It seems I made a weak attempt to balance the silence, said something to the effect that "we need to remember that not everyone holds that particular view about homosexuality." Authority issues compelled their resistance and my confusion about making space for students' voices. That day especially, I was torn by the realization that teachers cannot make students say what they think students might be thinking. Neither can they always say what they themselves are thinking; I had a fear of shutting down participation. What kind of power would that be, turning my "critical thinking" on students to model an involved counterargument? Many of them were deeply grounded in a religious faith which did not encourage deviance from so-called traditional values. They complained to me about the "liberal" agenda in the textbook. They felt angry and threatened, and I learned that after class they would gather for coffee, bash the textbook and its assignments, and find consensus with one another.

The experience of teaching untidy social discourse in front of one's supervisor was an emotional and intellectual challenge for me: it not only compelled me to seek an "appropriate" or "fair" balance of student voices, it also demanded that I understand my own place within that discourse—and teach composition effectively. Sometimes, I completely forgot that I was in that room leading students to "reread America" so that they could become more compelling writers. I could only react to what I knew about each of them as thinkers and believers—people shaped by their life experiences, confronting a curriculum which required them to challenge that shaping process, both individually and socially.

It is interesting that much of a teacher's identity is inextricably bound to her own sense of being able to effectively control situations such as the ones mentioned above. What, finally, was my "partner" thinking? Who would I *be* as the teacher? That all-important question of "What work will we do today?" gained a complexity when Russel entered my classroom. As I walked the line between theory and practice, my perceptions of my own role blurred, and sometimes my teaching became a performance aimed at two significantly different audiences. I was on the boundary, both teacher and student. What if Russel did not agree with a particular decision or act? What if he chose not to support me? Would he fully perceive my agenda? Would he "accurately" translate that agenda when he sat down to write about what happened in the classroom?

My collaborator's participation in small group activities, his frequent meetings with case study students, his access not only to their written work but to my evaluative feedback—all served to increase my awareness of the "imbalance" in our professional experience. Because I feared coming across as unappreciative, I hesitated to raise even the most respectful challenge of his role in my classroom, a role which significantly contributed to students' learning. When confronted with opportunities to assert my own authority as teacher I often remained silent. Once, in a conference, my student Amy mentioned with some frustration that Russel had firmly steered her away from a topic she really wanted to write about: military cover-up of extraterrestrial life. It crossed my mind then that I probably would have handled the conference differently. Amy and I would have entertained a discussion about audience issues and assignment goals as they related to her chosen topic. Ultimately, though, my role was governed by my sense of what collaborating should be with a senior colleague: better not to say much about the incident and to keep pushing forward.

Such situations imply a tangle of audience issues. Russel's research data would be determined in large part by the relationships he managed to build with the students and with me. We, in turn, could not help but be influenced by the authority he represented. And when faced with the dilemmas and unpredictable moments inherent to teaching composition, I found myself struggling to feel like a "collaborator" rather than a "subject." There is something very personal about how teachers ultimately translate and encourage critical ideas, how we build a classroom community. I tried once, in a journal entry, to explore this feeling of vulnerability:

> He is the researcher reading me as I read my students—who are also reading me. I remember at the beginning of fall quarter sensing what evaluative criteria might be used to gauge my classroom performance and thinking, "Russel and I are different. He will be watching for a structure, terminology, a kind of science—and I will be encouraging boundary reformulation, creative definitions and intuition."

Experimentation of any kind involves risk, and I found myself wondering about a reading which would be "cast from above" (Edelsky and Boyd 7). I knew that in our project the translation of experiences and situations both inside and outside the classroom would evolve into an epistemological product. It would, to draw on Thomas Newkirk's discussion of ethics in qualitative research (this volume), go through a series of "renderings" until it represented a text of "real power" about the activity of all parties involved. How, finally, would *my* story get told?

Russel Durst's Perspective on the Collaboration

The button on my bulletin board reads, "Question Authority." But increasingly in my professional life as a college professor and, in the last few years, composition program director, I find *myself* in the role of authority. In this situation, it is not so easy to "fight the power," as Public Enemy puts it in Spike Lee's *Do the Right Thing.* In terms of developing curriculum, hiring and evaluating faculty, scheduling, setting program policies, working with new graduate assistants, assessing students, helping to resolve student-teacher disputes, deciding who gets money, and representing the program both within and outside the university, I frequently face issues of authority and how best to exercise it. As director, my impulse is as much as possible to share power—and the responsibility that accompanies it—with my colleagues who teach in the composition program. This approach comes in part from my experience and ideology as a composition teacher who attempts to decentralize the locus of authority in the classroom, to push students to take greater and greater responsibility for their own development as writers. As a researcher, my impulse is similar. I have been engaged in numerous collaborative research and writing projects, always with colleagues who are peers as well as good friends. These collaborations are among my most satisfying professional experiences. There have been some conflicts and disagreements, to be sure. However, conflict and disagreement are part of the collaborative process, can indeed be quite helpful at times, and my overall experience of collaboration has been a very positive and productive one.

It was in this context of a history of successful and enjoyable collaborations that I talked with Sherry about working with me on a study of students' developing analytic abilities and the teacher's role in that development in freshman English. I knew I wanted to study a freshman English class, and my original plan was to do the research myself, with the teacher and the students serving as the subjects of the study. But my research orientation was changing at this time, as I began to move toward a less hierarchical way of doing research, an approach that was beginning to receive a good deal of attention in composition studies. Motivated by Sandra Harding's pioneering work in feminist inquiry, Gesa Kirsch's discussion of this approach in the context of composition studies, and Hull and Rose's work with basic writing students, I resolved to try a more participatory and egalitarian form of research. In this new (to me) approach I would work closely and collaboratively with a teacher-researcher, instead of observing from "above." I would get to know students in a different way as well, tutoring them and participating in the class, rather than just interviewing them and examining their written work. I would also focus more, in a self-reflexive way, on my own assumptions and opinions as a researcher, teacher, and administrator, rather than assuming the detached, pseudo-objective stance of the traditional empiricist. Coming from a background as a traditionally trained psycholinguistic researcher, and never having done a classroom-based, qualitative study before, I was intrigued by this new approach, which seemed both more humane and far better contextualized than other approaches to studying what went on in writing classes. I resolved to try it out.

Sherry was an obvious choice for a collaborator. With a background in composition studies, creative writing, and folklore, she was well respected in the department and known for designing interesting classroom activities and assignments, which many others would borrow. She had already given a number of papers at national conferences. She had distinguished herself in virtually all the courses we offer and was looking for research experience. Having just read a piece by Roen and Mittan (professor and graduate student, respectively) enthusiastically advocating collaborative scholarship, I felt very encouraged about the project.

However, to an extent that I had not fully realized, this was still "my" study, which I had conceived, was directing, and had asked Sherry to take part in. It was not as fully collaborative as projects I had worked on with faculty colleagues (though I have found that one never knows at the outset just how collaborative—in terms of shared work and commitment—a project is going to be; work roles often evolve). As director of the writing program of which Sherry's class was a part, and as her professor and mentor, I brought a considerable amount of authority to the project, more than I was initially aware of when I asked her to collaborate. Further, I brought in even more authority by virtue of being the observer of her teaching performance; there is a measure of "silent" power simply in being the one who enters a class and takes note of what goes on there. My main research agenda in observing Sherry's class was to examine how students responded to, made sense of, resisted, and engaged with classroom activities and explanations.

At the same time that I was observing Sherry's class sessions, I was also visiting the classes of the new graduate teaching assistants, critiquing and giving them feedback on their teaching, a very different kind of observation. Somewhat to my surprise, I found myself falling into an evaluative as opposed to interpretive or research-oriented stance in Sherry's class. My field notes, in which I tried to record as much as I could about what was happening in class, occasionally reflect this evaluative perspective, which was usually positive but sometimes negative. For example, a little more than halfway into the first quarter, regarding the "Author of the Day" activity, in which each student picked a day to read something, anything, they had written, I made the following comment:

> Author of the Day—Wu read a poem she'd written in 7th grade about the boy she liked, real "moon, June, spoon" kind of stuff. Yuck. I really question the value of this activity. Most of what I've heard in this class and in others that have started doing it has been real junk, not just average but awful, the worst rhyming verse, the most banal sentiments.

Sherry had introduced this activity into the department (adapted from Donald Daiker of Miami University), and many other teachers had begun using it, but I was beginning to have doubts about how students were approaching "Author of the Day." However, in my discussions with Sherry concerning the research project, I generally avoided making these evaluative comments because I did not want her to think she was being judged constantly on her teaching. We concentrated on issues concerning the research, mainly having to do with how students were making sense of the curriculum, class activities, and writing assignments. But I did feel I was holding back somewhat and not being completely frank about my perceptions of the class. The problem here is that I was having a hard time separating out my different roles. My own multiple agendas, the different positions I hold in my professional life, and the varying perspectives these positions require were complicating my reading of the class and the teacher.

As a researcher investigating classroom dynamics, it was not terribly important that I had doubts about "Author of the Day." However, these doubts were not completely irrelevant to the research either. I sensed increasingly that many students were taking the activity rather lightly; they were generally afraid to risk much self-disclosure in their pieces or significant departure from the class norms that had been established; they were churning out bland, formulaic, unchallenging texts. I viewed this trend as indicating a form of resistance to the critical reflection and risk taking Sherry was trying to encourage in the class. As a program director and teacher, I wondered whether these students were really doing college-level work in their "Author of the Day" pieces. It occurred to me that the fact that "Author of the Day" was an ungraded assignment probably had a lot to do with how students approached the task; it's no secret that most students give higher priority to graded work. For me, then, all of these perceptions were interesting and a part of the picture of the class I was developing. But I was uncertain about how to—or even whether I should—discuss these program-related misgivings with my collaborator. In the end, we did discuss the issue briefly, and Sherry explained and defended her use of the activity. Yet once again I felt as if I were rewarding Sherry's generosity in letting me into her class and her willingness to work with me on the project by providing another gratuitous critique of her teaching. Once again, we were no longer collaborative partners, and I had moved, rather ambivalently but by my own choice, into the role of authority figure.

Power and Authority in Collaborative Research

Historically, English departments have been wary of collaborative work, departing as it does from traditional models of humanistic scholarship and posing problems for tenure and promotion decisions. Even in the social sciences and education, where collaborative work is more common, published discussions of the nature of such work and how to carry it out are extremely rare. Examination of five major guides to qualitative research reveals very little on collaboration. For example, Bogdan and Biklen, who entertain one of the most extensive discussions, include nothing specifically about collaboration, and only about one page on what they call "team research," providing commonsense advice about keeping lines of communication open and making clear each person's role in the project (202–03). Because of this lack of extended critical discussion, those wishing to engage in collaborative research have largely had to come up with their own guidelines and approaches.

One recent discussion of collaborative inquiry focusing specifically on power disparities is an essay by Carole Edelsky and Chris Boyd, university researcher and elementary teacher, respectively. As a researcher, Edelsky refuses even to place herself in the position of evaluating and critiquing the teachers she collaborates with. She will work only with teachers she perceives to be outstanding, arguing that "if the teacher and I are supposed to be peers—co-researchers—then I cannot be in a position to want to improve her practice" (9). Edelsky's refusal to critique arises in large part out of a desire to put her collaborator at ease about opening up her classroom to a nationally known researcher. And indeed, Boyd says, "The initial impact of this research project on my teaching shocked me. I was frozen; I couldn't teach" (10). An accomplished teacher who had herself published work on whole language teaching, Boyd had been friends with Edelsky even before the study, and yet the reality of letting the researcher into her class, along with the expectation that they would be doing research, initially "had an almost paralytic effect" on her teaching (9).

Apparently Boyd was able to work through her initial paralysis, and the two went on to have a satisfying collaboration. However, Edelsky's unwillingness to consider being critical of her co-researcher points to problems common in classroom-based collaborative research. On the one hand, such a policy may deflect some of the anxiety that can develop when a researcher enters a teacher's class to observe. And in attempting to remove herself from the "superior" university professor/ "lowly" classroom teacher dichotomy, Edelsky showed a genuine respect for her collaborator and for teachers in general. On the other hand, her anticritical stance raises important questions about the nature of collaborative research. How can a researcher truly know, before the collaboration, that she will find nothing to be critical of in the collaborator's classroom? Is it really possible, or even desirable, not to be critical in a project which demands careful analysis of the people being studied, as well as self-scrutiny and reflexivity on the part of the researchers themselves? Can the "higher-status" and "lower-status" collaborators really assume a "we're all just friends here" stance and leave deeply entrenched power differentials at the classroom door? Such a stance would seem to ignore an important aspect of the relationship between the collaborators, a relationship which should itself be critically interrogated as part of a qualitative research project.

In our collaboration, we found the distribution of authority very much affected, but not completely determined, by our respective positions in the English department hierarchy. Both of us exercised different kinds of authority in the study; though a graduate student, Sherry was not completely subordinate or without voice. As the classroom teacher, she was in a very real sense an expert. She had a much more detailed understanding of what was happening in class, what the purpose of an activity was, and how particular students were doing than did Russel, the participant-observer. Her knowledge—and her authority—were critical in the collaborators' making sense of students' patterns of development as well as overall classroom dynamics. She also established authority by being assertive about her own position on issues, as in our discussion of the "Author of the Day" activity, and by negotiating power rather than letting Russel impose his own views and plans on the project.

This is not to deny the authority possessed by Russel, with his greater institutional power and experience in the field. It is only to suggest that we struggled in our collaborative research to establish what Henry Giroux calls a "border pedagogy." Such a pedagogy "provides educators with the opportunity to rethink the relations between the centers and the margins of power" and "challenges those institutional and ideological boundaries that have historically masked their own relations of power behind complex forms of distinction and privilege" (247). While Giroux uses the term "border pedagogy" to refer to teacher-student interactions in the classroom, we think the concept can be extended to describe the pedagogical component of our own collaborative process. In situations where our differing degrees of status and power could not help but take the foreground, we struggled, in the words of Mortensen and Kirsch, to achieve "a *dialogic* model of authority, one which infuses authority with ethics" (557). Our collaboration has provided us with an opportunity to interrogate these issues of authority and institutional hierarchy. Without denying our differing degrees of status and power, we view our work together, and collaborative work in general, especially that between colleagues with varying degrees of power, as an opportunity to move away from a traditional notion of authority as autonomous, role governed, and inflexible. Collaborative work offers chances to experiment with a feminist-inspired view of authority as, at least in part, negotiable, committed to building community, and sensitive to the well-being of all participants (Schweickart).

Our collaboration also allowed us to examine the closely related issue of gender and power. In a sense, our roles recapitulate traditional power relations, with a subordinate woman and a more powerful male authority figure. But one can also view the collaboration as an attempt to challenge the conventional gender hierarchy by offering a "less powerful" woman research experience that would empower her as a graduate student specializing in composition. Recently the field of composition has heard calls for replacing autonomous authority in teaching with an "ethic of care" (Noddings), a more collaborative institutional model which involves opening up and negotiating issues of power and authority rather than ignoring or exploiting them. Researchers willing to apply such an ethic not only in their interactions with the individuals they study, but also in their work with "unequal" collaborators are well positioned to challenge and revise the longstanding tradition of inequality between institutional members.

Where Conflict and Collaboration Converge

In order to develop models of research which allow for the kind of "nonhierarchical, empowering, and emancipatory" collaboration Edelsky and Boyd envision, we need first to acknowledge—even critically appreciate—situations which are hierarchical, subordinating, constraining (or, as Boyd herself suggested, "paralytic") (9). Mortensen and Kirsch's call for "rethinking notions of objectified, stable, autonomous authority" between students and teacher in the composition classroom can help us consider what it would mean to rethink collaborative research in composition (557). A redistribution of rhetorical power means not only that collaborators' differing perspectives would need to be interrogated as part of a study, but also that the students being "researched" would have a greater voice than has traditionally been the case in composition inquiry. Researchers' interpretations of students and teachers would have to compete with their interpretations of themselves. Storytelling would get untidy, unwieldy. (In our classroom study, we tried as much as possible to let students speak for themselves, but that is a subject for another essay.)

Discussing resistance in the humanities toward collaborative work, Roen and Mittan point out that collaboration can also mean treasonous cooperation with an occupying enemy and that, partly for this reason, many in the academy find it "frightening, unfamiliar, dangerous even"

(303). While it is dispiriting to think that one's collaborator could actually be "an enemy occupying one's country," the comparison suggests that researchers may hold a space they feel compelled to protect from border crossers. It was not until the two of us shared a classroom context (one in which we both had very significant—but different—investments) that we began addressing the oft-hidden ties between the concepts of power, collaboration, and "enemy." Before cross-collaborators can work "synergistically" (Roen and Mittan 302) the enemy element in power ought to be considered. How is a "frightening, unfamiliar, even dangerous" territory defined not only by newcomers to the field, but by veterans? Not only by junior colleagues, but by senior colleagues? In other words, what specific dynamics alter what it means to work together such that participants must vie for balance and control of their researcher roles?

We support recent calls in the field for an increase in collaborative research, but those considering collaboration should be aware that they risk conflict, threats to their power, dangerous questions, intrusions, and the general unpredictability which often characterizes such work. Roen and Mittan, like Ede and Lunsford, Edelsky and Boyd, Hudelson and Lindfors, and others who advocate collaboration, are part of the larger move in academia to consider and even celebrate "other" knowledge (see Sullivan, this volume). Thus, in their "mini-handbook for co-conspirators," Roen and Mittan offer some practical suggestions: (1) make collaboration a normal part of your work; (2) don't be afraid to approach others about collaborating; (3) leave ego out of it; (4) choose your collaborators carefully; and (5) learn from the example of other successful collaborative teams.

Yet before implementing these suggestions, one might consider more carefully the complex nature of authority. Mortensen and Kirsch argue that power differences "endlessly shift within and across social contexts" (558), whether we choose to acknowledge them or not. In the face of such shifting, Roen and Mittan, citing "political and economic realities of life in academic departments" (302), speculate about the prospects for broad acceptance of collaborative work in a field that still valorizes individual accomplishment. However, we suggest that these realities will only begin to change when researchers themselves critically address the political dimension of their collaborative relationship. For us, this scrutiny yielded several alternative ways of conceptualizing and carrying out collaborative research.

As one way of dealing with the political dimension, we have learned the importance of what we call *grounding for power* in such research. Ede and Lunsford have emphasized the need to establish clearly defined roles for "junior" and "senior" collaborators. This defining process may be an excellent starting point; nevertheless, it does not address the complexity of identifying the boundaries where those roles can (and often should) be challenged. Just as we have tried to overcome the individualist ethic to "do it myself because I'll get the job done quicker, better, righter, etc.," so too as junior and senior collaborators we have struggled against an uncritical acceptance of institutional and social roles. For the senior partner in a collaboration, grounding for power might include reexamining one's own sense of professional authority, negotiating boundaries previously not considered, inviting a kind of participation which may exceed the expectations of the junior colleague. In other words, the senior colleague is responsible for assisting the junior colleague in a kind of *authority building.* And while it is easiest to name the junior partner as the "marginalized" voice, in the end such labeling may do little to serve emancipatory goals for collaboration. Our experience has taught us that the junior partner, too, needs to ground for power—by admitting her own accountability for having a voice in the research. This move to establish a firm footing in the research can involve negotiating boundaries that seem intimidating but can ultimately help one to gain entrée to the field. In other words, the junior colleague is responsible for assisting the senior colleague in a kind of *authority balancing.*

In addition, our trust and respect for one another strengthened—and our research efforts improved—when we were able to talk openly about the problems of collaboration. Newkirk (this volume) suggests that senior researchers are often responsible for "seductions" of the people they do research "on" and "with" and for breaches of trust when the researcher makes critical judgments without providing opportunities for response. Likewise, Boyd's "paralysis" may reflect the tendency for junior partners to resign themselves to the low end of an oppositional role. A project which admits the reality of institutional power will produce the kinds of situations often labeled uncomfortable—because they are honest. These concerns relate to the notion of standpoint epistemology, where research is grounded in an examination of how *all* participants "understand and represent their lives" (Wood 14). A standpoint posture which begins at the point of opposition seems a more appropriate means of developing a foundation of trust and respect not only between students and researchers, but also between co-researchers wishing to inquire into "the conditions that cultivate distinct understandings" in a given rhetorical situation (16).

Moreover, we were able to refine our methods of negotiation by admitting, rather than dismissing, the role of ego in a collaborative project. It is easy enough, as Roen and Mittan argue, to "believe that everything generated . . . is collective" (305). But what is harder to relinquish, finally, is rhetorical ownership. Behind every ego is a rhetor who believes in a particular salience, an *ethos,* an argument. Co-authorship can be granted, but a real challenge to collaboration comes when the goals of the research can be reappropriated in response to the "collective" understanding. Partners, even "unequal" partners, who attempt to negotiate these understandings make their work more fully collaborative. In "reciprocal ethnography," a term coined by feminist-folklorist Elaine Lawless, careful attention to such points of exigency produces a "multi-layered story" which "balances text and interpretation" (39). In other words, the construction of knowledge becomes much more than whether or not the researcher "got it right" (37). Instead, practice based on reciprocal understandings willingly complicates a final product by embracing heteroglossia. An experienced researcher confronted with a less theoretically sophisticated perspective on the part of a subject or collaborator can dismiss it or work to attribute it to the research context. Likewise, a junior researcher experiencing either confusion or informed disagreement can either remain silent (and therefore in "good stead") or risk possible conflict.

Finally, when we thoughtfully questioned examples from successful collaborative efforts, we were led to see what could be successful about our own. While we do not suggest that an oppositional stance is the only useful way to position oneself with regard to collaborative inquiry, we suggest that there is much to be gained by looking carefully and critically at existing work as it relates to one's own collaborative dynamic. Collaboration which "comes naturally" may sound promising, but if it ignores or dismisses what can be "unnatural," unpleasant, problematic, or institutionally difficult about such research, then important aspects of the collaborative work may go unexamined.

Our research partnership began with Russel's plan to study Sherry's classroom, but developed over time into a study of the politics of classroom-based research. We have come to understand that to look at a scene of instruction *is* to look politically. Throughout this experience, we continue to find that, as collaborators, we are constantly revising our relationship with one another. We have struggled to understand each other and ourselves as writers, readers, evaluators, teachers, mentors, leaders, and learners. Our conflict over the use of a racially charged term in the classroom, for example, took both of us by surprise, and in order to move forward together we had to practice what we were trying to teach students: to negotiate the often implicit ground rules underlying classroom activity. There have been times, even while composing this chapter, when our two voices could not become one. Ultimately, though, we have come to view this dissensus—and the subsequent understandings that have developed from it—as an important part of our work together.

Works Cited

Allport, Gordon. "Formation of In-Groups." *Rereading America: Cultural Contexts for Critical Thinking and Writing.* Ed. Gary Colombo, Robert Cullen, and Bonnie Lisle. Boston: Bedford-St. Martin's P, 1989. 85–101.

Bakhtin, M. M. *The Dialogic Imagination: Four Essays.* Ed. Michael Holquist. Trans. Caryl Emerson and Michael Holquist. Austin: U of Texas P, 1981.

Bogdan, Robert, and Sari Knopp Biklen. *Qualitative Research for Education: An Introduction to Theory and Methods.* Boston: Allyn and Bacon, 1982.

Bruffee, Kenneth A. "Collaborative Learning and the Conversation of Mankind." *College English* 46 (1984): 635–52.

Bullock, Richard, John Trimbur, and Charles Schuster, eds. *The Politics of Writing Instruction: Postsecondary.* Portsmouth: Boynton/Cook-Heinemann, 1991.

Cheney, George, and Phillip K. Tompkins. "Coming to Terms with Organizational Identification and Commitment." *Central States Speech Journal* 38 (1987): 1–15.

Ede, Lisa, and Andrea Lunsford. *Singular Texts/Plural Authors: Perspectives on Collaborative Writing.* Carbondale: Southern Illinois UP, 1990.

Edelsky, Carole, and Chris Boyd. "Collaborative Research: More Questions Than Answers." *Collaborative Research in Language Education.* Ed. Sarah J. Hudelson and Judith Wells Lindfors. Urbana: NCTE, 1993. 4–20.

Giroux, Henry. "Postmodernism as Border Pedagogy: Redefining the Boundaries of Race and Ethnicity." *Postmodernism, Feminism, and Cultural Politics: Redrawing Educational Boundaries.* Ed. Henry Giroux. Albany: State U of New York P, 1991. 217–56.

Harding, Sandra. "Introduction: Is There a Feminist Method?" *Feminism and Methodology: Social Science Issues.* Ed. Sandra Harding. Bloomington: Indiana UP, 1987. 1–14.

Hudelson, Sarah J., and Judith Wells Lindfors. *Collaborative Research in Language Education.* Urbana: NCTE, 1993.

Hull, Glynda, and Mike Rose. "Rethinking Remediation: Toward a Social-Cognitive Understanding of Problematic Reading and Writing." *Written Communication* 6 (1989): 139–54.

Karis, Bill. "Conflict in Collaboration: A Burkean Perspective." *Rhetoric Review* 8 (1989): 113–26.

Kirsch, Gesa E. "Methodological Pluralism: Epistemological Issues." *Methods and Methodology in Composition Research.* Ed. Gesa Kirsch and Patricia A. Sullivan. Carbondale: Southern Illinois UP, 1992. 247–69.

Lawless, Elaine J. "Women's Life Stories and Reciprocal Ethnography as Feminist and Emergent." *Journal of Folklore Research* 28 (1991): 35–60.

Mortensen, Peter, and Gesa E. Kirsch. "On Authority in the Study of Writing." *College Composition and Communication* 44 (1993): 556–72.

Noddings, Nel. *Caring, a Feminine Approach to Ethics & Moral Education.* Berkeley: U of California P, 1984.

Roen, Duane, and Geraldine McNenny. "The Case for Collaborative Scholarship in Rhetoric and Composition." *Rhetoric Review* 10 (1992): 291–310.

Roen, Duane, and Robert Mittan. "Collaborative Scholarship in Composition: Some Issues." *Methods and Methodology in Composition Research.* Ed. Gesa Kirsch and Patricia A. Sullivan. Carbondale: Southern Illinois UP, 1992. 287–313.

Schweickart, Patrocinio P. "Reading, Teaching, and the Ethic of Care." *Gender in the Classroom: Power and Pedagogy.* Ed. Susan L. Gabriel and Isaiah Smithson. Urbana: U of Illinois P, 1990. 78–95.

Terkel, Studs. "Mike LeFevre." *Rereading America: Cultural Contexts for Critical Thinking and Writing.* Ed. Gary Colombo, Robert Cullen, and Bonnie Lisle. Boston: Bedford-St. Martin's P, 1992. 87–94.

———. "Stephen Cruz." *Rereading America: Cultural Contexts for Critical Thinking and Writing.* Ed. Gary Colombo, Robert Cullen, and Bonnie Lisle. Boston: Bedford-St. Martin's P, 1992. 36–41.

Trimbur, John. "Consensus and Difference in Collaborative Learning." *College English* 51 (1989): 602–16.

Vygotsky, Lev S. *Mind in Society: The Development of Higher Psychological Processes.* Ed. Michael Cole, Vera John Steiner, Sylvia Scribner, and Ellen Souberman. Cambridge: Harvard UP, 1978.

Williams, Raymond. *Keywords: A Vocabulary of Culture and Society.* New York: Oxford UP, 1976.

Wood, Julia T. "Gender and Moral Voice: Moving from Woman's Nature to Standpoint Epistemology." *Women's Studies in Communication* 15 (1992): 1–24.

5 Dilemmas of Fidelity: Qualitative Research in the Classroom

Helen Dale
University of Wisconsin–Eau Claire

As qualitative research has become more accepted in composition studies, discussion surrounding it has increasingly turned to ethical issues. Perhaps that is so because many ethical aspects of qualitative research have not been clearly articulated. It also may be that the reflection involved in qualitative research invites us to see the political and ethical in classrooms—our own and those of others. Unquestionably, "ethical issues are floating constantly beneath the surface of what we [as researchers] do" (Miles and Huberman 289). In dealing with ethical issues, we also reveal our values and fidelities. Both Wendy Bishop and Michael Kleine, for example, speak to the need for first-person accounts and metanarratives of the experiences of writing researchers. While some such accounts exist, too often studies in composition research do not address the ethical dilemmas involved and rarely describe "the mind-racking sessions that produced them" (Smagorinsky xvii).

Teacher research, even more than other forms of qualitative research, affords us the opportunity to examine our own practice, and recently there has been a good deal of interest in that subject. The National Society for the Study of Education selected teacher research as the theme of its ninety-third yearbook (Hollingsworth and Sockett), and many in English education—Fleischer, Goswami and Stillman, Snyder, and Stock, to name a few—have explored its possibilities. Researching one's own teaching offers the possibility of meaningful change in classrooms and rich contexts for reflection. Although the motivation for such research is admirable, we need to recognize that the overlapping roles of teacher and researcher can create ethical tensions.

A recently published handbook on qualitative research devotes only one chapter to ethics and points out that there are no rules to follow to guide researchers through the "swamp" that represents those ethics (Punch 94). Much of the murkiness in that swamp is caused by the inherent tensions involved when a researcher has dual roles such as teacher-researcher or participant-observer. Part of what makes such research so unsettling is that the researcher frequently faces competing loyalties and treacherous politics. Does one owe allegiance to an institution such as a university or granting agency? To a teacher who has agreed to have us study her class? To the students we so often observe? All of these competing research loyalties involve ethical questions. By its very nature, qualitative research is "an ethical endeavor" (Ely 218) which is "value-laden" (Flinders 126). Margot Ely, in her book *Doing Qualitative Research*, frequently mentions ethical concerns. But the complex ethics and competing loyalties involved in qualitative research are more than a *concern*; that word does not show the depth of the problem when one is both teacher and researcher. *Dilemma* is a more appropriate word. Presumably, no researcher sets out to be unethical or to hurt those involved in research. Rather, qualitative researchers often must make decisions in which one individual's or group's needs take precedence over those of another individual or group. The choices researchers make are not between good and evil, but between two goods. This creates dilemmas of fidelity.

In this chapter, I describe the problems inherent in the overlapping roles of teacher-researcher and participant-observer, using a first-person metanarrative to illustrate ethical dilemmas involved in my own work. I was both researcher and co-teacher in a ninth-grade English classroom in a working-class, culturally diverse high school in the Midwest, conducting research for my doctoral dissertation. The fact that this was dissertation research exacerbated the ethical quandaries that might ordinarily occur. Not only did my loyalties to the teacher sometimes compete with my loyalties to students, but I also had to keep in mind my commitments to my dissertation committee and to the research process. I still had to prove myself. I did not adequately anticipate the extent to which competing fidelities would create dilemmas both during the study and in the telling of it. These dilemmas of fidelity did, however, lead me to examine the ethics of qualitative research on composing. During the study itself, uncomfortable situations arose and simply had to be dealt with. When such ethical or political dilemmas occur, they "often have to be resolved *situationally,* and even spontaneously" (Punch 84). Without adequate time or expert advice, I had to act quickly and risk making faulty decisions. Only later could I really reflect on my own "lived space" (Greene) and grapple with the underlying ethical issues involved in being teacher and researcher. The tensions of those dual roles continue today. Recently I was asked if I were going to write this chapter as a teacher or a researcher. The question itself made me realize that, no matter what my intention, I would be writing from a multiply determined position. Just as in my dissertation, where I entered the text as an actor, I occupy this text as an acting subject as well.

Fidelity to Teacher

The subject of my research was *student co-authoring,* a practice I had used in my eleven years as a secondary English teacher, and one I had found promising as a means of engaging students in the writing process. Since I knew of no other English teacher in the area who had students write together, I hoped to find a teacher who was willing to use co-authoring practices in the classroom in order that I might study them. I realized that this was a large request. I had met many cooperating teachers as a university supervisor of English student teachers and intended to ask a few of them about their interest in participating in such a study. But I only had to ask one: Carol, the classroom teacher in my dissertation study. We had gotten along exceptionally well from the first time we met. As she put it, "We had a background of talking about teaching." Carol agreed that I could conduct research on co-authoring but did not feel confident teaching it, so she invited me to co-teach a ninth-grade English course for the first quarter of the year. It was a generous offer. I looked forward both to teaching high school students again and to conducting research on co-authoring. I wanted it all. I wanted to be a participant-observer who was colleague and friend, to observe the classroom and also redistribute authority in it, to be a teacher and a researcher. I expected to learn a good deal about teaching from Carol, and she was eager to learn about co-authoring. And, in fact, each of us did learn from the other.

The dilemma of fidelity narrated here is not one of betrayal or of disrespect. Neither our friendship nor our professional relationship went wrong in ways that made us distrust one another. Instead, each of us made choices based on tacit assumptions that furthered our own interests. While the data being collected in that one ninth-grade English class were vital to my interests, Carol was understandably more concerned with her daily class schedule, the yearly curriculum, and the various demands on her time and attention. I had hoped to work with Carol on all ongoing aspects of teaching and research, but that was not possible because Carol did not have time to collaborate with me so fully. She had to respond to "the power of practical urgencies" (DiPardo 163).

We agreed to teach together in her last-period class so that we would have time to talk after school each day. Carol intended first to learn about co-authoring from me and then to introduce it into her other classes. In the spring I conducted a pilot study in her classroom, and over the summer we met to plan the fall quarter. The challenge was to balance our very different needs and purposes. I was "redirecting the curriculum for my own research purposes" (Snyder 202) and wanted time both to prepare students for co-authoring and to have them write together several times in three-day blocks. Carol wanted time to cover the literature her other ninth-grade class was reading so that she could begin a new unit with both ninth-grade classes at the beginning of the second quarter.

As we talked about the project throughout the spring and summer, we had high expectations of the project and of each other. My motivation for co-teaching and researching was both obvious and genuine. Carol's motivation was her desire to grow as a teacher. She later explained her interest: "I knew that this was something that was likely to have a lot of positive potential for my students and for me. That's why I agreed to it. This sounded like it was going to help me be a better teacher." Carol was thrilled at the thought of "talking about teaching English, getting ideas," and we shared mutual goals. "This was like almost something that's too good to be true because in a typical public school teacher's day, you know, there's so little time to talk about teaching. But to try new things . . . the possibility of something new, and the reinforcement of getting to talk about teaching was very exciting to me; that's why I signed on for this." Carol said she saw in this research "the possibility of doing something different." Inviting a researcher colleague into her classroom was a way for Carol to alleviate the isolation of teaching and to rekindle her enthusiasm.

There was yet another reason Carol agreed to co-teach one quarter, a reason related to writing instruction. She had told me in our early discussions about teaching that "I've got problems with the writing process that I can't seem to get over." When Carol referred to the writing process, she might have been referring to the one day at the beginning of the year when she explained to students the stages of the writing process, emphasizing prewriting and revision in her lecture. She did not use classroom time for students to work through writing and revision processes; she expected students to do their writing outside of class. True, Carol described the writing process for her students, but she did not have them compose for authentic audiences. Over the course of the quarter, our discussions gave Carol a different perspective on writing processes. As she said in an interview one month into the quarter, "Talking about the writing process the way I've been talking about it is completely not productive. We're discussing some things that I can readily identify as true about co-authoring. There's a promise in this from the start that maybe *this* is what's going to actually make this process happen, where anything *I* say really can't." Carol seemed to imply that, as a university researcher, *I* had the answers that she did not. Although that is what university researchers too often promise to deliver, I was not comfortable with that assumption. Michael Connelly and Jean Clandinin note that "collaborative research creates a political context among participants" (86). I was just beginning to understand the politics and power relations involved in the context we were creating. When I realized Carol was looking to me for ready answers, I began to note a different dimension in our interactions that "foreshadowed problems" in our working relationship (Mills 104).

As the study unfolded in the classroom where I was sometimes teacher and always researcher, small conflicts arose, largely unanticipated and seldom discussed. Typically, the conflicts revolved around issues of time and commitment. Carol's lack of time to work with co-authoring groups or discuss the research project was frustrating for both of us. What made the tensions so troubling to me was the personal commitment I had to the ethic of collaboration. Collaboration was central to the study not only for students who were co-authoring, but also for the teaching-researching partnership I had envisioned. I had hoped Carol would be an active partner. I did not want to be part of an all too frequent scenario in which the university researcher, though appearing to be collaborating, really does not include the classroom teacher in meaningful ways (Miller 17).

I had unarticulated hopes that were never quite realized. As one of Lily Tomlin's characters in the stage play *The Search for Signs of Intelligent Life in the Universe* says about wanting to *be* somebody when she grows up, "Now I realize I should have been more specific" (Wagner). And so I should have been. I had hoped we would co-teach a good deal of the time, but as it turned out, that rarely happened. Underlying my expectations for collaboration was the assumption that our beliefs about teaching and learning were more similar than, in fact, they turned out to be. Carol tended to see knowledge as more transmittable; I saw it as more socially constructed. Without consciously making a decision, we taught individually. Not only did it take less time to plan for individual teaching, but it also helped us to avoid a discussion of epistemology and teaching styles. It was simply the most efficient way to organize. When Carol taught, I took field notes and she saw my role as observer. When I taught, she tended to catch up on paper work. *Time* became a major factor in our working relationship. Because Carol had been appointed faculty adviser for the student newspaper just before the year began, she was even busier than she had been in previous years. She was stretched to her limit. There were days I felt guilty for complicating her already overly busy schedule. Time at the end of the day to talk about the class became rare, and that in itself was frustrating because a caring relationship requires dialogue (Witherell and Noddings 7).

I did assume, though, that when students worked on collaborative writing exercises, we would both circulate to observe students' processes and to get to know the student co-authors better. Again, Carol tended to find a quiet corner and use the time to work. My field notes in the third week of the quarter speak to my frustrations: "I asked Carol to help me observe—to get their personalities in groups so that together we could form [more permanent] co-authoring groups, but she just kept working. It's frustrating, but I also understand having to seize every available minute." When students wrote together later in the quarter, I still hoped Carol would circulate to be another set of eyes and ears observing student groups write. I hoped she would provide *inter-observer reliability* (Preissle and LeCompte 218), and that by observing students write together she would provide a "reality check" for me. But she rarely joined me in observing students co-author. Now it seems uncomfortably obvious to me why. Too often I failed to remember that her purposes were very different from my own. I did not adequately take into account her busy schedule. Matthew Miles and Michael Huberman remind us that while researchers "traffic in *understanding,* most study participants are preoccupied with *action*—how to work and live better" (292). Understanding is neither more nor less important than action. But those two purposes are different, and what seemed essential to me in our partnership was easily displaced for Carol by the real and varied demands on her time.

In retrospect, Carol herself realized that she could have learned a great deal about her students had she circulated more among the groups as they wrote together. When we met one afternoon the following summer, we discussed our mutual experience. We got together because Carol was preparing a talk for her high school colleagues about co-authoring and she wanted to consult with me; we were also thinking of writing an article for teachers about implementing co-authoring. We discussed how much teachers can learn about their students if they listen to them write together and, therefore, how important it is for teachers to circulate. After talking about the teacher's role while students are writing, the following conversation occurred.

Helen: [If teachers don't circulate] they're missing their opportunity to learn about the writers.

Carol: Right. And that's something we do have to say. It can't be like, "Well, I have a day to catch up because my class is collaboratively writing."

Helen: Right.

Carol: You know, what better time *is* there, I mean there's so much to be said about this. . . . And the times that we *were* out there. Well, we were out there all the time. Well, *you* were out there all the time. When *I* was out there, it was really hard in terms of my time.

Even when Carol realized the opportunity co-authoring offered the teacher to learn about her students' writing processes, she still saw co-authoring time and the responsibility for it as mine. Had I not been conducting research in her class, she would not have questioned the time spent with the seventh-period class. But when a researcher and teacher work together, it is perhaps inevitable and maybe even fitting that each prioritizes her goals differently.

I owed Carol fidelity for many reasons, not the least of which were her interest in co-authoring, her trust that I could help her teach the writing process, and the generous offer of her classroom. My fidelity to Carol was challenged by the pressing demands of my own agenda, which clearly diverged from hers. When the demands on her time affected her involvement in the study, we negotiated an unspoken agreement. She allowed me to continue the study, but primarily on my own. In turn, I took over some of her teaching, thus giving her time to catch up on her work. I am keenly aware that the scenario was less than ideal. Some might even question the ethics and motivation behind such an arrangement. It may appear that an expert university researcher dominated a classroom teacher—engaged in a process of "othering" her, to use Michelle Fine's terminology (70). But in this case, and perhaps more often than we admit, lack of full involvement in collaborative classroom research is of the teacher's own choosing and occurs because of competing demands on her time and energy. My dilemma was ironic. In giving Carol the time to do her own work, I had to abandon some of my ideals about research relationships and collaboration, ideals central to my belief system and to the paradigm from which I work.

In the end, both Carol and I wrestled with dilemmas of fidelity. She had obligations not only to the class I was working with, but also to her other four classes, to students who worked on the school newspaper, and to me. In many ways I was spread less thin. I had obligations to the students in one class, to her, and to fulfilling the university's requirements for dissertation research. Since my focus was more narrow than hers, Carol was the one who really had to sort through her pressing obligations. We all face dilemmas of fidelity in how we apportion our time and attention. The best we can do is continually assess our professional commitments. Although many projects are interesting, we need to be realistic about the number of commitments we can handle while still dealing fairly and ethically with the persons involved. After committing to projects, we need to be aware of competing allegiances, to be honest about ethical conflicts, and to allow for the constantly changing focus of our fidelities to persons, ideas, and ideals.

Fidelity to Students

The Role of Teacher

In this chapter I have described myself as both researcher and teacher; however, students did not always fully accept me as a "real" teacher with full authority even though both Carol and I had been in class each day. Teaching ninth grade was a humbling but enriching experience. My field notes reveal my awareness of "teacher" behavior. "I'm teaching the class now, and often I react as a teacher—telling Ken I was waiting for him to be quiet." At one point I express emotional turmoil similar to that of inexperienced teachers. "Carol was gone today and although I know all of the students' names, they acted like I was a sub. . . . I felt whipped when I left." That entry was followed the next day by the simple but victorious, "Today went much better."

In retrospect, it was probably good that students responded to Carol as the primary teacher. It was enough that, in forming independent co-authoring groups, I was redistributing some authority in the classroom. Had students not deferred to Carol, the result might have further altered the conventional teacher-student power dynamic, diluting her classroom presence and possibly creating an uncomfortable situation. Questions of authority were most frequently framed as questions about grades; students wanted to know, of course, who would be assigning them. And even though Carol explained that we would collaborate on their quarter grades, students tended to see me more as researcher than as teacher.

School Context

When research is conducted in schools, one can expect disruptions to the most carefully laid plans. There were the usual pep rallies, assemblies, and even a power failure to interfere with the schedule Carol and I had established, but nothing prepared me for the tragic accident that would happen. On the day before the last three-day co-authoring assignment was to be written, two sophomore girls crossing the street on their way to school were struck and killed by a car outside of the building. To say the least, this incident had a big impact on the students and even on the study. Because the event was so serious, I had to decide whether to go on with the research or to postpone it.

My greatest concern was for the students, some of whom knew the young women. School officials had set up a crisis counseling center in a very large room which I had been using for co-authoring groups. Thus I had to find an alternative space. I could not use a regular classroom because the groups would be physically too close to allow for good tape-recording conditions. So the decision whether to continue involved not only the students' emotional welfare, but also the logistical concern of having students scattered in various classrooms to write. Such an arrangement would make it impossible for Carol and me to observe all the co-authoring groups. It also interfered with the established co-authoring routine, thus undercutting a goal of my research proposal: that the students should co-author each time in the same place with the same recording equipment so that co-authoring with a tape recorder running would become routine.

I had decided to postpone the study unless the students wanted to proceed. I asked Carol to sound out the class while I was away from the room so that the students would not decide to continue just to please me. She talked to the class about the issue on the day of the accident, and the students told her they wanted to go ahead. The next day every student in the class was present, an unusual occurrence. The co-authoring sessions proceeded with students scattered in four different classrooms that were available that period. Whereas before I had the large room set up with tape recorders for each group, this time the students had to find their rooms, set up the recorders themselves, and settle down to work, part of the time unsupervised because Carol and I could not be in four places simultaneously. The time line of the study was preserved, but the data gathered over the three writing sequences were no longer collected under similar conditions.

Were I doing the same study today, I would not feel so torn. My full attention would be on the students and their welfare. But as a doctoral student with little power or authority, I had to make a judgment call and hope that my committee would approve of the decision I made and still believe in the integrity of the study. I wanted to honor relational ethics which rest on caring, respect, and involvement. By including

Carol and the students in my decision, I managed to honor those qualities. When the researcher is also the teacher, dilemmas of fidelity are
likely to arise. Since we cannot anticipate unexpected events such as the
accident, the best we can do is to consider as paramount the well-being
of those involved in our research.

Student Power and Marginalization

Anecdotal evidence and research findings suggest that increasing numbers of English instructors now place writing in a social context and
create more interactive writing classrooms. As this happens, issues of
power and marginalization among students become particularly significant. The most compelling of my dilemmas of fidelity involved the
question of intervention when I suspected students were being disre-
spectful to each other in co-authoring groups. My reasons for supporting co-authoring were—and are—idealistic but not unrealistic. Students
learning from one another in a noncompetitive environment can contribute from their strengths, and because in writing there are so many
areas in which to be expert, all students can contribute. But by the end
of the study, it was clear that some groups did not work toward such
positive ends. Even when I suspected that a group was not functioning
positively, I did not intervene because describing students' interactions
as they wrote was fundamental to the study. To get a sense of how well
groups were functioning, I audiotaped co-authoring sessions and circulated as groups wrote. Because I did not listen to all of the tapes while
the study was still ongoing, I had little specific knowledge of what students said to one another. Still, I could sense the ease or tension with
which a group worked and, at times, I felt uncomfortable about a few
exchanges I overheard.

One co-authoring situation in particular invited my intervention
as a teacher, but caused dilemmas for me as a researcher. Mark, Tom,
and Sheri did not really interact toward the goal of composing text. Although at first I had only a vague idea that this group was not functioning well, over time I observed that they were not productive, that Mark
was dominating, and that Sheri was vulnerable. It was only later when
I listened to the tapes that I discovered the extent to which that was
true. The primary reason this group functioned so poorly was that Mark
established a voice that was dominant and counterproductive. He felt
free to insult other group members, especially Sheri, with whom he took
on the role of inquisitor.

From the first day they wrote together, Mark implied that Sheri
was not "smart." He asked her if she had to pay to get her homework

done, and when she offered a good idea for the text, Mark retorted, "Where'd you get that idea? It's so un-you." The situation grew worse during the second collaborative assignment. Sheri was absent on the first of the three days devoted to writing about whether ninth graders should have required study halls. On the second day Mark took the first chance to confront her.

Mark: You want a free ride.

Sheri: I don't plan on it.

Mark: You're doing a good job so far. I'd like to hear what you think. Without saying what's in our paper. Let's go! Why? Why shouldn't they have study halls?

Sheri: Because they don't use their study halls, so what's the point of being there.

Mark: That's like saying we're going to be negligent anyway, so why make us be negligent in a study hall? That's pretty weak. Next thought.

Sheri: Okay. If you don't use your study hall and you're only in there to talk and bother other people—

Mark: That's *really* convincing. Let's go! I'm not going to lead this discussion. You're going to say something.

Sheri: I already did.

Mark: Other thoughts?

Sheri: Not really.

Mark: You're a lot of help. I know you're not a carrot. I know you have *some* ideas. Thoughts? Think of something. I have good ideas, but I won't say them 'til you come up with something.

I did not listen to that conversation on tape until just before the third and last co-authoring assignment. I was quite disturbed about what I heard and uncertain what to do about it. For the first time I realized fully the harm to self-esteem that could accompany co-authoring. I could not deny that writing together could put students in a precarious emotional position, something I had not previously given enough thought because I was so focused on the potential benefits of co-authoring. I was particularly concerned with the gendered nature of the problems in this group, but have chosen not to focus on gender here because, across all the groups, dominance was not based solely on gender.[1]

In this study I felt caught between my fidelity to students and to the research process. I thought that a "real" researcher probably would not intervene because that would somehow "contaminate" the study.

After all, one of my goals was to record what happened in these writing groups and explore the influence of affective and cognitive dissonance on the success of the group. But as a teacher I felt keenly that those involved in this study should be empowered by the process, not marginalized. My goal was twofold: I wanted to intervene without unduly disrupting the co-authoring process, and I wanted to give Sheri voice and to discourage Mark and Tom from harassing her. As it turned out, there was little I could do during the last co-authoring sequence. She would not be there two of the three writing days because she was on the golf team and had to leave school early. The day before the group began writing, I asked Sheri if she would put some of her ideas on paper as her contribution to the group. It was an alternative way to give Sheri voice without the interference of Mark and Tom. However, she did not write down any of her ideas for the group.

I was particularly concerned because Mark and Tom, knowing that Sheri would be gone for most of the writing project, had reason to be disgruntled with her. Furthermore, because the groups were in four separate rooms, neither Carol nor I could supervise them all of the time. I stopped in to that group's classroom four times during the period, and Carol also spent some time there. At one point I intervened, ostensibly as a researcher, to ask Sheri to move closer to the tape recorder so that she could be heard. In spite of our attempts at supervision, the one day Sheri was present she was still harassed. In one instance the group, discussing audience, decided on writing the paper as a letter to a public official. That led Mark to quiz the others, especially Sheri. He grilled her on the names of several officials, from the mayor to the secretary of state. Whenever Tom would try to answer, Mark would say, "Shut up," and redirect the questions to Sheri. Tom, too, began to harass her, saying, "Sheri has no point of view" and "I say we evict her." Somehow the context of this group encouraged an emotional brutishness.

The teacher in me would have addressed the problem head on. I might have talked to the group about the advantages of using every member's strengths and insisted on mutual respect within the group. But as a researcher I felt I should remain aloof and let events play out. Because I felt powerless to affect the situation, I was actually relieved that Sheri would not be in class on the last two co-authoring days. Without a doubt, this group and this example is a worst-case scenario distilled from more than sixty hours of co-authoring tapes. But many such scenarios probably play out in writing classrooms where we conduct research. It is disturbing that, in the name of written expression and education, we might seem to condone such behavior.

Certainly, the brutishness of Mark's dialogue is sanctioned in many venues outside of schools, and that is sometimes why students carry this discourse into our classrooms. In Mark's voice, we hear traces of other, authoritative voices. Rather than giving his peers equal play, he often assumed a borrowed voice with aggressive overtones, a strategy which silenced Sheri and intimidated Tom. This group shows us that students can internalize the worst of adult discourse. When this happens, our intentions to provide caring, inclusive pedagogies are undermined because interactions can still turn on issues of power and marginalization.

I was anxious to talk to all three members of the group to help me sort out what had happened. I conducted two sets of interviews. In the interviews that took place immediately after the study, I had the opportunity to talk to Sheri and Tom, but unfortunately could not interview Mark because he had no free periods and had other obligations after school. Although I encouraged Tom and Sheri to address openly what had gone on, neither was ready to do so. Tom complained about Mark judging him on mechanical skills. "With Mark, I felt I was making mistakes. I couldn't spell or do punctuation. He'd bother me about that. He'd jump on me." Sheri glossed over the negative aspects of the experience, saying she liked writing with others because "you can see how other people feel." When I encouraged her to talk about the experience, she did say that she felt ignored. "They wouldn't listen to me. . . . They cut me down when I said something."

In a second set of interviews, conducted seven months later, Sheri still was hesitant to talk about the experience, although she did indicate that "when I had something to say they'd just laugh at it. . . . They'd do anything to get me mad. . . . They'd bother me if I took my time to think about something. They'd get really impatient with me, especially Mark." I was eager to talk to Mark to see how he remembered the co-authoring experience at the beginning of the year. Interestingly, he accepted a good deal of responsibility for the dysfunction in the group. "Tom and I bullied Sheri around a lot . . . and that basically put her out of the picture." When I said I could see why Sheri would stop contributing to the group effort, he said, "We were hurting ourselves as much as anyone else." Mark seemed to have thought a lot about the situation and what went wrong. "The problem with Sheri was that she was really intimidated. It seemed like sometimes she had things to say, and you could tell, but she just didn't say them. You have to get rid of that somehow." When I asked Mark if he had gained anything from co-authoring, he responded, "No, I didn't, but I think I could have. If I would have been a little more quiet and listened to what everyone else had to say, I think it could have worked a lot better. I definitely learned that." What I learned from Mark was that, as a teacher and researcher, I should have given more guidance. I should have anticipated that when students work closely together and are interdependent, the potential is there for marginalization and even cruelty. When authority is redistributed in classrooms, students can fall silent instead of finding their voices; they can be marginalized as easily as empowered.

I was reminded of that lesson when I received a letter from the editor of the journal to which I had submitted an article based on this research. The editor criticized my lack of intervention, saying that it was a teacher's responsibility to see that students working in groups got along, that those with similar interests should have been grouped and chosen their own writing topic, and that the teacher should not only intervene in groups having problems, but should rearrange the groups and allow those who want to write alone to do so. The paragraph ends, "While it isn't possible for any researcher to guarantee that all students will benefit . . . at least none should continue in a negative situation." At first, I reacted defensively: I had to keep the groups intact to answer my research questions. My major professor stipulated that all groups should have identical topics. We all have to work with people we are not fond of. Students who prefer collaborative work must often work alone. I could have added to my list of defenses. I would not have been wrong, exactly. But I knew that at the heart of things, the editor had a point. My responsibility to the students should have superseded my concerns about the "integrity" of the research design. Had I anticipated problems and articulated an ethical approach to conducting research, integrity to students and research would not have been in conflict.

When Carol invited me to teach in her classroom, the study changed in more fundamental ways than I realized. Adding the role of teacher to that of researcher is not a simple expansion of duties; it affects perspectives and fidelities. I should have changed my stance more fundamentally than I did and foregrounded my responsibilities as a teacher. Being a teacher-researcher demands that you intervene when necessary (see Newkirk, this volume).

Writing instructors form student groups in part to equalize power relations, to act as facilitators rather than givers of knowledge, and to allow students to learn from each other. They want students to be safe in their classrooms and in groups within those classrooms. But when we redistribute authority by creating writing groups, we also redistribute control. While that is usually seen as a means of empowering students, redistributing control can also put students on emotionally shaky ground. We must consider the "rightness or wrongness" of our decisions and attend to the possibility of harm inherent in what we plan and do (Miles and Huberman 288).

Conclusion

By most standards, the research I conducted on co-authoring was successful. I received positive feedback on the study, Carol incorporated co-authoring into her classes, and the students said they liked writing together. But I could not ignore the problems that qualitative research uncovered, because such research foregrounds the particular and asks us to reflect on issues that otherwise might go unnoticed. I found myself struggling with competing loyalties. I was a guest and an observer in someone's classroom, but I was also a participant, a teacher, and a researcher. Certainly, those overlapping roles affected the classroom dynamic. I wanted co-authoring groups to proceed naturally, but when students are not respectful of each other, it is difficult to know when to intervene.

As researchers, we have the luxury of time and the impetus for reflection. Experience itself does not teach us as much as does the process of reflecting on experience (Britzman 218). Now that I have had time to reflect, I know I would handle differently the dilemmas this study presented. In working with a classroom teacher, I would be far more explicit. From the outset I would want to discuss our expectations of a collaborative research relationship and keep well in mind the demands on our time. In discussing mutual expectations, I would be as specific as possible, perhaps even identifying those expectations we each felt were central to our working relationship. While I am tempted to offer suggestions for collaboration that involve dialogue journals and frequent meetings, I have learned that we must negotiate a passage through such research, remembering the demands on a teacher's time and appraising honestly the value of our research on writing to the teacher and to her students.

In the future, I would surely approach differently the dynamics in co-authoring groups. I would make clear that co-authoring involves mutual responsibility for "interpersonal as well as intellectual tasks" (Noddings 168). I would discuss the potential for harm in writing groups and let the class arrive at guidelines for appropriate group interactions. While I could not guarantee that every student would be treated well, at the very least students would sense the ethic of respect in the writing classroom. If I were aware of problems, I would intervene more quickly and more freely; I would be more "teacherly" and would feel comfortable speaking to a student who seemed to be seizing control of the writing group at the expense of the other students. At the very least, no one should be harmed by participating in a qualitative study; I see that as a researcher's primary responsibility.

To encourage reflection on dilemmas of fidelity, I would follow the advice of Miles and Huberman and document ethical issues along with other data collected. That is one way to attend to problems that arise and to think through ethical solutions ahead of time (296). We should enter qualitative research assuming that someone could be harmed in some way, and then consider ways to avoid that likelihood (292). Had I anticipated ethical dilemmas early in the research design, I would have been better prepared, at least emotionally, to handle the competing loyalties that presented themselves. But even had I anticipated dilemmas, I could not have headed off all problems and risks. Dilemmas are inherent in qualitative research that takes place in classrooms because the context itself is so textured and rich that it would be presumptuous to assume we could control it.

Qualitative research demands that we establish relationships with participants—at once the best and the most problematic aspect of qualitative research. It is in balancing those relationships that we face our greatest challenges. As we compose our versions of others' experiences in a research story, our conflicts, and thus our choices, are exposed. That, in turn, reflects who we are and what we value. To do qualitative research in classrooms is to sort through ethical dilemmas; we need to anticipate competing fidelities and then proceed as inclusively and as carefully as we can. If we understand the potential problems, perhaps we can better prevent them. We may not have a map of the swamp that represents the dilemmas of fidelity inherent in qualitative research, but we can have a clearer picture of it.

Notes

1. Analyzing the gender issues revealed in students' co-authoring discourse is an undertaking too complex and lengthy to accomplish in this chapter.

Works Cited

Bishop, Wendy. "I-Witnessing in Composition: Turning Ethnographic Data into Narratives." *Rhetoric Review* 11 (1992): 147–58.

Britzman, Deborah P. *Practice Makes Practice: A Critical Study of Learning to Teach.* Albany: State U of New York P, 1991.

Connelly, F. Michael, and D. Jean Clandinin. "The Promise of Collaborative Research in the Political Context." *Teacher Research and Educational Reform.* Ed. Sandra Hollingsworth and Hugh Sockett. Chicago: U of Chicago P, 1994. 86–102.

DiPardo, Anne. "Stimulated Recall in Research on Writing: An Antidote to 'I Don't Know, It Was Fine.'" *Speaking about Writing: Reflections on Research Methodology.* Ed. Peter Smagorinsky. Thousand Oaks: Sage, 1994. 163–81.

Ely, Margot. *Doing Qualitative Research: Circles within Circles.* New York: Falmer P, 1991.

Fine, Michelle. "Working the Hyphens: Reinventing Self and Other in Qualitative Research." *Handbook of Qualitative Research.* Ed. Norman K. Denzin and Yvonna S. Lincoln. Thousand Oaks: Sage, 1994. 70–82.

Fleischer, Cathy. "Researching Teacher-Research: A Practitioner's Retrospective." *English Education* 26 (1994): 86–124.

Flinders, David J. "From Theory and Concepts to Educational Connoisseurship." *Theory and Concepts in Qualitative Research: Perspectives from the Field.* Ed. David J. Flinders and Geoffrey E. Mills. New York: Teachers College P, 1993. 117–28.

Goswami, Dixie, and Peter R. Stillman, eds. *Reclaiming the Classroom: Teacher Research as an Agency for Change.* Portsmouth: Boynton/Cook-Heinemann, 1987.

Greene, Maxine. "Multiculturalism, Community, and the Arts." Paper presented at the Convention of the National Council of Teachers of English, Pittsburgh. November 1993.

Hollingsworth, Sandra, and Hugh Sockett, eds. *Teacher Research and Educational Reform.* Ninety-third Yearbook of the National Society for the Study of Education. Chicago: U of Chicago P, 1994.

Kleine, Michael. "Beyond Triangulation: Ethnography, Writing, and Rhetoric." *Journal of Advanced Composition* 10 (1990): 117–25.

Miles, Matthew A., and A. Michael Huberman. *Qualitative Data Analysis.* Thousand Oaks: Sage, 1994.

Miller, Janet L. *Creating Spaces and Finding Voices: Teachers Collaborating for Empowerment.* Albany: State U of New York P, 1990.

Mills, Geoffrey, E. "Levels of Abstraction in a Case Study of Educational Change." *Theory and Concepts in Qualitative Research.* Ed. David J. Flinders and Geoffrey E. Mills. New York: Teachers College P, 1993. 103–16.

Noddings, Nel. "Stories in Dialogue: Caring and Interpersonal Reasoning." *Stories Lives Tell: Narrative and Dialogue in Education.* Ed. Carol Witherell and Nel Noddings. New York: Teachers College P, 1991. 157–70.

Preissle, Judith, and Margaret Diane LeCompte. *Ethnography and Qualitative Design in Educational Research.* Orlando: Academic P, 1984.

Punch, Maurice. "Politics and Ethics in Qualitative Research." *Handbook of Qualitative Research.* Ed. Norman K. Denzin and Yvonna S. Lincoln. Thousand Oaks: Sage, 1994. 83–97.

Smagorinsky, Peter, ed. *Speaking about Writing: Reflections on Research Methodology.* Thousand Oaks: Sage, 1994.

Snyder, Ilana. "'It's Not as Simple as You Think!' Collaboration between a Researcher and a Teacher." *English Education* 24 (1992): 195–211.

Stock, Patricia Lambert. "The Function of Anecdote in Teacher Research." *English Education* 25 (1993): 173–87.

Wagner, Jane. *The Search for Signs of Intelligent Life in the Universe.* New York: Harper and Row, 1986.

Witherell, Carol, and Nel Noddings. "Prologue." *Stories Lives Tell: Narrative and Dialogue in Education.* Ed. Carol Witherell and Nel Noddings. New York: Teachers College P, 1991. 1–12.

II Representation: Positionality, Subjectivity, and Voice

6 Ethnography and the Problem of the "Other"

Patricia A. Sullivan
University of New Hampshire

The reflexivity inherent in all ethnographic inquiry—the researcher's presence in the story she tells—is compounded for those of us who study acts of literacy, for we are writers writing about writers writing. The methodological lines that the ethnographer draws, however tentatively, between observer and observed are, for us, not only crossed but frequently erased. To write ethnographies about writing communities is, in a sense, to conduct inquiry in a room of mirrors. We are studying communities with which we already share some degree of membership. We collect and interpret "artifacts" with which we are already familiar, indeed whose forms and conventions many of us have taught as writing teachers. Not only is our narrative presence inscribed in the stories we tell, but our assumptions about writing and discourse are refracted in the very forms with which we tell our stories. In short, the literacy events of others—the purported subject(s) of our inquiry—are inevitably framed in our own literacies, and that composition we call an ethnography takes on the shadings and hues of our own palette. A central question, then, for those who write ethnographies about writing communities is: How can we conceive and reflect the "other," the not-us, in the process of inquiry such that we convey otherness in its own terms? How can we adequately transcribe and represent the lived experiences of others—inscribe an other's reality—in a text that is marked through and through by our own discursive presence?

What I am calling the "other" is the given, the precondition, of ethnographic inquiry. As R. S. Khare notes in "The Other's Double—The Anthropologist's Bracketed Self":

> For anthropologists, the Other . . . invariably translates into configurations of cultural similarities and differences, yielding that cultural distance—Clifford Geertz's "not-us"—that has always been "out there" in various degrees for anthropologists to record, interpret, and explain. If the anthropologist does not do so, the implicit argument is that others would not only remain "unaccounted" but they also could not be "counted" within the scientific (that is, also the dominant and privileged) discourse.

> . . . [I]dentifying the presence and consequence of the ever-
> varying cultural Other remains the life source of contemporary
> anthropology and the life blood of the anthropologist. (4–6)

How could ethnography survive, Khare asks, "if it *stops* assuming, appropriating, and representing the Other, and lets the Other be itself?"
(5). What Khare asserts of the anthropologist is no less true of the ethnographer in composition studies and education. The other is the life
source and life blood of our fieldwork. We seek to understand literacy
events and writing contexts that are at least once removed from our
own occasions and contexts for writing; we desire to learn more about
discursive practices and discourse communities other than our own.
But it is precisely this intellectual need to bring the other into account
that situates us in a problematics of subjectivity and representation, for
any account we produce must simultaneously inscribe and transcend
the self who produces it.

In this chapter I will examine epistemological, political, and ethical issues that the other raises for ethnographic research in composition
to propose that we think of ethnography not only as a methodology we
employ for the sake of new understanding, but as a social practice—an
engagement with a culturally significant other who has a decided stake
in the understanding our research is said to produce. If the other is the
enabling condition of ethnographic research, I will argue, then an ethnography must be both an adequate account of the literate practices of
others and accountable to those others. As we seek to understand and
render the lived experiences of others, our research should ultimately
aim to benefit those whose voices, texts, and circumstances make such
understanding possible.

Constructing the Other in Composition Research

The question—In what sense are we studying an other?—seems less
relevant in cases such as Shirley Brice Heath's well-known ethnography of the communities of Trackton and Roadville (*Ways with Words*) or
Danling Fu's study of the literacies and socialization processes of members of a recently immigrated Laotian family (*The Trouble Is My English*)—
in cases, that is, where there are obvious differences of class, race, age,
nationality, or social experience between the researcher and those she
studies. In such instances, ethnographic research in composition and
education may be likened to contemporary forms of cultural anthropology or urban sociology. The researcher is interested in the local patterns
and arrangements, the contexts, interactions, and relationships that affect

and shape the literate practices of a subculture nested within the larger, shared culture.

Heath's fieldwork among two working-class communities in the Piedmont Carolinas is still relatively rare among those studies that make up the bulk of ethnographic research in composition. More often, composition researchers undertake ethnographies in "fields" that are closer to home—professions, institutions, disciplines, and classrooms that entail minimal problems of access and require minimal dislocations (geographic, discursive, or otherwise) on the part of the researcher. Here I would include studies such as those by Stephen Doheny-Farina ("Writing in an Emerging Organization") and Geoffrey Cross (*Collaboration and Conflict*) where the researcher assumes the role of participant-observer to gain and render an "insider's" perspective on the individual roles and collaborative networks undergirding the writing of professional business documents. But even in such studies, where social or cultural difference is less marked, the status of the research*ed* community as other is never really in question. The ethnographer is still attempting to demystify the rhetorical practices of others, to make the strange familiar to readers outside the workplace that forms the site of the researcher's fieldwork.

Equally as often though, composition researchers are studying language ("our" use of language) at home (on our "home field"), as did Beverly Moss, who studied the rhetorical practices of a community to which she belonged, and Bonnie Sunstein (this volume), who studied contexts of literacy and learning as a participant-observer in a summer writing program at her own institution, the University of New Hampshire (*Composing a Culture*). In these cases, the question "In what sense are we studying an other?" remains. Are we studying an "other" if the similarities between ourselves and the communities we observe are more marked than our differences? If our goal is not to demystify an other's experience and thereby make the strange familiar, but to disturb the familiar, to question the lenses through which we perceive our own culture, our own communities, are we still doing ethnography?

It is precisely the composition researcher's need or desire to render the familiar strange, to invert the terms by which ethnography customarily proceeds, I would argue, that distinguishes the ethnographic work of the compositionist from that of the cultural anthropologist. This is a minor distinction perhaps, but it serves to demarcate the different starting point at which most ethnographic inquiry in composition begins. The anthropologist begins, as Khare says, with a "configuration of cultural similarities and differences," with a "not-us" that "has always been 'out there'" for the anthropologist "to record, interpret, and explain" (4–5). For those of us in composition, this configuration of similarities and differences is most often a construct of our inquiry. The other, otherness, arises from the questions guiding our inquiry, defined as other the moment we articulate a concern with or express a puzzlement about the literate practices of other selves. While ethnography itself, in any field, entails the assumption of an other—the positing of an other or not-us—the other we seek out in composition is not so much an already defined social construct, a sociological or demographic configuration, as it is a rhetorical construct defined (like audience) by the purpose of our inquiry. The moment we ask what it means to speak or write or learn in a given setting, even if that setting is our own, we set ourselves apart from those other selves who hold the possibility of understanding. We might ask ourselves who, indeed, is the other in such a moment—but an absent other already has rhetorical presence.

Thus it is not the ontological status of the other that renders ethnography in composition problematic. Ethnography, as Linda Brodkey writes, "proceeds from the possibility of understanding others on their own terms" (41). It is understanding others on their own terms that weds the compositionist and the anthropologist in a problematics of writing and representation, in a science that Brodkey calls "a very human science indeed" (26).

In his essay, "On Ethnographic Authority," James Clifford asserts that issues of ethnographic writing and the representation of otherness must be understood within the political-epistemological context in which ethnographic science has developed (*Predicament* 24). Clifford's hyphenation of "political-epistemological" calls attention to the double meaning that the word "authority" has in his title. As Clifford Geertz puts it: "Imperialism . . . and Scientism . . . fell at more or less the same time" (*Works* 132). The fall of scientism eroded the distinction between observer and observed that provided the basis for the ethnographer's claims to have rendered reality as it really was, unmediated by his own presence in the field, his own subjectivity on the written page. Once ethnographic science acknowledged the researcher's agency in the reality observed and described, the epistemological foundations of the ethnographic text—its status as knowledge—were called into question. If reality itself is no longer the guarantor of the truths inscribed in an ethnographer's text, where precisely is ethnographic authority located? Clifford puts the question this way: "If ethnography produces cultural interpretations through intense research experiences, how is unruly experience transformed into an authoritative written account?" (*Predica-*

ment 25). What is it, we might ask, that warrants the ethnographer's descriptions, analyses, and interpretations of the experiences he observes such that we find them credible, convincing, accurate? On what bases or principles can we ascertain that, in the story the ethnographer tells about other lives, he has been there, has gotten things right, has produced an accurate description, a plausible analysis, an appropriate interpretation?

The Anxiety of Authority

The anxiety of authority that has surfaced in positivism's wake has generated what Geertz calls a "preoccupation" with "the mechanics of knowledge" (*Works* 9). As Brodkey writes, "The controversy specifically raised by ethnographic narratives is . . . whether the researcher or the research methodology is telling the story" (26). Kenneth Kantor, Dan Kirby, and Judith Goetz's 1981 essay, "Research in Context: Ethnographic Studies in English Education," may be read in this light as a story of our own professional anxiety, a story that encodes our conflicted response to the promise ethnographic research seemed to hold for studies of the social contexts of writing and the threat it portended to normal (empirical) science. In Kantor, Kirby, and Goetz's essay, method and the mechanics of knowledge rule the day. Emphasis is placed squarely on techniques that will assure accuracy, validity, and reliability in the final product. Triangulation is introduced prescriptively as a systematic check on the researcher's subjectivity. Even the "thick description" that the ethnographer is said to produce, that the authors encourage incipient ethnographers to write, is portrayed as a matter, indeed as a consequence, of method rather than of the storyteller's art.

Janice Lauer and J. William Asher's chapter on ethnography in *Composition Research: Empirical Designs* similarly focuses on the mechanics of knowledge—on methods of data collection and analysis that provide the composition researcher with "a window on culture" (39). But though the authors acknowledge that "no ethnographer can be 'objective,' nor is that the goal" (42), they view the qualitative nature of ethnographic inquiry, arising from the researcher's observations and participation in the research site, as a methodological limitation, an epistemological liability. Indeed, the longest section of the chapter is devoted to ethnography's difficulties and problems, a sweeping list that includes "data overload," "first impressions," "confidence in judgment," "internal consistency," "base-rate proportion," and "replicability" of research results (46–48). As in Kantor, Kirby, and Goetz's essay, we find in Lauer and Asher's chapter a preoccupation with the mechanics of knowledge, only this time couched in an oppositional discourse borrowed from positivist science. An ethnographer "does not have the freedom to observe without restrictions and to report results as ultimate truth," Lauer and Asher tell us. "As in any good scholarship, issues of generalizability of observations and data and relationships among variables must be considered" (43). Methods such as triangulation and the cross-coding of data instrumentally restrict the ethnographer's freedom and correct for his or her subjectivity, thereby lending authority to the ethnographic account.

In discussions of ethnographic method that place the onus of ethnographic authority on the researcher, on the other hand, the researcher's subjectivity is not only acknowledged but often heralded as the most valuable component of ethnographic inquiry. In his essay "In Search of Subjectivity—One's Own," for example, Alan Peshkin contends that "one's subjectivity" is "insistently present" like "a garment that cannot be removed"; but subjectivity is "virtuous, for it is the basis of researchers' making a distinctive contribution, one that results from the unique configuration of their personal qualities joined to the data they have collected" (17–18). After presenting a self-reflexive case study to "uncover" all of the "subjective I's" in a field-based study he had completed, Peshkin advocates that ethnographers in education impose systematic checks upon their own subjectivities at all stages of the research process so that subjectivity might be "tamed." If the anxiety of authority has produced a preoccupation with the mechanics of knowledge, as Geertz says, it has also produced what Geertz calls "author-saturated texts" (*Works* 9), ethnographies where the author, in seeking the other, finds himself everywhere, an "everywhere" where Peshkin says the researcher "belongs"—"in the underbrush of [his or her] own prose" (20). Peshkin, of course, means to challenge both the transcendent epistemology implicit in Lauer and Asher's chapter, which maintains the possibility of an authorial "view from nowhere," and realist accounts of culture from which the authorial self has been bracketed or erased. He advocates in their place a self-reflexive epistemology and a rhetoric of unremitting authorial presence, a mode of ethnographic writing in which the ethnographer continually declares himself here, and here, and here. Peshkin's approach, increasingly employed in contemporary ethnography, raises a new problem, however, if it introduces to the ethnographic text, in Khare's words, "a self-reflexivity that dwells more on 'ours' and 'us' than on a genuinely power-sharing discourse with the Other" (12).

Speaking For . . .

Khare's use of the word "power-sharing" takes us to the "political" side of Clifford's hyphenated term, to Geertz's other fall—the fall of imperialism. In the postcolonial world we now imagine ourselves to inhabit, the concept of authority is also suspect, but on different grounds. Here, authority is undermined not by the eroded foundations of empirically derived truths, but by ideological inquiries into the nature of dominance, privilege, and hierarchy, by critiques of the relations of power that structure and maintain social interaction. Here, the question is not whether the ethnographer has gotten the other right, and hence has produced an account that can be taken as authoritative, but whether the ethnographer has a right to appropriate an other for the sake of knowledge and can "speak for" another without compromising the other's own powers of representation. The anthropologist's ventures into foreign lands to record and render the lived experiences of "exotic" others, to make strange cultures familiar to Western audiences, have been interpreted in the wake of imperialism as an attempt not simply to understand but to domesticate and assimilate the other. Feminist scholars have long advanced a similar critique of scientific method in general and of traditional anthropology in particular. Frances E. Mascia-Lees, Patricia Sharpe, and Colleen Ballerino Cohen, in an essay critical of those who would draw solely on "postmodern trends in epistemology and literary criticism" in seeking out new modes of ethnographic representation, note that "while anthropology questioned the status of the participant-observer, it spoke from the position of the dominant and thus for the 'other.' Feminists speak from the position of the 'other'" (11). Citing Clifford's assertion that "'culture' is always relational, an inscription of communication processes that exist, historically, *between* subjects in relation to power" ("Introduction" 15), the authors contend that

> what appear to be new and exciting insights to these new postmodernist anthropologists—that culture is composed of seriously contested codes of meaning, that language and politics are inseparable, and that constructing the "other" entails relations of domination—are insights that have received repeated and rich exploration in feminist theory for the past forty years. Discussion of the female as "other" was the starting point of contemporary feminist theory. As early as 1949, Simone de Beauvoir's *The Second Sex* argued that it was by constructing the woman as "other" that men in Western Culture have constituted themselves as subjects. (11)

In fact, the authors note, a fundamental goal of the new ethnography is similar to that of feminist theory: "to apprehend and inscribe 'others' in such a way as not to deny or diffuse their claims to subjecthood" (12).

Under the pressure of postcolonial and feminist critiques, the grounds of ethnographic authority have been opened to ethical rather than epistemological scrutiny. Brodkey's question—Who or what is telling the story, the researcher or the research methodology?—might be recast to ask: Who is telling the story, the researcher or the "researched"? Whose story, after all, is it to tell? The ethnographer might argue that she is trying to bring the other, the unaccounted for, into account, to bring untold stories to the attention of the academy (Brodkey). In seeking out families of Trackton and Roadville, children of recent Laotian immigrants, African American ministers, staff members of an insurance company, professors who teach writing in other disciplines, or teachers in summer writing programs, the ethnographer is simply trying to bring to light the unwritten behavior, speech, beliefs, processes, and rituals of the other, to draw the literacies of others into a clearing where they will have wider meanings, relevance, and social significance. But the question remains: What gives her the right to speak for another, to tell another's story? If this "what" is the academy itself, or knowledge itself, or research itself, then isn't the story she tells merely another chapter in the West's master narrative, in its grand story of discovery, appropriation, domestication, assimilation?

Let me recall for a moment the question Khare has posed: How can ethnography survive "if it stops assuming, appropriating, and representing the Other, and lets the Other be itself"? One of the most ingenious answers to this question I know of is provided by Denny Taylor (co-author with Catherine Dorsey-Gaines of *Growing Up Literate: Learning from Inner-City Families*). In her conference presentations, several of which I have had both the pleasure and discomfort of attending, Taylor in effect deconstructs the question: the surest way to ensure ethnography's survival (in a postcolonial world) is to let the other be itself, to literally be itself. Taylor routinely invites her informants—drug addicts, alcoholics, homeless persons—to share the stage with her, to compose and to tell their own stories in their own words, their own idioms. Taylor's is a politically vigilant form of ethnography, in effect a critique of the social structures and institutions that shape and often circumvent her informants' lives. Her presentations are calls to action, not merely research reports, and the effect of those previously muted voices speaking from the stage is moving and powerful. Invariably a member of the audience is moved to ask: How can we help? What can we *do*? Taylor has succeeded in bringing the heterogeneity of language, the Bakhtinian carnival, to life. She has merged the ethnographic self and other into a "speaking" text, a power-sharing discourse, a performance through which the voice of the other can be, is heard in its own terms. But this text is, at last, not a text but a performance, a carnival with all of the power and only the power of spectacle. Taylor's informants, her actors, seem strangely out of place on the conference dais from which they make their presentations, and they are visibly uncomfortable as they address their stories to the rapt academic audience that sits before them. And why shouldn't they be? They are uprooted from the streets and shelters and families that they call home. The stories these others tell are rendered in their own terms, but not on their own terms or turf. In bringing the other to the reader-auditor rather than the reader to the other, Taylor's performed ethnographies, unlike her account of inner-city families in *Growing Up Literate,* necessarily omit the conditions and contexts and circumstances—the textures—of lived experience that thick description and transcribed dialogue provide to locate the reader "there," to situate the reader where the other lives.

Thus, while we might laud the nature of Taylor's ethnographies as praxis and admire the way her refusal to represent an other allows the other to literally present itself, hers is not a solution to the problem of the other, at least not one that many of us in composition can adopt, because it is a refusal of writing. The refusal to write, to inscribe, to *re*present an other's reality may allow us to escape the mediative role we play as authors of that reality, but it also banishes from the scene of inquiry the very medium that defines composition and circumscribes our work as ethnographers. Clifford contends that "in analyzing the complex transformation" by which intense field experiences become circumscribed by an individual author "as an adequate version of a more or less discrete 'other world' . . . one must bear in mind the fact that ethnography is, from beginning to end, enmeshed in writing" (*Predicament* 25).

Just as ethnography inevitably involves an encounter with an other, it inevitably involves an encounter with writing, indeed it is enmeshed in writing, as Clifford says, from beginning to end. Those of us who write ethnographies about writing communities compose an other, construct an other, at the moment our inquiry begins. In asking about the literate practices of others, we "set the terms of discourse in which others thereafter move" (Geertz, *Works* 19). And so we are returned again to the room of mirrors—to the scene of writing where our fieldwork begins and to that composition we call an ethnography. The problem of representation is still before us: How can we get at and represent an other, and not the self, in the act of writing? How do we allow the other to speak itself, to speak on and in its own terms, rather than reconstitute the other in our own likeness? How can we create textual conditions that will allow others to speak in and through our texts with their own powers of recognition, representation, and persuasion intact? And lastly, how can we write not only about the other but for the other? How can we write ethnographies that not only exist for the sake of knowledge but that can be put to good use?

Subjectivity, Representation, Intervention

Postmodern and feminist ethnographers advocate experimental modes of writing that disrupt the conventional fiction of a unitary author and disperse authority across the various voices and points of view encompassed in the text. Self-reflexivity—the explicit rendering of one's own theoretical and political assumptions and beliefs as well as one's experiences and emotions in the process of fieldwork—is one such disruptive strategy, for in postmodern terms, the self-conscious, critically reflexive "I" that renders the experiences of others is a self-in-relation. The self, like the other, is perceived as a construct of the ethnographic encounter. The author both acts and is acted upon, both affects and is affected by— indeed is an effect of—the relationships and interpretations inscribed in the ethnographic text.

While the need for (critical) self-reflexivity has been emphasized in anthropological studies of cultural difference, I would argue for its importance as well in composition studies of writing communities, that is, studies in which cultural similarities seem more marked than differences. For once again, composition researchers most often undertake ethnographies that are closer to home, if not *at* home. Our field of inquiry is quite often academe itself: we undertake fieldwork in university classrooms and teachers' lunchrooms, and our informants are often students or other teachers. When studying literacy or pedagogy in such contexts, it is easy to forget that our own status as researchers, as academics, is itself a social location invested with diverse and contestable meanings. Just as whites tend to forget that they are raced when studying nonwhite minorities, academics often fail to take into account the various and localized meanings their academic status confers—the ways they (and by extension the academy) are read by others differentially situated within the academy or who are situated outside it. If our status is presumed as a given at the outset of study rather than as a formation in relationship to an other, we may miss opportunities to learn how we are being constructed and the effects such constructions have on the other literacies we then "uncover."

This lesson was driven home to me a few years ago at the Conference on College Composition and Communication (CCCC) annual convention in Cincinnati. The convention took place the same weekend as the quarter-final round of the men's NCAA basketball tournament, and conferees shared hotels with college teams from around the country. As I stepped into an elevator to return to my room one afternoon, I was met by three tall young men returning to theirs. We exchanged greetings as the elevator door closed, and one of the men asked me if "some sort of convention was going on." I said yes, a conference of college teachers, and briefly explained what the CCCC was about. He said, "You're all English teachers?!" I answered, "Well, yes, but most of us teach writing." Just then the door opened to my floor, and as I stepped out, I turned to wish the athletes good luck. Instead, I heard the young man's own parting words, just as the elevator doors closed behind me: "My God, you're my worst nightmare."

I have thought about this incident many times and have enjoyed telling this story to composition colleagues who appreciate as much as I do the joke it makes at our expense. But I have also been made aware that, as an English professor and writing teacher, I am the stuff of nightmare for at least one undergraduate student in this country. In *Textual Carnivals*, Susan Miller reminds us to ask how we are constructing our students in our teaching and research and to reflect on these constructions to uncover the ideological work that they do. But in these moments of critical self-reflection, I believe we also need to ask how our students are constructing us. When I reflect on that student's construction of me and its inescapable meaning—that a writing teacher embodies and portends threat (to self-esteem? an athletic scholarship? a career?)—I find I am not at all surprised and yet at the same time deeply disturbed, for it implies that writing teachers can and do inflict a kind of damage. I know of no writing teachers who would take pleasure in such a representation; even those of us who deliberately challenge our students' most deeply held values and beliefs do so with the intellectual interests of our students at heart. But this is precisely my point. What I heard conflicted with my own self-perception, my sense of what a writing teacher is and does, and thus with the values I thought I embodied as a composition professor. (On reflection, I also realize that, in only slightly different circumstances, I might well have been the one to feel threatened by the presence of three male athletes in a hotel elevator.) During that chance meeting, at least two cultures came together, each with its own culturally laden frames of interpretation. And those frames undoubtedly find their way into the more structured, institutionalized spaces of our writing classrooms when teachers and students encounter each other, and encounter each other as other.

If this anecdote may serve ethnomethodologically as a microcosm of the anthropological encounter, then it reminds us that even in the most familiar of settings—a writing classroom, a hotel elevator—we can encounter the self-other divide and the power relations functioning at its borders. But if we understand self-reflexivity as a confluence of subjectivities and not merely as a confrontation of static identities, then self-reflexivity affords us the possibility of a reciprocal relationship between self and other, researcher and researched. If we examine our assumptions, perceptions, interests, and desires in relation to others' expressed assumptions, perceptions, interests, and desires, we stand to disrupt the unitary authority of the ethnographic text because no single consciousness can hold sway. Both writer and other "set the terms of discourse" in which a cast of selves "thereafter move."

Self-reflexivity alone, however, is not enough to ensure that others will express their beliefs and desires, or that their stories will be told and heard in their own idiom. The self-conscious positioning of the writer-researcher in relation to an other still leaves open to question how others are to exercise their own powers of representation and thus how the ethnographer-writer is to produce what might be deemed a power-sharing discourse and not merely a text in which all the subjective I's are painstakingly uncovered. Geertz's "Notes on a Balinese Cockfight," an essay that appears in several composition anthologies, is an instructive text in this regard, for while Geertz's authorial stance is at once self-reflexive and self-effacing, ostensibly abnegating epistemological authority to the Balinese men and rituals he observes, the essay itself is wholly monologic: it is Geertz's story to tell, and the rituals "observed" are both rendered and interpreted through a decidedly Western and patriarchal lens. Linda Alcoff ascribes the problem that Geertz's text raises to rhetorical *ethos*, to "the problem of speaking for others." "The practice of speaking for others," she notes,

> is often born of a desire for mastery, to privilege oneself as the one who more correctly understands the truth about another's situation or as one who can champion a just cause and thus achieve glory and praise. And the effect of the practice of speaking for others is often, though not always, erasure and a reinscription of sexual, national, and other kinds of hierarchies. (29)

Alcoff rejects "an absolute retreat from speaking for" others, however, on the grounds that it "weakens political effectivity, is based on a metaphysical illusion, and often effects only an obscuring of the intellectual's power" (24). Barring an absolute retreat from speaking—or writing—for others, how might we conceive the act of authorship so that it neither privileges nor occludes the author's agency (and desire) in the account of the other she renders?

Interestingly, anthropologists who have broached this question often draw upon principles and a lexicon that distinctly echo scholarly work in composition studies, particularly theoretical and classroom-based studies of collaborative writing and learning. Clifford, for example, invites us to think of ethnography as "a constructive negotiation involving at least two, and usually more, conscious, politically significant subjects" (*Predicament* 41). He advocates that we move away from both hermeneutic and scientific "paradigms of experience and interpretation" toward "discursive paradigms of dialogue and polyphony" (41). Stephen Tyler claims that postmodern ethnography "foregrounds dialogue as opposed to monologue, and emphasizes the cooperative and collaborative nature of the ethnographic situation in contrast to the ideology of the transcendent observer" (203). A diverse range of composition scholars who have investigated and (or) practiced collaborative writing in their own classrooms and research are intimately familiar with the type of inquiry Clifford and Tyler seem to advocate (see, for example, Bruffee; Ede and Lunsford; Flower; Herrington; Reagan, Fox, and Bleich). The strategic assumption behind such an approach is that knowledge is constructed in a collaborative relationship with those being studied. Participants are involved in framing research questions, collecting and interpreting data, and commenting on, and sometimes in, the final text. Taylor and Dorsey-Gaines's *Growing Up Literate* is a ground-breaking ethnography in this respect because the researchers accorded the families they studied the integral role of participants—and not merely informants—at nearly every stage of their project. A number of studies have followed the pathway charted by Taylor and Dorsey-Gaines. Several serve as illustrative examples of what dialogic and collaborative modes of inquiry look like as textual practices and what they might achieve, rhetorically and politically, as modes of representation.

Elizabeth Chiseri-Strater's *Academic Literacies,* an ethnographic study of two college students, their writing teacher, and courses they took from faculty in other disciplines during a semester at a state university, employs dialogue as its primary methodological strategy. From the opening sentence of the book, "This book celebrates what college students know" (xv), to its concluding observation that "academic discourse communities cannot flourish without real dialogue" (167), Chiseri-Strater delimits a textual space in which the voices and perspectives of others move freely and audibly, uninhibited by the narrative presence and intellectual frameworks of their author. Although she is rhetorically aware of her own agency in the story she tells and the effect of her presence on those she observes, she continually gives the stage over to the literacy events and actors that are her subject—to the writing and speaking "others" who hold the possibility of understanding literacy in its many and varied permutations. Through journals kept by student informants, talk that takes place during class discussion and in small collaborative writing groups, interviews with faculty, and conversations that occur in the natural course of fieldwork, Chiseri-Strater creates a multivoiced and multivalent text, a dialogue into which she weaves her own insights and critical speculations, but which remains open to the counterintonations of her students and the dialectic participation of her readers. *Academic Literacies* is in many respects an exemplary ethnography, one which both inscribes and enacts a power-sharing discourse as the author enlists the voices of students and teachers to talk about what it means to be initiated into the culture of a university.

Danling Fu's ethnographic study of four Laotian refugee adolescents from a family recently immigrated to America similarly foregrounds the speech, writing, and drawings of the study's participants to effect a highly nuanced, multivoiced ethnography. *The Trouble Is My English* offers readers a sensitive and compassionate portrait of what it means to live "in between"—to move within the liminal space between actual cultures (Southeast Asia and southern New Hampshire) and to negotiate the culturally marked spaces of home and school, orality and literacy, memory and forgetting, childhood and adulthood. From the outset, Fu is interested in her young informants—Tran, Paw, Cham, and Sy—as "individuals" and not merely "representatives" of Laotian culture. She allows the four teenagers to dictate the story of their own lives, following their lead as they relate their personal histories, share anecdotes about their family, interpret classroom assignments—or, as is sometimes the case, remain silent. She devotes considerable textual space to these individual accounts, and though she self-consciously mediates between cultures, selecting and editing the conversations and compositions that will represent an other's reality, the fact that her informants offer divergent accounts of a shared past, express different desires for their new life in America, and relate their stories with varied skills in their second language leaves little doubt but that, in speaking for others,

Fu has positioned herself as a student of the other. The effect is a collaborative text born of a shared inquiry into the nature of literacy and learning across a formidable range of cultural and linguistic borders. Fu's conclusion, that an American school agenda "matches and mismatches [such students'] learning patterns" and "reinforces the marginalization of ethnic minority students in their school life by ignoring what they know and who they are" (xvi), arises from her methodology: she allows each adolescent to teach her what to say and how to say it, even as they are learning to speak and write—to negotiate a myriad of cultures and try out new identities—for themselves.

Near the end of his essay, "The Other's Double," Khare takes note of anthropologist Margaret Trawick's suggestion for an alternative way to approach the other: "It is to view the Other under 'love' rather than under a will to secure self-privilege and textual power" (15). He claims that "not only may 'love' as a producer of dialoguè and discourses better address the anthropologist's deeper personal motivations in studying the other, it may also encourage the anthropologist's self-privileging discourse to inspect itself from an angle other than that which reduces everything to issues of contested power and privilege" (15). In Chiseri-Strater's unflinching "celebration of what college students know" and Fu's compassionate rendering of four young lives between cultures, we can glimpse an ethnographic practice motivated less by the will to knowledge than by an ethic of care—what I think Khare and Trawick mean by love when they argue for its place in ethnographic inquiry. Working against the limited and limiting conception of literacy usually ascribed to college-level writers and the stereotypes frequently imposed on Asian students studying in the West, Chiseri-Strater and Fu stand alongside the other, take the other's side, to produce alternative accounts of—and ways to account for—practices of writing that take place daily in American schools and colleges. In these studies we find a type of research that is not only *about* the other but *for* the other, a research practice that is concerned at the level of methodology—and not simply in its implications—with the good that it might do.

Alcoff writes that "in order to evaluate attempts to speak for others in particular instances, we need to analyze the probable or actual effects of the words on the discursive and material context. . . . One must look at where the speech goes and what it does there" (26). While Alcoff offers this strategy as a way to evaluate the already written text, a way to gauge its political efficacy and moral value as scholarship, I believe such a strategy, used in tandem with self-reflexive, dialogic, and collaborative modes of representation, has value at all stages of ethnographic writing. If we ask from the moment inquiry begins what our speech will do, what effect it will have on those we study, then we acknowledge not only our own agency but our responsibility to effect what change we can when we encounter social inequities. While I am mindful of Shirley Brice Heath's personal stand against interventionist research practices, or what she terms her "own bias toward trying to keep apart what is happening (or what some might call 'basic research') from clinical interventions and critiques of individual teachers, curricula, and schools that have the goal of *changing* students" ("Madness[es]" 260), I am also convinced by ethnographer Margery Wolf's claims for a study she undertook in a small village in northern Taiwan: "When I began my research, there were no Taiwanese scholars who were the least bit interested in women's lives. I may not have always gotten it right, but Taiwanese *women* were taken seriously as agents as a result of my research and writing" (14). And while I am in agreement with Heath that we should not "overstate the power of writing [and] academic research" when we consider the effects of our fieldwork on the communities we study ("Madness[es]" 256), I share feminist Michelle Fine's belief that, unless researchers are willing to take activist stances and provoke change, "we collude in producing social silences through the social sciences" (206). If we consider at the outset where our speech is going and what it will do there, and if we enlist the voices of others to guide us along the way, trusting the other to teach us what we need to know, we will be less likely to fall prey to the temptation ever before us as academics to view research as an end in itself and the knowledge we produce as its own justification. As we continue to negotiate the textual and social complexities of ethnographic research in composition, we might think of our project as "attaching what is to what could be" (225), to use Fine's phrase, ever mindful that the ways we choose to render worlds from words have the potential to alter the spaces in which the other thereafter moves.

Works Cited

Alcoff, Linda. "The Problem of Speaking for Others." *Cultural Critique* 20 (1991–92): 5–32.

Brodkey, Linda. "Writing Ethnographic Narratives." *Written Communication* 4 (1987): 25–50.

Bruffee, Kenneth. *Collaborative Learning: Higher Education, Interdependence, and the Authority of Knowledge.* Baltimore: Johns Hopkins UP, 1993.

Chiseri-Strater, Elizabeth. *Academic Literacies: The Public and Private Discourse of University Students.* Portsmouth: Boynton/Cook-Heinemann, 1991.

Clifford, James. "Introduction: Partial Truths." *Writing Culture: The Poetics and Politics of Ethnography.* Ed. James Clifford and George E. Marcus. Berkeley: U of California P, 1986. 1–26.

———. "On Ethnographic Authority." *The Predicament of Culture: Twentieth-Century Ethnography, Literature, and Art.* Cambridge: Harvard UP, 1988. 21–54.

Cross, Geoffrey A. *Collaboration and Conflict: A Contextual Exploration of Group Writing and Positive Emphasis.* Cresskill: Hampton P, 1994.

Doheny-Farina, Stephen. "Writing in an Emerging Organization: An Ethnographic Study." *Written Communication* 3 (1986): 158–85.

Ede, Lisa, and Andrea Lunsford. *Singular Texts/Plural Authors: Perspectives on Collaborative Writing.* Carbondale: Southern Illinois UP, 1990.

Fine, Michelle. *Disruptive Voices: The Possibilities of Feminist Research.* Ann Arbor: U of Michigan P, 1992.

Flower, Linda. *The Construction of Negotiated Meaning: A Social-Cognitive Theory of Writing.* Carbondale: Southern Illinois UP, 1994.

Fu, Danling. *The Trouble Is My English.* Portsmouth: Heinemann, 1995.

Geertz, Clifford. "Deep Play: Notes on a Balinese Cockfight." *The Interpretation of Cultures.* New York: Basic, 1973. 412–53.

———. *Works and Lives: The Anthropologist as Author.* Stanford: Stanford UP, 1988.

Heath, Shirley Brice. "The Madness(es) of Reading and Writing Ethnography." *Anthropology and Education Quarterly* 24 (1993): 256–68.

———. *Ways with Words: Language, Life, and Work in Communities and Classrooms.* Cambridge: Cambridge UP, 1983.

Herrington, Anne J. "Reflections on Empirical Research: Examining Some Ties between Theory and Action." *Theory and Practice in the Teaching of Writing: Rethinking the Discipline.* Ed. Lee Odell. Carbondale: Southern Illinois UP, 1993. 40–70.

Kantor, Kenneth, Dan Kirby, and Judith Goetz. "Research in Context: Ethnographic Studies in English Education." *Research in the Teaching of English* 15 (1981): 293–309.

Khare, R. S. "The Other's Double—The Anthropologist's Bracketed Self: Notes on Cultural Representation and Privileged Discourse." *New Literary History* 23 (1992): 1–23.

Lauer, Janice M., and J. William Asher. *Composition Research: Empirical Designs.* New York: Oxford UP, 1988.

Mascia-Lees, Frances E., Patricia Sharpe, and Colleen Ballerino Cohen. "The Postmodernist Turn in Anthropology: Cautions from a Feminist Perspective." *Signs* 15 (1989): 7–33.

Miller, Susan. *Textual Carnivals: The Politics of Composition.* Carbondale: Southern Illinois UP, 1991.

Moss, Beverly. "Ethnography and Composition: Studying Language at Home." *Methods and Methodology in Composition Research.* Ed. Gesa Kirsch and Patricia A. Sullivan. Carbondale: Southern Illinois UP, 1992. 153–71.

Peshkin, Alan. "In Search of Subjectivity—One's Own." *Educational Researcher* 17.7 (1988): 17–21.

Reagan, Sally Barr, Thomas Fox, and David Bleich, eds. *Writing With: New Directions in Collaborative Teaching, Learning, and Research.* Albany: State U of New York P, 1994.

Sunstein, Bonnie S. *Composing a Culture: Inside a Summer Writing Program with High School Teachers.* Portsmouth: Boynton/Cook, 1994.

Taylor, Denny, and Catherine Dorsey-Gaines. *Growing Up Literate: Learning from Inner-City Families.* Portsmouth: Heinemann, 1988.

Tyler, Stephen A. *The Unspeakable: Discourse, Dialogue, and Rhetoric in the Postmodern World.* Madison: U of Wisconsin P, 1987.

Wolf, Margery. *A Thrice Told Tale: Feminism, Postmodernism, and Ethnographic Responsibility.* Stanford: Stanford UP, 1992.

7 Turning In upon Ourselves: Positionality, Subjectivity, and Reflexivity in Case Study and Ethnographic Research

Elizabeth Chiseri-Strater
University of North Carolina at Greensboro

Every version of an other . . . is also the construction of a "self."
—James Clifford, *The Predicament of Culture*

All researchers are positioned. Whether Barbara McClintock studying genetic transpositions in corn, Renato Rosaldo describing headhunting among the Ilongot tribes, or Robert Connors tracing the rise and fall of discourse modes, researchers are positioned by age, gender, race, class, nationality, institutional affiliation, historical-personal circumstance, and intellectual predisposition. The extent to which such influences are revealed or concealed when reporting data is circumscribed by the paradigms and disciplines under which we train, work, and publish.

All researchers are positioned whether they write about it explicitly, separately, or not at all. McClintock's feeling for the organisms she investigated was never part of her scholarly papers, but was disclosed in Evelyn Fox Keller's book about the influences of gender, academic training, and situational circumstances on the researcher's work. In composition studies, Connors's discussion of the methods and methodology of doing historical research is best depicted in his essay "Dreams and Play," where he demonstrates how the historian negotiates the personal and cultural preconceptions that shape such scholarship. Connors's essay provides methodological insights that are unavailable in any of his other articles on the historical movements or legacies within the fields of composition and rhetoric where his data are presented without their intellectual journey.

For ethnographers, writing about how we are positioned is part of the data. We are trained to keep field notes on how we negotiate entrance into a community, how we present ourselves to our informants, how we think our informants perceive us—in addition to writing about what we think is linguistically and socially significant in the culture under investigation. Some ethnographers have published their personal insights separately as field experiences (Powdermaker; Rabinow; R. Rosaldo; Sanjek; Wax; Wolf), while others have integrated subjective factors of doing fieldwork into their final ethnographies (Chiseri-Strater, *Academic Literacies*; Fishman; Perl and Wilson; Shostak; Taylor and Dorsey-Gaines). Whatever the presentational choice, I argue in this essay that readers of ethnographies should approach them critically: they should understand what researchers were positioned to know and what they were *not* positioned to know—and why.

The concept of positionality includes the ethnographer's given attributes such as race, nationality, and gender which are fixed or culturally ascribed. Such attributes require textual disclosure when they affect the data, as they always do to some degree. For example, a unique collection of essays called *Arab Women in the Field: Studying Your Own Society* provides good examples of how the fieldworkers—positioned as Arab women studying indigenous cultures—were restricted in their data access and in their researcher roles because of their gender (Altorki and El-Solh). While the ethnographers studying their home cultures found that being natives held certain advantages, they disclose the ways in which gender shaped how they were seen by others in the culture— often as single, American-educated, Westernized women. One of the key points of this collection of essays is the importance of foregrounding the influences of the fieldworker's persona: "The manner in which the fieldworker presents her or his 'self' . . . is a major aspect of the ethical implications of fieldwork" (20). This collection of essays suggests that disclosure of fixed or ascribed personal attributes is not optional but rather an integral part of the data.[1]

Positionality is also shaped by subjective-contextual factors such as personal life history and experiences, as revealed in the reflexive account by Renato Rosaldo in *Culture and Truth*. In his book, Rosaldo demonstrates how the accidental death of his first wife, Michelle, while conducting fieldwork in the Philippines, increased his understanding of the practice of headhunting among a native tribe there. Previously Rosaldo had lived among this Ilongot tribe and, with his wife, had studied their headhunting practices (M. Rosaldo). Yet it was not until after Michelle Rosaldo's death that he began to understand headhunting as a response to intense grief and rage over the loss of a close relative. Rosaldo's revised insights into this initially impenetrable cultural practice reveal how personal history—in this case with respect to death and loss—can affect positioning as a researcher and subsequent repositioning. Rosaldo writes that "nothing in my own experience equipped me even to imagine the anger possible in bereavement until after Michelle Rosaldo's death in 1981. Only then was I in a position to grasp the force of what Ilongots had repeatedly told me about grief, rage, and headhunting" (R. Rosaldo 19). Ethnographers need to reflect upon and write about how their situatedness or their terministic screens—to evoke Burke's phrase—influence an understanding of their data.

This essay will explore how the ethnographer's stance-position-location affects the entire ethnographic process: from data collection, theory construction, and methodological understanding, through the creation of the narrative voice and overall writing of the ethnography. As has been suggested, researchers are always positioned, but disclosure of that positionality has not always found its way into the final ethnography. And while there are now a wide range of studies available to illustrate the kinds of choices that ethnographers have made with respect to positionality, I have elected to illustrate these points with the qualitative work I know best: my own.

To illustrate what happens when a case study researcher does not position herself with respect to her informants or the context as part of her data, I turn to my early work, a set of case studies I completed more than a decade ago called "Composing in Context: Revision Strategies of Freshman Writers," what I might now describe as quasi-qualitative research.[2] In this work I report on the ways that six students learned to revise in their freshman writing courses. I argue that the "instructional context is one of the tools necessary to understanding the revision process," but in fact I never visited my informants' writing classrooms except to seek student volunteers (35). I seldom talked with them about their writing course "context"; instead, our weekly interviews focused on a list of prestructured questions about the students' revision processes (e.g., What changes did you make in this draft and why?). The omission of actual classroom description might be attributed to the cognitive paradigm under which I designed this study, or it may be due to the convention of evoking generic writing classrooms in much of the early work on composing processes. While many studies on students' composing processes published around that time were similarly decontextualized (see Bridwell; Perl; Pianko; Sommers), at least those researchers did not claim "context" as the key insight to student writing.

And yet context *was* the key to understanding these students' revision processes. But not necessarily the classroom context, since I did not gather data there. Rather, the researcher-informant relationship became an additional context where we explored much more than the revision process. Three of these students' personal stories are dramatic enough to have stayed with me. One student had been anorexic and her long narrative paper—"My Diet Toward Death"—depicted her difficult recovery and continued struggle with this disorder. Another student, whom I labeled the "reluctant reviser," wrote his way out of playing college football on a full scholarship at our university through a series of essays about his constant injuries and subsequent fear of being hurt. Still another student, whose mother had died from cancer the year before, used her freshman course to develop a better understanding toward the loss of her mother and her sense of being more adult than most of her peers. Our researcher-informant discussions, which often touched on personal connections between myself and these students, most likely affected how they began to see paper topics and their potential and realized choices in revising particular papers. Our relationship also gave them an additional interested audience for overhearing their decisions about changing both their texts and their actual lives.

Yet like many case study researchers in the early 1980s, influenced at that time by cognitive studies on writing processes (Flower and Hayes; Rose), I reserved no space to describe the researcher-informant relationship or to include my own subjective reactions to these students' writings. Instead, I displayed my "findings" on a large pullout chart which depicts the growth of revision from "base level" to levels 1, 2, 3, and 4. What I really learned about revision strategies of freshmen is included in one line in my "Results" section, where I suggest that "revision, as a process of changing writing, encourages students to write about personal change" (60). End of insight. By situating myself—both in my research approach and text—as objective and detached from my informants, I actually distorted my data through omissions about my research context and my researcher self. My rereading of this earlier research shows that objectivity and detachment in reporting data are neither possible nor desirable because many important insights about students' revision processes were excluded from my findings on that topic.

This initial type of case study work done by composition researchers—whom Stephen North calls "the Clinicians" (197)—has been gradually replaced by the work of those who are influenced far more by anthropology, phenomenology, feminist theory, and critical ethnography than by cognitive science. This change of direction in studies of writing processes and literacy is thoroughly traced in an extended article by Cathy Fleischer, who describes her own teacher-researcher development as one of learning to "conduct research *with* rather than *on* our students" (109, emphasis in original). Clearly my early case studies were conducted under what is now considered the positivist medical, industrial, or agricultural research model that limits the kinds of questions asked, the designs used to answer questions, and the kinds of findings reported (Mishler). Such a research paradigm did not demand or even welcome dialogic or discursive reflections about either the process or product of my research.

In ethnography, however, a major goal of the research process is self-reflexivity—what we learn about the self as a result of the study of the "other."[3] To achieve a reflexive stance the researcher needs to bend back upon herself to make herself as well as the other an object of study. Or as Barbara Myerhoff and Jay Ruby describe it, subject and object fuse (2). Turning in upon ourselves as researchers makes us look subjectively and reflexively at how we are positioned. Turning in upon ourselves prevents us from removing our selv(es) from our research process, from our connections with our informants, or from our written translation of data to text.

The issue at stake here becomes one of just how much of our selv(es) is needed to guide the reader through the narrative about the other(s). What do readers need to know and understand about the situatedness of the researcher and influences that affect her or his perspective that are relevant to an understanding of the informants in the culture under investigation? How much self-reflexivity is valuable to readers as a way of understanding the ethics and methodology of the research context? How are choices about self-disclosure made both on and off the page? Such questions about positionality haunt the ethnographer throughout the research process since, as Clifford Geertz has explained, positioning oneself during the field experience is subsequently connected to positioning oneself in the written ethnography: "Finding somewhere to stand in a text that is supposed to be at one and the same time an intimate view and a cool assessment is almost as much of a challenge as gaining the view and making the assessment in the first place" (10).

While there is no formula for locating oneself within this delicate ethnographic terrain, I would suggest that we take no more risk in adopting subjective and reflexive roles as researchers than we would in presenting ourselves as objective and detached, a stance that most postmodernist fieldworkers would reject. Recently Ruth Behar, author of *Translated Woman,* an engaging and subjective ethnographic portrait of Esperanza, a Mexican street peddler, has written about the inclusive impulse that drives some feminists and minorities as well as others to personalize their research: "What is drawing me and, I believe, other scholars to write personally is a desire to abandon the alienating 'metalanguage' that closes, rather than opens, the doors of academe to all those who wish to enter" ("Dare" 1). Moreover, unmasking relevant aspects of ourselves within our texts signals to our readers that neither we nor those we describe are "typical or representative" individuals from a culture, but rather "situated" individuals within a particular "time, place and social context" (Karamcheti 8).[4] Those aspects, then, of our researcher selves—our relationships with our informants and the research contexts specific and local to our study—will call for some measure of disclosure.

To consider how positionality affects the entire ethnographic process, I will turn to my own study, *Academic Literacies,* as an ethnography for scrutiny. In highlighting some of the important contexts for this study, I will try to show how the researcher's positioning relates to (1) theory construction, (2) methodological disclosure, (3) development of the narrative voice, and (4) writing of a polyphonic text. While some of these factors are rhetorical ones, they are all inherently connected with how the researcher is actually situated in the field, not just on the page.

Positionality and Theory Construction

An analysis of the data collected for *Academic Literacies* illustrates how a complex factor such as gender can drive theory and encourage reflexivity. Unlike the self-aware ethnographers of *Arab Women in the Field,* I was initially unconscious of my engendered researcher position and how it might affect my view of classroom interactions and my relationship with my informants. When gender issues gradually emerged as central to my study, I could not ignore them and slowly began to reflect on the ways that my data were being sifted through my terministic screens— by my role as female ethnographer and feminist. As I took on the perspective of my informants (Anna and Nick) on classes in their majors, I began to record gender-related (but not gender-specific) differences in language use and classroom interactions. In my ethnography, I employed no particular rhetorical trope to illustrate my growing awareness of gender-related issues except through narrative disclosure of its spiraling significance to all aspects of my study.

My first hint of the impact of differences in men's and women's learning patterns began during the collaborative writing projects undertaken in Donna Qualley's prose-writing classroom. In their journal entries, both male and female students expressed tension over loss of control, need for ownership, and struggle for power while co-authoring their papers. Yet it was not until Carlos, a student in Donna's class, wrote in his journal that he was "turning into a woman" (29) because of his collaborative partnership that I began to think more critically about differences in male and female learning styles. As I read about women's epistemological development and reflected further on this issue, I began to see collaboration as a mode of working that came more easily for many female students, mainly because of cultural models and expectations. Certainly it was true for Donna and me that, as we began to work together more closely, we found collaborative inquiry supportive and empowering. To illustrate the startling differences I saw between two ways of learning—collaborative and autonomous—I reprinted Carlos's journal entries side by side with those of his partner so that readers could interpret for themselves whether or not these two students approached the collaborative project with very different "ways of knowing" (28–30). It was a rhetorical decision on my part to share with my readers how I was reading my data and to open these ideas about gender and learning styles to further interpretations.

Theories about differences between men's and women's learning and discourse styles spilled over into my fieldwork and interviews with informants. When I started to transcribe tapes of reading and writing groups, for example, I realized that Nick, working with Carlos and two women, including Anna, dominated the talk throughout the session. In my analysis of the taped transcripts, I discovered that Nick not only talked more, but he interrupted and disagreed with the women in the group while at the same time he supported all of Carlos's topics (90–91). Since these findings reinforce much of the research by linguists on mixed-sex conversations, I continued to search, test out, and confirm gendered patterns of discourse in classroom settings outside the prose-writing classroom.[5]

My gradual awareness of Nick's linguistic dominance in Donna's class repeated itself in our own interpersonal relationship. In listening to our taped interviews, I came to realize how hard Nick worked to wrestle the floor from me and that he felt free to interrupt me as well. When I called his attention to this by playing a tape of our conversation for him, he explained our competing styles of talk not as a "biological" difference, but as a "social" difference caused by women's mothering and nurturing roles. Nick and I never fully agreed about the source of male dominance and female mutedness in conversation, but our discussion allowed us both to be more aware of differences and suggested discourse styles as a topic for us to co-investigate. At one point when I wrote about the differences between us, Nick read my manuscript and jotted in the margins, "Yes, I can be a real prick about it," which left me with a sense that self-awareness may not be enough to encourage change. At still another point in our work together, Nick was clearly frustrated by an inability to understand a short reading assigned from *Women's Ways of Knowing*. He came to our interview filled with disbelief and anger: "What *is* this new women's way of knowing? Why is it that I can't figure out the difference between separate and connected thinking? What the hell does it mean? Separate from what? Connected with what?" he demanded (89).

It was not until I followed Nick into his political science course, however, that I witnessed a context where his male dominance and combative presentational style were appreciated. For Nick, the talk in this seminar was what I called a "risky dialectical merry-go-round." To participate, he suggested, "You have to have some balls to stand up in that class and say something" (125).

And yet by the end of our semester of attending this class together, Nick was able to concede that this agonistic discussion style might not be so easy for women students because some of the commentary in class depended upon sports figures and battle metaphors that could be offensive to or outside the experience of some women. And it was Nick who reported to me that a woman student was "seriously crying her eyes out" one night after the political science seminar, crying over having been interrupted throughout the class discussion. This experience made it possible for Nick to see how women students might take classroom discussions far more personally than he did.

Through a comparative analysis of oral discourse and presentational styles in other classrooms, I recognized how strongly I felt about the importance of nurture and support for students in all college classrooms. My ability to piece together these feelings did not come easily because I did not and could not have anticipated the ways in which gender-related discourse and pedagogical beliefs shaped and affected my perspective on other college classrooms. My gender and training as a writing teacher positioned me to resist the noninteractive pedagogies—like agonistic debate and strict lecture format—used in other disciplines. Thinking about possible changes for the political science and art history courses would not have been possible without my students' own gendered perspectives on what kind of learning was valued in their majors and how these approaches affected their potential as learners. David Bleich has suggested that collaborative relationships between informants and researchers should shape our work: "The ethnographic researcher has to enlist the subjects of study as partners, as posers of questions, as people who can see and change their own experiences through interaction with 'outside' but politically interested teacher-researchers" (182).

Positionality and Methodological Disclosure

Ethnographies that omit the methodology of doing fieldwork disappoint me, because this information can reveal what a researcher was positioned to see, to know, and to understand. The omission of the fieldwork experience also hides the conflicts and tensions that all researchers inevitably face and can learn from. The only direct way for a reader to obtain information about how positioning affects methodology is for the researcher to write about it. Increasingly, ethnographers who research literacy and learning are including more information about their fieldwork. Andrea Fishman's *Amish Literacy* is a notable example of methodological disclosure. She writes that "doing ethnography is not at all like reading ethnographies" (206), implying that the neat narrative product does not at all resemble the disorderly research process. In the methodology section of *Academic Literacies*, "The Handwork of the Field Investigator" (183–97), I share how I designed and conducted my study through its various stages not so that others will imitate my design, organization, or analytic categories (since that is impossible), but to share some aspects of how I was positioned to gather my data—that is, how I chose my informants, conducted my interviews, analyzed my transcripts, discovered patterns, and grounded theories.

Aside from writing a separate chapter about methodology, researchers can use other ways of disclosing positionality throughout the ethnographic text. In my study, I included descriptions of how other(s) perceived me as the researcher, information derived from the professors whose classrooms I visited and from students in those settings. As a researcher, I presented myself as an older, white, middle-class, female doctoral student interested in undergraduate students' perspectives on writing and learning within the disciplines. While my role as *student* allowed me rapport with my informants, my status as *graduate student* in composition marked me as powerless for some of the professors whose classrooms I studied and who saw composition as a marginalized discipline (if in fact a discipline at all) within the academy.

Professor Adams, the political science professor in my study, was unabashedly amazed that I wanted to research student writing in the disciplines. He never understood, for example, why I came to his seminar when my informant, Nick, sometimes did not. And he was never clear about what I was actually using as my source of data, even though he saw me writing field notes and gave me permission to tape-record specific sessions of his class and to read some of his students' papers. When Adams and I met for lunch after the data had been collected, he mainly used that time to complain about university writing requirements, problems with students' grammar, and the overall decline in students' cultural literacy. However, the art history instructor, Professor Hall, who initially cautioned me that she taught "art history, not writing," warmed to me over time so that by mid-semester she called upon my expertise to help her design and respond to student assignments. She also asked me to tutor a student failing her course because of poor writing skills. When Hall gave me samples of her own professional articles, she realized in a reflexive way that she was not "born" knowing how to write art history and that her style had developed over time. She concluded that "if professional writers of art history go through a period of apprenticeship, then surely students need practice in how to write and think about the discipline as well" (70). By the end of the study, Hall accepted me as a literacy expert and altered her course syllabus and assignments quite dramatically to reflect what we had learned together. In spite of this success, throughout my field study in all the departments outside of English, I often felt more like someone who taught a service course than a scholar in an academic discipline.[6] Most of this feeling was due to other professors' lack of understanding about what takes place in a university writing course or in composition studies as a field.

Even my descriptions of other classrooms revealed my sense of holding an outsider position. Here is my cool version of my initial meeting of Professor Adams: "Professor Adams enters. He's tall and balding. After he places his tea mug at the head of the table to mark his place, he then leaves" (120). If Adams seemed to mark his territory in his political science seminar, in Hall's class I felt totally anonymous: "Adopting the perspective of a student, uninitiated into art history, I wildly write my field notes in semi-darkness. The noise of the slide machine weighs on the afternoon air, not enough to interfere with [Professor] Hall's voice but obvious enough to indicate there is a mechanical accompaniment to her talk" (58). Such descriptions helped locate me as dependent upon the insider information that my informants eventually shared with me because they were positioned as students in fields different from my own.

With my colleague Donna Qualley, whose prose-writing classroom I used as my entry into the study, I shared disciplinary training and educational philosophy. The time I spent researching her classroom ultimately resulted in her being the most receptive reader of the many drafts of my study. In my methodology section, I acknowledged that Donna read not only the many transcripts of interviews I had with her students, but also my field notes as well, correcting them as needed. For instance, she was willing to be described as a "nurturing" teacher, but did not see herself as a mother figure in her classroom (see *Academic Literacies* 24 ff). My conversations with Donna during my research made me aware of what I was best positioned to understand: how students read, write, and talk in other disciplines. Our conversations also underscored what was foreign and unfamiliar to me: particular disciplinary practices such as slide presentations, for example.

Donna's students, who readily folded me into their classroom as a "researcher and writing teacher," often wrote about how they made sense of my role(s). At one point Connie wrote in her collaborative journal about my interrupting their group work. She said that "it was good in a way" to have to explain things to me, but also that "much time was wasted" because the group felt they had to review everything "so that Elizabeth could understand it" (9). At another point, Angie included references to what she saw as my "thesis" in her response to Richard Rodriguez's essay. Angie wrote in her own piece called "Monkey Read, Monkey Think":

> Indeed we do borrow ideas from other people, and we even form some of our opinions by reading the opinions of other people. We see the world through our past experiences. An example would be Elizabeth's thesis on the recurrence of words and ideas in our class. The use of this concept was applied by many students after our workshop but not before. (*Academic Literacies* 22)

The observations of how others see us (whether accurate or not, since Angie had mistaken the topic of my study) afford good data on how we are positioned, data that we could obtain in no other way.

Both of my informants—Anna and Nick—read late drafts of my case studies about them, then commented on and corrected what I had written. While Nick commented on the product, saying that I had constructed "a fairly accurate portrait" of him, Anna said that she felt "weird" reading about herself because the case study was so "revealing." Revealing how the researcher works with his or her informants within specific contexts (in class, outside of class, during the writing process, after the study is over) is important because it shows how close the lens was held and how it shapes the reader's willingness to trust and believe the ethnographic account.

Positionality and the Narrative Voice

There are many rhetorical choices for inscribing positionality within an ethnography, so many options in fact that some ethnographers with traditional anthropological training feel attacked and confused by new ways of writing ethnographies. In contrast, other ethnographers welcome "hybrid" forms of "cultural representation" which reveal ethnography's potential as "modernist collage" and as "subversive critique" through a series of "dialogues, impositions and inventions" (Clifford 13–17). In order to draw attention to my positioning in relationship to my student informants and to the artificial act of writing about them, I included some of my personal journal entries in my final ethnography.[7] These entries, shown as quite distinct from my field notes, help establish the intersubjectivity between my informants' lives and mine. The following journal entries position me with respect to Anna:

> *Anna as both me and not me. Anna as an idealized younger version of myself, literate but not always articulate, artistic but seldom confident.*
>
> *As ethnographer I enter a world of subjectivity trying to put into words, what I cannot always say in words. . . .*
>
> *As a writer I worry over how to represent psychological time and space on the linear page. Where to begin and where to stop . . . how to break out of, or into, formal writing. In writing, my words serve as boundaries for her events, her images that struggle to remain mute. This translation of Anna's silent meaning becomes my own issue as I write.* (*Academic Literacies* 33)

The narrative voice of the journal entries established a tone of doubt, of tentativeness about both doing and writing ethnography. It constructed the ethnographer as a kind of secondary character, guiding the reader throughout the study. Not every researcher may want to disclose the messiness of making meaning of her data. My decision to contrast my field notes with personal journal entries disrupted any attempt at creating a confident, authoritative narrative persona. Instead, I both constructed and highlighted a narrative voice that relies on intuitive hunches and changing perspectives about the research. Linda Brodkey suggests that such a self-conscious and "critical" narrator helps the reader see that "all stories, including their own, are told from a vantage point" (71).

Locating oneself assertively and deliberately within a text reflects ethical, rhetorical, and theoretical choices on the part of the researcher. But not every reader will be convinced by or even be interested in this disclosure; some readers will think it self-indulgent to give too much attention to factors of positionality. The fear of constructing too large a role for the researcher is that such subjectivity may cause readers to question not only the textual voice of the researcher but the actual findings being reported about the "other"—data which are, of course, the reason for doing ethnography in the first place. This tension over unveiling the researcher's role is well illustrated in a review of my book, *Academic Literacies*, in which Gail Offen-Brown finds herself reacting quite strongly to my position within the text.[8] And as she begins to question my textual location, she also begins to question my ideas, data, and theories. She writes:

> The author's presence looms large: she is a self-aware artificer shaping the patterns of her informants' lives into a text; she is a participant in their lives, becoming their friend and, on request, offering pedagogical advice as a writing specialist to their professors. Because the author herself plays such a dynamic role, the reader's response to her persona and strong personal voice may influence the response to her ideas. (24–25)

Offen-Brown goes on to suggest that some parts of my book seemed to her at first "self-indulgent and irritating" because they called attention to the writer-narrator too much. And while she ultimately finds herself applauding my "honesty and intensity" as well as my "thoughtfulness and dedication," she may have—because of what she interprets as the invasive voice of the narrator—merely pushed the book aside.

Many contemporary ethnographers, particularly feminists concerned with representation of differentials in power structures, readily acknowledge their role as narrators writing about the other. They are conscious of *constructing*, not merely *representing*, the other as seen in more traditional foundationalist ethnography. Yet much agonizing continues over the professional risks involved in self-disclosure. John Van Maanen and others critique denuded ethnographers for foregrounding themselves while the findings about the other slide into the background. Margery Wolf, in agreement, cautions feminist ethnographers against toying with new ways of writing texts, suggesting that the techniques of reflexivity, subjectivity, and polyvocality which are now being celebrated by postmodernists may be used against women to devalue their work "as tentative and self-doubting" (135).[9]

Development of the tentative, self-doubting, reflective, and potentially intrusive narrator must be, then, a deliberate rhetorical choice as well as one that reflects the researcher's actual positioning within her field research. For example, while it is now possible for me to return to my earlier case studies on the revision process and be reflective about what was left out, it would be impossible to rewrite them in a reflexive way since I never collected data on differential issues of power and gender, personal relationships with my informants, and the ethical and political responsibilities of the research. At the time, recording subjective data was simply not part of my ongoing research process, and self-reflexivity was not then one of the goals of my study.

Positionality and Writing the Polyphonic Text

Closely connected with creating the self-scrutinizing and contemplative narrator is another rhetorical technique that reveals the researcher's location. As writing teachers, often times studying writing classrooms, we are in a situation to construct a polyvocal text by folding our informants' voices into our own. By drawing on the multiple written and spoken texts of our informants, the narrator can avoid to some degree colonizing or dominating the ethnographic narrative. We can open our texts for students to speak for themselves and create a polyphony of informant voices.

My student informant, Nick, offered a wide range of oral and written texts to choose from in shaping his case study. Where I based my earlier case studies only on assigned papers shared with me by my informants and on our taped interviews, with Nick I had additional data sources: his writing in two very different courses, prose writing and political science; his personal and academic journals; his peer group assessments and self-evaluations; my field notes from two of Nick's courses; tape transcripts of Nick talking in two courses; our weekly hourlong interviews for more than a year of working together; and many of Nick's drawings, scribbles, and caricatures completed in his classes. As researcher, I felt it my responsibility to stretch my text to include as many of Nick's texts as possible to illustrate his complicated literacies and to discuss how I gained access to them.

I wrote about Nick initially by marking the researcher-informant boundaries between us as formal and distant. I also recorded my sense of breakthrough and repositioning when he allowed me to read his personal journal, which recorded aspects of his everyday life that I would not otherwise have had access to.

Polyvocality in an ethnography creates a different kind of textual validity than one mediated by the univocal narrative. Since the reader—not just the researcher—has access to the textual data (at least part of it) that help inform theories and conclusions, he or she thereby assumes responsibility along with the researcher for figuring out how theories are being drawn. Sources for data triangulation also become clearer: when I suggest, for example, that writing for Nick is a kind of role playing in which he poses in many different garbs for different audiences, Nick's own texts corroborate this, as do the responses of others to his work. My theory of role playing is based on two sources: the feedback of his prose-writing teacher, who writes on one of Nick's drafts that "you are trying to keep me out, keep me at a distance with bravado and flash," and his peer group's request that he define his own "role" more clearly in one of his papers (94). And I have many data where Nick himself admits that writing is a kind of performance for him and that once a text is written, he never revises it. From many different sources—all readily available to the reader—I conclude that for Nick writing is a kind of staged performance.

The field of composition studies has developed what Gesa Kirsch and others call "methodological pluralism," with many of us now shuttling back and forth between literary studies and the social sciences, as well as drawing on the interdisciplinary resources of cognitive science, developmental psychology, feminist and critical studies, education, folklore, history, and anthropology. With such methodological diversity within a field, we need to be critically aware of the epistemological stances which guide our work. While neither polyvocality nor self-reflexivity nor methodological-theoretical disclosure—and, in fact, nothing—can ensure epistemological validity, the use of these discursive strategies more accurately conveys the dialogic way that ethnographers learn from their informants and from their field experiences. And in spite of some critiques of narcissistic self-representation in ethnographies, the stance of turning in upon ourselves as researchers seems a fitting one for those of us in composition studies who have always had to question our methods and methodologies. When ethnographic fieldworkers accept the challenge of researching literacy, it seems both ethically responsible and rhetorically sound for them to disclose their positions within the research process and in the resultant written text.

Notes

1. Since I drafted this chapter, another very useful collection of essays on gender and writing ethnography has been published. See *Women Writing Culture,* edited by Ruth Behar and Deborah Gordon.

2. This study, published by the New England Association of Teachers of English in *The Leaflet,* is based on my 1981 master's thesis of the same title.

3. My thanks to colleague Donna Qualley for her help in distinguishing between reflection and reflexivity. As she points out in "Writing and Reading as Reflexive Inquiry," to be reflective does not demand an "other," while to be reflexive demands both an other and some self-conscious awareness of the process of self-scrutiny.

4. For an insightful discussion of issues of writing about the other, see Indira Karamcheti's review of an ethnography wherein she questions the silencing of informant voices in anthropology, particularly non-Western voices. While I disagree with Karamcheti's conclusions, I find her discussion very helpful.

5. At the time I was conducting research for *Academic Literacies,* two books proved most useful in considering language differences among men and women: Francine Wattman Frank and Paula A. Treichler, *Language, Gender, and Professional Writing: Theoretical Approaches and Guidelines for Nonsexist Usage,* and Barrie Thorne, Cheris Kramarae, and Nancy Henley, *Language, Gender, and Society.* If I were doing this research today, I would also include Deborah Tannen's research on gender and conversational difference (e.g., *Gender and Discourse*).

6. The one exception to this was the field of outdoor education, a major that shared common epistemology and pedagogy with composition studies. I always felt quite at home in these classes.

7. My decision to keep a personal research journal throughout this project reflects my desire to separate some of the subjective and reflexive feelings I had from the data collected in my field notes. There is an obvious overlap or blur between these two kinds of records, and I found that keeping them in separate notebooks helped me sort through both kinds of data.

8. Overall the review is quite favorable, and I appreciate Offen-Brown's critique and the care with which she read my book.

9. In spite of Wolf's critique of subjectivity, polyvocality, and other experimental styles in writing ethnography, her own book, *A Thrice Told Tale,* is an example of a postmodern text. She gives three different versions of the same data. One tale is a short story, "The Hot Spell," based on the same experiences recorded in her field notes from Taiwan, which make up the second section of her book. The final telling is her academic article, "The Woman Who Didn't Become a Shaman," published in the *American Ethnologist.* In addition to her three tales, Wolf provides extended reflective commentary about all of her texts, which shows her own investment in reflexivity, subjectivity, and positionality.

Works Cited

Altorki, Soraya, and Camillia Fawzi El-Solh. *Arab Women in the Field: Studying Your Own Society.* Syracuse: Syracuse UP, 1988.

Behar, Ruth. "Dare We Say 'I'?: Bringing the Personal into Scholarship." *Chronicle of Higher Education* 29 June 1994: B1+.

———. *Translated Woman: Crossing the Border with Esperanza's Story.* Boston: Beacon, 1993.

Behar, Ruth, and Deborah Gordon, eds. *Women Writing Culture.* Berkeley: U of California P, 1995.

Bleich, David. "Ethnography and the Study of Literacy: Prospects for Socially Generous Research." *Into the Field: Sites of Composition Studies.* Ed. Anne Ruggles Gere. New York: MLA, 1993. 176–92.

Bridwell, Lillian. "Revising Strategies in Twelfth Grade Students' Transactional Writing." *Research in the Teaching of English* 14 (1980): 197–222.

Brodkey, Linda. "Writing Critical Ethnographic Narratives." *Anthropology and Education Quarterly* 18.2 (1987): 67–76.

Chiseri-Strater, Elizabeth. *Academic Literacies: The Public and Private Discourse of University Students.* Portsmouth: Boynton/Cook, 1991.

———. "Composing in Context: Revision Strategies of Freshman Writers." *Leaflet* 84.1 (1985): 35–44.

Clifford, James. "Introduction: The Pure Products Go Crazy." *The Predicament of Culture: Twentieth-Century Ethnography, Literature, and Art.* Cambridge: Harvard UP, 1988. 1–17.

Connors, Robert. "Dreams and Play: Historical Method and Methodology." *Methods and Methodology in Composition Research.* Ed. Gesa Kirsch and Patricia A. Sullivan. Carbondale: Southern Illinois UP, 1992. 15–36.

Fishman, Andrea. *Amish Literacy: What and How It Means.* Portsmouth: Heinemann, 1988.

Fleischer, Cathy. "Researching Teacher-Research: A Practitioner's Retrospective." *English Education* 26 (1994): 86–124.

Flower, Linda, and John R. Hayes. "The Cognition of Discovery: Defining a Rhetorical Problem." *College Composition and Communication* 31 (1980): 21–32.

Frank, Francine Wattman, and Paula A. Treichler. *Language, Gender, and Professional Writing: Theoretical Approaches and Guidelines for Nonsexist Usage.* New York: MLA, 1989.

Geertz, Clifford. *Works and Lives: The Anthropologist as Author.* Stanford: Stanford UP, 1988.

Karamcheti, Indira. "The Reproduction of Othering." *Women's Review of Books* June 1994: 7–8.

Keller, Evelyn Fox. *A Feeling for the Organism: The Life and Work of Barbara McClintock*. San Francisco: Freeman, 1983.

Kirsch, Gesa E. "Methodological Pluralism: Epistemological Issues." *Methods and Methodology in Composition Research*. Ed. Gesa Kirsch and Patricia A. Sullivan. Carbondale: Southern Illinois UP, 1992. 247–69.

Mishler, Elliot G. "Meaning in Context: Is There Any Other Kind?" *Harvard Educational Review* 49 (1979): 1–19.

Myerhoff, Barbara, and Jay Ruby. Introduction. *Crack in the Mirror: Reflexive Perspectives in Anthropology*. Ed. Jay Ruby. Philadelphia: U of Pennsylvania P, 1982. 3–35.

North, Stephen. *The Making of Knowledge in Composition: Portrait of an Emerging Field*. Upper Montclair: Boynton/Cook, 1987.

Offen-Brown, Gail. Rev. of *Academic Literacies*, by Elizabeth Chiseri-Strater. *The Quarterly* [National Center for the Study of Writing and Literacy] Spring 1992: 24–26.

Perl, Sondra. "Understanding Composing." *College Composition and Communication* 31 (1980): 363–69.

Perl, Sondra, and Nancy Wilson. *Through Teacher's Eyes: Portraits of Writing Teachers at Work*. Portsmouth: Heinemann, 1986.

Pianko, Sharon. "A Description of the Composing Processes of College Freshman Writers." *Research in the Teaching of English* 13 (1979): 5–22.

Powdermaker, Hortense P. *Stranger and Friend: The Way of an Anthropologist*. New York: Norton, 1966.

Qualley, Donna. "Writing and Reading as Reflexive Inquiry: A Reflexive Inquiry." Diss. U of New Hampshire, 1994.

Rabinow, Paul. *Reflections on Fieldwork in Morocco*. Berkeley: U of California P, 1977.

Rosaldo, Michelle. *Knowledge and Passion: Ilongot Notions of Self and Social Life*. New York: Cambridge UP, 1980.

Rosaldo, Renato. *Culture and Truth: The Remaking of Social Analysis*. Boston: Beacon P, 1989.

Rose, Mike. "Rigid Rules, Inflexible Plans, and the Stifling of Language: A Cognitivist Analysis of Writer's Block." *College Composition and Communication* 31 (1980): 389–400.

Sanjek, Roger, ed. *Fieldnotes: The Makings of Anthropology*. Ithaca: Cornell UP, 1990.

Shostak, Marjorie. *Nisa: The Life and Words of a !Kung Woman*. New York: Vintage, 1983.

Sommers, Nancy. "Revision Strategies of Student Writers and Experienced Adult Writers." *College Composition and Communication* 31 (1980): 378–88.

Tannen, Deborah. *Gender and Discourse.* New York: Oxford UP, 1994.

Taylor, Denny, and Catherine Dorsey-Gaines. *Growing Up Literate: Learning from Inner-City Families.* Portsmouth: Heinemann, 1988.

Thorne, Barrie, Cheris Kramarae, and Nancy Henley, eds. *Language, Gender, and Society.* Rowley: Newbury House, 1983.

Van Maanen, John. *Tales of the Field: On Writing Ethnography.* Chicago: U of Chicago P, 1988.

Wax, Rosalie H. *Doing Fieldwork: Warnings and Advice.* Chicago: U of Chicago P, 1971.

Wolf, Margery. *A Thrice Told Tale: Feminism, Postmodernism and Ethnographic Responsibility.* Stanford: Stanford UP, 1992.

8 Constructing Voices in Writing Research: Developing Participatory Approaches to Situated Inquiry

Ann M. Blakeslee
Eastern Michigan University

Caroline M. Cole and Theresa Conefrey
University of Illinois at Urbana–Champaign

This chapter is concerned with the occasions when composition researchers study academic communities that carry great intellectual prestige: for example, when they examine the discursive practices of scientists. In such situations, the views and approaches of composition researchers appear to be at odds with the intellectually sanctioned perspectives that drive science and much of academic inquiry. Thus researchers must often negotiate their own and their subjects' authority in the face of the subjects' expertise, prestige in academia, and high status in society in general. In carrying out such negotiations, composition researchers may face a dilemma: Should they make audible the voices of their subjects, even when they are dissonant with their own epistemological beliefs or those of contemporary humanistic and social scientific thinking? Or should the researchers mediate their subjects' voices so as to critique—or even silence—the voices and actions of subjects that may contradict their own and their field's beliefs? In this chapter we propose a middle ground: negotiating with subjects to find a common place where we can represent their voices fairly and critically while also allowing our subjects to critique our own methodology and interpretations.

More simply, we argue that two important notions of situated inquiry—voice and authority—cannot be reproduced without researcher mediation, and, as such, researchers need to create a space that allows for and encourages negotiation with subjects.[1] Our arguments underscore the need to reflect both on our voices and authority as researchers as well as on the voices and authority possessed by and attributed to our subjects. These arguments build on critical works in composition studies that address how the researcher positions herself as author in situated inquiry and how the researcher evokes her discipline in constructing research accounts (Bishop; Brodkey; Cintron; Clark and Doheny-Farina; Cross; Herndl). They also build on postmodern critiques of ethnography. For instance, Edward Bruner notes that works by Benson, Clifford and Marcus, Geertz, Rosaldo, and Turner and Bruner criticize the "objective, authoritative, politically neutral, usually white male observer standing somehow above and outside the text" (1). In sum, these scholars recommend a greater association and acknowledgment of the researcher with and in the text. Clifford Geertz, for example, suggests a need for "'Being There' authorially, palpably on the page" (23):

> The ability of anthropologists to get us to take what they say seriously has less to do with either a factual look at or air of conceptual elegance than it has with their capacity to convince us that what they say is a result of their having actually penetrated (or, if you prefer, being penetrated by), another form of life, of having, one way or another, truly "been there." And that, persuading us that this offstage miracle has occurred, is where the writing comes in. (4–5)

Statements such as Geertz's also suggest the significance of rhetorical strategy in constructing accounts of situated inquiry.

Another way of conceptualizing the concerns of postmodern scholars is expressed in Renato Rosaldo's satiric commentary on traditional ethnographies:

> Once upon a time, the Lone Ethnographer rode off into the sunset in search of "his native." After undergoing a series of trials, he encountered the object of his quest in a distant land. There he underwent his rite of passage by enduring the ultimate ordeal of "fieldwork." After collecting "the data," the Lone Ethnographer returned home and wrote a "true" account of "the culture." (30)

Few would dispute that the accounts we write of our fieldwork, whatever discipline we are from, can ever be unambiguously authoritative or true. Statements such as Rosaldo's encourage a concern with the researcher-researched relationship in situated work—more specifically, with issues of hegemony and appropriation in relation to the subjects we study. As researchers, we must therefore be alert to the ways we may appropriate our subjects, and we must try to minimize such appropriation. That is, we must be wary of how we interpret and use the voices of our subjects, and we must be alert to the potential consequences of our interpretations.

Scholars engaged in the debates concerning ethnographic research have proposed that we construct accounts that diffuse the colonial and dominating grip of researchers and portray the landscapes we study in more egalitarian ways (Clifford and Marcus). However, such proposals suggest that we can get beyond distinctions of power and authority when, in fact, we cannot. In contrast, we believe that the conditions and constraints of situated inquiry are features of such work that must be mapped and incorporated into our accounts. In addition, we believe that asymmetries in power and prestige in our relationships with our subjects must always be considered as we conduct our inquiries and construct our accounts. Given these factors, our concern is with proposing realistic alternatives for working out issues of authority and voice in our studies—alternatives that are responsive to our subjects, as well as to our research, ourselves, and our discipline.

In this chapter we argue, on the one hand, that it is naïve to assume that researchers can completely give up their authority in situated inquiry. After all, researchers formulate the initial research questions based on a theoretical and empirical understanding of the situation and then choose how to investigate those questions. Next, researchers are, as Margery Wolf suggests, responsible for sorting through the data and for evaluating the cultural significance of their observations for readers. As Sherna Gluck and Daphne Patai also point out, we cannot ignore that what reaches our auditors is a text produced, in large part, by researchers themselves (2). On the other hand, we argue that we should conceptualize our subjects not as passive objects of analysis, but as thinking subjects who may co-construct text and knowledge with us through negotiations and interactions, rationally and intellectually contributing to the research (see also Rosaldo).

Below we present ideas for implementing our proposed approach to situated inquiry. We suggest ways to construct voice cooperatively with our subjects, drawing on feminist and postmodern perspectives. We also incorporate, throughout our discussion, examples from the experiences of one of the authors (Blakeslee) who faced these issues in her research with physicists. These examples illustrate our recommendations.

Constructing Voice Collaboratively and Cooperatively

Interpretive Discrepancies

What initially prompted the questions that led to writing this chapter was an incident that occurred in Blakeslee's study of three physicists specializing in condensed matter theory.[2] Following her first published account of the physicists' rhetorical activities ("Readers and Authors"), her primary informant, Robert Swendsen, read, objected to, and openly challenged her claims about his group's collaborative activities.[3] The interpretive discrepancies that occurred in this situation, and the concerns they evoked for Blakeslee, led to a renegotiation between her and Swendsen of the arguments that were made and a subsequently revised account addressing the physicists' collaborative activities ("Collaboration").

The outcomes of Swendsen's disagreement with Blakeslee's account suggest features of the approach to situated inquiry that we propose in this chapter. We do not wish to suggest that Blakeslee's approach to handling the discrepancies can or should be generalized to other situations; it is impossible—as well as undesirable—to suggest one single procedure that researchers should follow. Rather, researchers must assess their sites of inquiry and strive to involve their subjects in the research to the fullest extent possible (e.g., by inviting and valuing their perspectives) and include them in ways that contribute productively to the inquiry.

Varying Definitions

Blakeslee's interactions with Swendsen after he responded to her account of his collaboration offer an example of how situated inquiry may become a cooperative endeavor through the combined agency of researcher and subject. In her *Technical Communication Quarterly* article, Blakeslee argued that the exchange that occurred when Swendsen's group asked three scientists to read and respond to their paper was a collaboration. She so labeled the exchange because of the extent to which the scientists' responses influenced the shape of the physicists' claims. That is, the physicists revised their arguments extensively on the basis of concerns raised by these readers, explaining that if they had not addressed these concerns, their ideas about the efficiency of the Monte Carlo method of simulating biological molecules may have been viewed as not credible within the communities they were addressing. On the basis of the foregoing observations, Blakeslee made the following claims:

> The outcome of these actions suggests ways in which authors may extend their collaborative networks to support their text production and inventional processes and to assist them in generating new knowledge that will gain the adherence of their auditors. The physicists used the knowledge they acquired from these collaborative interactions in a strategic manner to construct a persuasive account of their work. ("Readers and Authors" 24)

When Swendsen initially read Blakeslee's article, he felt that he had been misunderstood. He objected to how she applied the term "collaboration," arguing that the notion did not at all characterize the interactions in which he had engaged with the three scientists. That is, the connection Blakeslee drew between the physicists' interactions with their readers and their collaborative activities was not one that Swendsen would have drawn. In addition, he disagreed with the breadth Blakeslee assigned to the notion of collaboration.

Ironically, this disagreement is not unlike the discrepancies that exist in how collaboration is defined, more generally, in the field of composition. For example, in their book, *Singular Texts/Plural Authors*, Lisa Ede and Andrea Lunsford illustrate the variations in how writing scholars define collaboration by citing, among others, Nancy Allen, Dianne Atkinson, Meg Morgan, Teresa Moore, and Craig Snow. Allen et al. jointly define collaboration as an activity that entails the production of a shared document, substantive interaction among members of a group, and shared responsibility for the document. Deborah Bosley, another author Ede and Lunsford cite, defines collaborative writing as two or more people working together to produce a document. James Paradis, David Dobrin, and Richard Miller, also cited, examine as instances of collaboration documents assigned and edited by a supervisor and researched and drafted by a staff member. This conception of collaboration is broadened by Lee Odell to encompass the planning of documents. Similarly, Stephen Doheny-Farina and Paul Anderson each extend the definition to encompass the individual planning and drafting of a document that is then collaboratively revised (Doheny-Farina), as well as the peer critique of a co-worker's drafts (Anderson). Finally, some authors, such as James Reither, conflate collaboration and writing. This latter definition, by encompassing all of the social and contextual factors that may influence a writer and by suggesting that no writing occurs in isolation, supports social constructionist views of writing.

Of course, for interpretive purposes, any of these definitions requires that we explicate constituent terms such as "substantive," "shared," and "interaction." In addition, as Ede and Lunsford point out, each definition of collaboration depends on often unstated definitions of writing that tend to reflect ideological assumptions (15). They say that "the shifting and conflicting nature of the definitions revolving around the term *collaborative writing* seems to call not for simplification or standardization but for a Burkean complexifying" (16). With social constructionist theory encouraging complexity in understanding collaboration, writing researchers now possess an extensive repertoire of definitions of the notion that can be drawn into their studies.

Challenging Breadth

Blakeslee, in her paper, viewed collaboration as that activity contributing in a substantive way to the construction of a text, thereby extending the definitions presented by Allen et al. and Anderson. In response to this more inclusive use of collaboration, Swendsen said that "there is a question of whether the definition is useful or not, and I don't think the definition that I'm hearing, as being used in rhetoric, is useful because it's all-inclusive" (Personal interview, 12 Nov. 1993). Swendsen's definition of the term was much more restrictive. He said that for him "collaboration is two or more people working together to do an experiment or to perform a calculation to solve a problem. . . . That's basically the distinction—having someone work with you to solve the problem" (Personal interview, 1 July 1993). This was not the case, he said, in the situation with the three scientists who responded to the Swendsen group's writing: "The work was already done, and we wanted a response. Jim made the most important contribution but didn't actually help to solve the problem" (Personal interview, 1 July 1993). In other words, Swendsen distinguishes contributions made through interactions with colleagues from those made by co-workers engaged with one another in an investigation. Consequently, his definition of collaboration excludes the type of interaction in which the physicists engaged with the three scientists who read their paper:

> [Y]ou have a conversation . . . [l]et's say the conversation with Jim as an example. He wasn't a collaborator on this work, but he gave us valuable input in reaction to what we'd done. His purpose was not to solve the problem, and it wasn't, you know; what he said was not something that went towards solving the problem. . . . It was very valuable in terms of communication and telling us what our paper looked like and how it would be read. So that is something . . . which we acknowledge under useful conversations, and, uh, so that will go into the acknowledgment of the paper as something useful in some way to the paper—through conversation. (Personal interview, 12 Nov. 1993)

In light of these views, Swendsen considered Blakeslee's interpretations surprising and problematic:

> Well, you weren't addressing the paper to me. Your audience in this paper is not scientists. I think if you told me this was for publication in *Scientific American,* I would be, I would be quite surprised, and a bit upset, because I would, you know, foresee the flack you would get from scientists. Actually, I mean, when I think about it, I am surprised that the, that the word [collaboration] is used that widely without some other word being used in the, you know, to describe the more narrow classes. (Personal interview, 12 Nov. 1993)

An Alternative Conception

In subsequent discussions with Blakeslee, Swendsen offered what he believed to be a workable solution to these differing perspectives on collaboration. He suggested that as an alternative to using "collaboration" broadly defined, researchers in composition could employ various notions to describe a variety of interactions. Swendsen said that this would allow more apt descriptions of what occurs when scientists confer with one another to solve problems and to co-produce texts:

> You know, if you had a different word to describe that, that would be less surprising to me. I mean, you've just got this all-inclusive word that distinguishes nothing and it seems it makes it more difficult to talk about what's going on. I would have been less surprised if you had ten or twenty different, well, five or ten different words to describe different kinds of interactions, distinctions that would clarify different kinds of relationships, which doesn't seem to be the case. (Personal interview, 12 Nov. 1993)

Blakeslee found Swendsen's initial recommendation to use as many as twenty distinct terms cumbersome. However, the possibility of developing five to ten notions that could help to define such interactions more precisely seemed reasonable. As a result, she viewed his suggestion as a potential contribution to her field of knowledge. After careful consideration of his suggestions, she argued, finally, for distinguishing the various types of exchanges that may influence scientific authors.

Collaborative Negotiation

The interpretive discrepancies that occurred in this situation, and the concerns they evoked for the researcher, led to a collaborative renegotiation between Blakeslee and Swendsen of the claims that were being made and to a subsequent, revised account of Swendsen's rhetorical activities (Blakeslee, "Collaboration"). Specifically, by engaging

Swendsen more directly in the research, Blakeslee provided an opportunity for him to assist in constructing text and meaning for a subsequent account. In this second account, Blakeslee adheres to her original conclusion that social interactions between writers and readers play a central role in scientific writing and that the conflicts and tensions that may arise in these interactions can lead to better ideas and can advance knowledge in a field. (This is also true of the participatory approach to situated inquiry that we propose in this chapter.) However, whereas Blakeslee concluded her first paper by stating that relationships between authors and their readers are inherently social and ongoing—the rhetorical process in science entails an ongoing collaboration with readers, both actual and potential ("Readers and Authors" 32)—in her subsequent account she did not describe these interactions as collaborations ("Collaboration"). In short, she reconsidered her definition and use of collaboration because of her experiences with Swendsen. These experiences, and their outcomes, offer one example of how text and knowledge may be co-constructed when we view our subjects as partners in our inquiry. That is, we present this example for its illustrative value; it is not meant to suggest that researchers should reformulate their arguments and concepts every time disagreements occur. Whatever actions are taken in such situations must be determined thoughtfully by the researcher.

A Corrective to Silencing Subjects

Participatory and Cooperative Inquiry: Recuperating the Voices of Our Subjects

Now that we have considered an example of how situated studies can become more participatory, we wish to describe more explicitly the features we envision in such an approach to situated inquiry. First of all, we believe that we must make the voices of our subjects audible. When we foreground our own voices and interpretive schemes in our texts, often along with the voices and interpretive schemes of our disciplines, we risk silencing our subjects. We also risk losing the sociohistorical context of the practices being investigated if we impose our own or our field's frameworks too rigidly on the voices of our subjects. This is also a risk if we are constrained too severely by disciplinary and institutional strictures. The voices of our subjects should take precedence over an imposed or preestablished theoretical or rhetorical scheme (Anderson and Jack 18–19). This becomes particularly significant when we are the only voice—or the only link—that our subjects have to our world and to our audiences.[4]

As a corrective to silencing our subjects, we envision a research process that is more cooperative in character, as illustrated by the example of Blakeslee's research with Swendsen. We believe that situated studies of writing should be enterprises in which subjects act as partners with researchers during data collection and beyond. In adopting such a perspective, we must recognize the choices inherent in such research. At times we may be influenced or even forced to make choices that compromise the perspectives of our subjects as we interpret our data and as we consider our audiences—editors, referees, colleagues, funding and policy officials, reviewers of our tenure cases, and so forth. However, we are not, nor can we afford to be disinterested, impartial, and value-free observers.

Rethinking Traditional Dichotomies

A participatory conception of situated inquiry requires us to rethink the traditional dichotomy between researcher as active subject and researched as passive object of analysis (Cintron). As Rosaldo says, we must now "grapple with the realizations" that our "objects of analysis are also analysing subjects who critically interrogate ethnographers—their writing, their ethics and their politics" (21). Mary Catherine Bateson, likewise, comments on the need to reconceptualize the traditional researched-researcher dichotomy, noting,

> These resonances between the person and the professional are the source of both insight and error. You avoid mistakes and distortions not so much by trying to build a wall between the observer and the observed as by observing the observer—observing yourself—as well, and bringing the personal issues into consciousness. (161)

As researchers we must exhibit a greater willingness to learn *with* rather than from or about those we are studying. We need to view our subjects as rationally cooperating with us and contributing to our work. In short, we need to replace the old idea of describing culture in terms of our own schemes and categories with a new task, enabling conversations across the researcher-subject divide (see also Sullivan, this volume).

The increased involvement of subjects in our inquiry, we believe, will result in our adopting new roles as researchers. Rather than being arbiters who, in formulating interpretations, cast judgments on and exercise authority over the sites and subjects we study, we will become collaborators and mediators engaging with and involving our subjects more fully in our research and in our writing. These new roles, we believe, will facilitate researcher-subject cooperation, along with the selective processes we engage in to construct our accounts.

Authority and Voice: Achieving a Balance

The ideas we have presented above may seem contradictory to the claims we made earlier about the inevitability of the researcher's authority determining the direction of inquiry. In addition, we stated earlier our desire to acknowledge the actual conditions and constraints of ethnographic text production. Although we advocate acknowledging such conditions, which we take to include the authority of the researcher, we do not intend for such authority to determine completely the course and direction of our research so that it silences our subjects. In conducting studies like Blakeslee's, researchers may feel the need to assert their own authority in the face of their subjects' expertise and prestige (e.g., initially in her work with Swendsen, Blakeslee felt a need to demonstrate both her intelligence and her credibility as a scholar). However, researchers should not assert their authority at the expense of the authority or voices of their subjects. What we suggest, instead, is striving to balance the four elements of situated inquiry suggested by Geoffrey Cross.[5] For Cross, these elements include the research community, the researcher, the data, and our subjects (124). Although acknowledging the researcher's authority would seem to throw these elements out of balance, we wish to suggest that a disruption in balance need not occur and that our authority as researchers need not silence our subjects.

First, our texts are always embedded in issues of authority, power, and ideology, no matter how much we try to mitigate these issues (e.g., by involving others in their construction). Ethnographic texts present a particular and partial conception of reality that may be our own, our discipline's, our subjects', or, more likely, some combination of these and other influences. Carl Herndl, for example, argues for the need to recognize how the demands exerted by the institutions within which we work influence our discourse (331). He says of ethnographies, "As written texts they are part of an institutionally maintained discourse authorized not by their relationship to fact, but by their participation in the rhetoric shared by their community of readers" (322). As researchers engaged in situated inquiry, we maintain some amount of authority in relation to our subjects and to our sites of inquiry. We also possess some amount of expertise concerning the issues we plan to investigate. We enter the scenes of our research with theoretical perspectives that enable us to frame questions and to determine the most suitable course for our inquiry. Finally, we decide, ultimately, what information and artifacts are salient, how to interpret them, and what arguments to present to our peers. These choices are not unencumbered by institutional or ideological influences.

There is also a second side to this issue of authority. In *Women's Ways of Knowing,* Mary Belenky, Blythe Clinchy, Nancy Goldberger, and Jill Tarule say they let their subjects speak for themselves in their work. However, these scholars also acknowledge the processes of selection, contextualization, and filtering that occur in all ethnographies. Such selective processes, they say, allow them to amalgamate their subjects' voices—to look for common paths, experiences, strands, and themes— and to generalize from their diverse stories (55, 56, 88). Certainly, the selective processes Belenky et al. describe are, at least in part, the domain of the researcher. However, it would be naïve to assume that our subjects have no influence on these processes. In fact, subjects choose how to locate themselves and how to reveal themselves at any cultural moment. In addition, cultural pressures are always at work to position subjects and to shape what they disclose about themselves, leaving to researchers—oftentimes unassisted—the task of selecting what to represent. Therefore, in our research we must acknowledge not only the researcher's but also our subjects' authority, presence, and authorial signatures.

Constraints in Viewing Subjects as Participants

Ethical dilemmas and conflicting values may get in the way of realizing a more participatory approach to situated inquiry, making the principles we outlined above difficult to implement. As Gluck and Patai point out, seldom do our informants become true partners in the research process (2). For example, researchers may think that subjects have morally reprehensible values. In such cases, cooperation of the sort we envision would be extremely difficult. Dilemmas may also occur when researchers disagree with their subjects on crucial issues, or when researchers interpret their subjects' experiences very differently than their subjects do. Blakeslee's differing interpretation of Swendsen's experiences with the three readers, which caused Swendsen to feel misunderstood, is an example of such a dilemma. Similarly, Katherine Borland, in her account of constructing an oral history of her grandmother's life, addresses how she interpreted her grandmother's experiences much differently from the way in which the woman saw them herself. In such situations, researchers must somehow reconcile their competing understandings.

Time Constraints

It may also be, in some cases, that our subjects simply are not interested in collaborating with us. Or, if they are interested, they may lack enough time to participate with us more fully. This occurred in Blakeslee's research with Swendsen. After hearing Swendsen's concerns, Blakeslee decided that they warranted her consideration. Her response was similar to Borland's in that she recognized that her subjects' interpretations of events could contribute to her own understanding of them (Borland 71). Also like Borland, Blakeslee recognized the need to encourage an exchange of ideas—to grant interpretive space and to stretch to understand her subjects' perspectives (Borland 73–74). Specifically, Blakeslee became more sensitive to the uses of the term collaboration in her field. She also became concerned with considering Swendsen's and his field's conceptions of the notion. These concerns led her to invite Swendsen to co-author an article in which he could articulate his concerns about the claims Blakeslee had made about his group's collaborative activities.

Swendsen was willing to engage in such a project. He expressed his willingness to co-author a followup article in which he and Blakeslee would address the discrepancies in their thinking on collaboration and articulate their perspectives on the reasons for those discrepancies. However, as the deadline for the article approached, Swendsen realized that he would be unable to engage in this task to the extent that he wished (he had recently taken an administrative post at his university). Thus Swendsen agreed to substitute two extended informal interviews with Blakeslee for his part of the co-authorship. In these interviews, which still enabled Swendsen to participate in Blakeslee's research to a greater, albeit different extent, he offered input on his own and his field's views of collaboration. Blakeslee, in turn, revised her research goals to consider how Swendsen's perspectives could improve her understanding of the issues she was exploring.

Discrepancies in Expectations

Besides lacking time to collaborate with us, our subjects may also possess very different expectations about our projects, as well as about their roles in our research. They may end up feeling misunderstood, or even betrayed and violated by our statements about them or by the conclusions we draw, and thus insist that we omit various statements or perhaps even abstain from publishing our accounts. Borland addresses the stages that occur when, as researchers, we are delicately poised between the text we wish to produce and our relationships with our subjects.

During these stages, she says, conflicts may occur between our responsibilities to our informants and our need to interpret our findings. In short, our purposes in foregrounding, pointing out, and drawing connections between certain findings may differ from the intentions of our subjects. When such situations occur, we owe it to our subjects to consider their perspectives and to attempt to address and negotiate our differences.

Negotiating Discrepancies

Almost all researchers will experience one or more of the dilemmas we have articulated. Responsive researchers will attempt to address these dilemmas; however, efforts to respond may sometimes fall short. We wish that we could offer solutions for such circumstances, but in many instances they will need to be dealt with on a case-by-case basis. The very nature of the dilemmas—and their entanglement in the complexity of human relations—suggests that they defy easy solutions. Perhaps the best we can do is to make sure that as researchers we possess the proper disposition for conducting situated inquiry equitably with respect to our subjects. A participatory approach to situated inquiry works best when both researcher and subject are open-minded, engaged, and willing to learn from each other.

When we, as researchers, apply our own frameworks and perspectives too strictly, or when our subjects are unwilling to participate in our inquiry beyond their involvement as informants, our efforts to be inclusive may fail. Therefore, we must strive to approach our subjects and to interact with them in a manner that encourages a two-way exchange. As Kathryn Anderson and Dana Jack suggest, we should focus on our interactions with our subjects rather than merely on the task of gathering information from them (23). Here we may have something to gain from feminist approaches. Such approaches create conditions in which subjects are freer to take responsibility in research projects and in which researchers place themselves in a subjective, as opposed to an objective, position in relation to subjects. Such a stance, we believe, improves chances for a more truly dialogic relationship between ourselves and our subjects (see also Minister 36).

Contribution of Feminist Theory and Perspectives

Because of their inclusive character, feminist approaches to oral history and situated research suggest possibilities for obtaining more balanced perspectives of our subjects and for mitigating some of the dilemmas discussed. Feminist approaches support a concern with "unsilencing" subjects, particularly those who may be marginalized in some way from the "dominant" or mainstream culture. These approaches look for ways to include subjects' voices. Many of the strategies feminists offer for achieving this goal are consistent with a participatory approach to situated inquiry. These strategies include, but are certainly not limited to, the following:

- Writing collaboratively with subjects
- Asking subjects for clarification when necessary or possible
- Having subjects read the research to see whether they hear and recognize their voices in the work
- Negotiating and modifying those parts of the texts that subjects find questionable or inaccurate
- Presenting and maintaining subjects' "expertness" in their lives and in their ideas
- Hesitating to promote oneself too strongly as researcher, interpreter, and disseminator of knowledge

Feminist perspectives also advocate an antihierarchical approach to research in which subjects are not seen as objects to be studied, observed, or written about, but as co-originators of our inquiry (Rich 135). By allowing subjects to speak for themselves and to clarify or correct our interpretations of their ideas, we reduce the possibility of misnaming, misrepresenting, burying, or confusing our subjects' voices and perspectives. We wish to distinguish here the act of encouraging co-construction—with which these approaches and our own are concerned primarily—from the act of foregrounding it, as is suggested by theories of social construction. Social construction encompasses co-construction, which entails the notion of individuals deliberately and consciously engaged with one another in the act of making meaning, along with a range of other actions and influences.

Feminist perspectives encourage researchers, as well as readers, to acknowledge the biases that exist as we conduct and read accounts of situated inquiry; they also challenge those biases and their origins. For example, feminist perspectives are concerned with the influence of gender on researchers and acknowledge the gendered qualities of the research site, the researcher, and subjects. Along these lines Sharon Traweek writes, "The lab is a man's world, and I try to show why that is the case particularly in high energy physics: how the practice of physics is engendered, how laboratory work is masculinized" (16). Another example of how feminist perspectives challenge our biases is offered by feminist standpoint theory, which helps researchers and readers recognize that opinions and beliefs are culturally, socially, and politically situated (Harding). When research is conducted by ethnographers located in a dominant culture and possessing agendas associated with that culture, the information the researchers obtain will always be partial and perhaps even distorted. Our readers, however, will not always be able to recognize such distortions. Feminist standpoint theory offers a mechanism by which we can see things that those immersed solely in a dominant culture, by position or choice, cannot. This theory also encourages using current methodology for feminist goals: to write women's (and other marginalized individuals' or groups') experiences and voices back into society. By encouraging us to take women's and other subjects' locations and perspectives into account, feminist standpoint theory prompts us to account for the way we portray situations, events, and ideas.

Finally, feminist perspectives encourage approaching our research with a view toward multiplicity. Margery Wolf writes that when "human behavior is the data, a tolerance for ambiguity, multiplicity, and instability is essential" (129). Wolf also notes that there is an increasing blur between our responsibilities to our readers and to our informants (136–37). However, we wish to note that such tolerance of ambiguity and instability does not need to conflict with a balance of input from researcher, subject, data, and community. The goal of situated inquiries need not be unified, univocal accounts; instead, we should concern ourselves with writing into our accounts the experiences and voices of our subjects, no matter how multivocal, in a manner that is responsible to those subjects as well as to our readers and to ourselves (Ganguly). In sum, increasing our tolerance for multiplicity, as Wolf suggests, can assist us in taking into account women's and other subjects' locations and perspectives. Perhaps, then, Wolf's words are meant to sound the alert that without us our subjects may not have voices to correct or clarify what we say. Feminist approaches—recognizing and welcoming polyvocal, messy, nonlinear interpretations and presentations of data—can serve as impetuses for opening the boundaries of what is considered acceptable and accountable ethnographic research.

The Form of Our Situated Accounts

As suggested by many of the feminist and postmodern perspectives surveyed here, rhetorical strategy—how we textualize our findings—is yet another important concern in realizing a more participatory approach to situated inquiry. This includes the form of situated accounts, most often narrative because it is conducive to telling the lived experiences of our subjects. Simply put, stories are fundamental to how we live in and experience the world and how we write about it. Linda Brodkey supports this claim, saying that "narratives are one way to study how people imagine life to be, for themselves and for others" (46). She also says that "the most important lesson to be learned from ethnographic fieldwork is that experience is not—indeed, cannot be—reproduced in speech or writing, and must instead be narrated" (26). All ethnographies begin in stories (32), she argues, and inevitably deal with the narratives of lived experience (46). Extending these ideas, we present the following as a final argument: that considering the narrative style of our research allows us to examine how we position ourselves in relation to our subjects as well as how we construct our own and our subjects' voices in our accounts.

Through narration we make sense of our own experiences and lives as well as the experiences and lives of those we study. More specifically, narrative is the means by which we interact with and come to understand our subjects. For example, Alasdair MacIntyre notes that, because we live out and understand our lives in terms of narratives, the form of narrative is most appropriate for understanding the lives of others as well (197). Similarly, Jerome Bruner observes that we organize our experiences and our memories mainly in the form of narrative— "stories, excuses, myths, reasons for doing and not doing" (4). Stories are both rooted in society and experienced and performed in cultural settings. They bridge personal, social, and cultural divides. Further, stories allow us to recreate the lives and voices of our subjects more authentically.

Narrative form, however, is not without limits. In textualizing our research, we incorporate our subjects' narratives into accounts that are situated in the sociohistorical contexts of the settings we examine, as well as in the contexts of our intellectual communities. A limitation here is that all such narratives "are deeply entailed by disciplinary commitments, their validity limited therefore by other disciplinary interpretations of an experience, and by other experiences" (Brodkey 47). Likewise, Herndl cautions that, as written texts, ethnographies "are part of an institutionally maintained discourse" (322). In short, our accounts, of necessity, respond to the demands of the institutions, communities, and cultures within which we work (331).

Given these constraints, it is imperative that our reinscriptions of the stories of our subjects, to the extent possible, not be isolated and autonomous acts. As Brodkey recommends, our most urgent concern should be with how best to represent the relationship between ourselves, our methods, and our subjects (30). One alternative here is to involve ourselves to an even greater extent with our subjects as we engage in these processes. Such engagement can lead to a dispersal of our authority as researchers, making ethnography a more egalitarian endeavor and lessening the distance between ourselves and our subjects. Observer and observed can then learn from each other in the co-construction of reality through shared and negotiated understanding (Crapanzano; Krauss and Fussell).

Conclusion

In this chapter, we have viewed voice and authority as constructed phenomena and as features of situated inquiry that can never be reproduced without researcher mediation—and preferably negotiation between researchers and subjects. Our arguments underscore the need for self-conscious reflection on our voices as researchers as well as on the voices we give to our subjects. On the one hand, the researcher formulates research questions based on his or her understanding of the situation, chooses how to investigate those questions, and ultimately decides what data are valid and how to interpret and present those data. Therefore, we argue that it is naïve to assume that the researcher can give up his or her authority completely. On the other hand, we also argue that we should conceptualize our subjects not as passive objects, but as thinking subjects who may co-construct text and knowledge with us through negotiations.

In presenting subjects' responses to and ideas on the issues addressed in our research, we are not suggesting that our subjects represent the final authority on those issues. However, we are suggesting that a productive way to extend our understanding of the rhetorical issues under investigation may be to combine our *in situ* examinations with thoughtful considerations of the perspectives possessed by our subjects. This is our central claim. We believe, for example, that the tensions that occurred in Blakeslee's research with Swendsen are not uncommon in situated studies. We also believe that such tensions may become even more common if we seek to involve our subjects, increasingly, in our work. Subjects, understandably, are sensitive to the ways in which they are portrayed in our accounts and to the conclusions we draw about their behavior (Clifford and Marcus; Liebow; Rabinow; Whyte; Wolf). But if there is a difference between our informants' understanding of a notion and our own, we owe it to our informants to consider those differences thoughtfully and to determine how they may influence our conceptions and interpretations. In other words, we believe that the tensions that may arise between researchers and their subjects can be productive as well as instructive. The lesson they offer is that we must constantly reflect on and question our methods, our observations, and our interpretations.

In this chapter we have argued that we should view our subjects as contributing constituencies who engage actively in our studies and in our textualizations of our findings. We have also argued that we should be sensitive to interpreting our data in ways that do not perpetuate dominant-culture interests, especially when such interests may be at the expense of those we study. By incorporating these concerns into our work, we can diffuse further the researcher-object dichotomy, the hallmark of traditional anthropological inquiry and a central concern of postmodern theorists and feminist scholars. However, we must also bear in mind that the participatory approaches to situated inquiry that we develop will not be uniform across situations. Rather, the highly contextualized, situated nature of such inquiry will require us to consider these issues anew in each setting we enter.

Notes

1. The subjects we are most concerned with in this chapter are those who are in a more powerful or authoritative position with respect to the researcher.

2. In her study, Blakeslee was a participant-observer in the group of physicists for six months, during which time she attended all meetings of the group, interviewed each group member, and collected and analyzed all written documents produced by the group. She focused on the writing done by the group as well as on the physicists' work in general, because she views the two as interrelated. The group was working on the computer simulation of biological molecules, using a simulation methodology called Monte Carlo. Another methodology, molecular dynamics, had been the preferred method for conducting these simulations in biology and chemistry since 1980, when an article by two chemists claimed that it was more efficient than Monte Carlo. The physicists wished to challenge this claim. However, to do so they had to make their claims acceptable to unfamiliar audiences consisting of biologists and chemists. Physicists Djamal Bouzida, Shankar Kumar, and Robert Swendsen wrote and published the paper "Efficient Monte Carlo Methods for the Computer Simulation of Biological Molecules" while Blakeslee conducted her study of the group; the physicists' paper appeared in *Physical Review A*.

3. In this and other accounts resulting from this research, the actual names of the physicists are used. This decision was taken by the subjects, in

consultation with the researcher, because they felt they would be identifiable to their peers even with pseudonyms, given the highly visible nature of their work. Also, they expressed a belief that their positions as physicists were secure and therefore would not be threatened by accounts of their discursive activities.

4. In other words, because our subjects are seldom members of the communities that we address, we speak for them in these settings.

5. The balance we recommend is difficult to describe adequately; however, we attempt such a description here because we believe it to be important.

Works Cited

Allen, Nancy J., Dianne Atkinson, Meg Morgan, Teresa Moore, and Craig Snow. "What Experienced Collaborators Say about Collaborative Writing." *Journal of Business and Technical Communication* 1 (1987): 70–90.

Anderson, Kathryn, and Dana C. Jack. "Learning to Listen: Interview Techniques and Analysis." Gluck and Patai 11–26.

Anderson, Paul V. "What Survey Research Tells Us about Writing at Work." Odell and Goswami 3–83.

Bateson, Mary Catherine. *With a Daughter's Eye.* New York: William Morrow, 1984.

Belenky, Mary F., Blythe M. Clinchy, Nancy R. Goldberger, and Jill M. Tarule. *Women's Ways of Knowing: The Development of Self, Voice, and Mind.* New York: Basic Books, 1986.

Benson, Paul, ed. *Anthropology and Literature.* Urbana: U of Illinois P, 1993.

Bishop, Wendy. "I-Witnessing in Composition: Turning Ethnographic Data into Narratives." *Rhetoric Review* 11 (1992): 147–58.

Blakeslee, Ann M. "Readers and Authors: Fictionalized Constructs or Dynamic Collaborations?" *Technical Communication Quarterly* 2 (1993): 23–35.

———. "Collaboration in Science: An Articulation of Alternative Perspectives." *Collaboration in Technical Communication: Research Perspectives.* Ed. Rebecca E. Burnett and Ann Hill Duin. Hillsdale: Erlbaum, forthcoming.

Borland, Katherine. "'That's Not What I Said': Interpretive Conflict in Oral Narrative Research." Gluck and Patai 63–75.

Bosley, Deborah. "A National Study of the Uses of Collaborative Writing in Business Communications Courses among Members of the ABC." Diss. Illinois State U, 1989.

Bouzida, Djamal, Shankar Kumar, and Robert H. Swendsen. "Efficient Monte Carlo Methods for the Computer Simulation of Biological Molecules." *Physical Review A* 45 (1992): 8894–901.

Brodkey, Linda. "Writing Ethnographic Narratives." *Written Communication* 4 (1987): 25–50.

Bruner, Edward M. "Introduction: The Ethnographic Self and the Personal Self." *Anthropology and Literature.* Ed. Paul J. Benson. Urbana: U of Illinois P, 1993. 1–26.

Bruner, Jerome. "The Narrative Construction of Reality." *Critical Inquiry* 18 (1991): 1–21.

Cintron, Ralph. "Wearing a Pith Helmet at a Sly Angle: Or, Can Writing Researchers Do Ethnography in a Postmodern Era?" *Written Communication* 10 (1993): 371–412.

Clark, Gregory, and Stephen Doheny-Farina. "Public Discourse and Personal Expression: A Case-Study in Theory-Building." *Written Communication* 7 (1990): 456–81.

Clifford, James, and George E. Marcus, eds. *Writing Culture: The Poetics and Politics of Ethnography.* Berkeley: U of California P, 1986.

Crapanzano, Vincent. *Tuhami: Portrait of a Moroccan.* Chicago: U of Chicago P, 1980.

Cross, Geoffrey A. "Ethnographic Research in Business and Technical Writing: Between Extremes and Margins." *Journal of Business and Technical Communication* 8 (1994): 118–34.

Doheny-Farina, Stephen. "Writing in an Emerging Organization: An Ethnographic Study." *Written Communication* 3 (1986): 158–85.

Ede, Lisa, and Andrea Lunsford. *Singular Texts/Plural Authors: Perspectives on Collaborative Writing.* Carbondale: Southern Illinois UP, 1990.

Ganguly, Keya. "Accounting for Others: Feminism and Representation." *Women Making Meaning: New Feminist Directions in Communication.* Ed. Lana Rakow. London: Routledge, 1992. 60–79.

Geertz, Clifford. *Works and Lives: The Anthropologist as Author.* Stanford: Stanford UP, 1988.

Gluck, Sherna B., and Daphne Patai, eds. *Women's Words: The Feminist Practice of Oral History.* New York: Routledge, 1991.

Harding, Sandra. *Whose Science? Whose Knowledge? Thinking from Women's Lives.* New York: Columbia UP, 1991.

Herndl, Carl G. "Writing Ethnography: Representation, Rhetoric, and Institutional Practices." *College English* 53 (1991): 320–32.

Krauss, Robert M., and Susan R. Fussell. "Mutual Knowledge and Communicative Effectiveness." *Intellectual Teamwork: Social and Technological Foundations of Cooperative Work.* Ed. Jolene Galegher, Robert E. Kraut, and Carmen Egido. Hillsdale: Erlbaum, 1990. 111–45.

Liebow, Elliot. *Tell Them Who I Am: The Lives of Homeless Women.* New York: Free P, 1993.

MacIntyre, Alasdair. *After Virtue: A Study in Moral Theory.* Notre Dame: U of Notre Dame P, 1980.

Minister, Kristina. "A Feminist Frame for the Oral History Interview." Gluck and Patai 27–41.

Odell, Lee. "Beyond the Text: Relations between Writing and Social Context." Odell and Goswami 249–80.

Odell, Lee, and Dixie Goswami, eds. *Writing in Nonacademic Settings.* New York: Guilford, 1985.

Paradis, James, David Dobrin, and Richard Miller. "Writing at Exxon ITD: Notes on the Writing Environment of an R&D Organization." Odell and Goswami 281–307.

Rabinow, Paul. *Reflections on Fieldwork in Morocco.* Berkeley: U of California P, 1977.

Reither, James A. "Writing and Knowing: Toward Redefining the Writing Process." *College English* 47 (1985): 620–28.

Rich, Adrienne. *On Lies, Secrets, and Silence: Selected Prose, 1966–1978.* New York: Norton, 1979.

Rosaldo, Renato. *Culture and Truth: The Remaking of Social Analysis.* Boston: Beacon P, 1989.

Swendsen, Robert. Personal interview. By Ann M. Blakeslee. 1 July 1993.

———. Personal interview. By Ann M. Blakeslee. 12 Nov. 1993.

Traweek, Sharon. *Beamtimes and Lifetimes: The World of High Energy Physicists.* Cambridge: Harvard UP, 1988.

Turner, Victor, and Edward Bruner. *The Anthropology of Experience.* Urbana: U of Illinois P, 1986.

Whyte, William F. *Street Corner Society: The Social Structure of an Italian Slum.* 3rd ed. Chicago: U of Chicago P, 1981.

Wolf, Margery. *A Thrice Told Tale: Feminism, Postmodernism and Ethnographic Responsibility.* Stanford: Stanford UP, 1992.

9 A Text for Many Voices: Representing Diversity in Reports of Naturalistic Research

Lucille Parkinson McCarthy
University of Maryland Baltimore County

Stephen M. Fishman
University of North Carolina–Charlotte

Once ethnographic texts begin to be looked at *as well as through, once they are seen to be made, and made to persuade, those who make them have rather more to answer for.*

—Clifford Geertz, *Works and Lives*

N aturalistic studies assume that reality is socially constructed. The naturalistic researcher assumes the world is a negotiation among participants and settings—among various points of view, ways of thinking, and social-political forces in particular locales (Gergen; Lincoln and Guba; Mishler). As a result, we believe the heart of reporting naturalistic study is representing the negotiations among a situation's diverse voices, the interplay between different images and constructions by various members of a community. And since researchers themselves influence the situations they investigate, reports of naturalistic studies also attempt to be reflexive, to reveal the researcher's own voice, the biases which determine an investigator's organizing principles and research design. In summary, we characterize reports of naturalistic study by the following three goals:

1. To represent diverse voices in a particular situation and to describe their interplay and mutual influence. Diversity in this sense means the ways different voices conceive, imagine, and tell their stories.

2. To reveal the researcher's influence as he or she negotiates with informants. This includes a representation of the investigator's own biases and tacit knowledge.

3. To describe the emerging research design. This means reports of naturalistic inquiry show the research process—the entry of

the investigator into the setting, his or her ongoing negotiations with informants, and their continuing refinement of research questions and methods.

Given these goals for reporting naturalistic research, we believe successful studies are measured not by how closely they mirror a single reality, but by how profoundly they affect the participants (see Lincoln). In particular, a successful naturalistic study helps both informants and researchers become more self-conscious about their assumptions and constructions of the world. Such studies also increase participants' ability to take action on behalf of themselves or their group. In line with these criteria for evaluating naturalistic studies, we believe that certain textual forms are especially appropriate for reporting them.

Academic Discourse and Reports of Naturalistic Research

Although naturalistic studies gained acceptance in composition research in the decade of the 1980s, reports of such studies have been circumscribed by the character of academic discourse. Academic prose in general has been called "author-evacuated" as opposed to "author-saturated" (Geertz 9). It is discourse marked by third-person pronouns, the passive voice, and the suggestion that the text writes itself. Phrases like "The findings of this essay are . . ." and "This paper concludes that . . ." invest the researcher's conclusions with an aura of inevitability. The impersonal quality of academic discourse implies that research and writing are method driven, untainted by the interests or prejudices or even skills of the investigator (Brodkey; Elbow). By contrast, textual forms which represent the interplay of different voices, like narrative and dialogue, and styles which are more "author-saturated," like letters or confessional tales, are seen as too subjective and therefore inappropriate for academic publications.

Academic language poses at least two problems for reporting naturalistic studies. First, the single-voiced, monologic style of academic discourse makes it a difficult form in which to present the multivoiced situations the naturalistic investigator seeks to represent. Although the impersonal voice of academic writing can describe various interpretations or opinions, it is not well designed to capture the diverse ways informants go at the world and their diverse discourses, exactly what naturalistic inquiry aims to construct. Second, the research techniques of naturalistic inquiry are shaped by the interplay among investigator, setting, and informants. To present these techniques as if they occur in predetermined and rule-governed ways ignores the fact that naturalistic researchers have something of the craftsperson about them and that, as Geertz puts it, fieldwork is "always a messy, biographical affair." Just as academic language's resistance to narrative and dialogue makes it a difficult medium in which to reveal the interplay among diverse voices, so its avoidance of letter and confessional styles makes it an equally difficult medium in which to present the evolving quality of naturalistic methods.

Modifications of Academic Textual Forms by Naturalistic Researchers

For most of the 1980s, investigators presented their studies in traditional academic forms, relying heavily on the APA reporting style (see Berkenkotter, Huckin, and Ackerman; Doheny-Farina; Dyson, "Emerging Alphabetic Literacy" and "Second Graders"; Herrington, "Writing"; McCarthy). In such reports the researcher keeps his or her voice out of the text, informants' voices are heard only when quoted or paraphrased, and the piece itself is structured to conform to the scientific conventions of the APA style. These textual forms may be appropriate for research which assumes that a detached researcher using predetermined methods will produce context-free generalizations. However, they conflict with the goals of naturalistic research. (For a discussion of the positivistic assumptions underlying the *Publication Manual of the American Psychological Association,* see Bazerman, and for an analysis of how scientific conventions may distort naturalistic research reports, see Zeller.)

It is only in the last few years that naturalistic investigators have experimented with textual forms, seeking styles more reflective of the goals of naturalistic research. That is, more recent naturalistic reports have sought textual forms which capture the dialogic, mutually shaping interactions among investigators and informants. These textual experiments have taken a variety of shapes, including staged dialogue (see Berkenkotter and Parsons; Lewis and Simon), multiple interpretations of the same data (see Clark and Doheny-Farina), reflexive monologue (see Woolgar), drama (see Brodkey 108–66), oral history (see Weiler), and sequential informant-researcher narrative (see Anderson, Best, Black, Hurst, Miller, and Miller; McCarthy and Fishman). Texts of these sorts have been called "heteroglossic" by James Clifford, who draws that term from Bakhtin's analysis of the novel ("On Ethnographic Authority" 119). (For further discussions of textual representations of naturalistic research, see Anderson; Gitlin; Herrington, "Reflections"; Lincoln; Newkirk; Quantz and O'Connor.)

In the remainder of our essay, we discuss three of these heteroglossic experiments in more detail, focusing on how the researchers represent diverse voices within the research scene and how they reconstruct the interplay among them. We also speculate about the implications for researchers of these heteroglossic reports.

Textual Experiments with Naturalistic Research Reports

Textual Experiment No. 1

"Cross-Curricular Underlife: A Collaborative Report on Ways with Academic Words" (Anderson et al.) is co-authored by Susan Miller and five of her students at the University of Utah. It is an example of the reporting form we have called sequential informant-researcher narrative. Miller sets out to evaluate the success of her freshman composition course in preparing students for writing assignments across the curriculum. To accomplish this end, she might have observed her students in their second-quarter disciplinary courses—interviewing them, having them respond to questionnaires, analyzing their drafts and formal papers. Instead, she asks five students from her course to be not just informants, but co-researchers with her. At their initial meeting she lets them choose from two possible research topics, and, appointing them "participant-observers," arms them with a series of instructions and questions. By elevating the students' status from informant to participant-observer, Miller shares control of the project and opens the door for multiple interpretations. In fact, more than half of the twenty-five-page research article is devoted to interpretations constructed by the five students.

The opening sections of the article—"A Readers' Guide" and "Background"—are written jointly by the six collaborators, "we five students and one teacher" (11). These sections briefly describe Miller's freshman course, the purpose of the research, and the study's conclusion, namely, that Miller's composition class can only make a "limited" claim to prepare students for other lower division courses (12).

After these six pages of introduction, the rest of the article is divided into three sections of nearly equal length, the first two consisting of narratives written by the five students, the last written singly by Susan Miller. In the first section, "Observations of How Language Is Used in College Courses," each student presents his or her observations about two of their university classes. Each organizes what he or she says around a central theme which emerges as they analyze their data, the different themes revealing the students' varying perspectives and preserving their diverse ways of going at the world.

The second major subdivision of the article is called "When Learning and Language Intersect: Conclusions." In this part, students present their individual summations, each of which averages about three-fourths of a page. Again, the text preserves students' diverse voices, their diverse ways of constructing reality as they come to different conclusions about their second-quarter classes.

The final section of the report, Miller's five-page evaluation of her course in light of her students' data and interpretations, allows readers to contrast Miller's voice with those of her students. Whereas, for the most part, students speak colloquially in short paragraphs, Miller uses an academic style marked by citations and by longer sentences and paragraphs.

Implications of This Multivoiced Report

The result of Miller's decision to share control with her students is that the project generates not just one but multiple interpretations of students' learning across the curriculum. The result of her decision to report the study in a heteroglossic form is that readers get not only multiple interpretations, but also the various languages participants use to construct them. In this report, readers hear nothing like the author-evacuated prose of the dispassionate observer reporting universal knowledge. Instead, the language of the five students and their teacher is situated, emotional, committed, their findings not transcendent truth but the result of negotiations among particular inquirers in a particular context.

An outstanding feature of the textual form developed by Miller and her students is the way it privileges student language, in particular what Robert Brooke calls the language of student "underlife" (141). Because students talk to one another in their research group, and because they write their own research findings, the students' texts reveal their underlife, that is, their alienation from and their strategies for success within the educational system. For example, Worth Anderson says about his course in international studies,

> Although I was almost always there, I consistently slept through this class. Part of the blame for this had to rest on the teacher's testing techniques. He chose meaningless facts (give the population of Kinshasa), thrown out at any old juncture as a test question. . . . The lectures didn't have any discernible patterns. . . . I simply couldn't construct a reasoned pattern for all this chaos, so I gave up, went to sleep, and relied on dumb luck and (admittedly obfuscatory) writing to pull my butt through the tests. (Anderson et al. 17)

Another student, Cynthia Best, describes her sociology teacher as someone who

> lectured from an outline of key words on the overhead projector.
> Several people commented that his lectures were hard to follow,
> but I thought they weren't too difficult because he followed the
> book. In fact, at times he read straight from it! The professor had
> the habit of leaning on the lectern while he lectured and placing
> his hand on his chin (it almost covered his mouth!). (Anderson et
> al. 19)

Alongside the strong sound of student underlife, we also hear an
interplay of voices as students on occasion try out the more academic
tone of their professor. At points we find sentences like the following
from Brandt Miller's classroom observations: "There were several overlapping communities of student interaction in this class" (Anderson et
al. 22). Likewise, although Susan Miller adheres to the academic register, it is evident she has taken her students' findings seriously. Within
the academic voice of her conclusion there is an intimate quality of self-
evaluation, even despair, generated by her students' conclusion that in
some ways her course had been irrelevant to their experiences across
the curriculum.

In this collaborative study, the role of the researcher has changed.
Although Miller does not discuss this in the article, we believe that, in
co-authoring with her students, she has allowed both the research and
the report writing to become more complicated. Instead of researcher-
dictated methods and a well-ordered, unified text, Miller's opting to
share control of her study invites conflicting stories, loose ends, and
more questions than answers. For such a project the researcher must be
far more than an experienced practitioner of research methods. She must
also be an expert listener, patient negotiator, caring midwife, and skilled
editor. She must, in addition, be prepared to go down unanticipated
roads, ones which only open after the project begins.

Textual Experiment No. 2

The second heteroglossic text we examine is an article co-authored by
then-graduate student Magda Lewis and her professor, Roger Simon,
titled "A Discourse Not Intended for Her: Learning and Teaching within
Patriarchy." In certain ways this second article resembles the report of
Miller and her student collaborators. The research of Lewis and Simon
develops out of a shared classroom experience and, like the first article,
parts of this report are co-authored and other parts are written individually. However, whereas the article by Miller and her co-authors uses

the diverse languages of undergraduates and their professor to capture their multiple points of view, diversity in the Lewis and Simon report is based less on difference of language than on different gender-based interpretations of the same classroom events. Magda Lewis, the graduate student, speaks as academically as her professor, Roger Simon, both using an impersonal voice which relies heavily on citations.

The fifteen-page Lewis and Simon article begins with a two-page co-written introduction. This is followed by a ten-page staged dialogue with each author taking five alternate turns of at least half a page, each contribution headed by the author's name. The article ends with a two-and-one-half-page co-authored conclusion. In their introduction, the authors tell the purpose of their report: to present the different experiences of Lewis and Simon as they participated in a graduate seminar taught by Simon at the Ontario Institute for Studies in Education. The co-authors explain that their report's textual form came about because of their inability to find a common voice for their different experiences. In the introduction, they write that "the results of our search for a single voice were never satisfactory, as one or the other of us was unintentionally but inevitably silenced" (457–58).

In the ten-page staged dialogue which follows the introduction, the authors do not so much reply to one another as juxtapose their different theoretical assumptions and interpretations of classroom events. Lewis begins by reporting an encounter with a woman on a train who told about feeling invisible to male railway officials—the conductor, the steward, the railway's public relations representative. Simon follows with talk about the male-dominated education faculty of which he is a member. He also describes the development of the graduate seminar (in which Lewis was a student) which he called Discourse, Text, and Subjectivity. It was designed, he says, to examine questions concerning "the relations between language and power" (460). It is in Lewis's second speech that she relates the dynamics of Simon's seminar which led to the women students being silenced and which is the focus of the co-authored report. Lewis tells us that the men dominated the speaking as well as the course's theoretical and social agenda. In sections of the dialogue which follow, Simon presents his own dilemma, his recognition that by privileging theoretical discourse, "abstract and distanced language," he made his seminar an unsafe place for women" (464, 461). But, Simon tells us, he was helpless to find a solution to his dilemma—how to keep abstract male discourse from dominating and preventing the entry of female voices—since his course objective was to help students develop "theoretical fluency" (465). While Simon continues to speak in the dialogue about his frustrations, Lewis talks about the seminar from the women's side. She finds that their invisibility is either an imposed silence or a chosen one, "an ironic resistance to being silenced" (463). She relates the growing recognition by the seminar's women that their anger is collective, their effort to speak a struggle to defend their common experience and discursive forms. This anger builds until the women break their silence during discussion of a book focusing on how particular women describe their experiences within patriarchy (464).

In their co-authored conclusion, the collaborators draw implications from their data—their juxtaposed, conflicting interpretations and comments. This closing discussion, like Miller's in the first article, rests on interpreting the diversity which the heteroglossic textual form preserves. Lewis and Simon conclude that countering patriarchy requires not only women's descriptions of their silencing, but also men's exploration of their experience of privilege.

Implications of This Multivoiced Report

A significant feature of the heteroglossic form developed by Lewis and Simon is the way it allows them to juxtapose rather than debate their differences. Instead of using their dialogue to confront one another in point-by-point debate, their exchange gives both researchers space to present their experiences by using their own focus and sense of chronology. It is like two voice-overs for one piece of film, giving the reader a sense of the different ways these two people lived Simon's seminar. The juxtaposition rather than confrontation of difference also allows the reader to witness Lewis and Simon struggling to gain perspective on the patriarchal position and on the manner in which language reinforces patriarchal privilege. We see Lewis and Simon trying on each other's words in a development of diversity which seems to edge both of them toward new common ground in their conclusion.

Although Lewis and Simon do not set out originally to do research, their reconstructions of their classroom experiences are in line with assumptions of naturalistic research. Their staged dialogue allows readers to experience with them their struggles to articulate their assumptions about teaching and learning, language and power. Although Lewis and Simon do not discuss their methods for reconstructing their accounts—whether, for example, they drew upon "data sources" other than memory—they do mention their struggle to arrive at their dialogic textual form. Its effect, they say, was liberating. Had they chosen to report their classroom experiences in a single, blended "we" voice or in the author-evacuated style of much educational research, not only would at least one of them have been "inevitably silenced," but their aim of critiquing patriarchal, monologic discourse would have been undercut. However, because both student and teacher tell their stories in their staged dialogue, both are empowered, their voices re-created, their differences preserved.

Textual Experiment No. 3

The final heteroglossic research report we examine is our own: "Boundary Conversations: Conflicting Ways of Knowing in Philosophy and Interdisciplinary Research." Our study was a yearlong project in which McCarthy, a composition researcher, collaborated with Fishman, a philosophy professor, to study students' thinking and writing in his introductory course. We collected a variety of naturalistic data, focusing on five students in the fall of 1989 and five the following spring. We hoped to better understand both the nature of the philosophic discourse Fishman was asking students to learn as well as the classroom interactions that promoted or hindered their progress. Although we live in different states—Fishman teaches in North Carolina and McCarthy in Maryland—we decided to go ahead with the project, he motivated to improve his teaching, and she to try out a collaborative project in which she could share equal authority with a discipline-based teacher. We had observed other such teacher-researcher pairs and knew that, while their differences could produce exciting results, they also could test the researchers' openness and ability to share control. In fact, we had heard researchers compare these collaborations to marriage, saying that the ones that survived did so because the partners had learned to understand each other's frameworks and to respect their diverse points of view.

The diversity in our collaboration is different from the other two we described. Unlike Miller and her student collaborators who were distinguished from each other by academic status and language, and unlike Lewis and Simon whose diversity focused on gender, our differences centered on diverse attitudes toward research authority. Although McCarthy, as outside investigator in Fishman's philosophy class, wanted to give her informant equal voice, her desire did not translate easily into reality. The central story of our collaboration might be characterized as Fishman's struggle to achieve the place McCarthy had promised. Although McCarthy offered Fishman textual space in which to tell his story, we discovered that having an equal voice in research involves more than equal space in the report. It also involves giving one's informant-collaborators the opportunity to pursue their own questions, generate their own data, and formulate their own conclusions.

The heteroglossic textual form we developed is also quite different from those created by Miller and her students and Lewis and Simon. Because we wanted to publish in a journal requiring the APA four-part textual form—introduction, methods, results, and discussion—we had to preserve our differences within a positivist tradition characterized by its exclusion of multiple voices. This was especially difficult because we wanted to provide an account of Fishman's efforts to have his voice heard in the text. This meant creating space for a detailed narrative of our negotiations as collaborators, an account we refer to as a "confessional tale" (Van Maanen 73). In the story which follows we will show how we managed to incorporate narrative and confessional modes within the APA style. It's a story that describes our struggles to articulate our differences, share authority, and develop a heteroglossic form that honored both our voices.[1]

The research event with which we begin our story shows, first, how hard it was for us to articulate our differences because so much of what we know is tacit, and second, how hard it was for us to make each other's ways of knowing our own. This event occurred in early January 1990, when we first exchanged drafts of possible introductions to our article. All fall we had been collecting data from students and conversing frequently, McCarthy questioning Fishman in various ways about what constituted philosophy in his classroom and what counted as successful student writing there. At one point McCarthy asked Fishman point-blank: "What *is* philosophy anyway?" He replied, "I'm not sure I know. In any case I don't care so much that my students learn the conventions of philosophy as I do that they learn to celebrate their own voices, learn that they have beliefs and values that are worth exploring." "But, Steve," McCarthy responded, "I know you're working with students' own conflicts and questions, but you're using philosophic methods on them. I can hear that your methods are different from those of literary criticism or business or biology."

Just as it was hard for Fishman at first to articulate his disciplinary ways of knowing, so was it hard for both of us to articulate our tacitly held views of disciplinary initiation. What helped us eventually clarify our views was common reading we did. Fishman sent McCarthy sections from the *Encyclopedia of Philosophy* and various textbooks as well as passages from philosophers he admired, such as John Dewey, and we discussed these. McCarthy sent Fishman David Bartholomae's article, "Inventing the University," to explain her view that students must learn to speak the language of the professor, and Fishman shot back with sections from Peter Elbow's work, saying that good writing of any sort must come out of personal commitment. We were, during the fall of 1989, working to articulate our positions, identify our disagreements, and create a common language for talking about them. McCarthy was getting Fishman's perspective, we thought, and Fishman was getting McCarthy's.

We should have been alerted that this was not going to be so easy when Fishman responded to a manuscript McCarthy sent him in December. The manuscript reported a collaborative, co-authored study like our own, a naturalistic study in which the researcher, after a careful explanation of his methods, described the teacher's ways of knowing and teaching. But Fishman hated it. "This sounds like a treaty," he said. "Where are the conflicts? They've all been leveled. Sure, I hear the teacher's voice, but only as quoted by the researcher. And why all this talk about methods?"

Nonetheless, in early January 1990, we thought we could speak for each other and agreed we would each draft an introduction to our article, which we hoped to place in the composition journal *Research in the Teaching of English*. Fishman's eight-page draft arrived at McCarthy's house first, and McCarthy said to herself after reading it, "Oh no, this will never get published." It was a beautifully written narrative that captured our voices and our conflicts, but did not fill out the methods or the issues, nor did it set the piece in the ongoing disciplinary conversation.

And Fishman's objections to McCarthy's twelve-page draft echoed those he had made to the manuscript she had sent him the month before. He told her as tactfully as he could that she had not represented his views of writing fairly and that he found her tone too "sciency." McCarthy was, he said, keeping herself too much outside the piece, playing too much the role of white-coated, objective researcher. By contrast, in our report, Fishman said, he would be fully exposed. "Besides," he added, "you're *not* neutral. You influenced my teaching in the fall." And then Fishman raised the issue of authority, saying that by McCarthy's citing her own work and referring to herself by her last name and to him by his first, she was "making an implicit statement of who's in charge and whose voice counts."

At that point, we figured our being in different states was not such a bad thing, and each of us was probably considering a quiet research divorce. However, neither of us mentioned it, and this exchange did help us to further identify our differences. What we did not yet have, however, was a satisfactory textual form for dealing with them. So we let the introduction go for the time being. It was the only part of the article we thought we would have to agree on. Fishman, we had planned, would write a teaching autobiography, a personal narrative describing his own difficult initiation into philosophy. And McCarthy would construct the stories of several students' writing during their initiation in Fishman's class, stories based on the data we had collected in the fall.

If the three months before January 1990 were characterized by attempts to articulate our positions and by McCarthy's questioning of Fishman and trying on his language, during the next three months it was Fishman's turn. He read deeply in composition and ethnography, pieces McCarthy sent him as well as articles he found on his own. And Fishman's questioning influenced McCarthy's data analysis just as McCarthy's questioning the semester before had influenced Fishman's teaching. Although between January and March of 1990 we worked separately, McCarthy shared data with Fishman and frequently described to him the interpretations she was constructing. He often replied, "I see it a little differently," and his interpretations helped McCarthy rethink and, at times, reshape her own. This three-month period, in which we switched roles and continued to try out each other's language was a productive one for us. In late February Fishman told McCarthy he had surprised himself when, in a conversation with his dean about hiring, he had used the word "triangulation," and McCarthy reported she had just heard herself quote John Dewey to a colleague in English. This gradual taking on of each other's languages led to the second event we will describe.

This event, which occurred in March of 1990, helped us deal with the authority issue Fishman had raised in January. At the Conference on College Composition and Communication convention, we participated in an ethnography workshop, and there McCarthy gave a presentation in which she described Fishman as her co-researcher. Afterward, he shocked her by saying, "I *still* don't feel like we're co-researchers." He told McCarthy that he wanted to deal directly with data, not just comment on her interpretations of it. After having listened to McCarthy's taped interviews with students and having read transcripts of her interviews with him, he was, as he put it, suffering from "data envy." Furthermore, he was realizing that his own questions were not the same as hers. He was not so much interested in student writing as he was in classroom discussion—why were some classes marked by active student participation whereas others were silent? So we decided that Fishman would, on his own, collect and analyze data. In May 1990, after classes were finished, Fishman interviewed five spring semester students, imitating the methods McCarthy had used in interviews with five fall semester students. When he sent McCarthy the tapes, she was impressed and suggested a new plan for their research together. Again, we would divide our report into two parts, but this time Fishman would take responsibility for describing and analyzing his classroom community, while McCarthy would retain her focus on student writing. Furthermore, we agreed we would report our research in a heteroglossic form in which each of us could speak for ourselves. This decision was crucial for settling our conflicts over authority. Not only were we now both responsible for data collection and for answering our own questions, we had each agreed to write our own findings.

So all during the summer of 1990 Fishman worked with his data to construct findings about how his students learned during class discussion, and McCarthy analyzed hers, constructing the stories of two students' writing experiences in his class. Although we worked separately, we conversed and exchanged letters frequently, focusing on similar themes in both sets of data, namely, the ways students learned through conflict in what we were calling boundary conversations. In September 1990, after numerous conversations considering the relative merits of a monograph versus an article, we decided to proceed as originally planned, shaping our co-authored, heteroglossic report for *Research in the Teaching of English*. *RTE* gave us the audience we wanted and put no page limits on manuscript length. However, we were acutely aware that *RTE*'s four-part text form—introduction, methods, results, and discussion—is grounded in scientific rather than naturalistic assumptions. Fishman compared the four-part *RTE* structure to a sonata form and convinced McCarthy that it was a form we could "dance within." We could, that is, satisfy both *RTE*'s requirement of the scientific report form and our own desire to present our findings and research negotiations in our own voices. So from September 1990 until February 1991 we danced our multivoiced dance within the *RTE* form. (For further discussion of the uneasy coexistence of personal narrative and objectifying description in ethnography, see Clifford, "Introduction"; Geertz; Herndl; Pratt.)

We now want to describe the final form our article took. Our introduction, methods, and discussion sections are co-authored by the two of us. Since the time of our failed competition to write separate introductions nine months earlier, we had articulated our differences, equalized authority, and developed a common language. Thus we were able, in the fall of 1990, to write these three sections together, at times one of us drafting and the other refining, at times composing together.

In our article's introduction we use several familiar textual gestures to establish our authority in *RTE* terms. We cite numerous published works to contextualize our study, and then we create a gap in that literature, which we promise our findings will fill. However, two features of our introduction warn readers to expect something other than a scientific, objectified account. In our first paragraph we appear to be rolling the credits of a play or movie, introducing what we call our four principal characters, Fishman and McCarthy and two students, giving our ages and academic situations and explaining our various motives for participating. The second introductory signal we send readers is our announcement that our study has a central *image:* learning occurs, we say, in "boundary conversations." With these two moves, we are preparing readers for author-saturated as well as author-evacuated prose, for narrative as well as analysis.

In our second section, methods, we do some of the same double dance we did in the introduction. We again authorize ourselves in *RTE* terms by showing that we employ a mix of qualitative and quantitative methods, by referring to such concepts as triangulation and trustworthiness, and by citing previous work. In addition, we argue in the methods section for new textual forms for naturalistic research, an argument we again buttress with numerous citations. Thus in both our introduction and methods sections we were working, we now see, to get our feet in the door. In these first two sections we hoped to authorize our unorthodox, multivoiced third section—results.

In our results section we tell three stories in three distinct voices. Fishman begins with his classroom story, a piece whose title is that of a short story rather than a research report. He calls it, "When Upside Down Is Rightside Up." He first describes his goals for his students' learning and his view of philosophy. He then narrates one particular class discussion, asking the reader to relive it with him in order to *experience* our finding that students learn through conflict. Fishman concludes his story by focusing on himself and what he learned from this research. Although Fishman's account of his class discussion is based on data he collected, he seldom refers to them. Rather, he authorizes his account by the persona he constructs for himself—a caring teacher willing to examine his practices and admit his mistakes—and by the story itself.

McCarthy's piece follows Fishman's in the results section and tells the stories of two students writing in his class. McCarthy's title, unlike Fishman's, is that of a somewhat unimaginative composition researcher:

she calls her piece "Two Students Writing in Introduction to Philosophy." And, unlike Fishman, McCarthy positions herself outside her story, coming into the text only occasionally in the role of interviewer. Because McCarthy wrote her piece after Fishman wrote his, we think she may have been trying to compensate for Fishman's author-saturated story of lived experience. Trying to ensure that Fishman's radical departure from the third-person conventions of the APA style did not seal our fate with a rejection, McCarthy lets hardly a paragraph go by without mentioning, in scientific fashion, the data source or analytic method that grounds her interpretation, and she frequently cites other work that corroborates or extends her own. Just as during Fishman's writing, McCarthy pleaded with him, "Can't you mention a data source just once in a while?" during McCarthy's writing, Fishman asked, "Do you have to keep interrupting the students' stories with those citations?" He said, "It's like you're saying, 'And then the wolf quietly opened the door and went into grandma's bedroom. For other discussions of grandmas, see so and so.'"

If in McCarthy's piece she is more the scientific outsider than Fishman was in his, in the third part of our results section we are both stage center in our "confessional tale." Here we co-author the story of our research collaboration in a personal narrative we title "The Researchers' Boundary Conversation." We show our very unscientific struggles to articulate our tacit assumptions and to share authority, some of which we have just described above. We also show our conflicts and negotiations about emerging research design and data interpretation as well as describe our mutual influence throughout the project. And as if this were not dancing far enough at the edges of *RTE* assumptions about detached researchers and uncontaminated data, our confessional account, in addition to being autobiographical, is also self-parodying. In sum, our research story is a confessional tale which shows that, though we decided to tell certain stories, we might have told others had our negotiations worked out differently. We thus show that our truths are partial, constructed by annoyingly limited human beings whose motives never so much centered on finding truth as they did on improving our own teaching and research practices.

Although we place the story of our collaboration in the results section, it also fills out the methods section. We show how our fieldwork experiences were converted into two well-ordered classroom stories. Our fieldwork included discovering that giving the teacher his voice meant more than giving him a few pages to tell his story and more than McCarthy's teaching him how to talk like her. Rather, it meant granting him his own questions and agenda, his own data collection and analysis, and his own rhetorical style. And, of course, granting him all that reshaped both our inquiry and our ultimate textual representation of it.

Implications of This Multivoiced Report

Implications for the Teacher-Researcher. Our decision to give Fishman his voice radically changed our research design. It also changed the meaning of the project for him. He owned the research along with McCarthy, asking his own questions and working alongside her in data collection and analysis. This allowed Fishman to see his classroom in new ways and thus to change his practice, something we believe would not have happened had he remained only McCarthy's research subject. What, specifically, did he gain from his equal-authority role in our research project?

First, Fishman clarified his assumptions about his teaching practices and his subject matter. At the start of research Fishman was reluctant to say what philosophy was because he was aware there are so many competing definitions in the discipline's history. As a result of McCarthy's questioning, he realized that he *had* adopted a particular view of philosophy, and he understood for the first time his own commitment to that view. As a consequence, he could more forthrightly articulate this perspective to his class and accept responsibility for its central role in his decisions about classroom practices and required texts. He also became more self-conscious about criteria he was using to grade student papers. As the research process made these more explicit for Fishman, he could make them more explicit for his students.

Second, because Fishman participated in data collection and analysis, he got into his students' heads. He saw they were, at times, annoyed, confused, angry. He could see their problems and how his own failures contributed to them. As a result, he planned how he might help students by adjusting certain classroom interactions. Fishman's co-researcher status was, we believe, essential in achieving these insights and effecting change.

Fishman's experience of articulating tacit knowledge and acting to change practice is, as we have said, a goal for participants in naturalistic inquiry. And not only was Fishman so affected. In similar ways McCarthy came to see her research in a new light.

Implications for the Composition Researcher. How, specifically, did McCarthy profit from giving Fishman equal voice? First, just as Fishman needed McCarthy's outsider questioning about his discipline and his classroom, McCarthy needed Fishman's insider view. His close-up perspective on his students and his thirty years' experience with philosophic discourse helped her understand students' writing in ways she never could have done alone. She simply did not have the expertise in philosophy to understand the nuances of their struggles.

In addition, throughout the project, Fishman's questioning of McCarthy's research assumptions and procedures proved valuable. At first McCarthy was not sure why Fishman needed to understand these, but her openness to his probing and the discussions that we engaged in led McCarthy to rethink her approach. Although in theory she believed in the value of triangulation among investigators, and although she espoused the idea that research findings are socially constructed, she initially had trouble sharing authority with Fishman. Instead, she retained something of the detached-observer stance. As Fishman pushed McCarthy to share responsibility and give him equal voice, he required McCarthy to practice what she preached. Furthermore, as Fishman moved into co-researcher status, he was able to suggest research questions and analytical frameworks which reshaped and enriched the study.

Late in the project, as the benefits of giving Fishman his voice became clear, McCarthy and Fishman decided to give students their voices in the report as well. To this end, in May 1990, four months after fall semester students had completed Fishman's course, McCarthy asked the five students she had studied to write about their experiences in Introduction to Philosophy. She intended to include these students' stories in the research report without comment, in this way letting students speak for themselves. But this plan did not work. Unlike Miller's students' accounts of their various courses, these reports were all about one class, and as a series they seemed repetitive, dense, unengaging. They needed a narrative line to make them meaningful to the reader. Ultimately McCarthy provided that line, using these accounts in her own argument, quoting them to support her own reconstructions of students' experiences. Because we did not, like Miller, enlist students from the beginning as our co-researchers, our last-minute desire to give them their voices proved unsuccessful.

Recommendations to Researchers Planning to Do Collaborative Classroom Studies

We recognize several factors which were crucial to our collaboration's success. Although we did not understand these factors at the time, we have, in retrospect, identified their importance. In describing them, we offer a few words of advice to future researchers.

First, we believe researchers should approach the project willing to change, to discover, perhaps, that their present ways of doing things may not be achieving their intended consequences. If new insights and change are to occur, both teacher and researcher should be questioners. McCarthy did not fully understand the importance of this quality in the teacher-researcher when she agreed to collaborate with Fishman. However, it turned out that Fishman's inquiring mind, his questioning McCarthy at every turn, genuinely wanting to understand and share responsibility for the research—coupled with McCarthy's openness to such questioning—was central to our collaboration's success. It facilitated McCarthy's growth as a researcher and complicated and enriched our findings.

Second, we now realize that negotiation about the relationship between researcher and teacher is a continuing process. It cannot be settled once and for all at the start of work together. Although an initial understanding between collaborators about roles in research and writing is essential, any agreement should remain flexible. In our case, we tried several times to equalize responsibility, but it was not until Fishman was given his own research task that he was satisfied with his status. Although Fishman's expressions of dissatisfaction were not always easy for us to deal with, we had developed a climate of trust in which he could articulate them. We then worked to find avenues to redistribute authority in ways satisfactory for both of us. We also learned that equality is not so much doing the same things as it is a feeling of shared responsibility. No matter the exact distribution of tasks, both researchers must feel they are pulling equal weight if they are to retain their self-respect and be empowered by the project.

Third, we suggest that researchers consider including in their report, as we did, an account of their collaboration. In essence this subjects the researchers to the same sort of scrutiny they are focusing on the classroom. This accomplishes two goals. First, it renders explicit the assumptions about reality, knowledge, and method which shaped the collaboration. Readers can see the researchers' ways of going at the project as well as their conflicts and negotiations as they construct findings. Second, it also helps collaborators acknowledge negative findings. For example, what happens when the researcher believes that the teacher is *not* doing a good job, that the teacher's failures may be contributing to student confusion? In a project where the teacher is not a co-author, such a finding could be embarrassing. However, in co-authored work which includes a narrative of the research, the negative finding is not something to hide but, rather, an opportunity for inquiry into collaboration. In the research account, co-authors can describe how they constructed the negative finding, their reactions to it, and, perhaps, plans for change.

Finally, we suggest that co-researchers consider with care the audience for their heteroglossic report. Will they write for an audience of researchers as we did? Or will they write for a more mixed audience of researchers, teachers, and administrators as Miller and her students and Lewis and Simon did? A third option is to move outside the research community altogether and speak directly to teachers or students in publications aimed at these groups. Decisions collaborators make about audiences and forums for their work will, as we have shown in our account, profoundly influence the shape of their multivoiced report.

Conclusion

We conclude by returning to our own research story. When we learned in February 1991 that the editors of *Research in the Teaching of English* had accepted our heteroglossic research report, we were pleased. Although the acceptance was good news for us personally, of course, we think it was also good news for our field. Just three years earlier, Greg Myers suggested that it might be some time before we would see in composition studies new textual forms that call into question our yet unsure claims to academic authority. Our article's acceptance by *RTE,* and the increasing numbers of heteroglossic texts we are beginning to see in composition studies, may be a step toward recognizing that the forms we have borrowed from the scientific paradigm are neither natural nor native to naturalistic inquiry. It may be a step toward inventing forms of our own, forms that honor diversity, empower the voices of researchers and informants, and enhance participants' chances for understanding and change.

Notes

1. The following five paragraphs are taken from the confessional tale which appears in our actual research report (McCarthy and Fishman 460–61).

Works Cited

Anderson, Gary L. "Critical Ethnography in Education: Origins, Current Status, and New Directions." *Review of Educational Research* 59 (1989): 249–70.

Anderson, Worth, Cynthia Best, Alycia Black, John Hurst, Brandt Miller, and Susan Miller. "Cross-Curricular Underlife: A Collaborative Report on Ways with Academic Words." *College Composition and Communication* 41 (1990): 11–36.

Bartholomae, David. "Inventing the University." *When a Writer Can't Write: Studies in Writer's Block and Other Composing-Process Problems.* Ed. Mike Rose. New York: Guilford P, 1985. 134–65.

Bazerman, Charles. *Shaping Written Knowledge: The Genre and Activity of the Experimental Article in Science.* Madison: U of Wisconsin P, 1988.

Berkenkotter, Carol, Thomas N. Huckin, and John Ackerman. "Conventions, Conversations, and the Writer: Case Study of a Student in a Rhetoric Ph.D. Program." *Research in the Teaching of English* 22 (1988): 9–44.

Berkenkotter, Carol, and John Parsons. "Representing Knowledgeable Subjects' Perspectives in 'Polyphonic' Texts." Paper presented at the Convention of the Conference on College Composition and Communication, Boston. March 1991.

Brodkey, Linda. *Academic Writing as Social Practice.* Philadelphia: Temple UP, 1987.

Brooke, Robert. "Underlife and Writing Instruction." *College Composition and Communication* 38 (1987): 141–53.

Clark, Gregory, and Stephen Doheny-Farina. "Public Discourse and Personal Expression: A Case in Theory-Building." *Written Communication* 7 (1990): 456–81.

Clifford, James. "Introduction: Partial Truths." *Writing Culture: The Poetics and Politics of Ethnography.* Ed. James Clifford and George E. Marcus. Berkeley: U of California P, 1986. 1–26.

———. "On Ethnographic Authority." *The Predicament of Culture: Twentieth-Century Ethnography, Literature, and Art.* Cambridge: Harvard UP, 1988. 21–54.

Doheny-Farina, Stephen. "Writing in an Emerging Organization: An Ethnographic Study." *Written Communication* 3 (1986): 158–85.

Dyson, Anne Haas. "Emerging Alphabetic Literacy in School Contexts: Toward Defining the Gap between School Curriculum and Child Mind." *Written Communication* 1 (1984): 5–55.

———. "Second Graders Sharing Writing: The Multiple Social Realities of a Literacy Event." *Written Communication* 2 (1985): 189–215.

Elbow, Peter. "Reflections on Academic Discourse: How It Relates to Freshmen and Colleagues." *College English* 53 (1991): 135–55.

Geertz, Clifford. *Works and Lives: The Anthropologist as Author.* Stanford: Stanford UP, 1988.

Gergen, Mary M. "Toward a Feminist Metatheory and Methodology in the Social Sciences." *Feminist Thought and the Structure of Knowledge.* Ed. Mary M. Gergen. New York: New York UP, 1988. 87–104.

Gitlin, Andrew David. "Educative Research, Voice, and School Change." *Harvard Educational Review* 60 (1990): 443–66.

Herndl, Carl G. "Writing Ethnography: Representation, Rhetoric, and Institutional Practices." *College English* 53 (1991): 320–32.

Herrington, Anne J. "Writing in Academic Settings: A Study of the Contexts for Writing in Two College Chemical Engineering Courses." *Research in the Teaching of English* 19 (1985): 331–61.

———. "Reflections on Empirical Research: Examining Some Ties between Theory and Action." *Theory and Practice in the Teaching of Writing: Rethinking the Discipline.* Ed. Lee Odell. Carbondale: Southern Illinois UP, 1993. 40–70.

Lewis, Magda, and Roger I. Simon. "A Discourse Not Intended for Her: Learning and Teaching within Patriarchy." *Harvard Educational Review* 56 (1986): 457–72.

Lincoln, Yvonna S. "The Making of a Constructivist: A Remembrance of Transformations Past." *The Paradigm Dialog.* Ed. Egon G. Guba. Newbury Park: Sage, 1990. 67–87.

Lincoln, Yvonna S., and Egon G. Guba. *Naturalistic Inquiry.* Beverly Hills: Sage, 1985.

McCarthy, Lucille Parkinson. "A Stranger in Strange Lands: A College Student Writing across the Curriculum." *Research in the Teaching of English* 21 (1987): 233–65.

McCarthy, Lucille Parkinson, and Stephen M. Fishman. "Boundary Conversations: Conflicting Ways of Knowing in Philosophy and Interdisciplinary Research." *Research in the Teaching of English* 25 (1991): 419–68.

Mishler, Elliot G. "Validation in Inquiry-Guided Research: The Role of Exemplars in Narrative Studies." *Harvard Educational Review* 60 (1990): 415–42.

Myers, Greg. Rev. of *Science, the Very Idea,* by Steve Woolgar; *Science in Action,* by Bruno Latour; *Discourse and Social Psychology,* by Jonathan Potter and Margaret Wetherell; and *Knowledge and Reflexivity,* ed. Steve Woolgar. *College Composition and Communication* 39 (1988): 465–74.

Newkirk, Thomas. "The Aesthetics of Research." Paper presented at the Convention of the National Council of Teachers of English, Atlanta. November 1991.

Pratt, Mary Louise. "Fieldwork in Common Places." *Writing Cultures: The Poetics and Politics of Ethnography.* Ed. James Clifford and George E. Marcus. Berkeley: U of California P, 1986. 27–50.

Quantz, Richard A., and Terence W. O'Connor. "Writing Critical Ethnography: Dialogue, Multivoicedness, and Carnival in Cultural Texts." *Educational Theory* 38 (1988): 95–109.

Van Maanen, John. *Tales of the Field: On Writing Ethnography.* Chicago: U of Chicago P, 1988.

Weiler, Kathleen. *Women Teaching for Change: Gender, Class, and Power.* South Hadley: Bergin and Garvey, 1987.

Woolgar, Steve, ed. *Knowledge and Reflexivity: New Frontiers in the Sociology of Knowledge.* Newbury Park: Sage, 1988.

Zeller, Nancy C. "A Rhetoric for Naturalistic Inquiry." Diss. U of Indiana, 1987.

10 Culture on the Page: Experience, Rhetoric, and Aesthetics in Ethnographic Writing

Bonnie S. Sunstein
University of Iowa

[T]he optimal fieldworker should dance on the edge of a paradox by simultaneously becoming one of the people and remaining an academic. The term participant-observer reflects even as it shapes the fieldworker's double persona.

—Renato Rosaldo, *Culture and Truth*

When I write ethnography, I feel quiet guilt each time my informants speak and every time I enter their written words into my computer. As I transcribe conversations or work my field notes into a slick description, I worry. My informants, people in their own right, living in their own cultural spaces, enter my pages reincarnated. My processed version of them exists somewhere between *my* mind, *my* field notes, *my* computer, and eventually *my* reader. I write of these people but not necessarily for these people, use some of their words but not all of their words, understand a slice of their surroundings and histories but not the whole. I am everywhere and I am nowhere. My public writerly omniscience clouds their private right to exist. As I give them life on the page, I freeze them into time and space, depositing black words on a white paper backdrop for a reader none of us knows.

But I delight in writing what I have learned from my informants and their surroundings, hoping that my reader—and my informants themselves—will learn something from our work together. Yet I am a guilty academic voyeur, consciously reenacting a learned ritual for my own professional advancement. I need to remind myself that this silent, internal, tension-ridden performance, this alternating of personal quest, rhetorical rigor, aesthetic sensibility, and guilt, should be one that every ethnographic writer experiences. It is, as sociologist John Van Maanen writes, a "peculiar practice," as we represent "the social reality of others through the analysis of one's own experience in the world of these others" (ix). And it is, I hope, a continual, living dilemma—the heart of the researcher's data and the lungs of ethnographic writing. Our guilt, our art, and our scholarly rigor are both professional and personal, at once a dilemma and a delight. "The bright side of guilt," writes anthropologist Barbara Myerhoff, "is that it is an expression of a sense of responsibility for another's well-being" (27).

In composition studies, as we assume the responsibility for studying people inside their cultural surroundings and its corollary goal of making something of what we see, we enter a tangled tension—between presentation and representation—between our informants, their texts, ourselves, our texts, and our readers. It is a liminal tension, a state, as anthropologist Victor Turner describes, of in-betweenness: "The liminal period is that time and space betwixt and between one context of meaning and action and another. It is when the initiand is neither what he has been nor is what he will be. Characteristic of this liminal period is the appearance of marked ambiguity and inconsistency of meaning" (113). It resides in many human performances meant to offer sociocultural shifts or transformations—coming-of-age rituals, for example, initiation ceremonies, secluded retreats, or the gentle inadvertent social dramas we enact every day. Such experience is, Barbara Myerhoff and Deena Metzger remind us, "the great moment of teachability" (106).

Liminality lurks everywhere in ethnographic research and writing, especially as we investigate and interpret the cultural sites in which our informants work with words. As writing teachers, we know to encourage tension in our students' composing processes. Sondra Perl's "felt sense," Linda Flower's "writer-based prose," James Britton's "expressive writing," Donald Murray's "inner voice," and invocations of Lev Vygotsky's "inner speech" number among composition scholars' theoretical attempts to describe a kind of liminal state of articulation. These are the healthy habits of first-draft writing, liminal texts, that mark movement toward verbal transformation, the "great moment of teachability" in which our student writers begin to articulate meaning for themselves.

For researchers, too, this tension marks our experience as much as it does our informants' as we watch them write: positioning ourselves as participant-observers, feeling boundaries shift between objective reality and subjective experience, contemplating the private-public nature of our field notes, our taped conversations, and in our informants' written drafts. And for ourselves as writers, liminal tension exists as we choose rhetorical and aesthetic devices to render this living culture on the page. Out of these choices emerges a quiet but inevitable ethnographic guilt. We want to represent our informants—who expect we have safeguarded the messy truths of their lived experience and their words—inside our writing. Our readers, on the other hand, will expect a narrative that conveys information according to the conventions of an academic discipline. But sometimes such conventions interrupt the narratives that we have heard, seen, and read. Liminal tension seeps between storytelling in the field and our obligation to information in the text. And so the requirements of storytelling and information blur between the informants whose works we observe and render and the readers for whom we write.

As writing researchers engaged in ethnographic work, our guilt represents a dialogical responsibility to mediate between storytelling and information. We need to become more like storytellers, artisans engaged in the preservation of informants' voices and narratives—spoken and written. And our academic emphasis on convention must be tempered by a greater attention to craftsmanship, to the rhetorical and aesthetic principles that protect the power and cohesion of people's stories. Folklorist Elliott Oring observes, "Lives are not transcriptions of events. They are artful and enduring symbolic constitutions which demand our engagement and identification. They are to be perceived and understood as wholes" (222).

So, the very term *ethnography* is dialogical. It refers to both the procedure and the product of our research. It involves layers of cultural performance—ours and theirs—as we act out relationships with our informants, with our texts, and with our readers. Ethnography is the relationship between what goes on in a culture and how it appears on the page, a relationship dependent as much upon writers' lenses and tools as it is on those of a researcher. Ethnography must describe culture through the perspectives and words of those inside—the informants'— as well as outside—the researcher-writer's. It is a dialogical awareness, the point of which, writes James Clifford, is "to *decenter* the self, to focus neither on the (intimate) self nor on the (distanced) other but on the historically and politically constituted field of relationships between (and constituting) self and other" (qtd. in Roth 562).

In this chapter, I explore ethnographic writing as liminal performance, rich with the entanglements between informant and researcher, culture and text, truth and fiction, writer and reader. I draw from one work of contemporary anthropology, Barbara Myerhoff's *Number Our Days,* and illustrate with excerpts from my own book, *Composing a Culture,* to show how this liminal condition both problematizes our method and influences the experiential, rhetorical, and aesthetic strategies we use. And I offer some questions and categories to examine our choices as writing emerges from research.

We can learn much about writing from the vigorous conversation in postmodern and feminist anthropology about the researcher's responsibility to be both reflexive and representative (Benson; Buker; Clifford and Marcus; Crapanzano; Geertz; Recchio; Roth; Ruby; Watson). But we can learn far more as we read ethnographers' studies and examine their crafted texts (Behar; Fabian; Glassie; Myerhoff; Narayan; Wolf). And alas, there is no solution to the ethnographer's guilt. It is a productive guilt as we work with the words of some and render them for others.

The Performing Researcher: Looking for Culture

If ethnographers are to become preservers of story, as opposed to being dispensers of information, then our artistry must come with an appreciation, practically and theoretically, of verbal art. The study of people writing is akin to the study of "verbal art as performance" in any culture. Our informants negotiate meaning as they draft and craft inside a cultural context of others doing the same. Both the enactment and the study of "verbal art" in its own setting, as folklorists describe it—the cultural texts people construct—depend on three features: a performer who is an insider to the culture, a recognizable verbal performance, and an audience of insiders (Abrahams, "The Complex Relations" and *Singing;* Bauman; Schechner and Appel; Turner). These three roles are symbiotic; the performer depends on an informed audience, the performance occurs within understood cultural frames, and the audience responds with conventions appropriate to the culture (Bauman). Such cultural performances are spontaneous verbal art; they are unrehearsed, unscripted, and not often staged.

When we teach and study composition, we know that much of what constitutes a finished written product is, in fact, this very informal, unrehearsed, unscripted, unstaged process of talk, draft, and response—the "trying out" of words for a group of informed insiders. When we study sites of literacy, we see performances of verbal art, that is, we see "composing in context." And so it is when we write. Ethnographers who study verbal art must enact a doubly reflexive presence as they shuttle between roles—their own cultural performances of collecting, reporting, and writing their research, and the cultural performances of their informants who read, write, listen, and talk. "'Performance,'" writes Johannes Fabian of his studies of proverbs and theater in Shaba,

Zaire, "seemed to be a more adequate description both of the ways people realize their culture and of the method by which an ethnographer produces knowledge about that culture" (18).

And so, as ethnographers studying sites of verbal performance, we must represent the culture from the informants' perspectives as well as our own, folding both perspectives into text. Ethnography differs from other forms of nonfiction—reminiscence, oral history, character sketch, travelogue, new journalism—by virtue of its *cultural focus*. As we research, read, and write ethnographies, as we give in to the liminality inherent in the ethnographic position, it is useful to ask such key focusing questions as:

1. Where is the culture?
2. What is the researcher-writer's position in relationship to this culture?
3. Where is the history? Whose is it? Where does the researcher-writer find it?
4. What theory drives the researcher-writer's informants? What theory drives the researcher-writer?
5. What are the researcher-writer's sources of data?
6. What is the researcher-writer's position in relationship to the data and the text?

These questions offer a heuristic by which we can confront ethnography's tension and address our own positions as readers, writers, and researchers—between cultures, histories, artifacts, and theories. We see performances of verbal art, ours and our informants', as they sit inside the culture in which they occur. As we look for the culture, we must recognize ourselves as performers in "a state betwixt and between." As we attempt to fold the answers to these questions into our texts, as we move our performance toward the page, we make experiential, rhetorical, and aesthetic choices.

Myerhoff's full-length ethnography *Number Our Days* is a study of elderly Jews in a southern California senior center, most of them immigrants who raised their families into mainstream middle-class America, most of them forgotten and in poverty. She establishes the center as a culture by referencing their shared histories in pre-World War II eastern European shtetls, their common use of Yiddish-American expressions, and her surveys of the colorful artifacts and variegated lives both inside and outside the center.

Myerhoff recognizes what few writers do. She reflects upon and illustrates a liminal moment, taking the opportunity to render a cultural situation rich with performance and verbal art. Early in the text, for example, she crafts an unconventional "arrival narrative." Convention dictates that the researcher simultaneously explain her arrival upon the scene and invite her reader into a position upon the text. She must convey information to readers. She establishes the site and defines it first as a cultural one through the data sources she has gathered and the informants she has chosen to represent. Yet as an artisan, attentive to rhetorical and aesthetic principles of verbal art, Myerhoff crafts her text without violating her informants' words.

In her first chapter, Myerhoff constructs her own performance, her liminal presence—as researcher and writer—amidst her informants' performances. She draws her title from an informant's comment: "So what do you want from us here?" cleverly suggesting through her informant's perspective that there is, in fact, a culture there and that she is, in fact, an outsider to it:

> I wanted to focus on the Center, not myself, but it became clear that what was being written was from my eyes, with my personality, biases, history, and sensibility, and it seemed dishonest to exclude that, thereby giving an impression of greater objectivity and authority than I believed in. (30)

But as Myerhoff focuses in on her informants and their center culture, she gently weaves her thick store of data. Yet she feels discomfort. Were she to assume "greater objectivity," she would ignore an important part of the center's story, namely, her performance as a participant in the culture. And yet, as she moves her performance toward the page, she must find the rhetorical and aesthetic principles which keep subjectivity in check.

She does this with her informant Basha's words: *"Every morning I wake up in pain. I wiggle my toes. Good. They still obey. I open my eyes. Good. I can see. Everything hurts but I get dressed. I walk down to the ocean. Good. It's still there. Now my day can start. About tomorrow I never know. After all I'm eighty-nine. I can't live forever."* And then we read Myerhoff as she interprets Basha's words and introduces us to the senior center: "Death and the ocean are protagonists in Basha's life. They provide points of orientation, comforting in their certitude. One visible, the other invisible, neither hostile nor friendly, they accompany her as she walks down the boardwalk to the Aliyah Senior Citizen's Center" (1).

My own ethnographic study, far smaller in scope, presents a parallel arrival narrative—in the field and on the page. As an academic, my obligation was to synthesize and inform readers according to certain conventions. Like Myerhoff, I had connections to the culture I was investigating. I was, to some degree, sensitized to my informants' stories and my place within them. And that meant I was concerned about how information might override story. Bringing performance to the page, I assumed, as did Myerhoff, the reflexive stance of any performer. Aware of my obligations to both readers and informants, I knew that what I wrote would involve an ethical balance of creativity and convention—of storytelling and information. Like Myerhoff, I strove to write research that would, in fact, soften the distinction *between* story and information. Rhetorically and aesthetically, I sought story *as* information.

I studied high school teachers in a three-week summer writing program, most of them middle-aged, middle-class, and away from home—as I was. I saw the program as a temporary culture, a liminal moment in time and space for teachers who wanted to learn more about teaching writing. My task upon arrival was to establish what constituted this "culture" for these teachers: common experiences in the high school classroom, struggles with teaching writing when they did not write much themselves, their quest for renewal and affirmation, their need for a collegial community. I saw these consistencies, but I also saw ironies. Liminality and tension were keys to establishing this temporary three-week culture.

I open with an intertext, a section I call "Confessions of a Participant-Observer" (23). In it I describe the rather oddly surrealistic reversals of time and space I observed as the three weeks began: public school teachers dressed for summer heat ("everyone is wearing minimal clothing: tank tops, shorts, sundresses, sandals, running shoes"), middle-agers moving into student housing ("they cradle computer monitors and printers wrapped in blankets and pillows"), students acting as their counselors ("Claire is young to be a dorm mother and most of the people she helps are middle-aged"). I notice that even the physical space invites the sense of community which the program wants to foster—the buildings outside ("the dorms cluster around a common velvet-grass lawn and a well-tended forest encircles them. . . . Each views the campus from a different perspective"), and the furniture inside ("the four sofas are upholstered in student-proof blue tweed, armed in oak, and they form a square for conversation"). And I document my own history as I place the artifacts of my middle-aged life into my student quarters ("my mother-in-law's blue striped sheets, the yellow towels which were a wedding gift from my father . . . the family picture that's been on four different desks at four different school jobs. . . . Alone in the steamy afternoon, I inventory my belongings in this new environment. Stripped of their cluttered context, they represent relationships") (23–26).

A page later, in a deliberate attempt at reflexivity, I locate myself in the bathroom on the first morning of the program, emerging from a shower, having a conversation about writing with a woman who was weeping because she was afraid to write:

> [A]s I step out, I see a woman about my age. We share an awkward smile. . . . She is sobbing, and we are both grabbing at our towels. We hold a towel with one elbow as we brush our teeth and speak to each other in the mirror.
> . . . Today is the anniversary of her husband's suicide, and she wants to write about it, but she is afraid to share it on Friday. . . . Talking to her in the mirror, I try to reflect what I know about helping someone choose a topic. . . . She decides on the dog. (27)

At the end of this opening intertext, I begin to explain my research methods and theoretical frame by referring back to the shower episode, positioning myself as a researcher much as I had positioned myself as a writing teacher—awkwardly before the mirror:

> I do have a double persona here, like the mirror conversation in the shower room this morning. I am a writing teacher who is studying writing teachers and writing about it, living in my own culture in order to study it. Writing is not just my topic; it is also my method. My personal perspective will render this story, but it cannot smother it. (28)

Although my use of the bathroom mirror to suggest reflexivity might be too slick (or cheap) a rhetorical move, and reading Myerhoff might have inspired a more sophisticated rendering, it was a moment in my data collection that I felt represented the cultural focus I was aiming to achieve. There were no irrelevant details in my final text; I chose each one to illustrate my findings and my theory. I wanted this intertext to be far more than the obligatory "arrival narrative" in which the confident (usually male) anthropologist, wife by his side, stumbles into a colorful native ritual and begins his journey toward universal human truth. Like Myerhoff's reflexive arrival narrative, I needed to craft myself, my informant, her surroundings, and the story I was about to tell into text that readers would recognize as information but feel compelled to read.

As a writer, I meant my opening intertext to synthesize the setting, the surroundings, the characters, the scholarship, and my studied position amidst it all. Months after the experience, as I wrote, I chose my details from field notes and analytic memos, from data collected and theory employed, to illustrate and situate the cultural sweep I had studied. I devised the intertexts—short, triangulated, five-page moments between longer case studies—to illustrate the nonlinear, nonchronological structure of this temporary event. My intertext title, "Confessions of a Participant-Observer," was at once personal and analytical, I hoped, with an ironic little nod to the tradition of the arrival narrative. In short, the choices I made while attempting to answer the ethnographic researcher's questions were the choices any writer makes: choices of experiential, rhetorical, and aesthetic performance.

The Page as Liminal Space: Attending to Text

Attention to the language and form of an ethnographic text, anthropologist George Marcus writes, is the way we synthesize fieldwork and theory. It is an act of "deskwork as opposed to fieldwork" (qtd. in Ruby 171). The page itself becomes our liminal space as we assemble a text out of our written words and the words of our informants, somehow synthesizing our field experience, moving it draft by draft, layer by layer, toward a reader who is another insider in a different culture—one which requires our writerly sensitivity.

In another passage from her first chapter, Myerhoff explains that her own history affects her research subject, placing herself on the benches just outside the senior center. Throughout her text, we find, the benches are a critical site in her data. But they also function as an important metaphor to explain the tension between two lives her informants must negotiate—as insiders in the center and as outsiders to an ambivalent and sometimes hostile California oceanside community:

> I sat on the benches outside the Center and thought about how strange it was to be back in the neighborhood where sixteen years before I had lived and for a time had been a social worker with elderly citizens on public relief. Then the area was called "Oshini Beach." The word *"shini"* still made me cringe. As a child I had been taunted with it. Like many second-generation Americans, I wasn't sure what being a Jew meant. When I was a child our family had avoided the words *Jew* and *Yid*. (11)

As she uses the benches to reflect on her own relationship with those she studies, she uses the benches, too, as her metaphorical vantage point, as her informants do, to survey their immediate world. Members of the senior center culture, in this scene, negotiate their identities with cultures outside their own in this liminal space. In the following description, she analyzes patterns of behavior, ritual, and talk which will define much of what readers need to know as we enter the inner life of the center's political pulses. And she foreshadows the outlying threats to the center's safety as she surveys the surrounding cultural scene—a scene, she notes, that her informants intuitively avoid:

As the morning wears on, the benches fill. Benches are attached back to back, one side facing the ocean, one side the boardwalk. The people on the ocean side swivel around to face their friends, the boardwalk, and the Center.

Bench behavior is highly stylized. The half-dozen or so benches immediately to the north and south of the Center are the territory of the members, segregated by sex and conversation topic. The men's benches are devoted to abstract, ideological concerns—philosophical debate, politics, religion, and economics. The women's benches are given more to talk about immediate, personal matters—children, food, health, neighbors, love affairs, scandals, and "managing." Men and women talk about Israel and its welfare, and about being a Jew and about Center politics. On the benches, reputations are made and broken, controversies explored, leaders selected, factions formed and dissolved. Here is the outdoor dimension of Center life, like a village plaza, a focus of protracted, intense sociability.

The surrounding scene rarely penetrates the invisible, pulsing membrane of the Center community. The old people are too absorbed in their own talk to attend the setting. Surfers, sunbathers, children, dogs, bicyclists, winos, hippies, voyeurs, photographers, panhandlers, artists, junkies, roller skaters, peddlers, and police are omnipresent all year round. Every social class, age, race, and sexual preference is represented. Jesus cults, Hare Krishna parades, sidewalk preachers jostle steel bands and itinerant musicians. As colorful and flamboyant as the scene is by day, it is as dangerous by night. Muggings, theft, rape, harassment, and occasional murders make it a perilous neighborhood for the old people after dark. (4–5)

In these paragraphs, Myerhoff observes her informants performing their cultural roles, but she also explains her own performance as researcher and interpreter. Her choices as writer suggest far more than the obligatory arrival narrative (Geertz; Herndl). Her first chapter is far more than narrative. It is interpretation, analysis, argument, historical documentation, dialogue, and poetic description. She answers the ethnographer's questions by weaving sharp detail with anthropological interpretation ("bench behavior is highly stylized," "[t]he half-dozen or so benches immediately to the north and south of the Center are the territory of the members, segregated by sex and conversation topic," "[h]ere is the outdoor dimension of Center life, like a village plaza, a focus of protracted, intense sociability"). She documents months of recorded conversation by noting men's and women's separate topics, but also the topics—critical to their cultural history—which they share ("about Israel and its welfare, and about being a Jew and about Center politics"). In a blur of colorful nouns, she records the surrounding culture ("bicyclists, winos, hippies, voyeurs, photographers, panhandlers, artists, junkies, roller skaters, peddlers, and police. . . . Jesus cults, Hare Krishna parades, sidewalk preachers jostle steel bands and itinerant musicians"). The quick blitz flashes in poignant contrast against the elderly people on the benches, physically slow but verbally adept, oblivious to the scene. She uses the device of foreshadowing to alert us that the surrounding culture is a hostile one ("it is as dangerous by night. Muggings, theft, rape, harassment, and occasional murders make it a perilous neighborhood for the old people after dark"). She prepares us for the layers of culture we will experience on her pages.

Sitting on her informants' benches, Myerhoff locates herself in the background of their culture and writes from their perspective, sketching the lines of researcher's questions against their cultural map. As writer and researcher, she too engages in a cultural performance. She carefully constructs her own presentation of self (with a theoretical nod to Erving Goffman), she writes sociocultural drama (with a theoretical nod to Victor Turner) as she interprets it, with rhetorical and aesthetic rigor. As a Jewish woman of a younger generation and an ex-social worker, perched on the benches which define the boundaries between inside and outside, Myerhoff acknowledges her performance as researcher and writer.

Like Myerhoff, in our work as composition researchers we are reflexive participant-observers, insider-outsiders, writing about writers as they write in writing communities, and our art as writers affects the writing we study. Like Myerhoff, we can aim for a collective reflexivity, a polyvocal performance in which our informants share our space. But in composition studies, we face special challenges because our informants are also producing written texts. We collect multiple verbal data sources to study the processes of literacy in order to render them— our own talk and writing and the talk and writing of our informants. The data sources we use as we synthesize our experience on the page can fall into two categories, their verbal performances and ours:

Informants' Writing	**Researcher's Writing**
Formal writing	Quotations from field notes
Progressions of drafts	Quotations from analytic
Marginal comments, class	memos or journal
notes, etc.	Descriptive sketches
Journal entries	Chronological arrangements
Handouts, fliers, worksheets	Juxtaposition of the written
Notes or letters	and the oral
Responses to reading	Verbal snapshots—land-
	scapes, portraits
	Ideas for interpretive section
	headings

But, ironically, our final text must break these categories. It should conflate our informants' words and our own. The final text is the result of a gathered cacophony of verbal data which holds the clues to how we render what we see, hear, smell, taste, feel, and recognize from our scholarship. As we merge our informants' texts with "ours," the boundaries between these categories merge, too, as the page itself begins to resolve—for a verbal moment—the liminal quality of our researched experience.

In one section of my book which I called "Breaking the Rules in Style: Into Wishin' about Intuition" (80), a long case study chapter, I use an informant's note taped to my dormitory door to unfold and interpret a twenty-four-hour period of her reading and writing. My informant, a young teacher who named herself Therese, works her way through an obsession—that she lacks "intuition." In order to examine the thread of influences which led to her poem, I moved backward over twenty-four hours of data. I examined the finished poem and its drafts, her journal entry from that day and a later reflection on it, the books she was reading and her marginal notes, an audiotaped conversation between her and another teacher, a crumpled note which I extracted from a wastebasket, my field notes from her classes over two days, the questions I asked myself in my researcher's journal, and her own account in a taped interview.

To render it months later, I listened to the tapes, stared at my notes, stared at her notes, studied my field notes and memos from that twenty-four-hour period, played with the images and metaphors I was using to characterize her, named the section I was trying to write, and read theories about teacher development and writing anxiety. But foremost was my commitment to Therese's perspective; her words inside mine furnished me with our collective reflexivity. The title of the section came from a line in her poem, "Breaking the Rules in Style: Into Wishin' about Intuition." Her confusion about following rules and breaking them played out in the field notes and photographs I had collected as I observed her demeanor, talked with her about her background, and even noticed how she arranged her possessions. For my readers, it is four pages, about three percent of the published book.

I trace Therese's need for rules by illustrating with deliberate textual decisions to maintain the tension between her voice (in writing and talk) and my interpretation. Myerhoff uses the seniors' benches and the Venice boardwalk life as the locus of complex cultural negotiation—between each member of the community, and between the community and its cultural surroundings. She achieves a collective perspective—between herself and her informants—with textual devices drawn from her experience at the research site, attention to rhetorical requirements as she moves from her writing to her reader, and aesthetic decisions as she crafts the text itself.

As our research experience crawls into our written pages, we must discover and attempt to maintain liminal tensions, all the while recognizing that our informants and our readers may make conflicting demands. The choices we make as we create ethnographic text require our experiential, rhetorical, and aesthetic rigor. In the remainder of this chapter, I will offer examples of a few of the features of ethnographic text and outline a few others. I share these categories not as an exhaustive list, but to suggest strategies we ought to consider as we write:

Experiential	Rhetorical	Aesthetic
Field notes	Position as trope: the voice of the researcher	Metaphor as extension and definition
Expanded field notes		
Analytic memos, journals	The voice of the "other"	Informant as foil
Interview transcripts	Historical contexts	Concrete and sensory images
Photos, artifacts	Disclosure of methodology	The social drama
Informants' writing	Descriptive intertexts	The spatial gaze
Theoretical "frames"	Analytic section heads, titles	Ethnopoetic notation

First we must document the experience itself, the data collection in the time and space in which we lived it. These layers of data might include field notes, expanded field notes, analytic memos, notes from the theoretical work which shapes our view, and the other records of our fieldwork: tapes and transcripts, photos and collected artifacts, and—in our case especially—the body of our informants' formal and informal writing. Next, we must make conscious rhetorical choices as we think about how we will interpret the experience into text—first for informants, then for ourselves and for our readers. Aristotle's rhetorical categories, still an influence on our Western tradition of presenting both science and writing, implicitly push us to combine an *ethos* (position of the speaker), *pathos* (sensitivity to audience), and *logos* (information itself) to represent our work. And, as Aristotle reminds us, the shape of our rhetorical appeal is dependent on each situation. Finally, we must employ our knowledge of the writer's craft as we choose aesthetic means to represent what we have studied. Like a vivid and satisfying poem, a well-written ethnography needs artful design to allow the reader in.

The Experiential: Reflexive, Dialogical Performance

Fieldwork is a blur of sights, sounds, textures, tastes, and impressions which we must record any way we can: notes, memos to ourselves, journals, photographs, videotapes, scraps of paper, artifacts from informants. Like the unarticulable "felt sense," the "inner speech put to paper" of first-draft writing, we record mounds of chaos and write to discover how we will organize it. We experience the events of the field, collect representative artifacts, and haul it all toward text—a reflexive, dialogic process. It is an act in which, as researchers, we are caught between seeing and writing. The ethnographic fieldworker performs as mediator, and our field notes are the concrete objects of that mediation. The data collection refers back to the "other," our informant, and forward toward another "other," the reader. But as we do it we must retain a reflexive presence—monitoring our assumptions, our emerging theory, and our changing questions.

In a study of anthropologists' field notes, Jean Jackson identifies field notes themselves as liminal, deep with intense fears and fantasies. In her interviews, some researchers wished their field notes would become famous documents, others wanted them destroyed at their death, many feared that their field notes would burn. Jackson explains that especially the first fieldwork experience represents "a liminal period in our preparation as professionals. As in other initiation rites, items associated with such activities take on a heavy emotional valence and sacredness" (29). Researchers' notes, she reminds us, at any stage in our professional growth, reflect the fieldwork experience characterized by a heightened sense of responsibility and emotion as the fieldworker imposes an order upon the chaos she studies in a cultural site:

> Twilight is a temporal liminality, swamps a geographical one, lungfish a zoological example, hermaphrodites a sexual liminality. Liminality necessarily occurs when we impose classification systems upon the natural world; what is interesting is that it is a conspicuous feature in the symbol system of every culture, often accompanied by marked *affect*. (9, my emphasis)

Our sense of order and purpose is disturbed, and often our "affect" is heightened as we leave our daily lives to conduct research in a space and time rich with opportunities for reflection and reflexivity—ironically, because of its very difference from daily life.

And so, to maintain a reflexive presence in relationship to our fieldwork, we must own up to our position as mediators between the field site and the text. Quoting from our own analytic memos or research journals, cataloging our data sources in the text, and explaining our methods inside our narrative are all ways we reconstruct the field experience as we craft the final text. For our readers, we must explain the structure and categories we have chosen to impose on the mass of data we have collected. Again, I turn to Myerhoff. In this passage she recounts her field experience and shares her organizational dilemma:

> The amount and variety of information accumulated in a field study is overwhelming. There is no definite or correct solution to the problem of what to include, how to cut up the pie of social reality, when precisely to leave or stop. . . . Of the three hundred Center members I met and talked with about a half. . . . Of these, I knew eighty personally, and interviewed and spent my time with thirty-six. I tape recorded extensive interviews with these, ranging from two to sixteen hours, visited nearly all in their homes, took trips with them from time to time outside the neighborhood—to doctors, social workers, shopping, funerals, visiting their friends in old age homes and hospitals, following my subjects to convalescent homes and hospitals; I went to many funerals and memorial services. Apart from these excursions and my interviews with outsiders who knew Center people well—teachers, rabbis, local politicians, volunteers—I concentrated on the Center and its external extensions, the benches, boardwalk, and hotel and apartment lobbies where they congregated. (28–29)

Myerhoff inventories her experience for the reader, accounting for her data and the places, determined by her informants' daily activity, in which she collected it. She also explains the theories which framed her interpretation and folds those theories into her text. In the following example, she accounts for the complexity of the culture as she met it after thirty years of the center's existence, citing the classic anthropological work of Lévi-Strauss:

> Claude Lévi-Strauss had used the word *bricolage* to describe the process through which myths are constructed in preliterate societies. Odds and ends, fragments offered up by chance or the environment—almost anything will do—are taken up by a group and incorporated into a tale, used by a people to explain themselves and their world. No intrinsic order or system has dictated the materials employed. In such an inelegant fashion does the bricoleur or handyman meet his needs.
> Center culture was such a work of bricolage. Robust and impudently eclectic, it shifted and stretched to meet immediate needs—private, collective, secular, and sacred. (10)

Critics argue about Myerhoff's scholarly rigor—too much narrative and not enough of the "theoretical and conceptual trappings of the scientist," constructing a fiction rather than reporting qualitative social science (Whaley 39; Atkinson). But I believe it is her ability to smooth out her text, to write for her readers, that invites skepticism. Critics have said the same of Clifford Geertz (Olson; Roseberry; Shankman). There is an assumption that if an ethnographic account is engaging, it cannot be scientific. Geertz himself claims that contemporary ethnographies "look at least like romances as much as lab reports" (16). If the writer-researcher admits her position in the culture, I believe, nods to her own personal theoretical and conceptual biases, interprets it to highlight a cultural reality, and is able to spin a compelling narrative all at the same time, the work then may begin to *feel* more like a fiction. What distinguishes ethnography from fiction is that the experiential *is* rhetorical; the ethnographer achieves her epistemological position *with* her rhetoric. If we ask "what is this text *doing*" we see that it is the ethnographic experience itself that does the work and, coupled with the ethnographer's rhetoric and art, carries it to the reader. In my mind as a reader of ethnography, it is rather a dazzling display of academic performance, rich with a researcher's personal ethic, scholarly inquiry, and the techniques of rhetorical and aesthetic craft.

The Rhetorical: Textual Performance

As Geertz reminds us, "We have met the Unreliable Narrator and He is Us" (qtd. in Roth 555). To write ethnographically requires layers of textual performance; with it we owe a rhetorical responsibility to our informants, our selves, and our readers. We must choose textual ways to account for the researcher's, informants', and readers' positions. We must find tropes and devices to locate ourselves and our informants where we want them, and help our readers locate themselves as well. The rhetoric of ethnography merges perspectives; it achieves a momentary, singular, and unreliable sort of reliability.

Claiming positions in text involves decisions related to the sites we have studied, like Myerhoff's metaphor of the benches and mine of the mirror. As we make these choices, we must find ways, too, to include historical and methodological information. Careful choice of titles or analytic section headings (like Myerhoff's "So What Do You Want from Us Here" or my "Breaking the Rules in Style: Into Wishin' about Intuition," both drawn from our informants' perspectives) offer readers a window of analysis without interrupting the flow of text.

Each setting we study suggests different rhetorical decisions about the chronology or the shape of the narrative. In my book, although I focused on three people's summer experience, I wanted to illustrate others' as well. I chose to write intertexts, as I illustrated above, five- to ten-page triangulated verbal snapshots of other moments in which participants, their writing, and the surroundings fused to show other important features of the summer program's culture. The living context we have experienced as researchers must govern the shape of our written text.

Myerhoff's site is one which does not produce many written texts, but she renders a cacophony of verbal data: arguments, stories, prayers and proverbs, reminiscences, written artifacts, and other verbal and visual creations. As she tours her reader around the center, she notes advertisements and posters: "'Hot Kosher Meal—Nutritious—65 cents' . . . a program provided by state and private funds." She details hand-lettered signs in both Yiddish and English, "Today at 2:00 Jewish History Class. Teacher, Clara Shapiro. *Very educational.*" She describes the walls, decorated by the center elders, which slide us through their own cultural history: paintings of traditional ceremonies and shtetl life in Europe, portraits of Yiddish heroes, a mass of artifacts illustrating American acculturation ("a large, wooden Star of David illuminated by a string of Christmas lights"). A wall-length mural, painted by the elders, portrays "their common journey from the past to the present," a shtetl street scene, a boatful of immigrants arriving at Ellis Island, picketers bearing signs such as "Protest Treatment." Finally, in a rhetorical decision that is doubly reflexive, Myerhoff's sweep of her informants' walls brings us back to their life at the center: "The last sequence rendered the elders, seated on benches along the boardwalk and celebrating the Sabbath inside the Center" (12–13).

The Aesthetic: Artistic Performance

Rhetorical consciousness allows us to mediate between presentation and representation, rendering for our readers what we have gathered between our informants and ourselves. It is a necessary performance as we move from experience to text. But as we smooth out the text itself, we confront another kind of liminal performance. As writers who study writers, we want to create engaging text, and we know the strategies to use. They are the very artistic strategies, the "writer's craft" with which we have been writing and teaching for years. Metaphor and imagery allow for reader interpretation. Carefully chosen details placed in our narrative enrich our view of the social dramas we attempt to represent. Sensory images display the ethnographer's spatial gaze, the details of setting so important as we describe our informants' surroundings. We must choose, too, the verb tenses and notation systems we will use to display our informants' words—both spoken and written—in order to allow their perspective into our writing.

None of these aesthetic techniques can be disconnected, although all of them must be conscious choices folded into a smooth text. As we write, the boundaries blur between fiction and nonfiction, between poetry and prose. And ethnographer's guilt emerges as we use the writer's craft. "As I undid necklaces of words and restrung them," writes anthropologist Ruth Behar, "as I dressed up hours of rambling talk in elegant sentences and paragraphs of prose, as I snipped at the flow of talk, stopping it sometimes for dramatic emphasis long before it had really stopped, I no longer knew where I stood on the border between fiction and non-fiction" (16).

To illustrate techniques of aesthetic performance on the page, I will offer another set of excerpts from Myerhoff. In her chapter called "Needle and Thread: The Life and Death of a Tailor," she introduces Schmuel, an informant who not only became her guide and friend, but who serves several purposes in her text.

> As often happens, I established a particularly strong and gratifying attachment to one individual, and also as often happens, in addition to being particularly knowledgeable and articulate about the community, this person was also an outsider. "Schmuel the Filosafe," he was called, and in a very significant way he was my teacher, critic, and guide. . . . I have included my own voice in his chapter, for it proved impossible to expunge. His statements and retorts did not make sense without that, for he was directing his commentary to me. (29–30)

Myerhoff uses Schmuel as her textual foil and admits it. His metaphors assist her as she observes and interprets the center culture. His view as a less distant outsider gives her words and images to represent the social drama and the spatial gaze she renders. Together, informant Schmuel and researcher Barbara explore not just the culture of the center, but her purposes for doing the study in the first place. She acknowledges the polyvocal, collective perspective they achieve together:

> He was my foil and teacher, goading and challenging my interpretations at every point. In time, our differences became sharper and clearer and more often than not a source of mutual amusement. We knew each other for eighteen months. At the end of this time I could see things from both our perspectives at once. I have often wondered if this was his chief purpose in agreeing to work with me. Certainly it was one of his most valuable lessons. (40–41)

In a courageous textual move, Myerhoff builds an imaginary conversation with Schmuel—after his death—which furnishes her with a frame for the chapter which she creates from his perspective and documents with her data. Her words mixed with his offer a peek into the contingent nature of ethnographic writing—we are dependent on our informants to find ways to write them. In this imaginary conversation, she employs a metaphor Schmuel used often—a pin deflating a ball—to illustrate her own fears as a researcher, and the layers unfold as Schmuel's skepticism becomes a metaphor for her own research:

> You cannot tell someone "I know you." People jump around. They are like a ball. You take a pin and stick it in, make a little hole. It goes flat. When you tell someone, "I know you," you put a little pin in. . . . So what should you do? Leave them be. Don't try to make them stand still for your convenience. You don't ever know them. Let people surprise you. This likewise you could do concerning yourself. All this, I didn't read in any book. It is my own invention."
>
> Invented, I was afraid, specifically to warn me. Schmuel delivered this speech as we trotted down the boardwalk on the way to his house, our arms linked tightly, less for closeness than to regulate our gait. He set a fierce pace. He didn't believe in strolling. I didn't mind. It gave me courage to walk with him in this way, regardless of his reasons. (41)

Schmuel's "fierce pace" as they trot down the boardwalk gives Myerhoff courage. It is no accident that she creates this concrete image with verbs like "trot" and arms linked tightly. It is informant Schmuel who regulates researcher Barbara's gait—not as much for closeness as it is to signify her dependence on his perspective.

In my own work, as I tried to represent my informants' perspectives, I found that each person's view of her experience suggested a different aesthetic choice. And the choice itself offered me frames for analysis. One teacher, Susan, although she was not a major informant, served as my foil. Like Schmuel was for Myerhoff, through Susan's description of her experience I came to understand others, testing her perspective against mine. In an interview which I used to open the book and title my introduction, "A Little Bit of a Cult" (1), Susan describes joy and confusion, as she put it to me, "a strange coexistence of solitude and dependence":

> I'm understanding that to read is to write is to listen; they're all the same thing. . . . But what is this? There's more to this. . . . I almost felt as though I was in a little bit of a cult. . . . I got an uncomfortable feeling after a while, because I thought "These

people are teaching us more than this stuff. . . . Unless I make a
deep change, I'm not going to be making any change at all". . . .
That is scary for me, and I didn't know it until I thought about it
. . . just about two days ago. (10)

To analyze the transcript of my interview with Susan, I experimented with ethnopoetic notation, a procedure for analysis of oral
speech, developed by folklorist Dennis Tedlock for the purposes of studying Native American verbal art, and adapted by sociolinguist Deborah
Tannen for studying mainstream American conversation. Spaces and
line breaks suggest repetitions and pauses, often highlighting important segments of thought. Susan's oral descriptions offered me an interpretive frame when I noted them poetically:

> I'm understanding
>   that to read is to write is to listen;
>   they're all the same thing.
> But what is this?
>   there's more to this.
>   I almost felt as though I was in a little bit of a cult
>   I got an uncomfortable feeling after a while
>   because I thought,
> "These people are teaching us
> More than this stuff!!
>   unless I make
>   a deep change,
>   I'm not going to be making
>   any change at all"
> That is scary for me
>   I didn't know it until
>   I thought about it
>   just about two days ago.

Her speech foregrounded her thinking, which became critical to
my analysis of the cult-like experience many teachers mentioned in my
interviews. In this poetic rendering, based on the pauses in her conversation, I can see that she sets herself against "these people," the program. With a triple infinitive, she begins by quickly and fluently recounting the program's basic tenets ("to read is to write is to listen").
But I can see that she sets herself against the program ("these people")—
with her conversational pauses and her skepticism ("uncomfortable,"
"a little bit of a cult"). Mostly, though, I was intrigued by two important
repetitions ("unless I make a deep change / I'm not going to make any
change" and "I didn't know it / until I thought about it"). In those two
repeated phrases lay two major concepts: (1) that teachers must make
changes their own way, in their own time, as they discover a pedagogical

paradigm shift, and (2) that in order to do it, they need time and colleagues to think about what they already know. For Susan, her fear of "making a deep change" linked with her surprise as she realized that it had taken two days of intense thinking. For me, her words helped establish a conceptual frame: that teachers were not, in fact, "transformed" as they lived in the program's culture, but they were rather affirmed.

Rendering Susan's speech into poetry on the page led to closer analysis. For her, as it would be for me, it would take months, maybe years, before it all sorted out. My poetic version of this interview never shows up in the final book, but without it, I doubt that I would have captured the subtleties of her perspective, nor would I have realized her value to me as an insider whose hard thinking validated my own. Ethnopoetic notation is both an ethnographer's tool and an aesthetic device, but it is a publisher's nightmare. As Tedlock reminds us, white space is not a cost-efficient way to capture a culture's speech patterns in a book or an article. But by linking our knowledge of the art of poetry to our informants' talk, it offers a way to analyze what's important: the pauses and emphases, the combinations, selections, and repetitions of their words.

Negotiating the Liminal State: Becoming One's Own Direct Object

Our completed draft is as much a textual performance as it is a report of research. Anthropologist Margery Wolf explains, "The better the observer, the more likely she is to catch her informants' understanding of the meaning of their experiences; the better the writer, the more likely she is to be able to convey that meaning to an interested reader from another culture" (5). Reading ethnography, too, requires a jump into the writer-researcher's tension—as she works between cultures and makes choices which will craft her informants' world into words for her reader.

So we need to give in to liminality—in the field and on the page— as we force ourselves into a consciousness that assumes three perspectives at once—the researcher's, the informants', and the reader's. "The reflexivity of performance," writes Victor Turner, "creatively democratizes. . . . To be reflexive is to be at once one's own subject and direct object" (qtd. in Ruby 96). When writing is the topic as well as the method, as in our studies of the cultural sites of literacy, we must render the polyvocality that our informants' words create as they tangle with our own. As we craft a final text, we work with their words and ours, always with an eye toward our rhetoric and our art:

1. Whose views of reality are these? Mine, my informants', someone else's inside my informants' culture?

2. How do I know what I know? Who constructs this knowledge? I, my informant, my informant-as-persona?

3. Do I organize data my informants' way, my way, or some way they or I see it because of someone else's theoretical construct?

4. Am I representing a character, creating, or re-creating a person? What histories, contexts, frames, or screens constitute that person?

5. What is the sense of place I am building? What details of setting do I use to organize and locate what I see?

6. What is my evidence? What values and assumptions do I already bring to my interpretation of it? How did I collect this evidence? Where? Under what conditions?

7. What does my evidence show? About me? About my informants? About the others around them? What other ways might I represent this evidence?

8. What is the foreground? Who describes it? I, or the people I portray? What other foregrounds are there? What backgrounds might there be? Described in whose voices?

9. Might I shift point of view and tell a similar story?

Whatever ways we decide to answer these questions, we construct a text amidst textual choices: ours and our informants'. And while we render their culture on our pages, our ethnographer's guilt sneers back. It is a nagging reminder, noisy with reflexive presence, productive as we organize and systematize our informants' words and works toward our text and craft it for our readers. We exercise our creative options, conscious of our power as academic storytellers. But we must recognize that our work captures only one particular slice—a single, cultural moment. Wolf writes:

> The anthropologist listens to as many voices as she can and then chooses among them when she passes their opinions on to members of another culture. The choice is not arbitrary, but then neither is the testimony. However, no matter what format the anthropologist/reporter/writer uses, she eventually takes the responsibility for putting down the words, for converting their possibly fleeting opinions into a text. I see no way to avoid this exercise of power and at least some of the stylistic requirements used to legitimate that text if the practice of ethnography is to continue. (11)

I never resolve my ethnographer's guilt, nor do I ever hope to. But I expect that as I conduct research in sites of literacy and render those cultural moments on the page, as I exercise my choices of experience, rhetoric, and aesthetics, I will be able to fold my "others'" words and perspectives into my writerly omniscience. In one more rhetorical move to conclude this essay, with hopes of rendering its own liminal performance and employing the voice that assisted me on these pages, I return to Myerhoff for the final words. Her work with the elders in the center was a tangle of both personal and professional guilt, which she describes with reflexive, rhetorical, and textual beauty:

> Diffuse and even irrational guilt plagued me until I had to laugh at myself. I had become a tasteless ethnic joke, paralyzed by Jewish guilt: about my relative youth and strength, about having a future where they did not, about my ability to come and go as I chose while they had to await my visits and my convenience, when I relished food that I knew they could not digest, when I slept soundly through the night warmed by my husband's body, knowing the old people were sleeping alone in cold rooms. . . . I considered quitting. It was unbearable to abide the countless ways in which Center people used guilt, often unconsciously, intending not to hurt. But after a time I accepted the fact that one cannot be "made" guilty. One volunteers. (27)

Acknowledgments

Much gratitude goes to my colleagues Julie Cheville, Hanna Griff, Pat Sullivan, and Elizabeth Chiseri-Strater, who are the silent significant "others" in this text.

Works Cited

Abrahams, Roger D. "The Complex Relations of Simple Forms." *Folklore Genres.* Ed. Dan Ben-Amos. Austin: U of Texas P, 1976. 193–214.

———. *Singing the Master: The Emergence of African American Culture in the Plantation South.* New York: Pantheon, 1992.

Atkinson, Paul. "Ethnography or Fiction: A False Dichotomy. Response to Whaley." *Linguistics and Education* 5 (1993): 53–60.

Babcock, Barbara. "Reflexivity: Definitions and Discriminations." *Semiotica* 30 (1980): 1–14.

Bauman, Richard. "Verbal Art as Performance." *American Anthropologist* 77 (1975): 290–311.

Behar, Ruth. *Translated Woman: Crossing the Border with Esperanza's Story.* Boston: Beacon P, 1993.

Benson, Paul, ed. *Anthropology and Literature.* Urbana: U of Illinois P, 1993.

Britton, James, Tony Burgess, Nancy Martin, Alex McLeod, and Harold
     Rosen. *The Development of Writing Abilities (11–18).* London:
     Macmillan, 1975.

Buker, Eloise A. "Rhetoric in Postmodern Feminism: Put-Offs, Put-Ons, and
     Political Plays." *The Interpretive Turn: Philosophy, Science, Culture.* Ed.
     David R. Hiley, James F. Bohman, and Richard Shusterman. Ithaca:
     Cornell UP, 1991. 218–44.

Cheville, Julie. "The Ethnographer as Performer: Staging Self and Other in
     Text." Paper presented at the Convention of the National Council of
     Teachers of English, Orlando. November 1994.

Clifford, James, and George E. Marcus, eds. *Writing Culture: The Poetics and
     Politics of Ethnography.* Berkeley: U of California P, 1986.

Crapanzano, Vincent. "On the Writing of Ethnography." *Dialectical Anthropol-
     ogy* 2 (1975): 69–73.

Fabian, Johannes. *Power and Performance: Ethnographic Explorations through
     Proverbial Wisdom and Theater in Shaba, Zaire.* Madison: U of Wisconsin
     P, 1990.

Flower, Linda. "Writer-Based Prose: A Cognitive Basis for Problems in
     Writing." *College English* 41 (1979): 19–37.

Geertz, Clifford. *Works and Lives: The Anthropologist as Author.* Stanford:
     Stanford UP, 1988.

Glassic, Henry. *Passing the Time in Ballymenone: Culture and History of an Ulster
     Community.* Philadelphia: U of Pennsylvania P, 1982.

Herndl, Carl G. "Writing Ethnography: Representation, Rhetoric, and
     Institutional Practices." *College English* 53 (1991): 320–32.

Jackson, Jean E. "'Deja Entendu': The Liminal Qualities of Anthropological
     Fieldnotes." *Journal of Contemporary Ethnography* 19 (1990): 8–43.

Murray, Donald. "Teaching the Other Self: A Writer's First Reader." *College
     Composition and Communication* 33 (1982): 140–47.

Myerhoff, Barbara. *Number Our Days.* New York: Dutton, 1978.

Myerhoff, Barbara, and Deena Metzger. "The Journal as Activity and Genre:
     Or Listening to the Silent Laughter of Mozart." *Semiotica* 30 (1980): 97–
     114.

Narayan, Kirin. *Storytellers, Saints, and Scoundrels: Folk Narrative in Hindu
     Religious Teaching.* Philadelphia: U of Pennsylvania P, 1989.

Olson, Gary. "The Social Scientist as Author: Clifford Geertz on Ethnography
     and Social Construction." *Journal of Advanced Composition* 11 (1991):
     245–68.

Oring, Elliott. "The Arts, Artifacts, and Artifices of Identity." *Journal of
     American Folklore* 107 (1994): 211–47.

Perl, Sondra. "Understanding Composing." *College Composition and Commu-
     nication* 31 (1980): 363–69.

Recchio, Thomas. "On Composing Ethnographically: Strategies for Enacting Authority in Writing." *Rhetoric Review* 10 (1991): 131–43.

Rosaldo, Renato. *Culture and Truth: The Remaking of Social Analysis.* Boston: Beacon P, 1989.

Roseberry, William. "Balinese Cockfights and the Seduction of Anthropology." *Social Research* 49 (1982): 1013–028.

Roth, Paul A. "Ethnography without Tears." *Current Anthropology* 30 (1989): 555–69.

Ruby, Jay, ed. *A Crack in the Mirror: Reflexive Perspectives in Anthropology.* Philadelphia: U of Pennsylvania P, 1982.

Sanjek, Roger, ed. *Fieldnotes: The Makings of Anthropology.* Ithaca: Cornell UP, 1990.

Schechner, Richard, and Willa Appel, eds. *By Means of Performance: Intercultural Studies of Theatre and Ritual.* Cambridge: Cambridge UP, 1990.

Shankman, Paul. "The Thick and the Thin: On the Interpretive Theoretical Program of Clifford Geertz." *Current Anthropology* 25 (1984): 261–79.

Sunstein, Bonnie. "'Ce Que J'eprouve': Grainstacks, Writing, and Open Spaces." *Education and Culture* 11 (1994): 17–27.

———. *Composing a Culture: Inside a Summer Writing Program with High School Teachers.* Portsmouth: Boynton/Cook-Heinemann, 1994.

Tannen, Deborah. *Talking Voices: Repetition, Dialogue, and Imagery in Conversational Discourse.* Cambridge: Cambridge UP, 1989.

Tedlock, Dennis. "The Spoken Word and the Work of Interpretation in American Indian Religion." *Myth, Symbol, Reality.* Ed. Alan Olson. South Bend: Notre Dame UP, 1980. 129–44.

Turner, Victor. *From Ritual to Theater: The Human Seriousness of Play.* New York: Performing Arts Journal Publications, 1982.

Van Maanen, John. *Tales of the Field: On Writing Ethnography.* Chicago: U of Chicago P, 1988.

Vygotsky, Lev. *Thought and Language.* Cambridge: MIT P, 1962.

Watson, Graham. "Make Me Reflexive—But Not Yet: Strategies for Managing Essential Reflexivity in Ethnographic Discourse." *Journal of Anthropological Research* 43 (1987): 29–41.

Whaley, Terrence. "Ethnography or Fiction: An Essay on Confounding Reader Response in Barbara Myerhoff's *Number Our Days.*" *Linguistics and Education* 5 (1993): 39–51.

Wolf, Margery. *A Thrice-Told Tale: Feminism, Postmodernism, and Ethnographic Responsibility.* Stanford: Stanford UP, 1992.

III Social and Institutional Contexts

11 Engendering Ethnography: Insights from the Feminist Critique of Postmodern Anthropology

Roxanne D. Mountford
University of Arizona

In his essay, "The Narrative Roots of Case Study," Thomas Newkirk suggests that composition researchers should shift their focus from trying to legitimize the "objectivity" of their case studies to trying to legitimize the "narratives" they tell about their student subjects. Newkirk writes:

> Early attempts to justify the case study (and qualitative research in general) were, as Stephen North has pointed out, schizophrenic. Researchers claimed to adhere to traditional standards of objectivity and methodological rigor, while at the same time pushing the narrative potential of the case study form. (131)

However, as our field matures, Newkirk suggests that critical concern can now shift from the method to the rhetoric of the ethnography or case study. He writes, "The issue is not, as positivistic researchers have argued, the problem of bias or the lack of objectivity. Rather, it is one of polyvocality" (148). Turning to the work of James Clifford, in particular, Newkirk calls for ethnographers and case study writers to "allow discordant voices into the [fieldwork] account, voices that complicate the moral judgments readers will make" (148).

Newkirk is not alone in citing Clifford as an authority on the question of representation in ethnographies. Several major articles on ethnographic writing published around the same time as Newkirk's essay cite Clifford's "On Ethnographic Authority" and the volume edited by James Clifford and George Marcus, *Writing Culture: The Poetics and Politics of Ethnography*, as authorities on the question of how to write a politically and poetically savvy ethnography (Kleine; Herndl; Clark and Wiedenhaupt). In turning to these postmodern scholars of anthropology, Newkirk and others open our field to a full-fledged "rhetoric" of ethnography, that is, a recognition that ethnographies are interpretative, written within a historical moment, and culturally and politically interested. In his essays, Clifford has drawn on the work of Bakhtin and Barthes to describe the experience of reading ethnography ("On Ethnographic Authority"). By describing ethnographies as "persuasive" rather than "scientifically valid," Clifford draws attention to the textual nature of ethnographies and the responsibility of ethnographers to write in such a way that their own biases are highlighted.

However, as David Bleich has noted, working from the conclusions of Clifford and other postmodern scholars of anthropology is limiting for building a socially responsible rhetoric of ethnography (176–81). For while this scholarship has been responsible for bringing to light experimental forms of ethnography (the so-called new ethnography) that break from the old objectivist forms, it has also been widely criticized for ignoring the older, more established experimentation by feminist anthropologists. For Bleich, the primary problem with postmodern anthropology is that it embraces the textual while ignoring the ethical issues in conducting fieldwork. However, I wish to offer a different caution: without importing feminist anthropology into our field alongside the more popular postmodern treatises, we may unwittingly miss the opportunity to explore how our gender—and our informants' gender—plays a role in ethnographic study. I begin this essay by introducing the feminist critique of postmodern anthropology and then go on to present examples of engendered ethnographic writing from Zora Neale Hurston's *Mules and Men* and *Tell My Horse*. I end with some principles for writing engendered ethnographies in our field.

Genealogies of the New Ethnography

James Berlin describes the project of cultural studies as mapping "the ways social formations and practices are involved in the shaping of consciousness, and [how] this shaping is mediated by language and situated in concrete historical conditions" (101). While here Berlin's focus is on the definition of cultural studies, it is also the founding principle behind postmodern scholarship in anthropology. Cultural studies is about the task of discovering how culture—high and low—is produced, received, and interpreted by individuals. Scholars in cultural studies share the insight that "subjectivities are produced, not given, and [should] therefore be the objects of study" (Johnson qtd. in Berlin 101). That is to say, standpoints are never innocent. This insight brought about a crisis in mainstream anthropology, since ethnographies—the product of anthropology—were considered scientifically valid after Bronislaw Malinowski, who in the 1920s set the standards for conducting valid fieldwork and writing accurate ethnographies. As a result of this insight, anthropologists no longer believe in the innocence or truth of their ethnographies.

Within mainstream anthropology, these insights are generally traced to Clifford Geertz, who wrote about the production of ethnographies. He coined the phrase "anthropologist as author" and began to describe the writing of ethnographies not as recording scientific observation, but rather as crafting literary interpretation. The shift in metaphor was profound, since traditional ethnographies, though often beautifully written and deeply literary, tend to hide what Foucault calls "the author function" (Boxwell 608). Franz Boas, considered by most historians and anthropologists to be the founder of modern anthropology, wrote in 1928 that fieldwork "requires . . . that the investigator free himself from all valuations based on [his] culture. An objective, strictly scientific inquiry can be made only if we succeed in entering into each culture on its own basis" (qtd. in Boxwell 609). While the latter goal—seeing a culture through the native perspective—is still the goal of ethnography, Geertz has led the field to understand the fictional quality of ethnographies.[1] That is, ethnographies are crafted and, as with all examples of rhetoric, are persuasive because of the author's skill, not the ethnography's inherent scientific validity. Geertz inspired a movement to describe the production of ethnography, leading to works like Roy Wagner's *The Invention of Culture*, that claims "every culture, including the anthropologist's own, is 'invented'" (qtd. in Boxwell 610).

However, this genealogy came into question around the time Clifford and Marcus's edited volume, *Writing Culture: The Poetics and Politics of Ethnography*, was published.[2] No one questioned the importance of this collection, one of the best known in cultural studies and anthropology. In it, the ten invited scholars explore not just whether but how ethnographies reflect the politics and culture of their authors, and how the poetics of some ethnographies demystify the relationships between the anthropologist and his or her subjects. Through their efforts ethnographies once classified as "fiction" or considered methodologically flawed now may be read along with the "canon" of new ethnographies—that is, reflexive, postcolonial cultural accounts that are considered to experiment with the limits of anthropological representation of "the Other" (Mascia-Lees, Sharpe, and Cohen 8–9). By treating ethnographies as texts—as competing stories serving or disrupting the hegemonic gaze of the West—this collection would seem to offer a way of recuperating ethnographies that fall outside the canon, including ethnographies by women anthropologists who were never validated by the field. However, the genealogy most interesting to these scholars is clearly not outside the mainstream. One of the feminist critics of this collection writes, "This latest school of ethnography, which advertises itself as 'experimental,' continues to valorize men's ethnographies, while ethnographies written by women are again consigned to the margins" (Visweswaran 27). Nearly all the texts considered by the scholars in this collection are classics in the field; furthermore, not one feminist was invited to participate in the seminar.[3]

The feminist anthropologists who have responded to *Writing Culture* have decried its nearly universal dismissal of feminist theory as a significant intellectual tradition in which to ground a "poetics and politics" of ethnography (Gordon; Visweswaran; Mascia-Lees, Sharpe, and Cohen; Kirby). Clifford tries to account for this absence in his introduction by noting that the volume was limited to those attending his "advanced seminar." He claims none of these scholars wrote from a feminist perspective for the volume because "feminism had not contributed much to the theoretical analysis of ethnographies as texts" and furthermore that "where women [ethnographers have] made textual innovations . . . they [have] not done so on feminist grounds" ("Introduction" 20). However, as Mascia-Lees, Sharpe, and Cohen show, in his own essay in the volume, Clifford cites as his primary example of ethnographic innovation Marjorie Shostak's *Nisa: The Life and Words of a !Kung Woman,* an ethnography he labels "feminist" (Mascia-Lees, Sharpe, and Cohen 13). Of this inconsistency they write that Clifford "reveals not only that he clearly knows of at least one feminist ethnography that has employed 'unconventional forms of writing,' but also that he prefers to write about feminists rather than inviting them to write for themselves" (Mascia-Lees, Sharpe, and Cohen 13). Of course, feminist anthropologists have been writing about the subjective gaze of anthropologists at least since the early 1970s, when two collections of feminist criticism of anthropology were published: Michelle Rosaldo and Louise Lamphere's *Woman, Culture, and Society* (1974) and Rayna Rapp Reiter's *Toward an Anthropology of Women* (1975). Had Clifford and Marcus considered the feminist literature in anthropology, as well as the considerable body of feminist literary criticism, it would have been impossible to draw a genealogy that neatly eliminated all feminist contributions to the subject.

The denunciation of Clifford and Marcus has been swift, voluminous, and ongoing. In addition to a flurry of articles in such feminist journals as *Signs,* two major collections of essays have been published documenting the rich history of feminist anthropologists' discussion of the question of how an anthropologist should represent herself as a gendered subject in an ethnography and the general lack of such consideration by most men in the field. Those collections—Micaela di Leonardo's *Gender at the Crossroads of Knowledge: Feminist Anthropology in the Postmodern Era* and Diane Bell, Pat Caplan, and Wazir Jahan Karim's *Gendered Fields: Women, Men, and Ethnography*—each begin with a genealogy of feminist contributions to the questions set forth by Clifford and Marcus, demonstrating how absurd Clifford's claim that "no innovations in ethnography have occurred from a feminist ground" really is. As Diane Bell puts it, "The gendered nature of our fields has been left to women anthropologists to ponder and feminist scholars to critique, and even then their work has been largely ignored. Neither the burgeoning body of ethnographic literature by women writers nor feminist theorizing about the difference gender makes have set the disciplinary agenda" (1).

Gender as a Rhetorical Act

The problem is that, when cultural studies and anthropology on the whole consider the question of culture, including how we experience culture, how it represents us, how we establish relationships with each other, and how that produces culture, the question of how people experience the world as gendered beings tends to drop out of the picture. This is a significant oversight within anthropology because no fieldwork occurs without gender playing a role. When I studied women preachers in the field, I did so as a woman scholar and student, and that gender reference was significant not only to me but also to the women I studied. My informants asked me questions about my experiences as a woman in the university and as a girl in the evangelical church in order to understand whether or not I would be a sympathetic researcher. Gender was a touchstone also, as I came to see, in much of the ministers' professional practices. For instance, I noticed that they preached with frequent reference to their own gender (Mountford). While the gendered nature of my relationship with my informants was obvious to me, it is not obvious to all ethnographers. Bell argues that "women have been conspicuous for their consideration of the impact of their presence in the field as an element in their ethnography. Theirs is the gender-inflected voice, which cannot masquerade as universal; they have a standpoint and cannot pretend otherwise" (2).

However, it is *not* the case that men's position has ever been without gender inflection. Thus the irony of Clifford and Marcus producing a collection elucidating the position of the author in ethnographies without consideration of gender. The problem is that, to this point, men ethnographers have not written reflexively on their own male standpoint. David Morgan is one of the few male anthropologists to explore this problem. He argues, "Men . . . have to work against the grain—their grain—in order to free their work from sexism, to take gender into account. The male researcher needs, as it were, a small voice at his shoulder reminding him at each point that he is a man" (qtd. in Back 218). In his article "Masculinity and Fieldwork in a South London Adolescent Community," Les Back takes up Morgan's challenge by rereading his own ethnography of a South London neighborhood in terms of gender. He discovered as he reread transcripts of interviews that, although he thought he was studying race issues, in fact he often was experiencing the effects his own gender had on the interview situation. For instance, if he stopped to talk to girls in a club, his male informants intervened. If he met girls in private outside the club, he discovered that they resisted his questions. He realized in part that he caused the resistance by aggressive questions (for instance, by trying to get two white girls to talk about their attitudes about race), a technique he realized was based in part on his own masculinity. But in addition, it was a feature of the culture he studied that women resisted male authority whenever they could, sometimes by engaging in "'cussing' exchanges" (225). He had ignored these issues in his ethnography.

Back's article is a daring throwing down of the gauntlet to Clifford and Marcus, whom he charges with creating "a significant diversion for those who are serious about developing a sensitivity to the gender-loaded contexts in which fieldwork takes place" (217). Back argues that what is needed from male anthropologists such as those Clifford and Marcus gathered in Santa Fe is critical reading that brings to light the gendered nature of *men's* ethnographic writing (in addition to inviting the feminists to come out to play). However, Back says, "Sadly, for too many of my male colleagues the issues of 'sex and gender' in cross-cultural fieldwork rarely moves beyond a discussion of 'sex and sex'!" (230). While Back is speaking of an extreme—locker-room swapping of fieldwork sexual conquest narratives—clearly the trend of men in the mainstream of the discipline to leave an exploration of gender and subjectivity to feminists, and to marginalize them and the subject, must end if significant reforms in cultural studies and anthropology are to go forward. To ignore feminist work is to continue to tolerate inequities in the field, to continue to build genealogies that exclude women who already have made valuable contributions to cultural studies, and to miss the opportunity to study an important aspect of culture.

At issue, as Back illustrates, is that gender is rhetorical in two ways: (1) in the way we perform our fieldwork (how we interact with our informants, how we present ourselves, and how we view the research) and (2) in the way we write our ethnographies. These categories are fluid: if I am aware that I am taking up "girl talk" with a woman informant, I am more likely to write reflexively about this encounter. In Back's case, a failure to recognize his performance of gender caused a significant oversight in his research and later in his ethnography. Most importantly, however, is the recognition of power as a backdrop to gender. While postmodern scholars of anthropology have noticed inequalities between races, cultures, and economies, they are often unaware and uncritical of the power held disproportionally by men in cultures and institutions throughout the world.

The Poetics and Politics of Zora Neale Hurston's Ethnographies

How, though, does one "write gender"? Perhaps the best way to illustrate some principles in writing gender is to discuss the work of women ethnographers who have been neglected by the field of anthropology. Like the field of rhetoric, anthropology has done little research into the history of its women practitioners. However, one of the implications of the work of Geertz and Clifford and Marcus is that ethnographies once dismissed as too literary or unscientific may now be recuperated. For if, as Geertz suggests, ethnographies are always fictions, then those ethnographers who chose to write in ways that highlight the fictional quality of their work could be considered foremothers of the genre. In the period between Boas's and Malinowski's work, the two men most validated for their ethnographic work during this time, there was a great deal of experimentation going on among ethnographers. In particular, Boas's student Zora Neale Hurston was experimenting with ethnography as genre, producing works marked by an attention to the ethnographer's place as a raced, classed, and gendered being in the fieldwork setting. As I will show, her ethnography is innovative from a number of perspectives, but, most importantly, from the perspective of gender.

From a postmodern perspective, Hurston's two ethnographies, *Mules and Men* and *Tell My Horse*, are innovative for two reasons: first, Hurston chooses as her standpoint an insider's position, including her own past experience as an artifact to be studied, and second, she creates narrative frames in which she herself becomes a participant in the events that led to the telling of folktales. These techniques allow her to speak authoritatively about the "black experience," an experience she wanted black elite and white audiences to appreciate on its own terms. In writing this way, of course, Hurston was faced with the dilemmas of being a native insider in general, but not always an insider to the particular southern communities she studied. In writing her ethnographic accounts, she puts into play this dilemma, thus, as Barbara Johnson points out, deconstructing the too easily dichotomized terms "insider" and "outsider." In Hurston's work, these terms are constantly up for negotiation.

For instance, to illustrate her allegiance with the "bottom-folks" (*Dust Tracks* 245) and to explain to a white audience the black experience (which included her own), she writes in a passage at the beginning of *Mules and Men*,

> Folk-lore is not as easy to collect as it sounds. The best source is where there are the least outside influences and these people, being usually under-privileged, are the shyest. They are most reluctant at times to reveal that which the soul lives by. And the Negro, in spite of his open-faced laughter, his seeming acquiescence, is particularly evasive. You see we are a polite people and we do not say to our questioner, "Get out of here!" We smile and tell him or her something that satisfies the white person because, knowing so little about us, he doesn't know what he is missing. The Indian resists curiosity by a stony silence. The Negro offers a feather-bed resistance. That is, we let the probe enter, but it never comes out. It gets smothered under a lot of laughter and pleasantries. (4)

Through this passage Hurston illustrates the complex relationship she has with the research and the audience. The passage is a general statement about research, yet the researcher here (and the audience) is white. Hurston identifies herself not with the researcher (which she is) but with the community researched. The passage is meant to illustrate why Hurston has to be careful with the way she presents herself to the community. Thus we are left with a complex picture: to the reader (a white person), Hurston (the researcher) is presenting herself as black and a native of the community she is researching. However, to the community, the subject of her research, she is not merely (only) the "Zora" they knew, but also urban, college-educated, and therefore somewhat alien— more like the white researcher she is describing in the passage than the native she presents herself to be in the ethnography.[4] Traditional ethnographies, in contrast, feature a "distanced" ethnographer who makes few, if any, self-references. The self-reference in this passage is what Clifford has called "reflexivity."

While the above passage is somewhat more typical of reflexivity in the "new ethnography," the final passage in *Mules and Men* is both brilliant and unique in its subtlety. *Mules and Men* is written as a travelogue. Hurston describes her efforts to collect New World African folklore in the South (primarily in Florida communities). The characters she meets tell her folktales, which she records for the reader in the characters' own words. Included in the book are Hurston's difficulties and successes in gaining access to and the trust of the people from whom she hopes to hear stories. After introducing the last of a series of "hoodoo" practices, she abruptly ends the book with a folktale, to which she tacks on one phrase of her own:

> Once Sis Cat got hongry and caught herself a rat and set herself down to eat 'im. Rat tried and tried to git loose but Sis Cat was too fast and strong. So jus' as de cat started to eat 'im he says, "Hol' on dere, Sis Cat! Ain't you got no manners atall? You going set up to de table and eat 'thout washing yo' face and hands?"
>
> Sis Cat was might hongry but she hate for de rat to think she ain't got no manners, so she went to de water and washed her face and hands and when she got back de rat was gone.
>
> So de cat caught herself a rat again and set down to eat. So de Rat said, "Where's yo' manners at, Sis Cat? You going to eat 'thout washing yo' face and hands?"
>
> "Oh, Ah got plenty manners," de cat told 'im. "But Ah eats mah dinner and washes mah face and uses mah manners afterwards." So she et right on 'im and washed her face and hands. And cat's been washin' after eatin' ever since.
>
> *I'm sitting here like Sis Cat, washing my face and usin' my manners.* (*Mules* 251–52, my emphasis)

This ending could be read as a challenge to the entire project of "objectivity" (which Hurston says in her autobiography is the "genius" of her teacher Franz Boas, whom she calls the "greatest anthropologist alive" [*Dust Tracks* 182]).[5] Hurston is challenging the very notion that a representation of "truth" is ever possible. The reader is cast as the white researcher "probing" what he or she should not be probing; while Hurston, the narrator, casts herself as a storyteller-liar (like her informants). As Sis Cat, she uses her manners, but somewhat after she has "used" her readers. The passage throws into question whether or not *Mules and Men* itself is an example (at least at some level) of Hurston's own "resistance" and therefore, perhaps, not "true" in the Enlightenment sense. The brilliance of this ending is that it points out the very essence of ethnographic writing: that it is, after all, a cultural construction.[6] This passage is all the more remarkable when we consider that

Hurston was writing long before anyone was supposed to be writing "new ethnography."

Hurston's experimentation with the ethnographic form has implications for how gender issues can be explored in ethnographies. Among Hurston's concerns in *Mules and Men* and *Tell My Horse* is women's independence. Like Janie Crawford, the heroine of *Their Eyes Were Watching God,* Hurston illustrates the problems and opportunities brought about by her gender. Not shy about using her flashy car and good looks to attract attention, especially of male informants, Hurston writes unapologetically in *Mules and Men* about offering rides in her car to anyone who will tell her folktales (11). Offering up these glimpses of her research "style," Hurston illustrates not only her own performance of gender, but also how gender plays out in the culture she is studying. In one sequence of stories in *Mules and Men,* she describes a "toe-party," one of the cultural practices she is illustrating in her ethnography (13–17). By showing how she gets there (driving some of her informants) and with whom she dances (other informants), she is able to illustrate the texture of the culture as well as her standpoint within it. It is not all good: in one story (told with humor and a little seriousness), Hurston tells how she narrowly escapes murder at a juke-joint by a woman who is jealous of her (179). But this information reveals Hurston's own performance of gender and the expectations of gender held by the culture she studied.

Hurston continues this pattern in *Tell My Horse,* her rich study of African-based voodoo rituals in Haiti and Jamaica. As in *Mules and Men,* the narrative frame for *Tell My Horse* is a travelogue, with Hurston paratactically organizing the voodoo rituals she encounters around stories of the particular characters she meets. Although she is unfamiliar with the culture she studies, she portrays herself within the narrative as a southern black woman in the culture and therefore implicitly argues that she is far more of an insider than perhaps others might be. She accomplishes this task by occasionally employing phrases from her childhood community of Eatonville and by narrating circumstances in which her cultural perspective differed from that of the African diaspora she encountered. It is from this standpoint that she explores issues of gender. For instance, in one passage, Hurston tells about a disagreement she has with one of her informants over "woman's place." Her informant explains that he has no use for educated women, women being meant to "love and comfort" men (20). Hurston writes, "I assured him that he was talking about what he didn't know" (16).

Artfully using this encounter to introduce a voodoo ritual, Hurston reports that her chauvinistic informant led her to "specialists who prepare young girls for love" (17–18), a kind of geisha training for the fiancées of influential men. In narrating the story of her introduction to these rituals, which she was invited to witness, Hurston seemingly adopts a traditional anthropological innocence. Ishmael Reed appears to take this reading in his introduction to *Tell My Horse*. He writes, "Hurston describes, without sermonizing, the Jamaican practice of cultivating geishas for the delight of prospective grooms. . . . Ironically, many of today's feminists would consider such [lack of sermonizing] to be 'retrograde'" (xiv). However, there is a second voice in this episode, and in this voice Hurston is much more "feminist" than Reed seems to recognize. In describing the preparation of the bride for the consummation of her marriage, Hurston focuses her attention on the complex (and quite homoerotic) rituals in which the old woman "touches" the bride to arouse her:

> [The old woman] carries this same light-fingered manipulation down the body and the girl swoons. She is revived by a mere sip of rum in which a single leaf of ganga has been steeped. Ganga is that "wisdom weed" which has been brought from the banks of the sacred Ganges to Jamaica. The girl revives and the massage continues. She swoons again and is revived. But she is not aware of the work-a-day world. She is in a twilight state of awareness, cushioned on a cloud of love thoughts. (19)

While Reed, reading as a man, identifies with the groom, a figure whom Hurston mentions only from the point of view of the bride, Hurston clearly stands with the women, winking and nudging and focusing on the rituals themselves, which she describes as extremely pleasurable for the bride. Her narration carries a cultural perspective, but it is not the one Reed finds; rather, Hurston is celebrating what she finds to be a healthy attitude about sex the old woman teaches the young bride. Her feminist perspective on women serving men and not having careers is clearly stated in the prior passage. Thus this section, which Reed clearly believes is antifeminist, is, in a complex way, rather more celebratory of women's wisdom in sexuality.

Tell My Horse, like *Mules and Men*, is the conscious work of a storyteller. Its writing is crafted to celebrate the telling of the tale. Hurston's literary use of language is in keeping with her overall view of rhetoric as performance, of representation as the "lies" told in storefronts throughout the South. Though she gives mock reverence to the "objectivity" loved by Boas, her teacher, she clearly did not write within the confines of his rhetoric of ethnography. Representation of a culture she had researched—research which she called a "formalized curiosity" and "poking and prying with a purpose" (*Dust Tracks* 182)—is a narrative event no less colorful and fictional than writing a story or playing the dozens at the corner. It is Hurston's attention to her relationships with her informants, her presentation of herself as a woman of southern black culture, and her overt statements about the narrative quality of her ethnography that make her what I would call, in mock reverence to postmodernists like Clifford, a *pre*-postmodern feminist ethnographer.

Principles for Rhetoric and Composition Researchers

What we learn from Hurston's ethnographies is the importance of rhetoric and composition scholars writing and then scrutinizing the narratives they tell about themselves and their informants. Until now, this self-scrutiny has been focused on class and race. For instance, in his article "The Tidy House," David Bartholomae notes that composition researchers have been too invested in the liberal narrative of "saving" students. By constructing students as "outsiders," our profession has been guilty of ethnocentrism. The solution is to consider students' "home cultures" as viable and to find ways to include those cultures in the classroom. This perspective is shared by Newkirk as well as several other scholars (Bridwell-Bowles; Pratt; Heath). However, few scholars focus on the ways their own gender interacts with the gender of their student informants—and when they do, they do not describe that process.

For instance, in his article on ethnography, Bleich showcases the ethnographic observations of a woman student in his class, Ms. S, who reflected on her experience of being the only woman in an all-male classroom. He writes,

> Like most young men unaware of how sexism works and its part in the ideology they take for granted, many class members expressed an almost unending series of sexist and homophobic opinions, noted in Ms. S's restrained remark about "the words of the women whose stories we read and the male opinions expressed in class." Obviously, my own efforts to oppose those remarks appeared to Ms. S as feminism "through a filter of male vision." As a woman, Ms. S really was alone. (188)

Later, Bleich notes that he laughed at one sexist joke directed at Ms. S: "Even though [the joke] was funny (and to the extent that I laughed, I participated in its sexism, in spite of the opinions I otherwise advocated), it was gratuitous since it was not personally provoked by anything Ms.

S said" (188). Bleich presents the ethnographic observations of Ms. S, his student, because they were, in his view, "ideologically disruptive" for the class of all-male students. And, for him, this is the kind of ethnography that should be written. However, though he hints that his own behavior needed changing, he does not narrate the relationship he had with his students and the class so that it is possible to see what he means when, at the end of his essay, he writes, "[Ms. S] is teaching us that traditional constraints [on teaching] are too rigid" (192). Does he mean that he should have intervened more when his students made sexist remarks? Stopped laughing at "gratuitous" jokes? (What about *any* sexist jokes? Why just gratuitous ones?) The point is, we would learn more about the dynamics of gender in Bleich's classroom if he described his role in creating a setting in which men students feel comfortable telling sexist jokes. It is *not* the case that male students will tell sexist jokes with just any teacher at the helm. They do not, for instance, tell sexist jokes in my classes. The ethnographic opportunity lies in explaining why they do so in Bleich's classes but not mine. Is it the gender of the teacher? A level of disapproval or lack thereof? These are the kinds of issues that can be explored through reflexive ethnographies.

If we consider gender to be a significant rhetorical act in all field studies, there are at least two ways we must focus our attention in order to represent gender in ethnographies: first, in paying attention to our rhetorical poses as ethnographers, and second, by paying attention to the way we represent these poses and our informants' poses in our ethnographies. By "poses" I mean something like "being in drag" (Butler): there are many more than just two ways to "do" gender, and even when we perform it, we are endlessly mutating those "ideals" we think we are imitating. However, as Bleich suggests, there is an ideological commitment involved in conducting field research, whether we are aware of it or not. Therefore, our "drag" or "pose" is terribly important to narrate as we write ethnographies. We may not be able to perform Hurston's cultural reflexivity (that is, her ability to write parts of her ethnography in the style of her home culture). But it is crucial that we begin to write about our gendered ways of conducting and writing field research. In the sections that follow I will suggest some ways to do so.

1. View Gender Dynamics as Creating Cultural "Spaces"

What does it mean to view communication as "gendered"? Hurston's performance of gender in the "toe-dance" episode in *Mules and Men* illustrates the way in which gender defines a "space" for both Hurston and her informants to interact. Like a barroom, courtroom, or other "location" associated with specific communicative practices, gender dynamics create a "space" where ritual behaviors are well defined. These ritual behaviors change and can be changed to some extent, but for most human groups, the gender of group participants signals a space in which certain kinds of behavior are expected. For instance, one study suggests that when faced with a male professor at the head of the classroom, students expect to be in a location in which their emotional response will be irrelevant to the discussion. When faced with a female professor, students expect to be in a location in which their needs and emotions are relevant and managed sensitively. These expectations are powerful and affect almost every aspect of the classroom interactions; male and female professors are often "punished" in student evaluations for deviating from the expectations associated with their gender (Statham, Richardson, and Cook).

However, according to Carol A. B. Warren, "gender conformity and deviation in a given culture are processual, dialectical, and reflexive: They change over time, they are related to one another, they affect not only relationships with respondents but also categories used in interpretation" (60). Therefore, ethnographers must learn as much as possible about a culture's expectations of the "spaces" gender creates and how an ethnographer's dress, talk, and behavior "signal" those spaces. As an example, Warren notes that "a Western woman going to Burma has to be informed that wearing fresh flowers in her hair will be well received, [whereas] a woman going to the local district attorney's office does not have to be told that this same body adornment will seem slightly strange to the legal natives" (61). Similarly, many women professors in the United States avoid wearing dresses with lace and other traditionally feminine trim because such adornment signals a "space" in which intellectual issues are not taken seriously.[7]

When conducting fieldwork, an ethnographer's performed gender (that is, dress, talk, and behavior) powerfully signals informants about the kind of space they are entering when talking to the ethnographer. Therefore, it seems that an ethnographic account would include self-reflection on the fieldworker's performance of gender. In Hurston's ethnographies, the self-reflection of gender is offered indirectly, by way of the stories she tells about how she was able to collect folklore. Hurston keeps the focus on the cultural performance she learns she must offer to her informants. At the beginning of *Mules and Men* she suggests she would be refused information if she sounded too "educated" (4). Instead, she offers them a woman who is willing to engage in the flirting and hijinks of a woman of the culture. She illustrates this change, significantly, by showing her readers the language she used while collecting folklore (evocative, rich, of the people) and by illustrating how she moved in and out of the communities she studied.

2. Explore the Power Associated with Gender

First, consider the role of the woman ethnographer in a male-dominated setting. Warren reports that "women fieldworkers in male-dominated organizations have experienced several dimensions of male dominance: not only sexual hustling, but also assignment to traditional female roles and tasks such as mascot, go-fer, audience, butt of sexual or gender joking, or 'cheerleader'" (37). We have few glimpses of how women ethnographers handle this sexist behavior, primarily because such treatment has been perceived by women ethnographers as possibly compromising the legitimacy of their work (Warren 38–40). Hurston chose to narrate moments of sexism as moments of solidarity between herself and the women informants she studied, for example, in showing how she resisted one of her informants' contention that women should not be educated (*Tell My Horse* 16–20). According to Warren, this solidarity is the direction of much feminist ethnography—study of and solidarity with women across cultures, and "feminist-revisionist ethnographic genre[s]" in which the "ethnographer's and the respondent's relationship is one of mutual transference and transformation" (40). Warren uses as her example Marjorie Shostak's *Nisa: The Life and Words of a !Kung Woman,* an ethnography written in two voices: Nisa's and Shostak's. The advantage of this approach is that the reader is able to see something of the texture of the relationship between the ethnographer and her informant. And, while this relationship can never be "known," even by the ethnographer and her informant, polyvocal texts can evoke for the reader a sense of the nature of that relationship and thereby something of the power dynamic between them.

While it is easy to narrate instances in which we connect with our informants, it is more difficult to describe moments when we do not. But, in some ways, this information is just as important to understand. Back was unsuccessful in his attempts to interview teenage girls in the London neighborhood he studied. Hurston writes that she was occasionally run off her fieldwork sites. At the beginning (when she still talked with her university voice), she was ignored. Shostak had to pay Nisa in order to get her time and attention. All these situations show the ways in which researchers were resisted by informants when the ethnographic relationship was not mutually beneficial. How do we discover ways to conduct "socially generous" research (Bleich 176)? One way is to include this question in our ethnographies so that we can learn from each other. How do we get our informants' time? What do we need to offer to follow them around? Interview them? Observe? What does our research offer them? Of course, gender offers a "space" for this conversation to be negotiated. Race is another "space." For the one in power culturally (sometimes, but not always, the researcher), the exchange may involve throwing down one's own power. For instance, Warren describes the experiences of Norris Brock Johnson, an ethnographer who studied a midwestern elementary school. At first, the women teachers resisted his questions and acted, from his estimation, suspicious of him. He discovered that his gender was a problem in this environment, for the only men the teachers were involved with were the principal, who approached them condescendingly, and the custodians, who harassed them (by, for instance, interrupting them in the middle of a lesson to fix something in the room). They thought the researcher was a spy sent by the administrators. Johnson learned he had to acknowledge the teachers' expertise in order to gain their trust. By asking them about their teaching, listening to their views, and acknowledging their competence, he distinguished himself from the men who used their power in ways the teachers found oppressive. He could not ask his own questions until the gender dynamic had shifted (Warren 17–18).

When Hurston encountered this level of suspicion, she looked for ways to change the power she unwittingly projected. For instance, upon entering one town, she discovered among the men "a noticeable disposition to *fend* [her] off" (*Mules and Men* 65). She writes, "This worried me because I saw at once that this group of several hundred Negroes from all over the South was a rich field for folk-lore, but here was I figuratively starving to death in the midst of plenty" (65). Finally she noticed the problem: her car. "The car," she writes, "made me look too prosperous. So they set me aside as different. And since most of them were fugitives from justice or had done plenty time, a detective was just the last thing they felt they needed on that 'job'" (65–66). Her solution was to give herself an identity that allowed her to establish trust:

> I took occasion that night to impress the job with the fact that I was also a fugitive from justice, "bootlegging." They were hot behind me in Jacksonville and they wanted me in Miami. So I was hiding out. That sounded reasonable. Bootleggers always have cars. I was taken in. (66)

Ellen Cushman calls this research dynamic "reciprocity" and suggests that there are issues of democracy at stake in the development of our relationships with our informants. Reciprocity can range from pay or services to the collegiality Johnson and Hurston offered their informants. Cushman, for instance, offered tutoring and counseling in exchange for the time and information of women in an African American urban neighborhood. An ethnography should reveal the nature of reciprocity and, most importantly, examples of when the reciprocity failed. Hurston documents some of the lessons she learned about language, dress, and behavior that allowed her access to the people and their folktales in *Mules and Men*. For instance, in one town she learned her dress caused her informants to feel inferior. She narrates the encounter:

> "Miss, you know uh heap uh dese hard heads wants to woof at you but dey skeered."
> "How come, Mr. Pitts? Do I look like a bear or panther?"
> "Naw, but dey say youse rich and dey ain't got de nerve to open dey mouf."
> I mentally cursed the $12.74 dress from Macy's that I had on among all the $1.98 mail-order dresses. I looked about and noted the number of bungalow aprons and even the rolled down paper bags on the heads of several women. I did look different and resolved to fix all that no later than the next morning. (68–69)

Whereas in traditional ethnographies this information is hidden, in reflexive ethnographies like Hurston's, this information is offered to explain something about the power dynamic between the ethnographer and her informants and how the ethnographer handles the conflict.

3. Use the Informants' Own Words

Finally, there is no clear way to "know" how our own performance of gender affects our informants and the research. Therefore, in addition to writing reflexively, it is crucial that we offer the reader some access to the words of informants.[8] In the traditional ethnography, ethnographers write a seamless report of the various aspects of culture they studied. Such ethnographies do not allow the reader any access to information about individual members of the culture or to any information about how the fieldwork was conducted. In contrast, the "new ethnography" described by Clifford as well as the work of early women anthropologists such as Hurston reveals greater reflexivity by the ethnographer along with increased access to the words of individual members of the culture.

In the case of Hurston, the individuals are introduced within a narrative and then quoted at length. For instance, after describing the morning rituals of a swamp-gang whom she studied, Hurston re-creates the first conversation she overheard:

> Joe Willard was sitting with me on the end of a cross-tie when
> he saw Jim Presley coming in a run with his bucket and jumper-
> jacket.
> "Hey, Jim, where the swamp boss? He ain't got here yet."
> "He's ill—sick in the bed Ah hope, but Ah bet he'll git here
> yet."
> "Aw, he ain't sick. Ah bet you a fat man he ain't," Joe said.
> "How come?" somebody asked him and Joe answered:
> "Man, he's too ugly. If a spell of sickness ever tried to slip up
> on him, he'd skeer it into a three weeks' spasm."
> Blue Baby stuck in his oar and said: "He ain't so ugly. Ye all
> jus' ain't seen no real ugly man. Ah seen a man so ugly till he
> could get behind a jimpson weed and hatch monkies."
> Everybody laughed and moved closer together. Then Officer
> Richardson said: "Ah seen a man so ugly till they had to spread a
> sheet over his head at night so sleep could slip up on him." (*Mules*
> 73)

Hurston is able to accomplish several tasks through offering her informants' words in the text as dialogue. First, she gives her largely white
audience a sense of the diversity, individuality, and dignity of the members of the culture she studied. Second, she is able to work in the ethnographic information—in this case, the "woofing" of the swamp gang—
in the form that she heard it. Third, she is able to give a sense of the
context in which the folktales she studied are told, including where she
was sitting and how she participated in the conversation.

Some experimental ethnographies include informants' words with
little commentary by the ethnographer (e.g., Clark and Wiedenhaupt;
Kirsch). However, this method is weak if the ethnographer does not
speak to the important power dynamics which, I suggest above, are so
critical in an "engendered" ethnography. In her ethnography of women
academic writers, Gesa Kirsch offers an explanation of her interview
techniques, including her efforts to make the interview process a "cycle
of conversation" and her relationship with the women involved
nonhierarchical (she even asked her assistant, a graduate student, to
interview the graduate students in the study so that all the interviews
were conducted between women of equal rank) (33–35). In contrast, we
learn little about the undoubtedly tricky dynamics of the research situation in Beverly Clark and Sonja Wiedenhaupt, an essay co-authored by
Clark (the teacher and ethnographer of Wiedenhaupt) and Wiedenhaupt
(the student and informant). It is difficult to see what role Wiedenhaupt
had in the creation of the final essay (which is crafted as a "dialogue"),
or her view of the potential power issues between her and Clark. In
addition, Clark does not describe her fieldwork strategies in the case

study. I am suggesting that playing with the poetics of ethnographies, including our use of narrative and dialogue, should come alongside explanations of the politics of those ethnographies if we are to "engender" our already gendered ethnographies. Clark and Wiedenhaupt break ground in the area of poetics (Wiedenhaupt, the student informant, is quoted at length), but leave unanswered many questions about the politics of their relationship.

Hurston offers a way to do both tasks at once. In addition to writing a poetically brilliant representation of her fieldwork, she also focuses on the tricky dynamics of race, class, and gender that she had to negotiate as she conducted her fieldwork. Her method—including herself as a participant member of the ethnographic account—is an approach that allows her research to be understood in a deeper way. We can see her performance of her gender, race, and class in the field, and we can also read at length the words, folktales, and traditions of her informants. As Back has suggested, for ethnographic accounts to avoid the gender bias of mainstream anthropology, we will need to conduct and write our fieldwork as though we—as well as our informants—are gendered beings, with all the rituals, language, and power plays that go along with this cultural conditioning.

The cautionary tale I have told of the "ethnography debates" in anthropology suggests that scholars in composition and rhetoric would benefit from looking to feminist anthropology for examples of a "poetics and politics of ethnography." Sadly, mainstream anthropology has generally ignored the contributions of experimental ethnographers like Hurston, as well as the genealogy of feminist contributions to the question of ethics and representation in ethnography. Diane Bell writes:

> The apparent isomorphism of these two fundamental critiques—
> feminist and postmodernist—of the ethnographic endeavor is at
> best illusory, at worst misleading. The "other" of postmodern
> writing is distanced from self by geography, and cultural, racial
> and ethnic identity. It would appear that feminist critiques are
> more unsettling. They reveal that the "other" of the feminist—
> namely, the beneficiaries of patriarchy—are the very authors of
> the "new ethnography" who, under the guise of democratizing
> ethnography through plurivocality, avoid scrutiny of their own
> power. (8)

Therefore, when we turn to scholarship in anthropology for help in developing a rhetoric of ethnography, we would do well to include feminist contributions—including the work of Zora Neale Hurston, a foremother of the experimental ethnography. Without this important work, we neglect an aspect of culture common to us all.

Acknowledgments

My heartfelt thanks to David Hess, Terese Guinsatao Monberg, Ellen Cushman, and the editors for their help with this essay.

Notes

1. Geertz's best statements on the rhetoricity of ethnographies were published after *Writing Culture* appeared (see *Works and Lives: Anthropologist as Author*). However, Clifford, Marcus, and other authors in the volume had copies of the lectures Geertz delivered in 1983 on which *Works and Lives* was based.

2. A little background on *Writing Culture* is necessary to understand the nature of the ensuing controversy. In 1984 Clifford and Marcus were invited to organize one of the School of American Research's prestigious "advanced seminars," a weeklong discussion set in the hills overlooking Santa Fe on grounds owned by the school. Only ten people are invited to attend any given seminar, and those ten are to be the most distinguished scholars in the field. Clifford and Marcus, following the thread of Geertz's argument, proposed that the seminar be devoted to "the making of ethnographic texts" (vii). The nine men and one woman who were invited were anthropologists or scholars of anthropology who had, as Clifford and Marcus put it, "questioned disciplines and genres in their recent work"—that is, scholars who had conducted critical analyses of ethnographic texts, including not only classic traditional ethnographies but also travelogues and other literatures with an ethnographic focus. The essays resulting from the ten participants' working papers presented at the seminar were collected and published in the volume *Writing Culture,* one of the most well-known edited collections in cultural studies and anthropology.

3. Mary Louise Pratt, the one woman invited to the seminar, apparently did not define herself as a feminist, for Clifford addresses the question of why no feminists were invited to the seminar in his introduction to *Writing Culture.*

4. For a discussion of the dilemma of researching one's own community, see Beverly Moss, who refers to Hurston's strategies for collecting folklore in Eatonville, her hometown.

5. Hurston writes, "I was extremely proud that Papa Franz felt like sending me on that folklore search. As is well known, Dr. Franz Boas of the Department of Anthropology of Columbia University, is the greatest anthropologist alive, for two reasons. The first is his insatiable hunger for knowledge and then more knowledge; and the second is his genius for pure objectivity. He has no pet wishes to prove. His instructions are to go out and find what is there. He outlines his theory, but if the facts do not agree with it, he would not warp a jot or dot of the findings to save his theory" (*Dust Tracks* 182).

6. Johnson writes of this passage, "If, as Hurston often implies, the essence of telling 'lies' is the art of conforming a narrative to existing structures of address while gaining the upper hand, then Hurston's very ability to fool us—or to fool us into thinking we have been fooled—is itself the only effective way of conveying the rhetoric of the 'lie'" (328).

7. Of course, professional women also find themselves condemned for wearing clothing and hairstyles that are too "masculine." This no-win situation is described with poignancy by Naomi Wolf (37–48).

8. See also Newkirk's "Seduction and Betrayal in Qualitative Research" (this volume). Newkirk offers this strategy for avoiding the betrayal of informants. Since I view all ethnographies as constructed, I assume that even the most carefully crafted ethnography will betray "the truth." Another way to approach the ethical problem Newkirk addresses is to conduct fieldwork that is "for" the informants. Kirsch describes her research this way: "[T]his study aims to produce research *for* women, not just about women" (35). In a similar way, Hurston identifies *with*, not against, her informants. But even when conducting good faith research, the ethnographer constructs the world she writes.

Works Cited

Back, Les. "Gendered Participation: Masculinity and Fieldwork in a South London Adolescent Community." Bell, Caplan, and Karim 215–33.

Bartholomae, David. "The Tidy House: Basic Writing in the American Curriculum." *Journal of Basic Writing* 12 (1993): 4–21.

Bell, Diane. "Introduction 1: The Context." Bell, Caplan, and Karim 1–18.

Bell, Diane, Pat Caplan, and Wazir Jahan Karim, eds. *Gendered Fields: Women, Men, and Ethnography.* New York: Routledge, 1993.

Berlin, James A. "Composition Studies and Cultural Studies: Collapsing Boundaries." *Into the Field: Sites of Composition Studies.* Ed. Anne Ruggles Gere. New York: MLA, 1993. 99–116.

Bleich, David. "Ethnography and the Study of Literacy: Prospects for Socially Generous Research." *Into the Field: Sites of Composition Studies.* Ed. Anne Ruggles Gere. New York: MLA, 1993. 176–92.

Boxwell, D. A. "'Sis Cat' as Ethnographer: Self-Presentation and Self-Inscription in Zora Neale Hurston's *Mules and Men.*" *African American Review* 26 (1992): 605–17.

Bridwell-Bowles, Lillian. "Discourse and Diversity: Experimental Writing within the Academy." *College Composition and Communication* 43 (1992): 349–68.

Butler, Judith. "Imitation and Gender Insubordination." *The Lesbian and Gay Studies Reader.* Ed. Henry Abelove, Michèle Aina Barale, and David M. Halperin. New York: Routledge, 1993. 307–20.

Clark, Beverly Lyon, and Sonja Wiedenhaupt. "On Blocking and Unblocking Sonja: A Case Study in Two Voices." *College Composition and Communication* 43 (1992): 55–74.

Clifford, James. "On Ethnographic Authority." *The Predicament of Culture: Twentieth-Century Ethnography, Literature, and Art.* Cambridge: Harvard UP, 1988. 21–54.

———. "Introduction: Partial Truths." *Writing Culture: The Poetics and Politics of Ethnography.* Ed. James Clifford and George E. Marcus. Berkeley: U of California P, 1986. 1–26.

Clifford, James, and George E. Marcus, eds. *Writing Culture: The Poetics and Politics of Ethnography.* Berkeley: U of California P, 1986.

Cushman, Ellen. "Rhetorician as Agent of Social Change." *College Composition and Communication* 47 (1996): 7–28.

di Leonardo, Micaela, ed. *Gender at the Crossroads of Knowledge: Feminist Anthropology in the Postmodern Era.* Berkeley: U of California P, 1991.

Geertz, Clifford. *Works and Lives: The Anthropologist as Author.* Stanford: Stanford UP, 1988.

Gordon, Deborah. "Writing Culture, Writing Feminism: The Poetics and Politics of Experimental Ethnography." *Inscriptions* 3.4 (1988): 7–26.

Heath, Shirley Brice. *Ways with Words: Language, Life, and Work in Communities and Classrooms.* Cambridge: Cambridge UP, 1983.

Herndl, Carl G. "Writing Ethnography: Representation, Rhetoric, and Institutional Practices." *College English* 53 (1991): 320–32.

Hurston, Zora Neale. *Dust Tracks on a Road: An Autobiography.* Philadelphia: J. B. Lippincott, 1942.

———. *Mules and Men.* 1938. Bloomington: Indiana UP, 1978.

———. *Tell My Horse: Voodoo and Life in Haiti and Jamaica.* 1938. New York: Perennial Library, 1990.

———. *Their Eyes Were Watching God.* 1937. New York: Perennial Library, 1990.

Johnson, Barbara. "Thresholds of Difference: Structures of Address in Zora Neale Hurston." *"Race," Writing, and Difference.* Ed. Henry Louis Gates Jr. Chicago: U of Chicago P, 1986. 317–28.

Kirby, Vicki. Comment on "The Postmodernist Turn in Anthropology: Cautions from a Feminist Perspective," by Frances E. Mascia-Lees, Patricia Sharpe, and Colleen Ballerino Cohen. *Signs* 16 (1991): 394–400.

Kirsch, Gesa E. *Women Writing the Academy: Audience, Authority, and Transformation.* Carbondale: Southern Illinois UP, 1993.

Kleine, Michael. "Beyond Triangulation: Ethnography, Writing, and Rhetoric." *Journal of Advanced Composition* 10 (1990): 117–25.

Mascia-Lees, Frances E., Patricia Sharpe, and Colleen Ballerino Cohen. "The Postmodernist Turn in Anthropology: Cautions from a Feminist Perspective." *Signs* 15 (1989): 7–33.

Moss, Beverly J. "Ethnography and Composition: Studying Language at Home." *Methods and Methodology in Composition Research.* Ed. Gesa Kirsch and Patricia A. Sullivan. Carbondale: Southern Illinois UP, 1992. 153–71.

Mountford, Roxanne D. "The Feminization of the 'Ars Praedicandi.'" Diss. Ohio State U, 1991.

Newkirk, Thomas. "The Narrative Roots of Case Study." *Methods and Methodology in Composition Research.* Ed. Gesa Kirsch and Patricia A. Sullivan. Carbondale: Southern Illinois UP, 1992. 130–52.

Pratt, Mary Louise. "The Arts of the Contact Zone." *Profession 91.* New York: MLA, 1991. 33–40.

Reiter, Rayna R., ed. *Toward an Anthropology of Women.* New York: Monthly Review P, 1975.

Rosaldo, Michelle Zimbalist, and Louise Lamphere, eds. *Woman, Culture, and Society.* Stanford: Stanford UP, 1974.

Shostak, Marjorie. *Nisa: The Life and Words of a !Kung Woman.* New York: Vintage, 1981.

Statham, Anne, Laurel Richardson, and Judith A. Cook. *Gender and University Teaching: A Negotiated Difference.* Albany: State U of New York P, 1991.

Visweswaran, Kamala. *Fictions of Feminist Ethnography.* Minneapolis: U of Minnesota P, 1994.

Warren, Carol A. B. *Gender Issues in Field Research.* Beverly Hills: Sage, 1988.

Wolf, Naomi. *The Beauty Myth: How Images of Beauty Are Used Against Women.* New York: Morrow, 1991.

12 Writing, Rap, and Representation: Problematic Links between Texts and Experience

Jabari Mahiri
University of California, Berkeley

Can rap music with its powerfully influential oral, lyrical, visual, and written components be used effectively to bridge the chasm between streets and schools? Can its thematic content, critical perspectives and electric presentational styles be used to jump-start some students out of their apathy toward writing in school? Can it be used effectively to demonstrate connections between the strategies for its production and the production of other literate texts? Can it be used to motivate students to become producers of texts in schools, drawing on the capital of their own life experiences? These are key questions I asked in a recent research project, "African American and Youth Culture as Bridge to Writing Development."[1]

Many educators are attempting to find ways to build on cultural and personal experiences of students to enhance their literacy development. Rap music is an authentic cultural experience for the majority of African American youth. According to Catherine Tabb Powell, rap "emerged from the streets of inner-city neighborhoods as a genuine reflection of the hopes, concerns, and aspirations of urban Black youth in this, the last quarter of the 20th century" (245). However, capturing and representing this particular aspect of students' lived experiences in the formal contexts of schools poses variegated problems for both teaching and learning. These problems in some ways mirror the problems of capturing and representing lived experiences in qualitative research. This chapter explores how these processes can duplicate and ultimately illuminate each other even as one, qualitative research, tries to comprehend the other.

This research project was supported by a federal grant through the National Center for the Study of Writing and Literacy (NCSWL), and it took place in junior English classes at two urban high schools. It centered on a curricular intervention designed to help students become critical consumers of popular culture texts: to develop their skills in writing similar texts, and to transfer these analyses and writing skills to the production of other literate texts. The intervention specifically attempted to incorporate the pervasive appeal of selected aspects of rap music and culture—its thematic content and critical voice and its oral, lyrical, and visual styles—to motivate student writing. The premise that we can build on the lived experiences of students in schools is predicated on the notion that we can actually incorporate their authentic experiences into classrooms. My study revealed how this notion gets complicated in various ways for research, for teaching, and for student writing.

Research Pretexts

An initial concern emerged at the level of researcher access to the material of study, and it had several dimensions. In order to get the project funded and later implemented in school sites, a disclaimer had to be made that only positive aspects of rap music would be used. A key question, of course, was: Whose meaning should be used to define "positive"—the researcher's, the granting agency's, the school administrators', the focal teachers' (the two teachers in whose classrooms the intervention took place), the students', their parents', rap artists', the media's? This concern is ultimately connected to issues of censorship and power. To what extent does requiring rap to be positive (by whatever definition) distill its essence and make its representation in classrooms something other than what it is in the lives of young people? The flip side of the call for positivity is the notion that rap is really inherently negative, and at the root of this notion is the question of rap's legitimacy.

Perceptions of rap music are ultimately socially constructed, and its legitimacy has been continually challenged by societal institutions, especially the mass media. For example, on the basis of an analysis of all the articles on rap that appeared between 1983 and 1992 in the three most widely circulated news magazines in the United States and Canada (*Newsweek, Time,* and *U.S. News*), Julia Eklund Koza makes a compelling case that the vast majority of these articles "reinforced a link between rap and specific negative themes" (183). She further notes that the significance of these magazines' negative representations of rap should be seen in the light of theories "that negativity is a strategy of containment that tends to reinforce dominant ideologies" (184). Tricia Rose further argues that strategies of containment associated with rap music and culture extend even into physical spaces. For example, she illustrates how policies of containment are reflected in stringent permit procedures and other obstacles of access to the venues in which rap concerts and associated events take place.

My research decisions and designs had to acknowledge the power and politics that militate against the legitimacy of the specific personal and cultural representations associated with rap. But this, of course, raised a key ethical dilemma. We decided that the best way to resolve this dilemma with respect to *implementation* was to fully involve our focal teachers and students in the decision-making process as to which selections of rap would be used and why. This strategy provided a format for addressing some of the ethical and political considerations of rap's legitimacy in a way that encouraged both the voicing and negotiation of students', teachers', and researchers' concerns. On the other hand, we decided that the best way to resolve the dilemma with respect to *funding* was to provide explicit information and rationales as to how and why rap music could be a viable tool for learning. Still, questions were raised during the funding process that foregrounded ways in which rap and other popular cultural materials remain contested within and contained outside curricular space.

In an earlier study, "Micro-Voices: Computers and Underprepared Writers," in which I was both teacher and researcher, I had found it useful to uncouple curriculum content mastery and writing skill development in order to see them independently before deciding how they could best work together.[2] I had seen how many approaches to teaching writing required learning particular content in conjunction with, or in extreme cases requisite to, the development of writing skills. I incorporated this orientation to curriculum into my project on African American and youth culture. When federal evaluators met to review this and other NCSWL projects, I presented the position that, for purposes of writing development, the role of curriculum content was to serve the development of writing skills specifically. Several people in the meeting were clearly uncomfortable with this position, and finally one evaluator asked, "But what about Shakespeare? Are we going to just leave him out of the curriculum?" In answering, I referred to a recent poster from the Young Shakespeare Conservatory (endorsed by the *San Francisco Chronicle*) which had a picture of Shakespeare "crossed up" in a rapper's pose over the words "Meet the Grandaddy of Rap."

My response points to a tension in public perceptions of rap. While the media may characterize rap negatively, there is also a business strategy to commodify rap's cultural products, a process that legitimizes commercial messages for certain markets even as educators filter these same messages out of school settings. In referring to the conservatory poster, I was not attempting to justify the commodification of such cultural products, but rather to question resistance to using *any* of them in education. Yet some of the questions for the project implied that even if rap and other popular cultural materials could be shown to have prodigious effects on students' writing development, they might still not be seen as a legitimate means to this end because they circumvent the canon. At times this concern for canon was sublimated in challenges to rap's thematic content, to its use of explicit language and images, and to its viability as an oral-lyrical medium to the production of writing.

Some critical pedagogues answer this concern in a way that I support: they call for a more pervasive role for popular culture in schools, not as a simple substitution for "high" culture, but where both meet the test of relevance to student-centered learning as a criterion for inclusion (see, for example, Aronowitz and Giroux). To further answer the evaluators' concerns, I noted that rap music often presents an extended, intricate, oral text rendered in either a critique or story form or in some combination of the two. This oral text, with which many African American and other youth are already quite familiar, is usually accompanied by or easily transformed into a written text. (An example of ways these oral and written texts can be linked will be discussed later.) But the connection I drew in my study went beyond the textuality of rap lyrics. A key hypothesis of the project was that students' knowledge of particular strategies used in *oral* rap texts—particularly self-referential structures—could serve as a point of departure for making explicit the arguments and descriptions in the comparable *written* rap texts and, ultimately, in a variety of other literate texts. This heuristic use of rap texts is similar to how researcher Carol Lee employed signifying structures in African American language to build pedagogical scaffolding that helped African American students develop their skills of literary analysis.

There was another interesting textual consideration that contrasted with academic and mass media challenges to rap's legitimacy. Student responses on questionnaires, along with other background research, led us to a number of descriptive and critical sources about rap music and culture, as well as about youth culture generally. It quickly became clear how important it was to go well beyond the many pieces of academic research, commercial research, and mass media articles in order to comprehend the rapid movement and mutations of this culture. Magazines like *Vibe, The Source,* and *Details* became key sources for understanding this exploding cultural phenomenon. So much has been written about the artists, issues, aesthetics, and performances of rap music and culture that it would have been possible to base the entire intervention on text-based material without ever engaging actual rap songs and videos in the classes. But this would not have been consistent with the project's intent to explore possible links between oral and written texts, and to do so in a context, school, where students seldom encounter rap texts as part of the official curriculum.

The absence of rap texts from the curriculum is ironic because many such texts employ sophisticated rhetorical strategies and raise substantive philosophical questions that can be explicated in the same manner as any academic or other school-sanctioned text. Commentary on such rhetorical and philosophical complexity can be found in two brief examples: a *Vibe* magazine interview by Alan Light with "the artist formerly known as Prince," and a *San Francisco Bay Guardian* article by Donnell Alexander on the "culture clash" between rappers and hip-hop journalists.[3] The *Vibe* interview centers on the controversy caused when the man once called Prince used the occasion of his thirty-fifth birthday to inform the world that he was changing his name to a symbol, visual but not audible. The *Bay Guardian* article, on the other hand, centers on the increasing antagonism developing between rappers and some of the young African American journalists who critique their work. On occasion this antagonism has spilled over into physical confrontations.

Both the interview and the article focus on issues and ideas that have a place in college courses on theories of literacy or on theories of literary criticism. The interview, for example, seriously considers conceptualizations and functions of oral versus written language. In this case, they are latent in an artist's identity quest, a quest that demands an uncoupling of our traditional associations between signs and sounds. Exploration of issues raised in the interview could contribute to a fundamental understanding of how we make meaning, and thus sense of the world. The article on the hip-hop controversy is just as densely packed with considerations of authorial intention, textual ownership, and intellectual property rights and responsibilities. Both the article and the interview reveal intriguing complexities associated with textualizing lived experience. The potential use of these kinds of thought-provoking texts in schools is clearly more a question of their legitimacy, their acceptability, than of their viability for prompting learning.

Doing the background research for the project revealed another dimension of the problem of researcher access to the material of study—

an intergenerational dimension. The use of face-to-face interviews, questionnaires, and even informant stories had severe limitations for gaining insight into how young people actually engaged rap music and culture and other popular cultural experiences. It would have been much better to have been a participant-observer in actual out-of-school settings, but there was an interesting researcher-informant discontinuity based on age (though not ethnicity) that accentuated problems of gathering valid representations of youth culture.

Student informants in our target classrooms knew much more about the artists and issues we were investigating than we did as participant-observers, but they were sometimes reluctant to reveal this knowledge to researchers like myself, the age of their parents. To some, the idea of representing their experiences with rap music and culture to older adult researchers who were attempting to textualize them in field notes was seen as basically uncool. Fortunately, my two graduate student researchers were in their mid-twenties and were to some extent able to facilitate continuity of perspective between the students and other members of our teacher-researcher team. But essentially, in order to do this project, we had to continually struggle to gain legitimacy in the eyes of some of the students—even as rap itself continued to struggle with challenges to its legitimacy in society at large.

Teaching Contexts

The intergenerational dimension revealed itself also in the actual context of teaching during the curricular intervention. Though both focal teachers completely supported the project and had already experimented with rap music in their classes, the one who had taught high school for about six years ended up being much more comfortable than the other when it came to presenting and leading activities that incorporated the curricular materials we had jointly developed. The other focal teacher—an elegant African American woman who has been a successful urban high school English teacher of mostly African American and Latino students for more than twenty years—felt that she was not being as successful with students who currently occupied her classes. Somehow, these students' rhythms of learning seemed out of sync with a cadence of teaching that had worked well for her in the past. She initially saw the intervention as a way to breathe more life into her classroom toward the end of the school year. But it turned out that the experienced teacher was not so comfortable presenting and leading activities based on our curricular materials, and she began to feel that her students did not really accept her teaching them about rap music and culture. Essentially, the experienced focal teacher sensed that her students were resisting being taught about "their" lived experiences by someone they located outside those experiences.

Very little research addresses teaching situations in which the students are "authorities" and may know significantly more about the topic than their teachers do. As my ethnographic research attempted to apprehend processes of cultural representation in writing, it became clear that some methodological concerns were complicated by the nature of the cultural material represented. One of these concerns regarded the extent to which our results should be tied to the comfort levels and capabilities of the two teachers in presenting this nontraditional curriculum. These concerns were further accentuated when the more experienced teacher and I agreed that I would actually present parts of the curriculum because her students seemed responsive to me leading some activities.

This responsiveness may have stemmed from the fact that on several occasions while introducing the project to the classes and trying to get the students motivated to participate, I was challenged by some students to perform a rap myself. Though I was ambivalent, I decided, for two reasons, to take up the challenge. First, I felt these students were looking for a sign that I had some connection to rap beyond my obvious desire to do research on it. More importantly, I *had* performed a rap before, and it had gone over pretty well. When I had been a high school teacher more than five years earlier, I attempted to show my students the correspondences between the lyrical and rhetorical strategies of Chaucer's *Canterbury Tales* and contemporary rap poems. To demonstrate, I had memorized "The Miller's Tale" along with a rap song that linked thematically with the tale, and performed them both to a background beat from Digital Underground. Frankly, it has always amazed me that I not only didn't forget, but that I quite literally could not forget both pieces once I had memorized them and performed them in "rap-like" form. For the students in my research project, I told the story of this rap experience rather than reenacting it, but this seemed to be enough to placate their concerns about our motives for bringing rap into the curriculum.

However, bringing rap into the curriculum involved more than convincing funding agencies, school administrators, teachers, and ultimately students of its viability as a pretext for writing development in the context of school. Another key consideration in situating these materials in the curriculum was tied to the mutability of student interests in them. During the time it took to develop rap materials into curricular texts, many had already become passé in the minds and lives of the students. The process unfolded as follows. We first devised ways to incorporate student input into curricular choices of issues, themes, and forms of cultural production to be addressed. Then we accumulated and categorized materials in relationship to several themes that emerged as focal points in the curriculum. These materials included newspaper and magazine articles; short stories; visual materials such as ads, pictures, and album covers; the written texts of songs along with corresponding oral texts on compact discs or cassettes; and some audio-visual materials such as television specials on rap and television commercials that used rap to sell products. From among these materials we selected models that would allow us to demonstrate rhetorical correspondences with other texts of edited English. We then discussed and agreed upon the particular instructional strategies to be used in presenting the materials to students. But despite our careful planning, we had not anticipated nor could we fully compensate for the ephemeral shelf life of the texts we had hoped students would accept as authentic representations of rap music and culture.

Writing Texts

The two graduate students who were site managers for my project noted early in the study that the majority of students they observed in the focal classrooms strongly disliked having to do any kind of writing within the school setting. The strength of this resistance was characterized in the following snip of dialogue which occurred between our most experienced teacher and one of her students:

> *Student:* Man, we can't do this—I hate thesis statements. You think it's easy 'cause you got hella college degrees . . .
>
> *Teacher:* I've taught this year after year, and students just eat it up.
>
> *Student:* Yeah, well, we're not that hungry. [students laugh]

We found that the students' resistance to writing in school was quite pronounced. Interestingly, it was not always the act of writing itself that was resisted, but rather the topics and conventions of academic writing specifically. As part of our background research, we tried to look at the kind of writing being done by students on their own. Some students flat out refused to share their work with us, while others stated that their writing was too personal to show us. The samples we did collect, however, confirmed our beliefs, along with the implications from studies on vernacular writing by researchers like Miriam Camitta, that "writing was an important and valued activity among [urban] adolescents" (230). We also found that many of the students in our study had high regard for the talents of their peers who wrote their own poetry, stories, or rap lyrics.

We were successful in getting students to write fairly expansively during the intervention, and at this point in our analysis of their writings we see a number of our contentions supported. Specifically, we have identified rhetorical correspondences between rap texts and other edited English texts and have found that selections of these texts can be used jointly as models to motivate student writing. One example from the intervention, a rap video titled *I Used to Love H.E.R.* by the group Common Sense, will be used to illustrate some possible oral-text, experience-text, and curriculum-text links and to underscore how some of these links can be problematic.

I Used to Love H.E.R. describes the evolution of rap music by personifying it as the experiences of a young girl growing into adulthood. The theme of the song is revealed in the changing relationship of the lead singer to this maturing girl. "I met this girl when I was ten years old, and what I loved most, she had so much soul." He describes how fresh she was when she first started out on the East Coast, when she was free in the parks, "when she was underground, original, pure, untampered, a down sista. Boy, I tell ya, I miss her." But she changed when "she broke to the West Coast." And though she was already creative, "once the man got to her, he altered her native. Told her if she got an energetic gimmick then she could make money, and she did it like a dummy. Now I see her in commercials, she's universal. She used to only swing it with the inner city circle." The last section of the song chronicles the extent to which she has been slammed and taken to the sewer; it qualifies the singer's lament for his lost love.

We showed the short video of *I Used to Love H.E.R.* and used it as a lyrical-visual text to prompt discussion. The students amazed us and their teachers with their ability to explicate rhetorical strategies and thematic considerations. They demonstrated a clear understanding of personification and other metaphorical features in this text, and they provided in-depth discussion and analysis of the thematic features. In fact, they had more sophisticated perceptions and more background information about some of the provocative issues that the text raised than did any member of our teacher-researcher group. Such issues included concerns about "studio gangsters"—rappers whose only real experience with violence and street life is when they sing about it in the music studios—and the commodification of rap music and styles. The video had no curse words in it, but the students gave extended critiques to social, political, and racial implications of the use of words like "nigga." They also spoke to issues such as drug use, violence, and the denigration of women, and they answered questions about the nature of creativity and cultural authenticity that the song raised. The students were able to continue and extend this line of critique when we later provided the written text of the song, and we were also able to demonstrate how the written text of the song was highly consistent with conventions of edited English.

Since the discussions (and the video itself) addressed the commodification of rap in the marketing of everything from Coke to cars, we videotaped several soft drink commercials that were permeated with rap music and images for use in classes to extend the discussions. The commercials also became a prompt for writing when the students decided they wanted to script and produce their own commercials. This led to considerations of persuasive writing, the conventions of which students were eager to learn more about so that they could incorporate them into their texts. For this part of the intervention, the classes were arranged into groups of five or six students. In groups, students critiqued one another's writing and negotiated the creation of one script for video production. Then they worked together to direct, perform, and videotape their commercials. After each group shared its production with the rest of the class, each student wrote critiques of the commercials. Our focal teachers noted that the students' work and writing for this part of the intervention was perhaps the most inspired period of learning during the entire school year. The teachers also noted that some students who had only done marginal work in the class during the rest of the school year had come alive and worked hard on their scripts and had even taken leadership roles in their group work.

Interestingly, I eventually realized that almost every student commercial implied that the product being sold would resolve or compensate for some deficiency that women were perceived to have. At first I thought this might merely be a coincidence, but when I discussed it with the other members of our teacher-researcher team, all agreed that this outcome was too consistent for it to be merely coincidental. The team was concerned that the messages and images from rap culture (and from American culture at large) that denigrate women had become so pervasive that the students might be reproducing them in their own work unconsciously and unquestioningly. Women on the teacher-researcher team were especially concerned that as women they had not initially recognized or questioned this trend in the students' productions. We decided that even the video *I Used to Love H.E.R.* contributed to this problem. It had been chosen because it chronicled the way rap's pristine form had been transformed ("raped" and "prostituted") by commercial interests and other societal forces. But at the same time, the video characterized women as powerless, easily corrupted, and dependent on men—the lead singer in this case—to save them from their frailties.

We later tried to address this problem in class discussions with the students. Since we had had earlier discussions about the negative characterizations of females that often occur in rap music, students were somewhat sensitive to this issue. Yet they were surprised that they had unconsciously reproduced similar negative characterizations of their own. We elaborated with examples of how African Americans as a race are often portrayed negatively in the mass media and explored some of the ways that these images are sometimes internalized and revealed in self-deprecating attitudes or self-destructive behaviors. But this occurrence also made our teacher-researcher team more aware of how using rap lyrical, visual, and written texts to facilitate the production of student writing could also potentially contribute to the reproduction of problematic cultural perceptions.

Crisis of Representation

Norman Denzin and Yvonna Lincoln, in their introduction to the *Handbook of Qualitative Research,* outline five historical moments—traditional, modernist, blurred genres, crisis of representation, and postmodern—that reveal key aspects of the evolution and conduct of qualitative research. They note that these moments simultaneously operate in the present, and all are important for understanding issues and tensions in qualitative research (7–11). Qualitative research as well as teaching and writing are all fundamentally acts of representation. Attempting to make these representational acts authentic for their varied audiences is inherently problematic. This chapter illuminates the crisis of representation by focusing on the problems that arise when we research and teach controversial content that is related to the lived experiences of students.

I have shown that representations of rap are not only contested within curricular space, but at the same time complicate our considerations of curricula. The production and presentation of meanings in the curriculum represent established views of social reality that are selected and reinforced by institutional and societal power structures. Elizabeth Ellsworth notes that "meanings are not direct reflections of the world or of people, but are actively made and always mediated by interests and histories of dominant groups" (100). Rap and other popular cultural material challenge the validity of these meanings as representations of social reality for many students. Rap texts bring into their critique (and potentially into the classroom and writing experience) perspectives on class, race, gender, ethnicity, power, and authority that are disruptive of the received curriculum and in the classroom culture. But such disruption also carries the baggage of representations in crisis.

In designing and conducting research that engaged these issues, I found that the difficulties of capturing and representing lived experiences for students in school partially mirrored the difficulty of capturing and representing lived experiences in qualitative research acts. Denzin and Lincoln note that "a double crisis of representation and legitimation confronts qualitative researchers" (10) as part of the assault on the ethnographer's authority, and that "these two crises blur together, for any representation must now legitimate itself in terms of some set of criteria that allows the author [and the reader] to make connections between the text and the world written about" (11). Similarly, it could be said that a double crisis of representation and legitimation confronts student writers as part of the continued assault on student authority, for their representations must legitimate themselves in terms of some set of criteria that allows student authors (and their teachers and other readers) to make connections between their texts and the rap culture or popular cultures they have written about them. In this way, issues of legitimation for students who inscribe rap and popular cultural experiences in their written texts both illuminate and are illuminated by the corresponding issues of legitimation that ethnographers face as they represent sociocultural experiences in their written texts.

My research project pushed beyond traditional structural and cultural borders to trace inroads in curriculum and instruction that might authentically engage student writers. In becoming ethnographers of student experiences with rap music and in hip-hop culture, we not only made connections appropriate for learning in schools, but we also learned a bit more about where points of connection could be made between youths and adults. We routinely ask students to study things we value in the adult world, but our success with students also depends on our efforts to understand things students deem important in theirs.

Notes

1. The final report on this study is filed with the National Center for the Study of Writing and Literacy, University of California, Berkeley.

2. "Micro-Voices: Computers and Underprepared Writers" is presented in my *Shooting for Excellence: African American and Youth Culture's Role in New Century Schools* (New York: Routledge, forthcoming).

3. "Rap" and "hip-hop" are sometimes used interchangeably. "Rap" refers more specifically to the style of music itself "that entails talking, or 'rapping,' to a rhythmic musical background," according to Powell (245). The term "hip-hop" also includes the cultural styles, images, attitudes, and products that surround and are often subjects of rap music.

Works Cited

Alexander, Donnell. "Critical Beatdown: The Culture Clash between Rappers and Hip-Hop Writers Erupts into Violence." *San Francisco Bay Guardian* 7 Sept. 1994: 37–42.

Aronowitz, Stanley, and Henry A. Giroux. *Postmodern Education: Politics, Culture, and Social Criticism.* Minneapolis: U of Minnesota P, 1991.

Camitta, Miriam. "Vernacular Writing: Varieties of Literacy among Philadelphia High School Students." *Cross-Cultural Approaches to Education.* Ed. Brian Street. Cambridge: Cambridge UP, 1993. 228–46.

Common Sense. *I Used to Love H.E.R.* Videocassette. Relativity Records, 1994.

Denzin, Norman K., and Yvonna S. Lincoln. Introduction. *Handbook of Qualitative Research.* Ed. Norman K. Denzin and Yvonna S. Lincoln. Thousand Oaks: Sage, 1994. 1–17.

Ellsworth, Elizabeth. "Representation, Self-Representation, and the Meanings of Difference: Questions for Educators." *Inside Out: Contemporary Critical Perspectives in Education.* Ed. Rebecca A. Martusewicz and William M. Reynolds. New York: St. Martin's P, 1994. 99–108.

Koza, Julia Eklund. "Rap Music: The Cultural Politics of Official Representation." *Review of Education/Pedagogy/Cultural Studies* 16 (1994): 171–93.

Lee, Carol D. *Signifying as a Scaffold for Literary Interpretation: The Pedagogical Implications of an African American Discourse Genre.* Urbana: NCTE, 1993.

Light, Alan. "The Man Who Won't Be Prince." *Vibe* Aug. 1994: 45–51.

Mahiri, Jabari. *Shooting for Excellence: African American and Youth Culture's Role in New Century Schools.* New York: Routledge, forthcoming.

Powell, Catherine Tabb. "Rap Music: An Education with a Beat from the Street." *Journal of Negro Education* 60 (1991): 245–59.

Rose, Tricia. "'Fear of a Black Planet': Rap Music and Black Cultural Politics in the 1990s." *Journal of Negro Education* 60 (1991): 276–90.

13 Social and Institutional Power Relationships in Studies of Workplace Writing

Jennie Dautermann
Miami University (Ohio)

Any adequate understanding of the dynamics of written communication within a discourse community depends on some grasp of the political and social forces which shape the production (and reception) of the texts that appear there. In order to address current social theories of writing which challenge simplistic views of authorship, audience, and even the nature of text, qualitative research on workplace writing must account for the social and material conditions in which the discourse of the research itself arises, as well as the ways language appears to function in specific communities. Such an accounting may necessarily imply negotiating the researcher's own authority so as to create a rhetorical space in which a project's participants may claim dignity and authority—a space where readers may formulate alternative, perhaps contending accounts of the work and lives narrated on the ethnographer's page. Drawing on my own experience as a researcher, I argue here that this accounting must deal with at least the following issues: (1) defining the researcher's own roles in the target culture amid the conflicting loyalties that such roles may represent, (2) gaining access to the conflicting and multiple realities of the site and making reasonable inferences from those experiences, and (3) finding ways to preserve the perspectives of the participants, the researchers, and the sponsoring disciplines while addressing the requirements of research publication.

Such an approach to writing research implies a much larger view of context than has sometimes been assumed by research designs which focus on close readings of specific texts, genres, or specific writing behaviors. Carl Herndl, whose early workplace research emphasized text analysis in a workplace context (Brown and Herndl), has recently called for a broader social agenda for composition research (Herndl). Many researchers now look to Mary Louise Pratt's image of contact zones to describe the multiple intersecting layers that comprise the context of written discourse, or to the material and metaphorical communities discussed by Joseph Harris. My own discussion here assumes that both the discourse of a research site and the consequent discourse it inspires in the researcher's own community represent such multiple intersecting layers in both metaphorical and material dimensions.

Studying writers in a hospital context (Dautermann, "Writing"; Dautermann, "Negotiating") has brought me to a sense of the difficulty of actually addressing Herndl's injunction to incorporate "material, institutional, and ideological constraints" into workplace writing research (320). Workplace research which looks beyond the materials and products of writing requires methods which account for the ways social issues connect with the work of specific writers. Such methods are still evolving, and of course every context presents new challenges which can make the previous theoretical choices irrelevant or the hard-won techniques of previous projects unworkable. But in a larger sense, writing studies that address social issues can appear threatening to the institutions and organizations under study and thus threaten researcher access as well. We have not yet found adequate ways to critique the assumptions of institutions and cultures while depending on their good graces for the continuation of our work.

I was certainly committed to the importance of noting the social and cultural constraints of the hospital project from the beginning, identifying such constraints as part of the overall "context." But as my involvement there matured, I began to see more clearly that many of the arrangements for access to the hospital became observations in their own right. Negotiating access, collecting, analyzing, and reporting this work put me in a position to experience the institutional practices and ideologies of the hospital in a rather direct way even though I was not a full member of the community in my own right. Thus understanding my own struggle often helped me understand the experiences of the writers at Good Hope Hospital as they negotiated the fluid and contingent realities of composing in this institutional setting.

Situating the Consultant-Researcher Roles in the Institutional Culture

Since critical workplace writing research generally requires access to a writing site over extended time periods and some form of close working identity for the researcher, I took on the role of paid consultant in the hospital in order to establish that identity and to build trust between myself and the nurses. The consulting arrangement gave us a common task to work on together. Such arrangements, however, also imply some commitment to the goals of the organizational gatekeepers who fund the consulting relationship. Thus they have been criticized for corrupting the researchers' critical stance on the one hand or for constituting conflicts of interest on the other (see Adler and Adler; Harrison).

Even in cases where ethnographers do not intend to "criticize" in the commonest sense, those who control access to an institution may fear misrepresentation of their community. Since a critical perspective suggests an activist approach that aims to uncover such issues as class, gender, institutional power, and social interaction—issues which may not always be apparent to the informants themselves—researchers taking such an approach must be prepared to interrogate an institution's centers of power as well as the discourse on its margins. Such work requires generous access conditions and the ability to record unselfconscious expressions of these relationships (see Kincheloe and McLaren).

In the case of Good Hope Hospital, conflict much older than my project determined the institutional politics I encountered long before I arrived. I originally began work at Good Hope as part of what might be described as a "communication audit," although we did not call it that at the time. At the request of the nursing department, my first task was to collect a record of the documents housed on each nursing unit and to study how those documents were being used. This survey was intended to be a preliminary step in reorganizing and revising the entire nursing department's regulation system. During this early involvement with the nursing department, I learned that the nurses themselves had elected to carry this work forward after a previous hospital-sponsored project had been canceled by upper-level administrators because of perceived cost to the hospital. So despite a corporate commitment to reducing paper work throughout the hospital, support for systematic work on the nursing regulations had been reduced to activities the nurses could do within their own budget and on their own time. Thus our project in the nursing department enacted a modest form of resistance to the greater hospital administration.

Being hired as a consultant by the nursing department specifically aligned me with the interests of nursing and set me in opposition to a number of other hospital interest groups. However, it also helped clarify which of the gatekeepers were due my primary loyalty.

The project's situation in the institutional hierarchy meant that all reports of the work itself were articulated to upper administration by the nurses themselves. The nursing director explained our work to the top managers and returned their responses to us softened by her interest in the project's success. Within the division, members of the writing group frequently interpreted our work to the nursing hierarchy as well. So even though I had some access to the nursing director, I was also shielded from her by the writing group leaders. Both situations, while taking me "out of the loop" as a consultant, gave me valuable insights as a researcher into the sorts of strategies nursing staff members used to further their own goals in this institutional culture. These conditions also put me into a space where my work was explained upward in the institutional hierarchy by people supportive of the work and anxious to protect my involvement. Therefore, the nurses themselves mediated a number of conflicts that might have arisen regarding my ability to take a critical view of the hospital as an institution. These conditions told me a good deal about the position of nursing in the larger institution, placed me in a position of support for the nurses' subtle assertion of their own authority, and gave a proactive slant to my research even before I understood its significance.

Fortunately, this unusual set of circumstances reduced my dependence on the good will of the highest administrators of the hospital, but it is not something every researcher can expect to encounter. I can imagine a number of other conditions in which entry into an organization could be arranged through access to less powerful groups in the institution. Such an approach might counteract the tendency of writing researchers to select members of powerful groups for study and certainly fits with Donna Haraway's suggestion that taking the perspective of less powerful social groups offers an important way to reinvent research "objectivity" (395). Indeed, much workplace writing research has focused on the work of engineers, scientists, upper-level managers, and others with considerable prestige in the larger culture. Such people tend to occupy positions that enable them to participate in the development of official institutional discourse on internal policy matters. Studying less powerful groups may open our work up to the counterdiscourses that also inform an institution's climate and affect the work of those more commonly studied. Such "back door" communities generally seem to represent little threat to the institution itself, and the researcher's affiliation with them may thus appear correspondingly less threatening to gatekeepers.

Conflicting Loyalties between the Consultant-Researcher Roles

Even though I was protected from direct conflicts with hospital management, the nursing department sought permission from upper management when I asked to tape-record the writing sessions I began to have with a number of head nurses after the unit survey was completed. I was told at the time that one hospital administrator expressed reservations about my request to use the project as a research site. He suggested that the hospital should avoid "paying her to write a dissertation on our time." I assumed this sentiment to be connected to the need to guarantee that the hospital would receive adequate return on its investment in my time with the nursing staff and that my work with the nurses would be focused on hospital goals rather than on those of my own research.

Since the work and the observations occurred at the same time, it was difficult to define the two activities in ways that could discriminate between billable hours and my own research time. But I assured the nursing director that there were indeed two tasks—(1) working with the writers, and (2) observing and recording their writing processes for later analysis. I offered to balance the hours I recorded with contributed time for which I would not bill the hospital. Since that offer seemed to satisfy the administrators' objections, I eventually donated all the hours I spent building a small computer database that served as the project index, entering its data, and writing instructions for using it. Taken together, all of these projects returned considerably more donated hours to the hospital than I spent recording and interviewing the writing group.

Although this strategy did not really separate my consulting from the observations, it did provide a guarantee that the hospital's funds would not necessarily be spent on my research time. In addition to the donated time, I also used the consulting fees in the nursing department's interest when I purchased software and other supplies to use on the project at home. Looking back, I am not convinced that reciprocation at this level was really necessary, since my consulting role provided a concrete service to the hospital. I may have billed too modestly for my time, but I think those actions were a result of my concern for keeping myself on the generous side of the consulting equation. This arrangement, however, ensured that combining consulting with workplace research was not particularly financially profitable in my case. Since support for research such as this is rare enough, I felt fortunate to have the consulting fees to pay for tapes, recording equipment, and transcribing help. I used up nearly all the consulting funds to support the research in these ways, so the nursing department at Good Hope actually did fund my research in an indirect way through the consulting fees. In return, they received a great deal of consulting help, a database design for housing their documentation index, and a good many hours of data entry. These accommodations represented my cooperation in the nursing department's efforts to carry on a project despite skepticism and diminished support from the institutional hierarchy. It thus further involved me in the acts of resistance the project represented.

Besides aligning me with the concerns of the nursing community itself, my status as a consultant for nursing yielded additional benefits. It gave me direct access to the texts which defined nursing activity in the hospital, made me welcome in the main nursing office, provided me with an identity badge which gave me passage into controlled areas of the hospital, and established a credible role for me in the nursing environment. The nursing station survey acquainted me with departmental organization inside nursing and gave me access to ways current policy documents were being used. It also gave me a reason to be in the nursing units and to listen to ways people responded to my work with the documents. Had I chosen to become a hospital volunteer rather than a paid consultant, I could have moved about in some of these same spaces, but my credibility and my alignment with nursing might have been less clear and my understanding of the relationship of nursing to the larger institution might have been much less rich.

Despite this positioning of my work in the nursing domain, some conflicting loyalties remained between my consulting work and my research. The nurses themselves articulated a similar conflict of loyalties when they expressed reservations about whether the information I carried outside might eventually embarrass the hospital in the larger community. Several issues relating to public perceptions of the hospital led people to request that my recording equipment be turned off, which blocked my ability to document certain portions of the nurses' experiences. In cases where the collaborative writing group made such a request, I always complied, because my work with them produced ample evidence of their ways of dealing with sensitive issues in a wide variety of circumstances. But I fought back when I thought one such request threatened my ability to document a specific conflict between the interests of nurses and those of others such as hospital administrators and staff physicians.

The conflict appeared in a Head Nurse Council meeting where the nursing supervisors discussed a new hospital policy on the use of a specific drug in the institution. During a break, the nursing director asked that I not record this part of the meeting, but I persuaded her to allow me to continue the tape by explaining that the discussion of the sensitive issue would not be transcribed and that the contextual information I would collect during the discussion would have important consequences for my research. Of course I have not transcribed that conversation and have only referred to it indirectly in my reports. In important ways, my sense of how members of the nursing department perceived their own need to mediate among various hospital authorities was first suggested at this meeting. But when I look back, it was probably not necessary for me to record the meeting in order to learn that. Rather, it was important for me to hear the discussion and to see the ways nurses protected the hospital's local reputation in their own terms. Knowing this made me better able to interpret their subsequent comments about institutional practices, but I found ample evidence of many such conflicts once I had learned how to listen for them.

In the early stages of the work, I feared that my influence on the writing group would interfere with the writing activity itself and produce research into my own teaching rather than a record of the group's authentic efforts. As most researchers do, I worried that my own influence might distort the writing culture of the collaborative group. True to my worst fears, my presence in early meetings not only distorted, but completely dominated the writing group's work for a while. As I listened back through tape recordings of our early writing sessions together, my voice seemed frustratingly prominent, and the nurses seemed to be listening, as students sometimes will, for clues in my talk about what they should do. Sensing that the role of consultant rendered my words more powerful than I had expected, I struggled for several weeks to make my role in the collaborative writing sessions less prominent and to encourage the nurses to do what they had defined as their own job—to do the writing.

This deference to my advice surprised me at first because of the definition of the consulting role as the nurses had originally described it. From the nurses' perspective, the first prerequisite for any consultant invited to help with department projects was a nursing education. (When first introduced to people in the department as a consultant, I was almost always asked if I were a registered nurse.) Since I am not trained as a nurse, I was not considered qualified to deal with the content of the writing project, and thus only able to advise. The definition of the project from the beginning specified that the nurses themselves would "do the writing" so (I assumed) as to prevent my taking over the project or ghost writing materials which could be both inaccurate and inappropriate to local needs.

But while I expected that this consultant-researcher distinction would establish the nurses as the dominant writers, it was not quite that simple. The nurses' own attitudes about writing made this choice a difficult one for them. The nurses I met generally expressed apprehension and even loathing about the work of composing and frequently lamented that I could not do it for them. So despite their doubt that I was qualified to serve as a project writer, the nurses' own resistance to writing made the members of the writing group rather receptive to suggestions on my part. My conflict in this area helped me to see how difficult it was for the nurses to get beyond their own ambivalence about my involvement in the project. Feeling unprepared to write, they looked to me for help and advice. Yet it was difficult for them to find a way to trust me to speak for nursing concerns without being a nurse myself.

Those early sessions in which I talked entirely too much did not produce a great deal of appropriate work on the project and set us off in some unproductive directions. But together we eventually began to sort out my consulting role, their own writing role, and a productive working relationship between the two. The nurses were certainly right that I was not qualified to articulate local policy matters. My lack of nursing education made me particularly apt to misunderstand technical issues, and my strangeness to the local community made me unable to participate fully in understanding the institutional consequences of decisions which seemed perfectly neutral to me. Such dissonance often provides the sites for the discourse of negotiation, something I needed as a researcher and consultant, but more importantly, a phenomenon I began to see as essential to the institutional culture of nursing in this hospital. Indeed, our own negotiations within the writing group mirrored negotiations I subsequently saw group members engaging in with administrators, fellow nursing department heads, and a dizzying array of interest groups to which they had some form of responsibility. So once again, access and research arrangements led me to a richer understanding of the context in which the nurses worked.

This very ownership of the project by the nursing department and their caution about giving an unqualified person too much responsibility for the content of the documents provided valuable ways to offset the potential undue exercise of my consulting role. Some of the members expressed a confidence that their work was a way to increase their own institutional influence in the hospital and wanted that effect to be specifically attributable to nursing. Eventually the nurses themselves began to enjoy explaining things to me as they learned to value my outsider's perspective and my ability to name an issue when they could not find adequate closure for their own deliberations. But my ignorance meant that many things generally left unsaid among the nurses had to be explained to me as an outsider, and relationships well understood among the group members sometimes had to be patiently spelled out for me. Such explanations enriched the observation tapes every time we met, but made me (as they had predicted) a less efficient consultant. I think my billing strategy, explained above, may have also been informed by the need to acknowledge the conflicts I felt between what I offered the nurses in the way of consulting help and what they actually needed.

I also carried this ownership concern in the back of my mind throughout the subsequent analysis and writing phases of my research. My presence had pressured people to attend meetings they might have missed in order to attend to other pressing matters. My influence had added confusion to a task they saw as much more straightforward than I did. And at times, my inexperience required so many explanations and digressions in the meetings that I felt I had made them far less productive than they could have been without me. But most of all, the nurses' articulate ownership of the writing project constantly reminded me that I did *not* own it and that my research gave voice to people who did not need me to speak *for* them, but who had generously allowed me to work *with* them. I have tried to honor that trust even though the forums in which I have discussed this work tend to be quite remote from the spaces in which their voices generally are heard.

Preserving Access to the Competing Realities in a Site

Researchers who study the activity of institutional writers have a chance to ask about who determines certain defining features of an organization: the content of its public discourse, the forms of that discourse, the nature of discourse production, and the roles of specific individuals who take up the discourse in various ways. In doing so, such projects give a concrete face to the understanding of power structures in a discourse context. Such work requires access to the voices of both the powerful and the marginalized members of a community. Thus research that attempts to account for cultural constraints on writing may need to be designed in ways that balance the perspectives of groups with varying degrees of institutional influence even in cases where these groups do not perceive power differences themselves. Because my access to the powerful elements of hospital and medical cultures was both mediated and interpreted through the language of the nurses, I learned a great deal about the institutional forces that shape the experience of hospital nursing by listening to what these nurses feared, by observing the authority figures they deferred to, and by recording the evasions and subterfuges they felt it necessary to employ.

As I continued to work in the hospital over a period of months, I tried to be sensitive to both the public values being discussed in the writing group meetings and to the informal discussions of similar issues that occurred inside the group and elsewhere. I was not trying to triangulate my observations in the usual positivistic sense, but rather to attend to the alternative experiences which contend with each other in an institution's cultural dynamic. My hope was to get at the organization's formal and informal webs of human interaction. Frequently I ate lunch in the hospital cafeteria, and it was there one day that I noticed the apparent connection between official hospital roles and the clothes people wore. Surgery personnel in green scrub-wear were mostly sitting together in groups, while other clusters of people all tended to be wearing a similar garb—be it nursing whites or lab smocks. Some nursing administrators even wore "power clothes" of the business community. That day I began to understand how uniforms, smocks, and surgery gowns identified people in relation to their hospital function and something of why the debate over a nursing dress code I had witnessed had been so heated. The clusters at lunch tables represented social networks as well as functional teams, but they also represented hospital status.

The dress code discussion had pitted high-prestige nursing groups in areas such as surgery, recovery, and specialty labs (where uniforms were provided by the hospital) against staff nurses and aides, whose more generic patient care duties were not so subsidized. To have a uniform dress code in the hospital nursing units, therefore, would only affect those people who purchased their own wardrobes, and hospital "favorites" would thereby be making a significant imposition on these other groups. I heard discussions of this issue in an official meeting of all unit head nurses, in the writing group, over lunch with a group of floor nurses, and in a private conversation with their head nurse (and advocate). The motivation to improve patient perceptions of the hospital nurses and to make the hospital look more like a conventional clinical environment came from a small group of traditionally minded nurses. But since such new rules would only affect a small part of the nursing department staff, those who would be affected fought against a dress code change throughout my two years of visiting the hospital. This debate among the nurses simmered, but was never satisfactorily resolved during my observations.

The contradictions I observed between the managerial and bedside roles of the head nurses in the Good Hope study also required that I look at the community through the variety of lenses that its members did. Serving at the border between administrative and clinical functions of the hospital, the experience, discourse, and responsibilities of head nurses span two major institutional forces important to a hospital's culture. Understanding head nurses as first-level managers required attention to the larger administrative affairs of the hospital and to official texts. But since the head nurses also continued to participate in patient care activities on the nursing floors, their writing decisions were also clearly tied to the hospital's clinical discourses and to issues of concern to floor nurses, bedside aides, orderlies, and department clerical personnel. It was necessary to know about each of these perspectives before I would make any sense of the highly charged discussions that arose when we tried to rewrite the policies that affected these groups in different ways.

The shifting articulation of various hospital constituent interests seemed to be a major concern of head nurses. I noticed that the discourse of individuals changed as they spoke up for different interests in the writing sessions. No record of any single conversation was adequate to represent the way individuals argued for each of the various factions over time. I began to see the writing group work as more than a negotiation between individuals with diverse interests; it became a microcosm of the views represented by most of the interest groups affected by the policies we were attempting to revise. Group members did not hesitate to bring their own personal and departmental interests into the writing context, but they also evidenced desire to account for the interests of other groups as well. Even further, they frequently repeated the arguments of regulators, legal staff, physicians, administrators, and accreditation boards. Thus their writing time was often spent trying out such arguments on each other and working toward a synthesis that would satisfy local conditions and be acceptable as well to the various groups that would need to approve or to enact the policies they established.

Members of the writing team spoke both as individuals and as community representatives as they negotiated policy matters affecting the wide variety of organizational interests that had to be pleased. My own commitment to the various factions being tenuous, I was rarely pressured to take sides in these discussions among the writing group members. However, some nurses who identified themselves with the project, but who rarely attended group meetings, offered conflicting views of the project in their interviews and invited me to participate in criticism of it.

In a further attempt to get at a variety of perspectives not adequately covered by my direct observation, I ended my project at Good Hope by interviewing all the regular group members individually as well as representatives of some of the primary departmental interest groups. I also met with all of the nursing administrators to whom the head nurses reported and with a number of head nurses who had not participated in the writing group—some of whom had supported the project from a distance and some of whom preferred to write their own unit materials outside the group's influence.

In these interviews I asked each person about her own writing history, her opinions about the project, and her perceptions of the hospital hierarchy and culture. Because I chose to ask open-ended questions, few people saw the interviews as a space for open critique of the hospital's power arrangements, although some saw it as a chance to criticize the project itself. I learned a good deal in these interviews about community attitudes toward writing and the tendency for nurses to devalue their own writing that was not "creative" or "publishable" in some traditional way. But it was my writing group observations, more than my interviews, that provided insight into what contributed to the hospital's strong, hierarchical organization.

Making Inferences and Drawing Conclusions

One of the most treacherous stages of qualitative research is the time when the researcher has returned from the field to work with the materials collected and to make sense out of what she has experienced. There are, of course, multiple levels of such experience. There is the record of the actual observations, there are the impressions and possible explanations that infuse the acts of analyzing such data, and there is the inevitable need to select relevant material from all these sources to create the ethnographic report.

I found analysis and report of the work to require continual self-examination as well as frequent return to the data itself. Of course there is a need to preserve the authentic experience of the study's participants, but events recorded in qualitative studies cannot be repeated. By the time analysis and report are complete, the "realities" of the community have long since shifted, and the report becomes a historical account.

Such accounts must at last put away the tendency to entertain all possible explanations and to take some stand on interpreting the experience.

I am pretty sure the need to let the experiences "settle" and to find some ways of dealing with the mountains of data pushed me to try to achieve some distance from the nursing community as I began to describe the writing events there. I did, of course, maintain some contact with the most active nurses and discussed with them several drafts of my work as the reports emerged. However, things were *not* the same anymore when I returned. The feeling of closure I had after the last interviews somehow represented a release, a definite end to the events of the study. Of course, the nurses' project itself was *not* finished and took a number of different turns after I left. The problems that the writing group sought to address did not all go away, and I had a difficult time dealing with the idea that, for all our efforts, we had not achieved many of the goals the nurses had set for the project.

After that first moment of relief, I worked primarily by re-creating the experiences in my memory as I sorted, analyzed, and revisited the materials. Each time I did so, I had the feeling that I was re-creating the context in yet another way, and each time a number of alternative interpretations seemed equally plausible. So my qualitative researcher habits—of withholding judgment, of continually watching for new ways of thinking about the site, of keeping open to the unfamiliar—infused my interpretation and writing, thereby displacing the sense of confidence I had assumed other researchers must surely have achieved by the way their reports showed focus, substance, and assurance.

Throughout the analysis I compared my evidence across media, across informants, across time, and across contexts and felt much more comfortable when those comparisons could contribute to a consistent picture of the forces that had informed our work together. But each time I chose one explanation and began to act on it—to inform subsequent analysis or to become part of the emerging report—I felt at some level as if I were falsifying the experience by choosing only one of the many interpretations that the evidence might warrant.

I also often felt like something of a spy when those interpretations opened up questions of institutional power and its effects on the writing of nurses in this context. A good deal of what I reported came from indirect observation, from participants unable or afraid to speak to issues of institutional power. I worked from material collected in unguarded moments, from hints that appeared when writers had trouble with definitions, articulations of policy, or imagining the responses to their work by their co-workers or supervisors. I made inferences from the ways people referred to authority figures, from the ways they described their own reasons for accepting the status quo, and from the euphemistic language they sometimes chose to describe hierarchical relationships. Sociolinguistic analysis of turn-taking, conversation patterns, and local jargon gave some of this interpretation substance. I certainly learned a great deal about the hospital's culture by noticing who controlled conversations, what sort of issues recurred without resolution, and which issues were resolved by administrative edict.

One particularly revealing conversation illustrates this indirect evidence. I recorded three regular members of the group in a conversation in which they were trying to persuade a less active group member to accept a course of action agreed to in a meeting she had not attended. I observed the regular members using rather heavy-handed rhetoric to convince their less connected (had she marginalized herself?) colleague. The discussion became quite heated and went on much longer than the issue seemed to merit. I wondered why it was so important to convince Leah to agree with the group's approach. I knew the discussion offered a significant record of the shared group values employed as grounds for the logic directed toward Leah, but I could not account for the emotional tone of the discussion. At my request, group members reflected on this conversation in a subsequent meeting; they offered a number of possible reasons for their feelings and Leah's resistance. I also discussed the incident with Leah herself. Such reflective discussions created a space where we could explore the political dynamics of the writing project and where I could gain access to local explanations of the incident. But eventually it was my own choice of interpretations that made its way into the record of this incident. As researcher, my role implied a privileged status in the eventual records of the work. Understanding this position still makes me uncomfortable and presses me to look for more alternatives to the traditional report format that privileges the researcher's voice so much.

Representing the Various Perspectives

I struggled throughout the writing and rewriting of the Good Hope study to find adequate ways to integrate the diverse perspectives of the hospital environment while satisfying the demands of the various publication forums in which I thought the research might appear.

I have found it particularly difficult to devise effective ways to integrate participant voices in research reports of this work. I do not know that I have found ways of adequately making the nurses' owner-ship felt in reports of the research, and my reports have been criticized by reviewers for veiling the nursing voices too much. Given the com-plexities of exploring the interactions and social relationships of a group of people, I find it difficult to reproduce the dynamic of the collabora-tive events without reducing the reports to discussions about the nurses as "a group." Individual personalities get subsumed in general state-ments about the climate while my own voice seems to dominate de-scriptions of the work.

For one thing, the complexity of issues taken up in the study de-manded a much broader perspective than any one of the participants was able to articulate in pointed, telling statements. Indeed, most things people said need so much explanation and contextualizing that insert-ing them in my reports threatens to disrupt the finely focused discus-sions demanded by the constraints of publication in journals. Complex discussions of the many perspectives, influences, audiences, and con-straints on the writing of a hospital nurse need a good deal of explana-tory space if the conditions are to be anything but sketched.

Yet I am myself technical writer enough to believe in summary and to use it to set limits around potentially lengthy explanations. Set-ting limits is essential: if today's academic reading habits are such that an 800-page novel elicits resistance, then it is hard to imagine many readers willing to tolerate the 2,000-plus pages of some qualitative re-search reports I have seen. So with limits in place, my personal sketches of the individuals I encountered capture but a fraction of the rich expe-riences each person brought to the group writing task. Furthermore, the shifting loyalties these individuals represented as they constantly tried to articulate views through the hospital's various discourses made it difficult to name any position consistently taken by any given group member.

The desire to protect individual identities and preserve anonym-ity also pushed the reports toward discussing the activities of the group rather than the ideas and practices of individuals. My rather unsatisfac-tory solution to this dilemma has been to talk about the writing group as a team and to erase the individual identities of the participants in any but a superficial way. This somewhat totalizing approach to describing the writing group's activity still makes me rather uncomfortable when I think of the resulting loss of individual voices and the richness each brought to the discussions.

In order not to lose the flavor of the hospital conversations en-tirely, I eventually chose to include snippet transcripts in my reports as illustrations of the sort of occasions that prompted my interpretations. Such excerpts are inserted into my own text at appropriate places, but are separated from my own analysis by boxes to highlight the distinction between nurses' voices and my own. This excerpting of conversational moments does enough damage to the fabric of the group dynamic that I could only rarely find a way to justify further appropriating the voices of group members by quoting them within my own sentences.

Attempts to reclaim writing research from positivistic paradigms have led researchers to emulate the conventions of literary or historical prose in which a singular author surveys a broad array of material—in this particular case, a collection of texts and artifacts—in order to render a sensible account of it. Within this schema, incorporation of participant voices functions as does literary quotation. Indeed, some reports of qualitative research appropriate entire narrative structures from literary models. In my own work, I eventually came to feel rather like a spinner of fictions rather than a reporter of research—something I had previously criticized in the work of John Van Maanen. I began my project thinking that he was far too free with his comparison of ethnography to fiction, but came to see just how much I was "fictionalizing" even when I was handling objective-looking data. One way I posit the distinction between ethnography and fiction for myself is to invoke the notion of "aim" from modern rhetorical theory (for instance, see Kinneavy). Research such as mine has a specifically liberatory and political aim, which makes it distinct from a great deal of (but, of course, not all) creative fiction.

Furthermore, the turn toward "telling tales" does not adequately address the questions of negotiating the vast divide between being too specific on the one hand and too general on the other. Many qualitative researchers have reached out to alternative narrative structures, such as inserting individual biographies between analytic chapters, as Gesa Kirsch did in her recent book. We could think about other radical approaches such as situating columns parallel on a page, constructing hypertexts, adopting participant personas, or writing other sorts of texts that follow the conventions of fiction or poetry. Yet none of these approaches feels completely right to me, and most would be difficult to get published in the forums that academics consider to be "serious intellectual spaces." In addition, we do not execute such radical texts very well yet, because their conventional instability makes it hard for readers to negotiate their slippery surfaces. However, while we push toward greater critical perspectives in ethnographic reports of workplace environments, we must carve out new conventions for such work as we become both better writers *and* readers of qualitative research.

In my experience, this battle to achieve an acceptable voice and presentation for ethnographic work promotes the isolation of a researcher. Inasmuch as it does so, it also runs somewhat counter to the social theories that inform this chapter, as well as much current thinking about the nature of discourse itself. Consider the figure of the humanistic researcher. If such a researcher is in fact an author—a connection not too difficult to draw, I believe—then we must recognize that the autonomous researcher, like the autonomous author, is dead.[1] So if we are serious about social construction of knowledge, it is important to authorize and practice collaborative methods for analyzing and reporting our research as well as for collecting it. And for a number of practical reasons, such collaborations offer a much better approach to respecting the rights of researchers to reasonable workloads.

Collaborative research among colleagues in both a researcher's discipline and in the disciplines that organize the workplace research site could add more evenly matched voices to the analysis and report-writing stages of inquiry. Choosing collaborators from disciplines closely related to the research site also opens up the number of scholarly forums in which research might be reported. Pairs of researchers could write articles for journals in both their disciplines, thereby bringing important balance to the presentations in each case. Sadly, such teamwork may remain rare until we devise disciplinary structures that value collaborative interdisciplinary projects and co-authored publications. I promote collaborative research as an ideal, knowing that there are few opportunities for it in current institutional settings, and knowing firsthand how much time, flexibility, and compromise it requires.

Nevertheless, if in the course of reporting research it becomes necessary for participant voices to yield to the researcher's own voice, it would be helpful if that voice were to remain in some sense collaborative. And it will remain collaborative so long as the researcher acknowledges that, as an author, her words are inevitably shaped by the words of others—including those of workers in other disciplines she studies. The benefits of such collaborative voicing are clear: it can serve a wide variety of audiences, from other working writers, to students learning to write, to scholars who lack experience in discourse beyond the classroom.

In summary, researchers and readers of research alike need to remember that ethnographic inquiry into workplace writing puts us all into political and ethical spaces even when we do not actively seek them. It is an overtly political move to plan a worksite study and, as my access to Good Hope shows, the nature of such politics may be incorporated into the very arrangements for the research itself. As well as being political, workplace research is also, by definition, interdisciplinary. This interdisciplinarity means that the researcher must be prepared to struggle with the cultural dynamics particular to the discipline under study—and perhaps unfamiliar from the researcher's point of view. To stand astride disciplinary boundaries is to enrich and complicate that point of view in ways that defer closure in workplace research.

Closing Note

I offer this discussion with some sense that its value may accrue more to me as a researcher than to those who have yet to undertake such study. Indeed, in my several drafts of this chapter I have grown successively more frank and less sure of my own choices, yet correspondingly more productive. To those who aspire to observe workplace writing using qualitative methods, the community of composition researchers offers few guarantees for recognition, for firm conclusions, and for confident reflection on a job well done. I remain convinced, however, that those who study writing must value the experience of connecting with working writers and share in some measure in their struggles to make language work for them. I feel no need to apologize for my own effort to do that. In fact, I believe that such efforts may be the only way for both writers and writing researchers to come to understand the complexity of written discourse. A firm commitment to assess our own involvement and a critical perspective are important elements of how that understanding shall eventually be achieved.

Notes

1. I am aware that my concrete view of collaborative research probably underplays the influence of source texts, conversations at national conferences, and the contributions of peer reviewers (see Roen and Mittan). But those influences, important as they are, function on a primarily metaphorical plane. I refer here to actual material collaborations among face-to-face research teams—like what we expect students to do when we ask them to write together, or like my Good Hope consulting work.

Works Cited

Adler, Patricia A., and Peter Adler. *Membership Roles in Field Research.* Newbury Park: Sage, 1987.

Brown, Robert L., Jr., and Carl G. Herndl. "An Ethnographic Study of Corporate Writing: Job Status as Reflected in Written Text." *Functional Approaches to Writing: Research Perspectives.* Ed. Barbara Couture. Norwood: Ablex, 1986. 11–27.

Dautermann, Jennie. "Writing at Good Hope Hospital: A Study of Negotiated Discourse in the Workplace." Diss. Purdue U, 1991.

———. "Negotiating Meaning in a Hospital Discourse Community." *Writing in the Workplace: New Research Perspectives.* Ed. Rachel Spilka. Carbondale: Southern Illinois UP, 1993. 98–110.

Haraway, Donna. "The Bio-politics of a Multicultural Field." *The "Racial" Economy of Science: Toward a Democratic Future.* Ed. Sandra G. Harding. Bloomington: Indiana UP, 1993. 377–97.

Harris, Joseph. "The Idea of Community in the Study of Writing." *College Composition and Communication* 40 (1989): 11–22.

Harrison, Michael I. *Diagnosing Organizations: Methods, Models, and Processes.* Beverly Hills: Sage, 1987.

Herndl, Carl G. "Writing Ethnography: Representation, Rhetoric, and Institutional Practices." *College English* 53 (1991): 320–32.

Kincheloe, Joe L., and Peter L. McLaren. "Rethinking Critical Theory and Qualitative Research." *Handbook of Qualitative Research.* Ed. Norman K. Denzin and Yvonna S. Lincoln. Thousand Oaks: Sage, 1994. 138–57.

Kinneavy, James L. "The Basic Aims of Discourse." *College Composition and Communication* 20 (1969): 297–304.

Kirsch, Gesa E. *Women Writing the Academy: Audience, Authority, and Transformation.* Carbondale: Southern Illinois UP, 1993.

Pratt, Mary Louise. "Criticism in the Contact Zone: Decentering Community and Nation." *Critical Theory, Cultural Politics, and Latin American Narrative.* Ed. Steven M. Bell, Albert H. Le May, and Leonard Orr. Notre Dame: U of Notre Dame P, 1993. 83–102.

Roen, Duane H., and Robert K. Mittan. "Collaborative Scholarship in Composition: Some Issues." *Methods and Methodology in Composition Research.* Ed. Gesa Kirsch and Patricia A. Sullivan. Carbondale: Southern Illinois UP, 1992. 287–313.

Van Maanen, John. *Tales of the Field: On Writing Ethnography.* Chicago: U of Chicago P, 1988.

14 Ethics, Institutional Review Boards, and the Involvement of Human Participants in Composition Research

Paul V. Anderson
Miami University (Ohio)

Among the contexts for composition research in the United States is a federal policy designed to assure that the human participants (whom it calls "subjects") are treated ethically. Part of the United States *Code of Federal Regulations*, this policy establishes criteria for most types of research that involve human participants, and it requires that colleges, universities, hospitals, and other institutions that receive federal funds for human-participant research create committees, named Institutional Review Boards (IRBs), to assure that researchers adhere to these criteria.[1] When composition researchers are planning studies covered by this policy, they must design their projects in ways that conform to its requirements. Additionally, the researchers must submit descriptions of their projects to their Institutional Review Boards, which may take anywhere from a few days to several weeks to reply. If the IRBs find any shortcoming in the researchers' plans, they have the power and responsibility to disapprove the studies or require modifications they believe necessary to protect the participants' privacy, welfare, or dignity.

The federal policy does provide exemptions for a few types of studies, including some that are conducted by composition researchers. Even for exempt studies, however, researchers probably need someone else's approval before beginning their projects. Many colleges and universities prohibit researchers from declaring their own studies exempt. Researchers must obtain an independent determination of their projects' status.

As a researcher, as a person who sometimes teaches graduate seminars in qualitative research methods, and as a member of my own university's Institutional Review Board, I can attest that this federal policy has tremendous potential to both assist and frustrate researchers. Some researchers express gratitude for help they have received from an IRB in identifying ways to better protect their participants. Other researchers express annoyance, even resentment, that they must obtain permission to conduct projects they believe present no discernible risk to participants. Furthermore, composition researchers sometimes find that they and their IRBs encounter difficulty in determining how the policy, which was created with biomedical research primarily in mind, applies to composition research.

Regardless of their attitudes toward the federal policy, researchers may be placing not only their participants but also themselves and their institutions at risk if they fail to comply with it. Every institution covered by the policy is required to monitor for violations and report them to the appropriate federal agency. Additionally, suspicion of violations can trigger a federal investigation (Ellis, Memo on compliance). Violations can lead to ineligibility for federal research funds for both the researcher and the institution.

My purpose in this chapter is to provide a framework within which composition researchers can understand the nature of the federal policy, its rationale, and its sometimes ambiguous application to their studies. Because the requirements and language of the policy have been shaped significantly by the circumstances surrounding its creation, I will begin by briefly recounting the policy's history. Then I will describe its implications for composition research, sketch the administrative structures it establishes, tell how IRBs process research plans, explain some of the key criteria the policy requires IRBs to use, and discuss several areas of ambiguity that can perplex both composition researchers and the IRBs that review their projects.

History of the U.S. Policy for Protecting Human Participants in Research

The history of the U.S. policy for protecting the human participants in research begins in a place quite remote from contemporary composition studies: the Nuremberg Tribunals, at which Axis war criminals were tried for atrocities committed during World War II.[2] At one tribunal, twenty-three Nazi physicians stood accused of perpetrating extreme cruelties, often resulting in death, against concentration camp prisoners in order to study the human response to the ingestion of poison, intravenous injection of gasoline, extended immersion in ice water, and other torturous treatment. The physicians argued that they had merely engaged in justified biomedical research. In response, the judges wrote the *Nuremberg Code,* a ten-point statement of the conditions under which human experimentation can be conducted. Two of the code's cardinal points became fundamental in subsequent U.S. policy. The first is that it is "absolutely essential" that every human research participant give voluntary consent after being fully informed about the research, including its nature, duration, and purpose, as well as "all inconveniences and hazards reasonably to be expected" and "the effects upon his [*sic*] health or person which may possibly come from his participation."[3] Second, the research can be conducted only if the risks to participants are justified in terms of the benefits that could result from the knowledge that might be gained (*Trials of War Criminals* 181–82).

First Policies in the United States

In the United States, the first federal policies concerning the use of human research participants were written in the late 1940s and early 1950s by the Atomic Energy Commission and the Department of Defense. However, these policies were not widely followed or even widely known within the agencies that issued them. In fact, the Department of Defense classified its policy top secret, meaning that only senior Defense Department officials could read it. The policies have come to light only recently through investigations into numerous hitherto secret radiation experiments conducted on thousands of unsuspecting U.S. citizens by government agencies and their contractors (Gallagher; Hilts; United States, Dept. of Energy).

The general public and Congress did not become concerned about the treatment of research participants until the 1960s. The preceding decades had seen a tremendous growth in the amount and popularity of biomedical research involving human volunteers, which brought such medical breakthroughs as penicillin and the polio vaccine. Most of the public and most elected officials trusted individual researchers, their professional disciplines, and their institutions (e.g., hospitals, medical research centers) to guarantee that human participants were treated ethically. In the early 1960s, however, this faith was eroded by the exposure of studies that treated participants in an egregiously unethical manner. For example, in the early 1960s, during extensive hearings concerning the possible revision of the Pure Food and Drugs Act (1906) and the Food, Drug and Cosmetics Act (1938), evidence was mounting in Europe that thalidomide, a sedative prescribed to pregnant women, could cause devastating deformities in their fetuses. In the United States, tha-lidomide was still considered experimental, but congressional hearings disclosed that some physicians were prescribing it to patients without notifying them of this fact and without obtaining their consent (*Evolving Concern;* Lear). Because of congressional alarm over such practices, the 1962 Drug Amendments required physicians to inform patients when they planned to use an experimental drug and to proceed with that plan only after receiving patients' consent. However, the amendments did not establish any mechanism for verifying that physicians were actually adhering to these requirements, and they did not apply to the many forms of human-participant research in which experimental drugs are not used.

Beginnings of the Current Regulatory System

In the late 1950s, officials in the National Institutes of Health (NIH) had also begun to doubt that all medical researchers and their institutions could be trusted to behave ethically in the numerous human-participant research studies that NIH sponsored. NIH Director James Shannon was disturbed to learn that one researcher had unsuccessfully transplanted a chimpanzee's kidney into a human being with partial support from NIH and that another researcher had injected live cancer cells into twenty-two feeble or seriously ill patients. Apparently, some of these patients were told they would be involved in an experiment, but not that they were being injected with cancer cells; others were incompetent to give consent. NIH's growing reluctance to trust researchers and institutions to treat research participants ethically was intensified by two publications: a 1959 monograph, *Experimentation in Man,* in which Henry K. Beecher discussed the application of the *Nuremberg Code* to the burgeoning amount of biomedical research in the United States, and a 1960 study by the Law-Medicine Institute that suggested that reliance on the self-scrutiny of researchers was not providing adequate protection for participants in biomedical research (Faden and Beauchamp 157–58).

Eventually, Shannon proposed to establish external ethical controls for all NIH-sponsored studies. He won the support of Surgeon General William H. Stewart, who in 1966 issued a Policy for the Protection of Human Subjects. It required every institution receiving research support from the Public Health Service (of which NIH was a part) to establish a committee of scientists who would provide ethical review of proposed projects. These committees were to consider three topics: the rights and welfare of the participants, the appropriateness of the methods used to obtain informed consent, and the balance of risks and benefits. No new, renewal, or continuation grant for research involving human participants could be awarded unless the institution sponsoring the project provided a written assurance that such a committee was in operation (Levine 209).[4] Stewart's 1966 policy is the beginning from which the current federal policy grew. The review committees it mandated are the seeds of the Institutional Review Boards from which composition researchers must now receive prior approval for projects involving human participants.

After the promulgation of Stewart's policy, concern about the treatment of research participants continued to mount, fueled by the exposure of additional unethical studies. In the most notorious of these projects, Public Health Service physicians studied the pathological evolution of syphilis in 399 African American males living in and around Tuskegee, Alabama, who were in the late stage of the disease when they were recruited for the study (Jones). These men were not told that they had syphilis but that they were going to be treated for a set of (syphilitic) symptoms that were thought locally to be caused by "bad blood." Actually, they were not treated at all, but underwent spinal taps and other nontherapeutic treatments. A group of 201 African Americans without syphilis were used as a control group. Begun in 1932 and originally planned to last six to eight months, the study continued for the next forty years! None of the infected men were given the best available treatment in the 1930s, nor were any given penicillin treatment after its discovery in the 1940s. Over the decades, while the researchers watched, the duped, untreated participants suffered the progressive effects of the disease. By 1946, their death rate was already twice that of the control group, but the study was not halted until 1972—twenty-six years later— when it came to the public's attention through an article in the *New York Times* (Heller). The public and many in Congress were especially disturbed that the study had proceeded so many years, even though it was well known in the Public Health Service and in the medical community. Between 1932 and 1970, it was reviewed and approved for continuation several times, and it was reported in thirteen articles in professional journals.

In 1974, against the backdrop of growing concerns about research ethics and under pressure from Congress, the Department of Health, Education, and Welfare (of which the Public Health Service was a part) elevated Stewart's 1966 Policy for the Protection of Human Subjects to the status of a formal regulation (United States, Dept. of Health, Education, and Welfare).

Application of Early Policies to Social and Behavioral Research

Of course, the risks involved with biomedical research differ greatly in kind and severity from those associated with most social and behavioral research, including composition studies. Nevertheless, Surgeon General Stewart's 1966 policy applied not only to the large amount of biomedical research conducted or sponsored by the Public Health Service (PHS), but also to the small number of PHS social science projects. Furthermore, the Department of Health, Education, and Welfare (DHEW) retained this broad coverage in 1974 when it elevated the PHS policy to a federal regulation that applied to all of DHEW, including its education and welfare divisions, which sponsored large amounts of social and behavioral research.

The continuing inclusion of social and behavioral research was rationalized, in part, by publicity surrounding several nonbiomedical studies whose researchers were criticized for treating their research participants unethically. These studies included Stanley Milgram's famous investigations of the phenomenon that led many defendants at the Nuremberg trials to argue that, when they tortured and killed innocent people, they were merely obeying orders. After telling participants that he was studying learning processes, Milgram instructed them to administer what they thought were electric shocks of increasing severity to another person—actually a confederate of the researcher—whenever this individual gave an incorrect answer in a learning exercise. Located in another room, the confederate (who was not actually given any shocks) screamed as if in pain when higher voltages were administered; recruits who wanted to stop were pressured by a researcher to continue. In some experiments, the confederate eventually fell silent, as if either unconscious or dead. Critics, led by Diana Baumrind, denounced this experiment for the potential psychological damage inflicted on participants, who, even after being told of the deception, were nonetheless aware of their capacity to be coerced into harming another person.

Objections were also raised to the deceptive procedures employed by sociologist Laud Humphreys in his study of men who commit impersonal homosexual acts in public restrooms. By playing the role of a "watchqueen" or lookout, Humphreys surreptitiously obtained some of the men's license plate numbers. A year later, claiming to be a health service employee, he showed up at their homes, asking for an interview.

And Philip G. Zimbardo was criticized for an elaborate experiment, planned to run for two weeks, in which college students played the roles of prisoners and jailers in a mock prison set up in a Stanford University laboratory. After six days, Zimbardo terminated his study because the "jailers" had begun to abuse the "prisoners" physically and psychologically. Critics argued that Zimbardo exposed the students to extreme stress and hazards they had not been informed about in advance and that the study exposed the students to these risks without hope of producing new knowledge about prison behavior.

Changes in the Scope of the DHEW Policy: 1981

Although social and behavioral research (including composition studies using social and behavioral science methods) had been covered by Surgeon General Stewart's 1966 PHS policy and by the 1974 DHEW regulation, the social and behavioral science research communities were largely unaware, until the late 1970s, that these policies applied to them. Their awareness increased largely because of discussions fostered by the National Commission for the Protection of Human Subjects of Biomedical and Behavioral Research (established in 1974) and by its successor, the President's Commission for the Study of Ethical Problems in Medicine and Biomedical and Behavioral Research. As the commissions published their reports and recommendations, controversy arose over the appropriateness of applying the DHEW policy to social and behavioral research. Pointing out that the policy had been created principally to address problems in biomedical research, some researchers suggested creation of separate regulations better suited to the social and behavioral sciences. Other researchers opposed any regulation whatever, arguing (1) that it would hamper social and behavioral research which presents little or no risk and (2) that the committees that review research plans would be overwhelmed with work if they were required to examine social and behavioral projects in addition to biomedical studies. In response, a 1981 revision of the policy exempted six types of studies that present little or no risk to participants (United States, Dept. of Health and Human Services, "Final Regulations"). The exemptions included some types of surveys and interviews, as well as some studies of normal educational practices. Later in this chapter, I will discuss the relevance of these exemptions to composition.

Another 1981 revision also had important consequences for composition research. Both the 1966 PHS policy and the 1974 DHEW policy applied only to federally funded projects. However, the National Commission recommended that new regulations be extended to all human-participant research conducted in the United States. This recommendation drew strong protests from many who felt that the federal government should not regulate research it did not fund. In its 1981 regulations, the Department of Health and Human Services (DHHS), which succeeded DHEW in 1980, took the middle ground. It decided against extending its policy to cover projects it did not fund, but it created a new requirement that all institutions receiving DHHS support for human-participant research must develop their own policies for protecting participants in *all* their projects, even those not funded by DHHS (United States, Dept. of Health and Human Services, "Final Regulations"). As a practical matter, many institutions simply adopted the DHHS policy as their institutional policy. Because so many colleges and universities received DHHS funds for at least one research project involving human participants, this new policy's impact on composition research was substantial. Most composition research that did not fall into the policy's exempt categories was now subject to federally mandated regulation—even projects that were not federally supported.

Creation of the "Federal Policy": 1991

As the preceding paragraphs suggest, the Department of Health, Education, and Welfare and its successor, the Department of Health and Human Services, played a central role in the development of federal policies for protecting humans from research risks. However, during the 1960s and 1970s, several other federal agencies also created policies for protecting participants in the research they sponsored. To eliminate the confusion caused by this plethora of policies, fifteen departments agreed in 1991 to adopt a single policy shared by them all. Often called the "Common Rule" or the "Federal Policy," it is nearly identical to the 1981 DHHS policy (United States, Executive Office of the President, Office of Science and Technology Policy).[5] In addition to DHHS, participating agencies included the Department of Commerce, Department of Defense, Department of Education, Department of Energy, Environmental Protection Agency, National Aeronautics and Space Administration, and the National Science Foundation—all of which are current or potential sources of composition research involving human beings.[6]

Implications of the Federal Policy for Composition Researchers

A basic question facing composition researchers as they plan any study that uses human participants is, "Must we receive prior approval before beginning our project?" In almost every case the answer is, "Yes."

However, as the preceding history of the Federal Policy indicates, a somewhat complicated set of considerations comes into play. The following paragraphs explain.

1. If the studies are sponsored by one of the fifteen agencies that adopted the Federal Policy, then they are probably subject to all the requirements of the Federal Policy. The only exceptions are studies belonging to one of the exempt categories introduced in the 1981 DHHS policy and incorporated into the Federal Policy in 1991. However, exemption under the Federal Policy does not necessarily mean exemption from review. Following advice by the federal Office for Protection from Research Risks, many institutions prohibit researchers from declaring their own studies to be exempt; the researchers must submit their studies for an independent determination of the studies' status (Howe and Dougherty; Ellis, "Research").

To obtain approval for projects that are not exempt, composition researchers must submit detailed descriptions of their research plans, usually called *protocols,* to their institution's IRB. Similarly, at institutions where exempt status must be certified, researchers typically submit applications for certification to their IRBs, although some institutions delegate responsibility for reviewing these applications to another group or person.

2. Even if the studies are not funded by one of the fifteen agencies, they are still subject to review if the researchers are affiliated with an institution that receives any funds for human-participant research from one of these agencies. As mentioned above, the Federal Policy requires each institution receiving such funds to create its own institutional policy for the protection of human participants in *all* of its research (subsection 103.b.1).

3. If the researcher is not affiliated with an institution that receives funds for human-participant research from any of the fifteen agencies, the researcher's studies may not be subject to any federal or institutional requirements, although an employer could adopt a policy for protecting research participants even if not required to do so. Of course, researchers who are not subject to the Federal Policy may nevertheless find it helpful to check their projects against the policy as part of their effort to treat their participants ethically.

IRB Structure and Responsibilities

Because Institutional Review Boards are responsible for reviewing protocols for all human-participant studies at most institutions, they are important groups for researchers to understand. When composition researchers submit their protocols to an IRB, they are interacting with a committee comprised mainly of their institutional associates who operate within a two-tiered structure. Introduced in rudimentary form by Stewart's 1966 policy for the Public Health Service, this structure represented a compromise between those who maintained that the PHS needed to directly regulate the research it sponsored and those who feared that the PHS would take an unduly authoritarian stance toward research if it directly oversaw all the projects it funded. In this compromise, general requirements are established at the federal level, but responsibility for interpreting and applying the requirements rests with the local IRBs at each research institution.

Federal stipulations concerning IRB membership represent another compromise. In the 1960s, many researchers maintained that the persons best qualified to judge the ethics of their projects were other members of their own professional disciplines. However, some members of Congress and the general public were skeptical that professional disciplines could be trusted to police themselves. A 1969 revision to Stewart's policy settled the issue by stipulating that, collectively, IRB members should be competent to judge research not only by the standard of professional practice, but also by those of "community acceptance" (qtd. in Levine 210). Subsequent revisions to the policy have preserved this compromise while providing additional specificity about IRB membership. At present, an IRB must have at least five members, including persons with expertise in scientific research but also including at least one member whose primary concern is outside science and one member who is not affiliated with the institution, possibly a businessperson, homemaker, or minister. To composition researchers, these stipulations concerning IRB membership mean their applications will be read by a complex audience, most of whom are probably unfamiliar with the traditions and practices of composition research.

As it reviews research protocols, an IRB engages in a very complicated task. The Federal Policy that it must interpret and apply is written in a dense, legalistic style, and the policy mixes precise instructions on some issues with general principles on others. To aid IRBs, the federal Office for Protection from Research Risks (OPRR) publishes a 300-page (plus appendixes) *Guidebook* (United States, Dept. of Health and Human Services, National Institutes of Health, Office for Protection from Research Risks). But the *Guidebook* itself addresses some issues by simply presenting a variety of interpretations, leaving individual IRBs to choose among them. OPRR also provides other aids, including a set of three videotapes intended primarily for new IRB members, and a series of policy memoranda entitled *OPRR Reports,* which are published at irregular intervals. As helpful as they are, all of OPRR's aids are themselves subject to varying interpretations. Moreover, as IRB members review research protocols, they must consider not only the Federal Policy, but also their institution's local policy.

One consequence of the two-tiered system established by the Federal Policy is that the same research protocol could receive different responses from different IRBs. These differences could result from differences in the local policies, different ways of interpreting the Federal Policy and the ancillary OPRR materials, or even differences in the kinds of studies that IRBs usually review. Anecdotal evidence suggests that protocols from the social and behavioral sciences (including composition) may receive much closer scrutiny at institutions where there is no biomedical research than at institutions where there is. The reason, according to anecdote, is that IRBs at institutions with biomedical research are accustomed to seeing studies involving such large amounts of risk that the risks involved with social and behavioral research seem much less worth worrying about.

How IRBs Process Protocols

When IRBs review protocols from composition researchers, they may use one of three processes, depending partly on which of three categories of research is being proposed.

The first category includes research the Federal Policy lists as exempt from its provisions. Researchers must contact their IRBs to determine whether their institutions recognize these exemptions (some do not) and whether the institutions require certification of exemption.

The second category of research is that which the Federal Policy identifies as eligible for an "expedited review," in which only the IRB chair or one or more experienced IRB members (but not the full committee) review the protocol (subsection 110.a). To be eligible for expedited review, a study must involve no more than minimal risk, and it must fall within one of ten specific categories (United States, Dept. of Health and Human Services, "Research Activities"). According to the Federal Policy, minimal risk means "the probability and magnitude of harm or discomfort anticipated in the research are not greater in and of themselves than those ordinarily encountered in daily life or during the performance of routine physical or psychological examinations or tests" (subsection 102.i). Examples include research involving moderate exercise by healthy volunteers and research on individual or group behavior where the investigator does not manipulate the participants' behavior and the research does not involve stress to the participants. If the reviewer(s) conducting an expedited review find no problems with a proposed study, they immediately give the researcher permission to proceed with the project. However, they cannot disapprove a research project; if they have doubts about a study or find deficiencies in its protections for participants, they must either work with the researcher to eliminate the problems or refer the protocol to the full committee. In their local policies, some institutions prohibit expedited review for one kind of study with special relevance to composition: studies involving children and minors. Some institutions forbid expedited review altogether.

The third category of research requires full-committee review. It includes all projects that are not exempt and are not eligible for expedited review. At many institutions, full-committee review is the most common type of review, even for composition research.

For both expedited and full-committee review, researchers generally need to supply the same information, though practices can vary. At a minimum, this information must address each of the criteria discussed in the next section; individual institutions can require additional information and specify the manner in which it is to be presented.

Criteria Used in IRB Reviews

The following sections describe the seven criteria listed in the Federal Policy that apply to composition research; an eighth applies to clinical trials in biomedical research (subsections 111.a and b). Because all seven must be satisfied for a nonexempt project to receive IRB approval, composition specialists must keep all in mind when designing their studies.

1. Risks Are Minimized

The first criterion derives ultimately from Hippocrites' maxim to "do no harm." Under the Federal Policy, an IRB must assure itself that researchers have done everything possible to minimize the risk of harm, paying attention to both the probability and magnitude of the harm. However, the policy contains no definition of "harm" and provides no instruction to IRBs concerning the types of harm they should consider.[7] Addressing this omission, the OPRR *Guidebook* describes four kinds of possible harm that IRBs should look for: physical, psychological, social, and economic (3-1–3-5). Especially important to composition researchers is the breadth of the *Guidebook*'s discussion of the last three types.

For instance, when defining psychological harms, the *Guidebook* includes "[s]tress and feelings of guilt or embarrassment" while filling out a questionnaire or talking with the researcher (3-3). Some interview-based composition research entails the possibility of such harms. Similarly, among social harms, the *Guidebook* includes "embarrassment within one's business or social group" if confidentiality is breached (3-5). Some ethnographic studies of writing in academic and nonacademic settings involve this sort of risk. Of course, it's impossible to eliminate *all* risks from a study. IRBs are responsible for assuring that the researchers have taken all reasonable precautions and designed their studies in ways that reduce the probability of harm or limit its severity or duration (3-6).

2. Risks Are Reasonable in Relation to Benefits

According to the Federal Policy, humans can be used in research only if the benefits likely to result from the research outweigh the risks to the participants. Consequently, IRBs are directed to conduct a systematic risk-benefit analysis of each project submitted to them.

   When assessing benefits, IRBs consider those that accrue to the individual research participant (for instance, through experimental treatment for a health condition) and to society at large (for instance, through the creation of new knowledge). If the benefit is knowledge, an IRB is to consider "the importance of the knowledge that may reasonably be expected to result" (subsection 111.a.2). When assessing potential benefits, IRBs are instructed to consider the soundness of the research design, because a poorly designed study cannot produce any benefit to offset even the smallest risk to participants.

3. Selection of Participants Is Equitable

IRBs are also required to see that the selection of participants is equitable. As the OPRR *Guidebook* explains (3-23–3-26), this criterion involves a pair of counterbalanced considerations. The first is to ensure that the burdens of participating in the research fall on the groups most likely to benefit from it. As an example of inequitable selection of participants, the *Guidebook* cites nineteenth- and early twentieth-century medical research in which most of the burdens fell on poor patients in hospital wards, while the benefits flowed at least as much to private patients. However, the *Guidebook* also notes that injustice can arise when a group is omitted from a research project. Examples include medical studies that focus primarily on white males so that beneficial knowledge is not obtained for women or minorities. While the regulation does not require that all studies have mixed populations, composition researchers who plan to look at only one particular social group (e.g., only women, only men, or only members of some particular racial group or social class) may be asked to justify—and perhaps modify—their selection of participants.

4. Informed Consent Is Obtained

From the time of the *Nuremberg Code*, obtaining the informed consent of each participant has been counted as a basic requirement for research involving humans. To satisfy the Federal Policy's requirements for informed consent, researchers must do three things.

First, they must fully explain their study to the people they are asking to volunteer. To assure that potential participants (or their parents or legally authorized representatives) receive all the information needed to make a fully informed decision, the Federal Policy details the information researchers must provide (subsections 116.a and b). Copies of the statements researchers plan to hand or read to the potential participants must be submitted to the IRB. Below, I quote the policy's requirements that are most obviously relevant to composition research; I have omitted requirements that apply only to biomedical research.

1. A statement that the study involves research, an explanation of the purposes of the research and the expected duration of the subject's participation, a description of the procedures to be followed, and identification of any procedures which are experimental;

2. A description of any reasonably foreseeable risks or discomforts to the subject;

3. A description of any benefits to the subject or to others which may reasonably be expected from the research;

5. A statement describing the extent, if any, to which confidentiality of records identifying the subject will be maintained;

7. An explanation of whom to contact for answers to pertinent questions about the research and research subjects' rights . . . ;

8. A statement that participation is voluntary, refusal to participate will involve no penalty or loss of benefits to which the subject is otherwise entitled, and the subject may discontinue participation at any time without penalty or loss of benefits to which the subject is otherwise entitled.

Despite the explicitness of this list, Sieber and Baluyot discovered that the problem IRBs most often find with the studies they review is the omission of important elements from the consent statements the researchers plan to give to potential participants. However, the Federal Policy does allow an IRB to authorize a study that omits or modifies some or all of these elements, but only when all four of the following criteria are satisfied: (1) the study involves only minimal risk of harm to the subject, (2) the waiver or modification will not adversely affect the participants' rights and welfare, (3) if appropriate, the participants will be provided with additional pertinent information after completion of the study, and (4) the research could not otherwise be conducted (subsection 116.d).

The second of the three requirements concerning informed consent stipulates that researchers must describe their studies to prospective participants in a way that is fully understandable by these individuals. The OPRR *Guidebook* emphasizes particularly the importance of avoiding jargon that may not be understood by potential participants (4-14). Although the *Guidebook*'s examples involve medical terms (e.g., use *bruise* instead of *hematoma*), composition employs its own set of specialized terms that must be translated into more ordinary words for some groups of research participants.

The third requirement is that researchers must recruit participants in circumstances where these individuals are free from any coercion or undue influence to participate. That's the reason, for instance, for the eighth point in the list of items that researchers must tell potential participants: if they decline to participate or if they withdraw from a study after it has begun, the individuals will not lose any benefits to which they are otherwise entitled. In order to assure that potential participants can make their decisions freely, IRBs carefully review researchers' plans for recruiting volunteers.

5. Informed Consent Is Documented

The general expectation of the Federal Policy is that researchers will have each participant sign a statement that he or she has received all of the information specified in the preceding section and that he or she freely volunteers to participate in the study. However, an IRB can also approve alternative means of obtaining consent. For instance, it might allow a researcher to present orally the information listed above and then ask participants to sign a statement acknowledging that the information was provided and that their participation in the study is voluntary. In some cases, IRBs will permit oral acceptance from participants, though usually such acceptance must be witnessed by a third person who may be required to sign an affidavit.

6. Provisions to Protect Confidentiality Are Adequate

As IRBs review protocols, IRBs are required by the Federal Policy to assure that if the participants in a study receive a promise of confidentiality, the researchers have planned adequate methods for fulfilling that promise. In composition research, as in other social and behavioral research, one method of protecting confidentiality is to obtain information in such a way that even the researcher cannot identify the person who supplied it. This can be accomplished, for instance, in a survey that is distributed to a group and returned anonymously. For interview-based and similar research in which the researcher does know who supplied responses, it is common to assign pseudonyms or numbers to records, to store records in a secure place, and to present research results (in publications, for instance) in ways that prevent readers or listeners from inferring any person's identity. IRBs typically review research protocols for all these protections.

7. Vulnerable Participants Are Protected

One of the major aims of the Federal Policy is to protect the rights and welfare of persons who might be especially vulnerable to coercion or undue influence when deciding whether or not to participate in a research project. Examples cited include prisoners and patients in mental institutions who, in the words of the OPRR *Guidebook*, "are confined under the strict control of people whom they must please and to whom they must appear cooperative and rational if they are to earn their release" (3-23). Another group identified as vulnerable is of particular relevance to composition researchers: children.

For research involving children, colleges and universities generally follow a DHHS requirement (made through a DHHS addition to the Federal Policy) that researchers obtain permission of a parent or guardian (45 CFR 46.408.b). In recognition of the importance of respecting the children themselves, these colleges and universities also follow the DHHS requirement that researchers obtain the assent of a child who is old enough and otherwise capable of understanding and making a decision about participating in a study. Since the DHHS policy defines children as persons who have not attained their legal majority, these requirements apply to much composition research.

The OPRR *Guidebook* alerts IRBs that students (including adults) can also be a vulnerable population. The *Guidebook* explains that many agree to participate in studies not because they freely wish to do so, but because they believe that if they respond favorably to a teacher's request they may receive better grades, recommendations for employment, and so on, or because they may fear that failure to participate may negatively affect their relationship with the teacher or faculty in general. The *Guidebook* also cautions IRBs to consider that student participants' confidentiality can be especially difficult to maintain in studies occurring within the close environment of a university. Composition researchers who are planning to involve student participants can expect careful IRB scrutiny of their plans for recruiting, obtaining informed consent, and protecting confidentiality.

Areas of Ambiguity for Composition Researchers

As mentioned above, IRBs can encounter substantial difficulty in determining how the Federal Policy applies to certain projects. Some ambiguities in the policy involve broad areas of research. Based largely on my experiences as a composition researcher and as an IRB member, the following discussion identifies five topics about which sufficient ambiguity exists that individual IRBs may respond in widely different ways to the same composition research project. It is important for researchers to remember that no matter how strongly they believe that any of these ambiguities should be settled in a particular way, the Federal Policy gives the final judgment to each local IRB.

Exemption for Educational Research

One area of ambiguity is the Federal Policy's exemption for "[r]esearch conducted in established or commonly accepted educational settings, involving normal educational practices, such as (i) research on regular and special education instructional strategies, or (ii) research on the effectiveness of or the comparison among instructional techniques, curricula, or classroom management methods" (subsection 101.b.1).

It is not entirely clear how this exemption applies to several kinds of composition research. Educational ethnographies provide an example. To begin, different IRBs might arrive at different interpretations of the phrase "normal educational practices." Composition is taught in myriad ways, some established, some novel, and many in between. A particular teaching strategy might be viewed as a normal educational practice by one IRB but as an unusual practice by another. Consequently, an ethnographic study of a course that uses this strategy could be judged eligible for exemption by the first IRB but not by the second one.

IRBs could also disagree about what constitutes "established or commonly accepted educational settings." Probably all would agree that classrooms are such places. In some educational ethnographies, however, researchers observe and interview students in dorms, campus dining facilities, or even off-campus locations, including the students' homes. Different IRBs might reach different conclusions about whether studies conducted partly or wholly in one or more of these settings are eligible for exemption.

Also, different IRBs might reach different judgments about the eligibility for exemption of ethnographies that involve interviews, not just observations. One locus of disagreement might be the topics discussed. For example, researchers might plan to interview students about the ways that their personal beliefs, family life, or ethnic background influences their responses to a particular class. IRBs might disagree over whether the interviews would move beyond "educational practices" to include personal and possibly sensitive information that could make the study subject to the Federal Policy's requirements.

Of course, even if an ethnography (or other type of composition study) fails to qualify for exemption, it can still be conducted if the researchers satisfy the IRB that the participants will be sufficiently protected. In most cases, failure to qualify for exemption means primarily that the researchers must submit their project for full IRB review and that they must employ informed consent procedures.

It is important to note, as the OPRR *Guidebook* emphasizes, that exemption from the Federal Policy does *not* release researchers from their ethical responsibilities to the research participants: it means only that the researchers' studies are not required to follow the Federal Policy's specific requirements (5-4).

Exemption for Survey and Interview Research

Another area of ambiguity in the Federal Policy is its exemption for "[r]esearch involving . . . the use of survey procedures [and] interview procedures . . . unless: (i) Information obtained is recorded in such a manner that human subjects can be identified, directly or through identifiers linked to the subjects; and (ii) any disclosure of the human subjects' responses outside the research could reasonably place the subjects at risk of criminal or civil liability or be damaging to the subjects' financial standing, employment, or reputation" (subsection 101.b.2). Of course, there are many types of surveys and interviews. A survey would seem clearly to qualify for exemption if it were distributed to a large group of people who returned responses anonymously, as in the anonymous forms used for student evaluations of courses. An interview would clearly be exempt if the interviewer recorded responses to multiple-choice questions without knowing the participants' identities, as in a telephone poll that uses random-digit dialing (United States, National Institutes of Health, Office for Protection from Research Risks 4-9). Less clear is the exemption's application to other types of surveys and interviews, such as the extensive case study interviews conducted by Gesa Kirsch for her study of *Women Writing the Academy.* Kirsch's IRB determined that her project was exempt, but my university's IRB would not have viewed her study as exempt (E-mail to author). Despite these ambiguities, one point is quite explicit for any institution receiving DHHS support for human-participant research: the exemption for surveys and interviews does not apply to studies involving children (45 CFR 46.401.b).

Distinction between Research and Practice

Related to questions about the exemption for "educational research" is some ambiguity about the distinction between research and practice. Within the paradigm of medical research, the question is how to distinguish formal research (which is subject to the Federal Policy) from a course of therapy where the professional observes the outcome of the treatment (which is not subject to the Federal Policy). Similarly, in composition research, the question is how to distinguish between the kinds of reflective practice that any teacher engages in and qualitative research designs in which the teacher is an observer or participant-observer. In fact, the movement in composition known variously as "teacher research," "classroom research," and "action research" seeks to erase the distinction between practice and research—and sometimes the distinction between researcher and research subject (Daiker and Morenberg; Goswami and Stillman; Ray).

   One way to determine whether particular instances of teacher research are research or practice may be to look at the methods used. In some cases, the teachers primarily reflect on what occurs during their normal teaching so that the "research" looks to the student very much like ordinary teaching. In other cases, they undertake various kinds of interventions or gather information about their students' beliefs, cultural background, and experiences that go beyond what students customarily are asked to provide so that the projects look very much like formal research. Another approach might be to look at the intended outcome of the research. In fact, the Federal Policy defines research in terms of outcome: "a systematic investigation, including research development, testing and evaluation, designed to develop or contribute to generalizable knowledge" (subsection 102.d). While we might quarrel with the epistemology underlying the policy's reference to "generalizable knowledge," we might also observe that its definition of research seems to include studies in which the investigator intends to publish the results. If we think along these lines, a teacher's study might be considered practice if a teacher-researcher intends only to learn how to improve his or her own teaching, but it might be considered research if he or she intends to write a manuscript about it for publication. Clearly, IRBs have much to think about when considering the boundary between research and practice, and different IRBs will inevitably come to quite different conclusions about this distinction.

Student Research

According to the Federal Policy, research is research whether the investigator is a professional or a student (subsection 102.f). However, many faculty have asked whether student projects in research methods classes are subject to IRB review. Some universities have established policies that say they are not. For example, Stanford University uses the term "research practica" to distinguish projects intended to develop students' methodological skills from studies intended to create or contribute to "generalizable knowledge" (Administrative Panel). However, other universities have reached other conclusions or have not addressed the question. It is important to note that Stanford makes faculty who supervise research practica responsible for assuring that student projects "follow the same guidelines as other research conducted at Stanford for protecting people's privacy, dignity, and welfare" (2). Stanford's policy also emphasizes that all instruction in research methods that use human participants should include discussion of the IRB process and its goals, and it classifies theses and dissertations as research rather than practica.

Conflicts between the Federal Policy and Academic Freedom

Another question with which IRBs sometimes must wrestle is the boundary between their responsibilities to protect research participants and the need to preserve academic freedom. The OPRR *Guidebook* acknowledges this issue in a passage where it observes that some IRBs have found ethical problems with studies that look at controversial or sensitive topics, such as "deviant" sexual behavior. The *Guidebook* warns that IRB objections based on such grounds violate academic freedom, and it instructs IRBs to focus on risks to the rights and welfare of the research participants, not on what the IRBs consider to be the propriety of the topic studied (5-5). However, the need to balance human protections against academic freedom can arise in many other situations. The most difficult case decided in recent years by my own IRB involved just such a question.

Because IRB proceedings are confidential, I cannot disclose the particulars of the case, but on the basis of that experience I can discuss two areas in which such a conflict might arise in composition research. The first is the selection of subjects. Suppose a research team wishes to study the ways male students respond to discussions of feminist perspectives in composition classes—or the ways female students do. In either case, the researchers might plan to interview only male or only female students. Presented with the protocol for such a study, an IRB might find itself in a quandary. On the one hand, it might be mindful of the OPRR *Guidebook*'s advice that medical studies should include women and minorities, not just white males, so that the research findings can benefit all persons at risk of the disease or condition under study (3-43). This consideration could lead the IRB to believe that it *should* require the researchers to interview both male and female students, since both are enrolled in classes where feminist perspectives are discussed. However, by requiring the researchers to change their plans for selecting participants, the IRB would also be ordering the researchers to change the research question they were going to investigate. And the IRB might think that requiring researchers to alter their research questions would infringe on the researchers' academic freedom to address the questions they thought most worth investigating. This consideration would lead the IRB to believe that it *should not* require the researchers to alter their plans to interview only females or only males.

An IRB could also encounter conflicts between participant protections and academic freedom as it reviews a proposed study's research procedures. For instance, imagine that a group of composition researchers wants to study student responses to readings that are by or about some minority group, such as a particular ethnic minority, gays and lesbians, or members of a particular religion. At the beginning of the semester, the investigators propose to interview student volunteers to learn what stereotypes, if any, they hold. During these initial interviews, the researchers will not respond to, or express, any judgment about what the students say. An IRB might believe that in these interviews the researchers would seem to the students to be endorsing negative stereotypes by listening nonjudgmentally to them. Moreover, the IRB might believe that in doing so, the researchers could impede the development of the students being interviewed and also negatively affect members of the groups about whom the stereotypes are held. On the other hand, the IRB might believe that it would be infringing on the researchers' academic freedom if it prohibited them from employing a widely accepted interview technique that the researchers, using their professional judgment, had selected for their study.

When such issues came up during my IRB's review of the case mentioned above, we disagreed about both the probability and severity of the risks involved with the proposed study. We also disagreed about how probable and severe risks must be in order for us to require researchers to alter their plans. And these disagreements led us into lengthy discussions about the correct balance between our responsibility to protect research participants and our responsibility to honor the academic freedom of researchers. As we worked through these issues, we corresponded and met with the researcher, who eventually modified several parts of the proposed study in order to provide what the IRB determined would be better protections for the research participants. Some of these modifications had only minor impact on the researcher's original design, but one change made it impossible for the researcher to pursue one of the research questions originally addressed by the proposed study. This outcome, however, is not the point of my necessarily veiled account of our deliberations on the case. The point is this: for IRBs there is not always a clear boundary between the need to protect research participants and the need to protect the academic freedom of the researcher. The boundary may seem especially fuzzy with research protocols in composition, where the possible harms are much less dramatic and less concrete than those involved with biomedical research.

Conclusion

In this chapter, I have described the two-tiered structure of federal and institutional policies that constitutes one context within which composition researchers conduct studies that involve human participants. These policies create constraints on research design and procedures, and they mandate certain practical steps that researchers must take before beginning their projects. For researchers at many institutions, the policies apply whether or not the particular studies are supported by federal funds; whether they are conducted by a faculty member, student, or other person associated with the institution; whether they involve quantitative or qualitative procedures; whether they occur in academic or nonacademic settings; and whether the participants are strangers or the researchers' own students and colleagues.

For several reasons, however, it is not possible to predict how a specific composition study will be viewed by a particular IRB. These reasons include the facts that the Federal Policy contains as much general guidance as firm dicta, that each local institution supplements the Federal Policy with its own policy, that both the Federal Policy and institutional policies require interpretation, and that the application of the Federal Policy to many kinds of composition studies is far from obvious. For the individual researchers, the most important advice about dealing with their IRBs is to make contact early. This early contact will give the researchers time to make any necessary adjustments to their projects before the planned start date, and it will give them time to educate the IRB about the nature of their research, if necessary. In fact, it is perfectly reasonable for a researcher to contact the IRB (or its chair) even before preparing the protocol in order to learn the IRB's interpretation of both the federal and local policies.

Acknowledgments

I wish to thank the following colleagues at Miami University for their suggestions: Janel Bloch, Jennie Dautermann, Susan Jarratt, Carol Willeke, and Chris Zahn. I am also grateful for helpful comments by Joan Porter of the Office for Protection from Research Risks and by another composition specialist who serves on an IRB, Ellen Barton at Wayne State University.

Notes

1. Institutions that conduct very little federally sponsored research may, with appropriate federal authorization, designate an Institutional Review Board at another institution as their reviewer. Institutions that conduct much of this kind of research often have several IRBs, each specializing in a particular type of research.

2. For more details concerning this history, see especially Annas and Grodin; Curran; Faden and Beauchamp, chapters 5 and 6; Katz; Maloney, chapters 1, 2, and 3; United States, Dept. of Health and Human Services, National Institutes of Health, Office for Protection from Research Risks, xviii-xx; and *Evolving Concern.*

3. Although the concept of informed consent received its most important publicity through the Nuremberg Tribunals, it had been developed and employed by earlier researchers. For instance, in his 1900 study of yellow fever, Walter Reed had each volunteer sign an informed consent form that communicated the risk involved and indicated the person's acceptance of this risk (*Evolving Concern*; Faden and Beauchamp 152–53).

4. Some institutions had peer review boards prior to the NIH policy. Because it was located within the Public Health Service itself, the most important policy to future developments was established in 1953 at the newly opened Clinical Center at the National Institutes of Health. Some private institutions had such review committees as well. In 1962, the Law-Medicine Research Institute at Boston University sent a survey to all university departments of medicine in the country. Of the fifty-two respondents, twenty-two reported having review committees (Levine 208).

5. Each of the fifteen agencies adopted the Federal Policy by incorporating its language in the agency's own "title" (or chapter) of the United States *Code of Federal Regulations.* A few agencies appended a small amount of additional material. When referring to the Federal Policy, some IRBs call it "45 CFR 46"; this is the abbreviation for the place where DHHS has incorporated the Federal Policy into its portion of the *Code* (Part 46 of Title 45).

6. The remaining agencies are the Department of Agriculture, Consumer Product Safety Commission, International Development Agency, Department of Housing and Urban Development, Department of Justice, Department of Veterans Affairs, Department of Transportation, and the Central Intelligence Agency. The Federal Drug Administration concurs with the Federal Policy, but has made selected changes in it to accommodate its own procedures. Some of the other fifteen agencies, including DHHS, created additional protections.

7. The Federal Policy does name some types of harm when discussing the kinds of studies that are and are not exempt from its regulations, but it provides no definition of the harm that IRBs are to look for when reviewing protocols that are not exempt. The harms named are "civil or criminal liability or . . . damag[e] to the subject's financial standing, employability, or reputation" (subsection 102.b.2).

Works Cited

Administrative Panel on the Use of Human Subjects in Behavioral Research. Memo on student research involving human subjects at Stanford University. Oct. 1987.

Annas, George J., and Michael A. Grodin. *The Nazi Doctors and the Nuremberg Code: Human Rights in Human Experimentation.* New York: Oxford UP, 1992.

Baumrind, Diana. "Some Thoughts on Ethics of Research: After Reading Milgram's 'Behavioral Study of Obedience.'" *American Psychologist* 19 (1964): 421–23.

Beecher, Henry K. *Experimentation in Man.* Springfield: Thomas, 1959.

Curran, William J. "Governmental Regulation of the Use of Human Subjects in Medical Research: The Approach of Two Federal Agencies." *Experimentation with Human Subjects.* Ed. Paul A. Freund. New York: Braziller, 1970. 402–54.

Daiker, Donald A., and Max Morenberg, eds. *The Writing Teacher as Researcher: Essays in the Theory and Practice of Class-Based Research.* Portsmouth: Boynton/Cook, 1990.

Ellis, Gary B. Memo on compliance oversight procedures. 5 Feb. 1993. Rpt. in United States. Dept. of Health and Human Service. National Institutes of Health. Office for Protection from Research Risks. *Protecting Human Subjects: Institutional Review Board Guidebook.* Washington: GPO, 1993. A5-47–A5-50.

———. "Research Activities that May Be Reviewed through Expedited Review." *OPRR Reports* 95-02. 5 May 1995.

Evolving Concern: Protection for Human Subjects. Washington: National Institutes of Health and Food and Drug Administration, n.d.

Faden, Ruth R., and Tom L. Beauchamp. *A History and Theory of Informed Consent.* New York: Oxford UP, 1986.

Gallagher, Mike. "Fernald Tested Outsiders' Body Parts." *Cincinnati Enquirer* 15 June 1995: A1+.

Goswami, Dixie, and Peter R. Stillman, eds. *Reclaiming the Classroom: Teacher Research as an Agency for Change.* Upper Montclair: Boynton/Cook, 1987.

Heller, Jean. "Syphilis Victims in U.S. Study Went Untreated for 40 Years." *New York Times* 26 July 1972: 1+.

Hilts, Philip J. "Panel Finds Wide Debate in 40's on the Ethics of Radiation Tests." *New York Times* 12 Oct. 1994: A1.

Howe, Kenneth R., and Katharine Cutts Dougherty. "Ethics, Institutional Review Boards, and the Changing Face of Educational Research." *Educational Researcher* 22.9 (1993): 16–21.

Humphreys, Laud. *Tearoom Trade: Impersonal Sex in Public Places.* Chicago: Aldine, 1970.

Jones, James H. *Bad Blood: The Tuskegee Syphilis Experiment.* 2nd ed. New York: Free P, 1993.

Katz, Jay, comp. *Experimentation with Human Beings: The Authority of the Investigator, Subject, Professions, and State in the Human Experimentation Process.* New York: Russell Sage, 1972.

Kirsch, Gesa E. *Women Writing the Academy: Audience, Authority, and Transformation.* Carbondale: Southern Illinois UP, 1993.

Lear, John. "The Unfinished Story of Thalidomide." *Saturday Review* 1 Sept. 1962: 35–40.

Levine, Robert J. *Ethics and Regulation of Clinical Research.* Baltimore: Urban and Schwarzenberg, 1981.

Maloney, Dennis M. *Protection of Human Research Subjects: A Practical Guide to Federal Laws and Regulations.* New York: Plenum, 1984.

Milgram, Stanley. "Behavioral Study of Obedience." *Journal of Abnormal and Social Psychology* 67 (1963): 371–78.

Ray, Ruth. *The Practice of Theory: Teacher Research in Composition.* Urbana: NCTE, 1993.

Sieber, Joan E., and Reuel M. Baluyot. "A Survey of IRB Concerns about Social and Behavioral Research." *IRB: A Review of Human Subjects Research* 14.2 (1992): 9–10.

Trials of War Criminals before the Nuremberg Military Tribunals under Control Council Law No. 10. Vol. 2. Washington: GPO, 1949. 181–82.

United States. Dept. of Energy. *Human Radiation Experiments: The Department of Energy Roadmap to the Story and Records.* Springfield: National Technical Information Service, 1995.

———. Dept. of Health and Human Services. National Institutes of Health. Office for Protection from Research Risks. *Protecting Human Subjects: Institutional Review Board Guidebook.* Washington: GPO, 1993.

———. ———. "Final Regulations Amending Basic HHS Policy for the Protection of Human Research Subjects." *Federal Register* 49.16 (26 Jan. 1981): 8366–91.

———. ———. "Research Activities which May Be Reviewed Through Expedited Review Procedures Set Forth in HHS Regulations for Protection of Human Research Subjects." *Federal Register* 49.16 (26 Jan. 1981): 8392.

———. Dept. of Health, Education, and Welfare. "Protection of Human Subjects." *Federal Register* 39.105 (30 May 1974): 18914–920.

———. Executive Office of the President. Office of Science and Technology Policy. "Federal Policy for the Protection of Human Subjects." *Federal Register* 56.117 (18 June 1991): 28001–032.

Zimbardo, Philip G. "On the Ethics of Intervention in Human Psychological Research: With Special Reference to the Stanford Prison Experiment." *Cognition* 34 (1973): 243–56.

Afterword: Ethics and Representation in Teacher Research

Ruth E. Ray
Wayne State University

This volume represents a significant progression in composition studies. The field has reached a point where researchers are confident enough to turn their critical gaze back onto themselves, analyze their own assumptions and predispositions, admit their uneasy relationships with the subjects of their inquiry, and question the rhetorical moves they make in writing about people, classrooms, and cultures. Though absolutely necessary to the maturing of the field, this kind of inquiry is almost as difficult to read as it is to conduct. Some readers may find themselves uneasy among these confessional tales, wishing, in the words of John Van Maanen, that the authors would conduct their "self-centered, anxiety work in private" (93). But such readings miss the larger point: *because* they are complexly nuanced, these tales provide far richer insights into the lives of literacy researchers and the contingencies of fieldwork in everyday classrooms.

In this chapter, I want to speak to the place classroom teachers play in the postmodern move toward reflexive inquiry. To do this, I look both backward and forward. I summarize some of the issues raised by contributing authors regarding teacher research, note what has not been addressed, and make suggestions for future inquiry on literacy conducted within the classroom. I focus on teacher research here because of the momentum it gained as a movement in composition studies during the 1980s (see, for example, Goswami and Stillman; Mohr and Maclean; Myers; Rudduck and Hopkins) and because of its potential for informing literacy studies in the next decade. A new generation of teachers is now being trained by some of the best education schools in the country to see their classrooms as sites of lifelong inquiry; university researchers must find ways to interact with and learn from these classroom scholars. I organize my discussion around three types of classroom inquiry, two of which are represented in this collection and one which is not: university researchers studying teachers; university researchers and teachers collaborating; and teachers initiating and conducting their own research in their own classrooms for their own purposes.

Researchers Studying Teachers

In her chapter on representation in classroom ethnography, Brenda Jo Brueggemann, following Michelle Fine, evokes the image of the hyphen between words as a space to be inhabited. Many of the authors in this collection are university researchers questioning the nature of the space between being a participant (part of) and observer in (apart from) someone else's classroom. This is the kind of inquiry that Marilyn Cochran-Smith and Susan Lytle call "research on teaching," which is distinct from "teacher research" (6–9). The participant-observer space in this relationship is full of conflict, for its inhabitants are continually faced with questions of purpose and allegiance: Why am I studying this place, these people? From whose perspective do I see and record? On whose behalf do I speak the "final results"? Who will benefit from this study? Thus we have Thomas Newkirk pondering the dilemma of whether an observer should intervene (become a participant) upon finding that a teacher is acting on prejudice or stereotype in relationships with students. The larger issue is one of allegiance: Are literacy researchers responsible to the field of composition studies, to the teacher who has generously opened the classroom doors to research, or to the students within that classroom? In this deliberation, the "field" is not an entity but an idea, an abstraction which allows the researcher to justify daily decisions on the basis of other abstractions, such as the creation of knowledge for a greater good. Conversely, the classroom is a material space inhabited by real people with lives and histories; from this place a researcher is inclined to make decisions on the basis of how someone else will react, recognizing that, although the field will embrace a critical interpretation of "literate practices," the teacher will likely feel betrayed by any "bad news" about her teaching (see Cheri Williams's chapter). Newkirk cautions us that when researchers choose to align themselves with the profession—and by extension their own professional enhancement—they may cause local harm to the people and schools they study.

If a funding source is added to the equation, as Jennie Dautermann's chapter suggests, the researcher may also find herself in allegiance with those who pay the transcribing bills. Sometimes what the funding source wants—in Dautermann's case, politically uninvolved consultation and computer services—is in conflict with what the field wants, such as critical analysis of the social and institutional relationships which affect writing in the workplace. Most literacy researchers who receive funding for their projects in and out of schools have not considered how the exchange of money will affect their allegiances, much less what to do about it. Dautermann struck a balance by providing some services "free of charge" and by not overtly researching (taping and asking questions) when the environment was especially charged with political tensions.

Researchers and Teachers Collaborating

Other authors in this collection address what it means to inhabit the space in the teacher-research alliance, where a university researcher collaborates with a teacher in the classroom. In some cases, the researcher is a co-teacher for the duration of the study; in others, the researcher observes a teacher and students together, interviews students, and discusses interpretations with the teacher. In both cases, however, the researcher still "owns" the project in terms of initiating and focusing the study, controlling the final writing, and publishing the results. Helen Dale, in her chapter on conflicting fidelities, and Lucille Parkinson McCarthy and Stephen Fishman, in a chapter on representing their own differences, illustrate some of the tensions between teacher and researcher in a collaborative relationship.

Dale, a university researcher and co-teacher in the class she is studying, finds herself conflicted between her two roles and wondering whether her allegiance should be to the field or to the students in her classroom. She finds that "adding the role of teacher to that of researcher is not a simple expansion of duties; it affects perspectives and fidelities." Just as there are differences in gender orientations, there are basic differences between teachers and researchers in their goals, values, and interpretations. Dale concludes that a researcher focuses on understanding, while a teacher focuses on actions in the world; a researcher observes and analyzes the classroom, while a teacher takes responsibility and intervenes in the environment to control student behavior. In terms of her research project, Dale acknowledges that the overlapping roles of teacher and researcher "can create ethical tensions." Still, it is clear in the end that her fidelities are to the researcher role, given that she is researching her teaching in order to write a dissertation so that she may become a professional researcher. The distinction in this case of teacher research is one of perceived identity: Dale is only *sometimes* a teacher but *always* a researcher.

McCarthy (a university researcher in English studies) and Fishman (a college teacher of philosophy) illustrate a slightly different teacher-research dynamic. McCarthy proposed the study as a "collaborative project in which she could share equal authority with a discipline-based teacher." They found, however, that "collaborative" does not necessarily mean "equal" or "the same." McCarthy was primarily interested in analyzing student texts, while Fishman was more interested in finding out how his classroom discussions worked in order to involve more students. Through Fishman's critiques of her interpretations, McCarthy came to realize that she actually "owned" the research, because she raised the questions and conducted the interviews, while putting Fishman in the position of respondent. When Fishman conducted his own interviews, he came to see his classroom in a different way and to change his teaching (thus changing the research environment for McCarthy). More interesting yet are the differences that arose in the course of their collaborative writing about the research for publication: Fishman's approach was narrative, raising situated truths, while McCarthy's was paradigmatic, raising more generalized truths, to evoke Jerome Bruner's terms. Despite their creative handling of these differences (they wrote narratives within a paradigmatic frame), one could argue that McCarthy still owned the study in a significant way: it was published in *Research in the Teaching of English* rather than in a journal of interdisciplinary studies. Although a collaboration of this kind cannot avoid the different orientations of teacher and researcher, it does overcome the ethical quandary of whether and how a researcher reveals "bad news" to the teacher. It also reminds us of the always unequal power dynamics between teacher and researcher, as does the chapter by Russel Durst (a senior faculty adviser and researcher) and Sherry Cook Stanforth (a graduate student and teaching assistant). In order to subvert some of these power imbalances, Cheri Williams, drawing on a history of teacher-research projects, calls for research that teachers themselves initiate and draw the researchers into, thereby encouraging interpretation from an emic (insider) perspective and avoiding what Newkirk calls "studying down."

Yet another version of teacher and researcher collaboration is exemplified in Jabari Mahiri's chapter on teaching writing through rap music. Mahiri's funded project, which involved a team of high school teachers and university researchers, raises significant issues about the limitations of both roles. One issue is the nature of teacher authority: both teachers and researchers came to question the appropriateness of teaching rap music to students who were far more expert—and up-to-date—on the subject than they were. In this setting, the teacher-researcher's reliance on veteran teaching status or academic credentials did not work to establish credibility among students. As an outsider to the students in terms of age, education, and cultural experience, Mahiri, a university researcher, had to convince the students that he had some connection to rap music beyond his desire to conduct research on a topic that appealed to his funding source. This situation raises another important point about the space between observer and participant: taking on the distanced observer status may carry some cachet in academe, but it makes people in the community suspicious—hence the attempts of many anthropologists to "go native." Another significant outcome of this study was the veteran teacher's questioning of her status in her own classroom. Always one to construct herself as a model to be emulated, the teacher found that this role removed her from the students' value and belief systems and limited her ability—and credibility—in talking about a subject which was much closer to their experience than to hers.

Teachers as Researchers

What this collection does not address are the issues that occur when a single person, the classroom teacher, inhabits the space between teacher and researcher. I am referring here to what is also called reflective practice or action research—forms of inquiry that are initiated, conducted, and published by the teacher. This type of teacher research offers another dimension to the discussion of ethical and representational issues in literacy research.

In this research situation, for example, the power dynamics are between teacher and student. It is the teacher who is "studying down" and must come to terms with all that entails. When teachers themselves conduct the inquiry, their work also problematizes the ethnographic ideal of understanding others on their own terms. For example, a teacher questions whether it is ever really possible to understand students on their own terms when the role of teacher is to evaluate and change students. And when the teacher must justify her evaluations to administrators and parents (as often occurs), she must defend herself on her *own* terms, as well as those of the school system. These kinds of conflicts indicate that the singular teacher-researcher is always deeply implicated in the school environment; the teacher is an "observant participant," but not a participant-observer (Florio and Walsh 91).

As a participant, then, the teacher-as-researcher has a perspective on classroom-based literacy research that is different from that of university researchers. For one thing, their inquiry starts from a different place. Teachers are motivated to do research by observing their classrooms, not by reading theories and others' research (Cochran-Smith and

Lytle). And teachers, as participants, assume the reliability of lived experience, while researchers, as observers, constantly stand back and question it. The goals of research are different, too. Teachers conduct research because of its transformative potential for themselves and their classrooms; researchers conduct research because of its transformative potential for their fields. These differences between participant and observer are significant. Teachers are immersed in the environment; researchers, no matter how reflective and participatory, are always at some remove from it.

Research that begins from the emic perspective of a participant, rather than the etic perspective of the observer, raises its own forms of ethical and representational issues. Teachers also must balance conflicting roles and allegiances when they do research. In *Composing Teacher-Research: A Prosaic History,* Cathy Fleischer, writing from the perspective of a graduate student teacher-researcher, discusses some of these conflicts:

> [W]e do have an underlying purpose in any research that we undertake in the schools. As a literacy worker and student of composition, I believe there are some better ways than others to teach students to write. As a "neutral" observer, that notion obviously colors my perspective; as a new friend of [a student], it sometimes makes our "professional" relationship difficult: I want to "suggest" ways to help her improve her writing (and she sometimes looks to me to help in that role), which makes me feel torn about my own purpose in conducting this research. Is my job simply to supply an anecdotal description of the literacy environment in this high school from [the student's] and Cathy's perspective? Or is it to effect change in one student? or in an entire system? . . . How can I separate my participant self from my observer self to write about the experience in ways which will be read kindly and seriously and help effect some change? (28–29)

The dilemma of whether merely to record or to change classroom behavior, and the level at which to direct this change, is especially significant for someone who is a full participant in the environment under study. As Fleischer's use of the adjective "kindly" suggests, the teacher is unlikely to construct her findings in ways that negatively implicate others or harm relationships. Further, the participant role of "teacher" is just as socially constructed as the role of "researcher": the good teacher is expected to cooperate in the environment and encourage students to learn within the established school system, while the good critical researcher is expected to challenge that system. But what if the teacher-researcher's findings point to the necessity of change beyond particular student behaviors or classroom interactions? What if the teacher comes to see the need for a major overhaul in curriculum and school policy? What if the inquiry leads to a critique of the American educational system in general? In an article on the teacher-as-researcher, James Berlin expresses his concern that change-oriented action research, as practiced in Great Britain, will be translated into a kind of teacher research in America that merely reifies the values of the institutions that support it. Fleischer is raising the same issue from the perspective of her own classroom: To what extent can teacher research be contestatory?

The challenges of conducting critical inquiry have been discussed by other teacher-researchers. In much of her work, for example, Janet Miller chronicles her experiences as part of a "critically oriented collaborative teacher-research group" that continually questions unexamined assumptions about the roles of teachers and administrators in the public schools (Miller and Martens 41). Miller and her teacher-research group believe that situating autobiographical narratives and analyses of their own teaching practices, assumptions, and expectations within larger social, historical, and political contexts might enable them to "break with submergence and transform" their classrooms and schools (Maxine Greene qtd. in Miller, "Teachers" 1). In their attempts to show relationships between the personal and political, Miller and her five collaborators—all K–12 teachers and administrators—have confronted the following issues in their personal narratives:

- The demands of elementary school students for constant nurturing and mothering, and the feminist teacher's ambivalent responses

- Parental and institutional expectations of teacher-as-nurturer that tend to reify early childhood education as "women's work"

- The ways in which women internalize and unconsciously act upon others' expectations of them as female teachers, even when these expectations are in direct conflict with their own goals and beliefs

- A school principal's characterization of his predominantly female staff as a loving "family" over which he is the presiding patriarch

- The tensions and gaps that arise in the school when an elementary school teacher, who is expected to be passive and submissive to authority, becomes an active, critically questioning teacher-researcher

- Conflicting constructs of oneself as "good girl" teacher and researcher who does her scholarship and reports it in the expected manner versus the critical, resistant feminist who challenges school-sanctioned forms of reporting

- The struggle to present oneself as an "authority" in one's teaching and writing without reinforcing or replicating unequal power relationships among elementary and secondary teachers

- Contradictory efforts to simultaneously *critique* and *engage in* acts of collaboration and emancipatory teaching and research ("Teachers")

In addressing these "situational discrepancies," Miller and her colleagues are disrupting the totalizing discourses which represent teachers as passive, unintellectual, atheoretical, and apolitical. Part of the challenge for them in writing autobiographically is to reinterpret themselves and their roles within the specific contexts of their own schools and classrooms. Miller's claim is that representing themselves in this way, particularly from feminist and neo-Marxist perspectives, has encouraged these teachers to review themselves within larger contexts of language, power, and authority that frame teaching practices and curricula. Through their writing, they reconceptualize teaching as a process that is not only historically and socially formed, but also individually created and re-created. With this understanding, they are better positioned to change their environments.

Another challenge for teacher-researchers is how to negotiate the role of students in the research. Because they are participants, rather than observers, teachers are more likely to conduct research *with* students rather than *on* students (Fleischer), thus sidestepping the representational issue of speaking *for* students, but raising other issues. The involvement of students has its advantages, for a study that lacks student representation can be decidedly skewed. Noticeably lacking in most research on teaching and much teacher-researcher collaboration are the perspectives of students in the classrooms under study. Newkirk makes this point in his critique of Brodkey's study of students' literacy letters; Brodkey interprets the "meaning" and significance of the letter-writing between her graduate students and those in an adult education class without ever consulting the students themselves. Thus her conclusions may be theoretically interesting but may not accurately reflect students' lived experience. Indeed, the fact that lived experience is not particularly relevant to Brodkey when she constructs her article illustrates the exclusionary perspective of the theoretical researcher. When teacher-researchers collaborate with students, rather than merely assigning them a place in the final write-up, they are constructing classroom "reality" as the co-creation of events by all participants. In this collaboration, if it is successful, a teacher-researcher learns to recognize her own lenses of interpretation and comes to see more clearly through them, while also learning to see through students' lenses (Fleischer 37). Here, students inhabit the space between student and researcher and are encouraged to speak for themselves, thus avoiding the position of "subjects" who are "spoken for" in someone else's study.

The question of how teachers will represent themselves in their written work also factors into teacher research. Teachers typically present the results of their inquiry, either orally or in written form, to other teachers. Here they must negotiate the tensions between teacher and researcher in an educational environment in which the two roles may be seen as contradictory. Many teachers, having experienced the gaps between educational research and their own classroom experience, often privilege the teaching role and disdain the research role. Thus teacher-researchers are in the position of learning to represent themselves as researchers in ways that are credible to their peers. They often do this by using narrative, descriptive, interpretive, and reflective discourses, presenting themselves as "researching teachers." This kind of self-representation is not as effective, however, when teachers seek to create more public knowledge beyond their own communities, because traditional researchers expect teacher-researchers to represent themselves as "teaching researchers." What literacy researchers need to understand is that teacher research is a distinct form of writing and representation that has value on its own terms. Cochran-Smith and Lytle make this argument clear:

> [C]omparison of teacher research with university-based research involves a complicated set of assumptions and relationships that act as barriers to enhancing our knowledge base about teaching. Researchers in the academy equate "knowledge about teaching" with the high-status information attained through traditional modes of inquiry. They fault teachers for not reading or not implementing the findings of such research even though teachers often view these findings as irrelevant and counterintuitive. Yet teacher research, which by definition has special potential to address issues that teachers themselves identify as significant, does not have a legitimate place. If simply compared with university research, it can easily be found wanting. Regarding teacher research as a mere imitation of university research is not useful and is ultimately condescending. . . . [I]t is more useful to consider teacher research as its own genre, not entirely different from other types of systematic inquiry into teaching yet with some quite distinctive features. (10)

Cochran-Smith and Lytle are saying, in effect, that teacher research (which is most often conducted in *writing* classrooms) has much more in common with the kind of postmodern composition research discussed in this volume than with the positivist educational research to which it is often compared.

The ethical dimensions of teacher research have barely been explored. To my knowledge, public schools have not developed the kinds of Institutional Review Boards (IRBs) that universities have established to oversee research protocols. Should they? As Paul Anderson makes clear in his chapter, federal guidelines stipulate that "research conducted in established or commonly accepted educational settings, involving normal educational practices," such as teaching strategies, curricula, tests, surveys, and observation of public behavior, is exempt from review unless the information is recorded in such a manner that human subjects can be identified or that disclosure of the subjects' responses could place them at risk or damage their reputations. However, many university IRBs do not automatically exempt research in educational settings, particularly if "vulnerable" populations are involved, such as young children, the cognitively and emotionally impaired, and others who may need a guardian to protect their interests. In these cases, usually a consent form is required, signed by a guardian or legal representative. It is not clear how many—if any—teacher-researchers conduct their classroom inquiry with the full consent of student participants or their guardians. It seems to me that consent is necessary, especially since the students' right to privacy is at risk and their choice to participate is in question. After all, if a teacher is conducting inquiry on her students in a particular school setting and reporting the results to colleagues within that setting, it would be very difficult to conceal the identity of individual students. Students also need to be informed about the research and offered the choice to refuse participation without affecting their standing with the teacher. And parents have rights, too: namely, the right to know when a teacher is researching the classroom, what the research will entail, what arrangements have been made for students who do not wish to participate in the study, and how the results will be used and disseminated. Having both sat on my university's IRB and conducted inquiry in my own classrooms that required full consent, I can say that these stipulations are not necessarily prohibitive. In fact, in my experience, the requirement to construct a consent form in language that students and community members could understand helped me clarify, for myself as well as others, the purposes and importance of my study. It also gave me the opportunity to talk with people about my research and address their questions and concerns beforehand, thus making the study more responsive to local needs and interests.

Why Should Composition Theorists Care about Teacher Research?

In recent years, much has been written about the significance of classroom-based research to the making of knowledge in literacy studies (Branscombe, Goswami, and Schwartz; Hollingsworth and Sockett; Knoblauch and Brannon; Lather; Phelps; Ray). Since my interest here is in the ethical and representational issues that arise through classroom-based research, particularly that conducted by teachers themselves, I suggest by way of conclusion two areas in which teacher research can inform university-based literacy research.

I have already alluded to the fact that teacher research, conceived as action research, is necessarily change oriented—even emancipatory, for some practitioners. It is a highly situated form of research conducted for the purposes of making schools better. Teacher-researchers begin with the assumption that they have a responsibility to improve the learning of students in their classrooms and communities. It is my contention that far more literacy research, including that initiated by university researchers, should be action research. Within the domain of action research, certain ethical issues are resolved. For example, if good research is change oriented, researchers should feel comfortable, in fact morally compelled, to intervene in the learning environment. In order to do this ethically, however, literacy researchers need to make their political agendas clear (to themselves and others) before they begin a research project. They also need to collaborate with as many teacher-researchers and student-researchers as possible, not just to assure that written representations of the study are polyvocal, but also to increase the likelihood that changes will actually occur in the environment as a result of the study and that these changes will be responsive to the needs of the people involved.

The involvement of researching teachers cannot be overestimated in achieving school reform. Cochran-Smith and Lytle remind us that teachers are in the best position to initiate change because they are most sensitive to the diverse cultural populations of their communities. A teacher can "observe, talk with other teachers and parents, get to know the community, and build her own networks of resources, projects, and services. In this way, she [builds] her own agenda for reform both within her classroom and within the school community" (82). This approach to change is more meaningful and effective than global solutions to problems proposed by researchers working at a distance from the community. Instead, "what is required in both preservice and inservice teacher education programs are processes that prompt teachers and teacher educators to construct their own questions and then begin to develop courses of action that are valid in their local contexts and communities" (63). Thus teachers are initially trained to see inquiry and change as central to their professional role, and they embark on a lifelong career of teacher research. Through Project START (Student Teachers as Researching Teachers) and the Philadelphia Writing Project, Cochran-Smith and Lytle are joining other organized teacher-researchers—including the various National Writing Project groups, the Prospect Center and School in Vermont, the Bread Loaf School of English, the Philadelphia Teachers Learning Cooperative, the Boston Women's Teacher's Group, and the North Dakota Study Group—in establishing programs which support a "life span" approach to classroom inquiry.

From the perspective of action research, issues of allegiance are resolved as well: researchers who study schools are accountable *first* to the students and the school community and *secondarily* to their academic disciplines. Local knowledge takes precedence over global knowledge, and the researcher becomes participant in the local environment. It would be unethical for an action researcher to enter a school or classroom with a rigidly established agenda, conduct a study with little or no involvement from teachers and students, interpret the data alone, publish the results in professional journals, and never bring the findings back into the classroom under study.

In addition to becoming more accountable to the people they study, literacy researchers can also learn more about representation by conducting action research. One way for a researcher to be accountable to the local school and community is to publish the results of literacy research through speeches to the school board, inservice presentations, and articles in newsletters and newspapers that reach students, parents, teachers, administrators, and community organizers. Researchers need to learn how to establish credibility through means other than institutional affiliation, tenure status, and publishing record, which often have little meaning for the general public. (Fleischer refers to such credentials as "academic armor.") They will need to learn to establish trust by presenting themselves as honest, informed, and genuinely concerned citizens. Their writing will need to be detailed and persuasive to the general public, avoiding theory-speak and undue abstraction, while remaining true to the insights of those theories. In short, researchers can learn something about writing by reading the work of teacher-researchers. Often, teachers are much more interesting writers and speakers than university researchers, simply because they know how to represent themselves in ways that influence the community.

All of this is to say that teacher-researchers can teach university researchers a thing or two about how to be responsible to the people they study and how to represent themselves in ways that convince others to consider alternatives to the status quo of teaching and learning. Their work reminds us of the crucial difference between representational issues that arise out of a desire to be politically and intellectually current and representational issues that arise out of a desire to change the way people read, write, and act in the world.

Works Cited

Berlin, James A. "The Teacher as Researcher: Democracy, Dialogue, and Power." *The Writing Teacher as Researcher: Essays in the Theory and Practice of Class-Based Research.* Ed. Donald A. Daiker and Max Morenberg. Portsmouth: Boynton/Cook, 1990. 3–14.

Branscombe, N. Amanda, Dixie Goswami, and Jeffrey Schwartz, eds. *Students Teaching, Teachers Learning.* Portsmouth: Boynton/Cook-Heinemann, 1992.

Cochran-Smith, Marilyn, and Susan L. Lytle. *Inside/Outside: Teacher Research and Knowledge.* New York: Teachers College P, 1993.

Fleischer, Cathy. *Composing Teacher-Research: A Prosaic History.* Albany: State U of New York P, 1995.

Florio-Ruane, Susan, and Martha Walsh. "The Teacher as Colleague in Classroom Research." *Culture and the Bilingual Classroom: Studies in Classroom Ethnography.* Ed. Henry T. Trueba, Grace Pung Guthrie, and Kathryn Hu-Pei Au. Rowley: Newbury House, 1981. 87–101.

Goswami, Dixie, and Peter R. Stillman, eds. *Reclaiming the Classroom: Teacher Research as an Agency for Change.* Upper Montclair: Boynton/Cook, 1987.

Hollingsworth, Sandra, and Hugh Sockett, eds. *Teacher Research and Educational Reform.* Yearbook of the National Society for the Study of Education, 93rd, Part 1. Chicago: U of Chicago P, 1994.

Knoblauch, C. H., and Lil Brannon. "Knowing Our Knowledge: A Phenomenological Basis for Teacher Research." *Audits of Meaning: A Festschrift in Honor of Ann E. Berthoff.* Ed. Louise Z. Smith. Portsmouth: Boynton/Cook, 1988. 17–28.

Lather, Patti. *Getting Smart: Feminist Research and Pedagogy With/In the Postmodern.* New York: Routledge, 1991.

Miller, Janet L. *Creating Spaces and Finding Voices: Teachers Collaborating for Empowerment.* New York: State U of New York P, 1990.

———. "Teachers, Autobiography, and Curriculum." Unpublished essay, 1990.

Miller, Janet L., and Mary Lee Martens. "Hierarchy and Imposition in Collaborative Inquiry: Teacher-Researchers' Reflections on Recurrent Dilemmas." *Educational Foundations* 4.4 (1990): 41–59.

Mohr, Marian M., and Marion S. Maclean. *Working Together: A Guide for Teacher-Researchers.* Urbana: NCTE, 1987.

Myers, Miles. *The Teacher-Researcher: How to Study Writing in the Classroom.* Urbana: NCTE, 1985.

Phelps, Louise Wetherbee. "Practical Wisdom and the Geography of Knowledge in Composition." *College English* 53 (1991): 863–85.

Ray, Ruth E. *The Practice of Theory: Teacher Research in Composition.* Urbana: NCTE, 1993.

Rudduck, Jean, and David Hopkins, eds. *Research as a Basis for Teaching: Readings from the Work of Lawrence Stenhouse.* London: Heinemann Educational Books, 1985.

Van Maanen, John. *Tales of the Field: On Writing Ethnography.* Chicago: U of Chicago P, 1988.

Index

Editors

Photo by Mary Jane Murawka

Gesa E. Kirsch is associate professor of English at Wayne State University in Detroit. She is author of *Women Writing the Academy* and co-editor of *Methods and Methodology in Composition Research* and *A Sense of Audience in Written Communication*. She is currently working on a book entitled *Ethical Dilemmas in Feminist and Composition Research*.

Photo by MVP Studio, Park Ridge, Illinois

Peter Mortensen is associate professor of English at the University of Kentucky in Lexington. His essays on literacy and rhetoric have appeared in *College English, College Composition and Communication, Reader, Rhetoric Review*, and *Rhetoric Society Quarterly*. He is currently completing two book projects: *Imagining Rhetoric: Composing the Women of Early America* (with Janet Carey Eldred) and *Illiterate Sorrows: The Uses of Illiteracy in Industrial America, 1880–1920*.

Contributors

Paul V. Anderson is professor of technical and scientific communication as well as composition and rhetoric at Miami University (Ohio). He is author of *Technical Writing: A Reader-Centered Approach* and *Business Communication: An Audience-Centered Approach.* In collaboration with Carolyn R. Miller and R. John Brockmann, he co-edited *New Essays in Technical and Scientific Communication.* His other writing on research methodology includes two chapters on surveys in *Writing in Nonacademic Settings,* edited by Lee Odell and Dixie Goswami.

Ann M. Blakeslee is associate professor of English at Eastern Michigan University. She is interested in rhetorical practice in science and technology and has examined the discursive practices of a group of theoretical physicists engaged in interdisciplinary work. She is also interested in the acquisition of rhetorical knowledge and in the rhetorical construction of consensus in multidisciplinary contexts.

Brenda Jo Brueggemann is assistant professor of English-rhetoric-composition at The Ohio State University. She is working on a manuscript, *Lend Me Your Ear: A Study in Deaf Culture, Language, and Literacy;* considering a collection, *Focusing on the Process: Research Narratives in Rhetoric and Composition Research;* teaching courses in literacy, rhetorical theory, research methods, and contemporary poetry; and mothering.

Elizabeth Chiseri-Strater is assistant professor of English in the Rhetoric and Composition Program at the University of North Carolina at Greensboro, where she is also director of English Education. Her research interests include literacy, collaboration, ethnography, and race-gender issues in the classroom. Her published works include an ethnographic study of undergraduates' reading and writing across the disciplines, *Academic Literacies,* as well as articles on portfolios and evaluation, collaborative writing, and the social aspects of journals. She and Bonnie Sunstein recently co-authored a book about doing field research, *Fieldworking: Reading and Writing Research.*

Caroline M. Cole is a doctoral candidate in the English Department's Center for Writing Studies at the University of Illinois at Urbana–Champaign. She teaches expository and professional writing classes, as well as a desktop publishing course. She is currently examining the influence of gender on writing instruction and on learning. In a recent study, she explored the influence of gender on students' perceptions of themselves as writers.

Theresa Conefrey is an advanced doctoral candidate in the Institute of Communications Research at the University of Illinois at Urbana–Champaign. Her research interests include the uses of oral and written discourse in scientific research laboratories and methodological issues in qualitative research. She teaches freshman writing courses in the university's Academic Writing Program.

Helen Dale is assistant professor of English at the University of Wisconsin–Eau Claire, where she teaches courses in composition, literature, English education, and cultural diversity. She is the 1992 recipient of the American Educational Research Association's Steve Cahir Award for Research on Writing and was a finalist in the 1994 NCTE Promising Researcher Award. Her research interests include collaborative writing, supervision of student teaching, discourse analysis, and qualitative research. Among her publications are articles in *Journal of Educational Research* and *English Journal* and a forthcoming monograph about collaborative writing in the NCTE Theory and Research into Practice series.

Jennie Dautermann teaches rhetoric, professional writing, and sociolinguistics at Miami University (Ohio). In 1993 she was a finalist in the NCTE Promising Researcher Award competition. She is currently editing a collection of articles, with Patricia Sullivan (Purdue University), on writing with computers in the workplace; *Electronic Literacies in the Workplace: Technologies of Writing* will appear soon from NCTE. Interested as well in writing in the disciplines and qualitative research across the curriculum, Dautermann has served as research consultant for NSF-sponsored projects in Undergraduate Mathematics Education, co-authoring several articles with the principal investigators of those projects.

Russel K. Durst is associate professor of English at the University of Cincinnati, where he directs the composition program. He is chair of the NCTE Standing Committee on Research and a member of the editorial board of *College Composition and Communication.* His recent publications include *Exploring Texts: The Role of Discussion and Writing in the Teaching and Learning of Literature* (edited with George Newell); articles in *Research in the Teaching of English, English Education,* and *Language and Learning Across the Disciplines;* and pieces in several edited collections. He is currently working on a study of the conflicting agendas of students and teachers in the college composition class.

Stephen M. Fishman teaches philosophy at the University of North Carolina–Charlotte. In 1983 he attended his first Writing Across the Curriculum Workshop and began studying learning and writing in his classroom. His work has appeared in *Research in the Teaching of English, College Composition and Communication,* and *College English.*

Melissa A. Goldthwaite, a student in the Master of Fine Arts program in creative writing at The Ohio State University, writes poetry and creative nonfiction and is interested in nature writing and spirituality. She is working on a project to make connections between rhetoric and composition and creative writing, studying the way in which some women researchers in rhetoric and composition use the form of the personal essay for their disciplinary writing.

Andrea A. Lunsford is distinguished professor and vice chair of the Department of English at The Ohio State University, where she teaches courses in the history and theory of writing and rhetoric. She is the editor, most recently, of *Reclaiming Rhetorica: Women in the Rhetorical Tradition* and co-author, with Lisa Ede, of "Representing Audience: 'Successful' Discourse and Disciplinary Critique" in *College Composition and Communication.*

Jabari Mahiri conducts research on the literacy learning of urban youth—particularly African American students—in schools and outside of them. His focus is on connections between oral and written language, student motivation and empowerment, effective teaching and learning strategies, and computer-mediated learning in multicultural urban schools and neighborhoods. He taught high school English in Chicago public schools for seven years. Currently, he serves on the NCTE Standing Committee on Research. He has research projects funded through the National Center for the Study of Writing and Literacy and the University/Urban School Collaborative Program of the University of California.

Gianna M. Marsella is pursuing her doctorate in nineteenth-century American literature at The Ohio State University. Her interests include popular fiction and women's writing and their intersections with issues of readership, authorship, and book promotion. She is also interested in composition studies and the political and institutional history of the academy. She teaches first- and second-level composition to undergraduates, works as a writing program administrator, and is a writing consultant in Ohio State's Writing Center.

Lucille Parkinson McCarthy teaches composition at the University of Maryland Baltimore County and has published naturalistic studies set in a variety of medical and academic contexts. In addition to her ongoing collaboration with philosopher Stephen M. Fishman, she has co-authored research with practitioners from psychiatry, nursing, history, and composition studies. Her books include *The Psychiatry of Handicapped Children and Adolescents: Managing Emotional and Behavioral Problems* (with Joan Gerring, M.D.) and *Thinking and Writing in College: A Naturalistic Study of Students in Four Disciplines* (with Barbara Walvoord).

Sandee K. McGlaun is currently pursuing a graduate degree at The Ohio State University, where she works as a consultant in the Writing Center. She is interested in exploring intersections between rhetoric and the theatre arts, as well as in examining the dynamics of collaboration in the composition classroom, particularly in relation to students' responses to teachers' comments on papers. In her spare time, she conducts dramaturgical research for one of Columbus's nonprofit theatres.

Roxanne D. Mountford is assistant professor of rhetoric and composition at the University of Arizona, where she teaches courses in writing, rhetorical theory, and research methods. She has written numerous essays and chapters on teaching writing and rhetorical theory through an ethnographic perspective; her work has appeared in the *Journal of Advanced*

Composition and *Research Strategies.* The focus of her own ethnographic and textual studies is feminist rhetoric in the context of professional discourse. Currently, she is studying a New York Court of Appeals judge and writing a book based on her study of three women preachers.

Thomas Newkirk is professor of English at the University of New Hampshire, where he has directed the freshman English program and continues to direct the New Hampshire Writing Program, a summer institute for teachers. He is the author of *More than Stories: The Range of Children's Writing* and *Listening In: What Children Say about Books (and Other Things).*

Jennifer Phegley is a doctoral student in English at The Ohio State University, with concentrations in nineteenth-century British literature and rhetoric and composition, focusing specifically on representations of authorship and readership in Victorian periodicals. She is currently working as an administrator in Ohio State's first-year writing program and as a co-editor for and contributor to the writing program's reader, *Writing Lives, Composing Worlds.*

Ruth E. Ray is associate professor of English at Wayne State University in Detroit. She is the author of many articles and chapters on literacy and teacher research, as well as *The Practice of Theory: Teacher Research in Composition* (NCTE, 1993). She is currently at work on a book about her ethnographic research on writing groups in nursing homes and senior citizen centers.

Rob Stacy is in his second year of the doctoral program in English at The Ohio State University. His scholarly interests include twentieth-century rhetorical theories, American environmental discourse and nature writing, and composition theory and practice. He is beginning a dissertation project on the rhetorical situation-discursive context of John Muir and the Sierra Club. In addition to teaching composition and rhetoric, he works as a consultant in the English Department's Writing Center.

Sherry Cook Stanforth is an advanced doctoral student at the University of Cincinnati. Her research interests are in composition studies, folklore, oral narrative, and contemporary ethnic American literature and orature. Her creative and academic work has appeared in *Indiana Review, MELUS,* and other journals. Recently, she co-produced a university video, *Making Large Classes Interactive,* which is in national release.

Linda Stingily, a doctoral student in English education, teaches first-year English in the Writing Workshop at The Ohio State University. She often uses the focus of autobiography to help students consider issues of representation as they make the transition from high school to college-level studies in composition. She has supervised the field experiences of and taught seminars for student teachers in English education at Ohio State and in 1995 was named Outstanding University Supervisor in the College of Education. Her dissertation work investigates how representations of teachers, students, and education in contemporary African

American novels can comment on scenes of learning more accurately and accessibly than such representations in conventional academic research reports. A university fellow at Ohio State in 1993–94, she was the recipient of the Ralph Bryson Award in English Education in 1995.

Patricia A. Sullivan is associate professor of English and director of the composition program at the University of New Hampshire, where she teaches undergraduate courses in composition and American literature and graduate courses in composition theory and research, critical theory, and cultural studies. Her publications include articles, chapters, and reviews in composition studies, as well as two edited books, *Methods and Methodology in Composition Research* and *Pedagogy in the Age of Politics.*

Bonnie S. Sunstein is associate professor of English Education at the University of Iowa in Iowa City, where she teaches courses in ethnographic research, nonfiction writing, and English education. She taught English in Massachusetts public schools and at colleges throughout New England. She is a member of the NCTE Standing Committee on Research. She is author of *Composing a Culture* and co-editor, with Donald Graves, of *Portfolio Portraits.* Her forthcoming book with Elizabeth Chiseri-Strater, *Fieldworking: Reading and Writing Research,* is an introduction to ethnographic research methods. Her chapters, articles, and poems about writing and teaching appear in many journals and books.

Rebecca Greenberg Taylor is pursuing doctoral work in rhetoric and composition at The Ohio State University. She hopes to study the multicultural movement in composition studies, emphasizing a rhetorical analysis of the ways in which multicultural anthologies affect students' constructions of one another. She is also researching feminist rhetorics and composition theory. Forthcoming publications include book reviews in *Focuses* and *The Composition Chronicle.*

Cheri L. Williams is assistant professor in the Division of Teacher Education at the University of Cincinnati, where she teaches courses in language and literacy education. Her research interests include emergent literacy development of both hearing and deaf children and reading-writing instruction in the primary grades. She has published articles on the emergent literacy development of deaf children in *Reading Research Quarterly, Sign Language Studies,* and the *American Annals of the Deaf.* Currently, she is investigating the use of interactive writing in a whole language kindergarten classroom for children who are deaf or hard of hearing.